Fairy Tales and the Art of Subversion

"... the most challenging study to appear on the subject for a considerable time."

The Times Educational Supplement

"Tracing the development of literary fairy tales from Charles Perrault through the twentieth century, Zipes argues that they constitute a discourse on 'civilization,' .... He avowedly seeks a political understanding of our notion of classicism and classical fairy tales. In doing so, he has produced a powerful work on the politics of culture."

The Journal of American Folklore

Routledge Classics contains the very best of Routledge publishing over the past century or so, books that have, by popular consent, become established as classics in their field. Drawing on a fantastic heritage of innovative writing published by Routledge and its associated imprints, this series makes available in attractive, affordable form some of the most important works of modern times.

For a complete list of titles visit
www.routledge.com/classics

Jack
Zipes

Fairy Tales and the Art of Subversion

The classical genre for children and the process
of civilization

With a new introduction by the author

 London and New York

First published 1983 by Heinemann Educational Books Ltd.

Published in 1988 by Methuen, Inc.

Published 1991 by Routledge

Second edition published 2006 by Routledge

First published in Routledge Classics 2012
by Routledge
2 Park Square, Milton Park, Abingdon, Oxon OX14 4RN

Simultaneously published in the USA and Canada
by Routledge
711 Third Avenue, New York, NY 10017

Routledge is an imprint of the Taylor & Francis Group, an informa business

© 1991, 2006, 2012 Taylor and Francis Group, LLC
Introduction © 2012 Jack Zipes

The right of Jack Zipes to be identified as author of this work has been
asserted by him in accordance with sections 77 and 78 of the Copyright,
Designs and Patents Act 1988.

British Library Cataloguing in Publication Data
A catalogue record for this book is available from the British Library

Library of Congress Cataloging in Publication Data
Zipes, Jack, 1937–
    Fairy tales and the art of subversion : the classical genre for children and
    the process of civilization / Jack Zipes, with a new introduction by the
    author.—2nd ed.
        p. cm.—(Routledge classics)
    Includes bibliographical references and index.
    1. Fairy tales—History and criticism. 2. Children—Books and reading.
    3. Socialization. 4. Moral development. I. Title.
    PN3437.Z56 2012
    398.209—dc23

                                                                    2011019189

ISBN: 978–0–415–61025–4 (pbk)
ISBN: 978–0–203–80525–1 (ebk)

Typeset in Joanna MT
by RefineCatch Limited, Bungay, Suffolk

For the Feisty Subversives in My Life:
Carol, Hanna, Schoena

Contents

Acknowledgments

This book was originally made possible by a Fulbright Grant from the International Exchange of Scholars, which allowed me to spend a year at the Johann Wolfgang Goethe Universität in Frankfurt am Main, where I taught and conducted research in 1981 and 1982. In particular, I am indebted to Klaus Doderer, former director of the Institut für Jugendbuchforschung, for the encouragement and assistance he provided me. During the course of my work I profited from various discussions with Thomas Elsaesser and from the suggestions of Roni Natov and Ralph Cohen, who published different and abbreviated drafts of chapters 3 and 7 in *The Lion and the Unicorn* and *New Literary History*. In addition, I should like to thank David Hill for his kind support and Caroline Lane and Betty Low for their fine editorial work in preparing this book for the first edition. In regard to the second revised edition, I am most grateful to Bill Germano for his advice and guidance and to Fred Veith for his valuable assistance. Finally, I want to express my gratitude to Sarah Blackmon for carefully taking charge and overseeing the production of this new edition and to Nicole Hirschman for her thorough copyediting of the manuscript.

INTRODUCTION TO THE ROUTLEDGE
CLASSICS EDITION

Fairy tales continue to pervade if not invade our lives throughout the world. They play an intricate role in acculturation, that is, in forming and reflecting the tastes, manners, and ideologies of members of a particular society. They have a powerful effect on how young and old behave and relate to their daily activities. Though seemingly universal, fairy tales serve a specific function in communicating the values and the various preoccupations of different nations. We have no idea exactly when fairy tales originated in oral cultures thousands of years ago, but we do know they were metaphorical stories that stemmed from basic human experiences and contained vital information that strengthened the common bonds of people living in small clans and tribes. Salient units of this information gradually formed the basis of narratives that enabled humans to learn about themselves and the worlds that they inhabited. These informative tales were not given titles. They were simply told to mark an occasion, to set an example, to warn about danger, to procure food, to explain what seemed inexplicable. People recounted stories in social contexts to communicate knowledge and experience. Though many ancient tales might seem to us to be magical, miraculous, fanciful, superstitious, or unreal, people believed them, and they were and are not much different from people today who believe in religions, miracles, cults, nations, and notions such as "free" democracies that have little basis in reality. In fact, religious and patriotic stories have more in common with fairy tales than we realize except that fairy tales tend to be secular and are not based on a prescriptive belief system or religious codes.

Fairy tales are predicated on a human disposition to social action – to transform the world and make it more adaptable to human needs while we try to change and make ourselves fit for the world. Almost all fairy tales involve a quest. Therefore, their focus, whether the tale be oral, written, or cinematic, has always been on the struggle to find magical instruments, extraordinary technologies, or helpful people and animals that will enable protagonists to transform themselves and their environment and make the world more suitable for living in peace and contentment. Fairy tales begin with conflict because we all begin our lives with conflict. We are all misfit for the world, and somehow we must fit in, fit in with our environment and other people, and thus we must invent or find the means through communication to satisfy and resolve conflicting desires and instincts.

Every society has developed some sort of civilizing process to motivate its members to cooperate and co-exist in peaceful ways. Tales are motivators, and as they were told and retold over vast periods of times, they were woven into the texture of the civilizing process, retained in our memories, and assumed different forms for social purposes that determined the nature of their genre. Fairy tales, often called wonder or magic tales in oral cultures, were means of communication that afforded storytellers and listeners the opportunity to imagine and contemplate worlds more just and ideal than their realities. The tales afforded moral and ethical pleasure while not preaching or prescribing how to act.

Fairy tales are rooted in oral traditions, and as I mentioned above, they were never given titles, nor did they exist in the forms in which they are told, printed, painted, recorded, performed, and filmed today. They evolved in traditions through imitation, memorization, replication, and re-creation. Folklorists generally make a distinction between wonder folk tales, which originated in oral traditions throughout the world and still exist, and literary fairy tales, which emanated from the oral traditions through the mediation of manuscripts and print and continue to be created today in various mediated forms throughout the world. In both the oral and literary traditions the tale types influenced by cultural patterns are so numerous and diverse that it is almost impossible to define the typical plot of a wonder folk tale or a fairy tale or explain the relationship between the two modes of communication. What is fascinating to study is how the oral and literary forms of the wonder/ fairy tale blended together once printing began to be developed in the fifteenth century in western civilization. The blend has been enhanced by other technologies such as audio-visual inventions of the late nineteenth century. Today the hybrid fairy tale has become more diversified and embellished. It has multitasks, and yet, it remains strikingly consistent in its major goal: to compel storytellers and listeners alike to explore the Freudian question of why humans are so discontent with civilization.

The focus of *Fairy Tales and the Art of Subversion* concerns the transformation and evolution of the literary fairy tale from the fifteenth century to the present and how and why the genre became a conflicted cultural field in which different social institutions and individual writers and artists used the tale either to bring about conformity or to question conformity to the dominant civilizing process of a society. Once print became an effective means of communication and was followed by audio-visual modes of communication up through the present-day Internet, the fairy tale was transformed and formed into paintings, moving pictures, cartoons, advertisements, plays, musicals, operas, toys, dolls, household artifacts, soap operas, and so on. In most western societies the fairy tale also had to be changed to make it more suitable or appropriate for children, for the fairy tales told in the oral tradition had never been explicitly told for children. Fairy tales do not belong to children. They are part and parcel of a general civilizing process that developed different tale types some of which were directly composed for children.

Due to their symbolical and secular contents that might have given and still give children "wild ideas" that their lives need not conform to the governing norms of society, fairy tales have generally been viewed as dangerous if not subversive by conservative religious and political groups. The fact is, however, that fairy tales can be both provocatively subversive and trivially traditional. With the rise of the middle classes in seventeenth-century Europe and North America and the massive influence of the Christian church and its various belief systems, the fairy tale was often cropped and altered in books for young readers to reinforce dominant religious and patriarchal attitudes about gender, mating, law, and order. Highly conservative mores and prescriptive codes were disseminated in such early works by François Fénelon (Collection of Fables Written for the Education of the late Monsignor the Duke of Burgundy, 1718), Sarah Fielding (The Governess, or Little Female Academy, 1749), and Madame Leprince de Beaumont (The Young Misses' Magazine, 1757) in the eighteenth century, and as literacy expanded and children's literature gradually developed into an industry in the nineteenth century, more and more pristine fairy-tale collections for children were published for children, primarily for middle and upper-class youngsters. The taming of the "wild" fantasies of the oral and literary fairy tales, what one might call sanitization, was quite common in the nineteenth century, and the classical tales of Charles Perrault, Madame d'Aulnoy, the Brothers Grimm, and Hans Christian Andersen underwent very curious adaptations for children due to explicit and implicit censorship. One of the most curious "infantile" sanitizations that took place in the nineteenth century was Edgar Taylor's 1823 adaptation of the Grimms' fairy tales in German Popular Stories. With the bizarre approval of the Grimms, who had also begun changing the tales in their own German collection to make them more suitable to the "innocent" souls of children, Taylor produced a second sweetened collection in 1826 and then added a third in 1839 called German Popular Stories and Fairy Tales as Told by Gammer Grethel. His "re-making" of the Grimms' tales led to yet another strange re-publication under the title Grimms' Goblins. Grimms' Household Stories published in 1876 by

Robert Meek, who wrote: "Fairy Tales are the earliest cultivators of the purest bias in the youngest and freshest of soils; they are the especial prerogative and boon of children's libraries. Their world-wide popularity, their boundless influence, form a striking contrast to that immense flood of writing distinguished by bad taste and low aims, which, if not positively pernicious, is at best vulgar trash. With no higher standard than the reading of Fairy Stories, children would ever, from these sources, learn how good and holy is virtue and benevolence — how bad and wicked is craft and cunning. Nay, moral lessons may be learned from these sources, not only by the little world of wondering, believing minds, but by many minds that have long since passed the age of wondering."[1]

In contrast to this sentimental and misleading view of fairy tales in the nineteenth century, the oral fairy tales continued to be told in all sorts of fresh, unlettered ways throughout Europe and America, and numerous writers such as E. T. A. Hoffmann, Charles Dickens, Hans Christian Andersen, George MacDonald, Lewis Carroll, and Oscar Wilde created highly innovative, sophisticated, and provocative counter-cultural fairy tales for children and adults that opened the genre to vast experiments by the end of the nineteenth century including "proletarian" tales and bawdy verse adaptations as well as vaudeville plays and the early silent films of Georges Méliès. The 1900 publication of L. Frank Baum's The Wizard of Oz in America led to a series of 14 utopian fairy-tale books, which pit the ideal world of Oz against the drab real world of America's Kansas. Baum's series was a direct subversion of the American civilizing process. Walt Disney followed Baum by making anarchical fairy-tale films in Kansas City during the early 1920s, but in the 1930s he reclaimed the fairy tale for conservative patriarchal values with his production of Snow White and the Seven Dwarfs (1937). Since that time the virtues of innocent virginity and pure love along with the justification of elitist hegemonic rule were championed in Disney's films and have been maintained by his corporation up to the present. Nevertheless, there are subversive elements in all of the Disney films and books. It is almost inevitable, for there has always been a subversive current in fairy-tale art and literature ever since their origination.

If we speak and use language to know the world and ourselves through metaphor, as George Lakoff and Mark Johnson maintain in Metaphors We Live By, the art of the fairy tale provides a means for understanding the real world through standard metaphorical clichés as well as through highly innovative articulations and inferences. Lakoff and Johnson write: "A great deal of everyday, conventional language is metaphorical, and the metaphorical meanings are given by conceptual metaphorical mappings that ultimately arise from correlations in our embodied experience. In short, metaphor is a natural phenomenon. Conceptual metaphor is a natural part of human thought, and linguistic metaphor is a natural part of human language. Moreover, which metaphors we have and what they mean depend on the nature of our bodies, our interactions in the physical environment, and our social and cultural practices. Every question about the nature of conceptual metaphor and its role in thought and language is an empirical question."[2]

Fairy tales are not unreal; they tell us metaphorically that "life is hard," or that "life is a dream," and their symbolical narrative patterns that assume the form of quests indicate possible alternative choices that we can make to fulfill our utopian disposition to transform ourselves and the world. The metaphors used in the composition of fairy tales are very much in touch with empirical reality. Fairy tales test the correlation between real social practices and imaginative possibilities that can be realized but are thwarted in our everyday interactions. Fairy tales interrogate the lack of correlation between real world practices and ethical idealistic options. Therefore, even the sentimental and contradictory happy endings in standard fairy-tale romances and Hollywood films are somewhat subversive in that they compel us to consider what is lacking in our lives that prevent us from fulfilling our dreams and utopian longings. Certainly, the contrived happy endings of standardized fairy tales are delusional and misleading. Yet, we must always ask that if the protagonists succeed in finding love, wealth, and contentment in fairy-tale melodramas, what is preventing us in reality from having the same success?

As long as there is discontent with the civilizing process, there will be fairy tales that will either project alternatives to the status quo or that will reconcile us to our social conventions and religious beliefs. In the twenty-first century there is no sign that the cultural production of fairy tales in all spheres of life has diminished. The mass media rely on fairy tales to transmit commercial and public messages throughout the world. We see, tell, and consume fairy tales every day on a personal level without even being aware that we depend on them to make it through the day. By no means do I wish to privilege the fairy tale above other significant forms of simple, effective narratives such as myth, fable, tall tale, proverb, legend, joke, and so on. All these genres are related to one another, and we relate to them to make our lives relevant. We create patterns and parallels to map our way through the intricate and inexplicable hazards that constitute human existence. Fairy tales as socially symbolic acts enable us to intercede in civilizing processes that deny the ethical fulfillment of the meaning of humanity. They speak out against passivity and exploitation. They conceive worlds of contestation in which the art of subversion ultimately reveals stunning truths that we try to avoid. But fairy tales are insistent and persistent, and as I asserted at the beginning of this introduction, they continue to be tantalizing. They pervade and invade our lives by telling us truths without telling us how to live those truths.

Jack Zipes
Minneapolis, March 1, 2011

Preface to the Second Edition

Originally published in 1983, *Fairy Tales and the Art of Subversion* has never gone out of print, I am pleased to say. But as time passed and I continued to do more work in the realms of folklore and fairy-tale studies, I realized that there were gaps in the book that needed to be filled. Fortunately, they were not enormous, and I am very grateful to Bill Germano and Routledge for granting me this opportunity to revise the entire book and to add two new chapters.

In the course of time, I have not changed my views about the historical development of the literary fairy tale, especially as it has been cultivated for children as part of the civilizing process, but many of my observations and interpretations have become more complex and more comprehensive thanks to changes in scholarly attitudes. In fact, before 1980, one could virtually argue that there was no such thing as fairy-tale studies proper. The literary fairy tale was a marginalized genre, and, if it was taken seriously, then it was by folklorists, who actually had a fraught relationship with what some considered to be a contaminated genre: either they studied and celebrated the fairy tale to show its roots in the oral tradition or they condemned it for defiling the "authentic" folktales. But ever since the 1980s, a more diverse and sophisticated appreciation and study of the literary fairy tale could be noticed, and scholars and educators became more aware of its significance as a genre that has wide ramifications for the civilizing of children and adults. I need only point to the enormous publication of books and essays on the fairy tale in North America and Western Europe, some included in my bibliography, not to mention the thousands of fairy tales and the appearance of such important journals such as *Marvels and Tales* and informative Web sites such as *Sur la Lune*. In short, the vast interest in the literary fairy tale has had a strong influence on my own work, and I have felt obliged to incorporate the findings of some of the research into the revised edition of this book along with stimulating ideas from such different thinkers as Theodor Adorno, Pierre Bourdieu, Marina Warner, and others even when I may not expressly cite them. My debt to Norbert Elias is clear.

The two chapters that I have added to the book concern the influence of the unique Italian writers Giovan Francesco Straparola and Giambattista Basile on the French writers of the ancien régime and the extraordinary impact of Walt Disney on the fairy tale. I believe that these chapters provide indispensable information and theses that help explain why we must examine the fairy tale as part of the intricate civilizing process in the Western world. Moreover, I have updated, expanded, and changed all the previous chapters so that they incorporate the more important recent research. About twenty years ago, a German scholar predicted that the fairy tale would lose its vital utopian significance in the twentieth century because the only writing, given the atrocities of the past century, that could be taken seriously had to be dystopian. There is a certain truth to this argument, but if one believes in civilization and in the virtues of civility, the fairy tale continues to play a role in the civilizing process not just as trivial amusement but, more important, as a subversive alternative to a process that has lost its touch with humanity.

Jack Zipes

1

FAIRY-TALE DISCOURSE: TOWARD A SOCIAL HISTORY OF THE GENRE

Language and style are blind forces. Writing is an act of historical solidarity. Language and style are objects. Writing is a function. It is the relation between creation and society. It is literary language transformed by its social destination. It is the form grasped in its human intention and thus tied to the great crises of history.
—Roland Barthes, *Le degré zéro de l'écriture* (1953)

Even though the fairy tale may be the most important cultural and social event in most children's lives, critics and scholars have failed to study its historical development as a genre. There are chapters on the fairy tale in histories of children's literature, essays and even books on the fairy tale for adults, in-depth psychological explorations of the fairy tale's effect on children, and structuralist and formalist studies of individual tales galore. But no history of the fairy tale for children, in particular, no social history. Just a gap.

Nonhistory is history. Or, the acceptance of the gap means that brief descriptive outlines and chronologies of the fairy tale pass for history. Perhaps the most remarkable outcome of the so-called historical studies of literary fairy tales for children is the sense one gains that these tales are ageless. The best fairy tales are supposedly universal. It does not matter when or why they were written. What matters is their enchantment as though their bedtime manner can always be put to use to soothe the anxieties of children or help them therapeutically to realize who they are. One should not dissect or study fairy tales in a sociopolitical context, for that might ruin their magic power.

Fairy tales for children are universal, ageless, therapeutic, miraculous, and beautiful. This is the way they have come down to us in history. Inscribed on our minds, as children and then later as adults, is the impression that it is not important to know about the mysterious past of fairy tales just as long as they are there and continue to be written. The past is mysterious. The history of the fairy tale for children is mystery.

Fredric Jameson claims that "history is not a text, not a narrative, master or otherwise, but that, as an absent cause, it is inaccessible to us except in textual form, and that our approach to it and to the Real itself necessarily passes through prior textualization, its narrativization in the political unconscious."[1] It follows, then, out of necessity that we write our own texts to gain a sense not simply of what has happened in reality but also of what has happened on psychological, economic, cultural, and other levels to free ourselves of the dictates of other sociohistorical texts that have prescribed and ordered our thinking and need to be disordered if we are to perceive for ourselves the processes that produce social structures, modes of production, and cultural artefacts. To write a historical text (or any text for that matter) implies that one has a worldview, an overall perspective of history, an ideology, whether conscious or unconscious, and that the writing of such a text will tend either to test this view or to legitimate it. Textual form depends on the method one chooses. We place a value on how and what we write.

Jameson talks about the necessity of developing a method of mediations that will enable us to grasp and evaluate history in the most comprehensive manner possible:

> This operation is understood as a process of *transcoding*: as the invention of a set of terms, the strategic choice of a particular code or language, such that the same terminology can be used to analyze and articulate two quite different structural levels of reality. Mediations are thus a device of the analyst, whereby the fragmentation and automization of the various regions of social life (the separation, in other words, of the ideological from the political, the religious from the economic, the gap between daily life and the practice of academic disciplines) is at least locally overcome, on the occasion of a particular analysis.[2]

Jameson's method could be called interdisciplinary but that would be too simplistic, for he does not want to bring disciplines together in a traditional positivist way to study literature from different statistical and strategic angles. Rather he wants to invent an ideological code and method that will subsume different approaches so he can grasp the underlying forces that have caused

gaps in history and prevented our understanding the essence of literary creation. He seeks to explore the political unconscious, and it is obvious that he
wants to develop many of the notions first elaborated by Roland Barthes in *Le
degré zéro de l'écriture* (1953) and *Mythologies* (1957). For Jameson the individual
literary work is a *symbolic act*, "which is grasped as the imaginary resolution of
real contradiction."[3] Such a definition is helpful in understanding the origins
of the literary fairy tale for children and adults because it immediately
perceives the process of writing as part of a social process, as a kind of intervention in a continuous discourse, debate, and conflict about power and
social relations. Jameson sees ideology not as something "which informs or
invests symbolic production; rather the aesthetic act itself is ideological, and
the production of aesthetic or narrative form is to be seen as an ideological
act in its own right, with the function of inventing imaginary or formal
'solutions' to unresolvable contradictions."[4]

Certainly one can speak about the single literary fairy tale for children as a
symbolic act infused by the ideological viewpoint of the individual author—
and here it is important to add that the fairy tale for children cannot be separated from the fairy tale for adults. The genre originated within an oral
storytelling tradition and was created and cultivated by adults, and as the fairy
tale became an acceptable literary genre first among adults, it was then
disseminated in print in the eighteenth century to children. Almost all critics
who have studied the emergence of the literary fairy tale in Europe[5] agree that
educated writers purposely appropriated the oral folktale and converted it
into a type of literary discourse about mores, values, and manners so that
children and adults would become civilized according to the social code of
that time. By the eighteenth century, the writers of fairy tales for children
such as Sarah Fielding and Madame Leprince de Beaumont *acted* ideologically
by presenting their notions regarding social conditions and conflicts, and
they *interacted* with each other and with past writers and storytellers of folklore
in a public sphere.

This interaction had already begun in Italy during the sixteenth century
and led to an institutionalized symbolic discourse on the civilizing process in
France that served as the basis for the fairy-tale genre. For example, writing
literary tales in France in the late seventeenth century, modeled on Italian
tales, was predicated on their acceptance at Louis XIV's court and in prominent Parisian salons. The oral tale had flourished for a long time in villages
and nurseries, part of a popular discourse, part of a discourse between
governesses and children of the upper class. It had even seen literary light in
the mass-marketed "blue books" distributed by peddlers for consummation
by peasants and the lower classes.[6] However, it was disdained as a literary
form by the aristocratic and bourgeois classes until it received courtly approval
through Madame de Maintenon and Fénelon; that is, until it could be

codified and used to reinforce an accepted discursive mode of social conventions advantageous to the interests of the intelligentsia and ancien régime,[7] which made a fashion out of exploiting the ideas and productivity of the bourgeoisie. There is an interesting parallel that one could draw with the institution of *conversation* at this time. A noncompulsive elegant mode of conversing was developed at the court and salons that paradoxically emanated from a compulsion to respect strict rules of decorum.[8] The speaker was compelled to be noncompulsive, and the audience was to be spontaneous in its reception of stories and exchange of remarks. The more folktales could be subjected to the rules of conversation, the more they were ornamented and accepted within the dominant discourse. This was the historical sociogenetic origination of the literary fairy tale for children. Writing fairy tales was a choice, an option exercised within an institution, a manner of imposing one's conversation on the prescribed fairy-tale discourse.

Jameson is again instructive in his definition of genre:

> Genres are essentially literary *institutions*, or social contracts between writer and a specific public whose function is to specify the proper use of a particular cultural artefact. The speech acts of daily life are themselves marked with indications and signals (intonation, gesturality, contextual deities and pragmatics) which ensure their appropriate reception. In the mediated situations of a more complicated social life—and the emergence of writing has often been taken as paradigmatic of such situations—perceptual signals must be replaced by conventions if the text in question is not to be abandoned to a drifting multiplicity of uses (as *meanings* must, according to Wittgenstein, be described). Still, as texts free themselves more and more from an immediate performance situation, it becomes ever more difficult to enforce a given generic rule on their readers. No small part of the art of writing, indeed, is absorbed by this (impossible) attempt to devise a foolproof mechanism for the automatic exclusion of undesirable response to a given literary utterance.[9]

In the case of the literary fairy tale for children as genre, it appears fruitless to me to begin a definition based on the morphological study of Vladimir Propp[10] or the semiotic practice of Algirdas-Julien Greimas,[11] as many critics have done. To be sure, Propp and Greimas are useful for comprehending textual structures and signs of the tales, but they provide no overall methodological framework for locating and grasping the essence of the genre, the substance of the symbolic act as it took form to intervene in the institutionalized literary discourse of society.

This becomes apparent when one reads the remarkably informative essay "Du Conte merveilleux comme genre" (On the Magic Folk Tale as Genre) by Marie-Louise Tenèze, who uses the works of Propp and Max Lüthi to grasp the kernel (un noyau irréductible) of what constitutes the magic of the folktale.[12] She begins with Propp's thesis that there are a limited number of functions in the magic folktale with an identical succession of events. The hero lacks something and goes in search of aid (intermediaries) to achieve happiness, most often marriage. The structure of every magic folktale conforms to this quest. Then she combines Propp's ideas with those of Lüthi, who sees the hero of a magic folktale as a wanderer charged with carrying out a task. Because the answer or solution to this task is known in advance, there is no such thing as chance or coincidence in a folktale. This accounts for the precise, concrete style of all the tales, and their composition is a detailing of the ways in which the hero takes steps to survive and complete his mission. According to Tenèze, the rich variety of folktales stems from the freedom given to each narrator to alter the functions and tasks within the fixed schema. Her synthesis of Propp and Lüthi leads her to the following formulation:

> The magic folk tale reveals itself in its very core to be like the narration of the situation of the hero between the "response" and the "question," that is between the means obtained and the means employed. In other words, it is the relation between the hero—who is explicitly or implicitly but always assured of *aid in advance,* guaranteed—and the difficult situation in which he finds himself during the course of action that I propose as the constitutive criterion of the genre.[13]

By combining Propp's thesis with Lüthi's, Tenèze endeavors to elaborate a structural approach that stresses the dynamics and changeability of the tale, avoiding the pitfalls of the static models of Propp and Lüthi. She draws an interesting parallel to the primitive North American Indian ritual of puberty described by Claude Lévi-Strauss in Tristes Tropiques,[14] where adolescents were placed in the wilderness and left alone to survive and develop a sense of power while they also were expected to become aware of the absurdity and desperation one would experience by leaving the social order. Tenèze believes that

> like the real hero of this custom, the hero of the magic folk tale ventures, alone and far from his familiar surroundings, to the perilous fringe of an exceptional experience capable of supplying him with a "personal provision of power," his insertion into the world—and thus, there is a magic solution to the absurd and desperate endeavor to leave the social order which is played out in the universe of fiction. Isn't the folk tale a response to the oppressive interrogation of reality?[15]

Like Propp and Lüthi, Tenèze favors the structural approach to explain the essence of the magic folktale. In other words, it is through the structure or composition of the tale that we can gain an understanding of its meaning or enunciation, what it is trying to communicate. The difficulty with this approach, as Tenèze realizes, is that, if all folktales have essentially the same "morphology" (even though the functions may be varied), they all express the same thing, some kind of universal statement about the plight of humanity. The form itself is its meaning, and the historicity of the individual creator (or creators) and society disappears. Such formalist approaches to folk and fairy tales account in great part for the reason why we tend to see the tales as universal, ageless, and eternal. The tendency here is to homogenize creative efforts so that the differences of human and social acts become blurred.

Tenèze is much too aware of the failing of the structural approach to be satisfied with it, for the second half of her essay on the genre explores other aspects that may help us define its essence such as its relation to myth and legend and to the narrator and community. In her survey of criticism dealing with reception aesthetics, she stresses the significance of specific narrators and their audiences, their norms and values, all of which must be taken into account if we are to grasp the core of the genre, especially the significance of its development. This leads Tenèze to conclude,

> When we envisage it in its concrete cultural formations, in spite of the character of the world which we recognize in it, the magic folk tale needs to be inscribed in the functional totality of the system of expression of the community in question. Even more than this, it needs to be situated in the life of this community itself. This is the research which must now be carried out in studies of the European folk tale.[16]

Whereas it is extremely difficult to study the historical origins and social significance of a folktale (the relationship between narrator and audience) because we lack a great deal of information about storytelling in primitive tribes and societies, it is not so difficult to define the historical rise of the literary fairy tale for children. It seems to me that any definition of this genre must begin with the premise that the individual tale was indeed a *symbolic act* intended to transform a specific oral folktale (and sometimes a well-known literary tale) and designed to rearrange the motifs, characters, themes, functions, and configurations in such a way that they would address the concerns of the educated and ruling classes of late feudal and early capitalist societies. What Tenèze amply discusses as the dynamic structure of the folktale is what August Nitschke[17] has evaluated in terms of autodynamics, heterodynamics, and metamorphosis of primitive tribes and modern societies. Nitschke maintains that every community and society in history can be characterized by the way human beings arrange themselves and perceive time, and this gives rise to a dominant activity (also called a line of motion). The perspectives and positions assumed by members of society toward the dominant activity amount to a configuration. The configuration designates the character of a social order because the temporal–corporeal arrangement is designed around a dominant activity that shapes the attitudes of people toward work, education, social development, and death. Hence, the configuration of society is the pattern of arrangement and rearrangement of social behavior related to a socialized mode of perception. In the folktale the temporal–corporeal arrangement reflects whether there are perceived to be new possibilities for participation in the social order or whether there must be a confrontation when possibilities for change do not exist. This is why, in each new stage of civilization, in each new historical epoch, the symbols and configurations of the tales were endowed with new meaning, transformed, or eliminated in reaction to the needs and conflicts of the people within the social order. The aesthetic arrangement and structure of the tales were derived from the way the narrator or narrators perceived the possibility for resolution of social conflicts and contradictions or felt change was necessary.

If we examine the vast group of European folktales of the feudal and early capitalist periods, those tales with which we are most familiar and that were recorded very early, that which is our legacy, we must bear in mind that their configurations and symbols were already marked by a sociopolitical perception and had entered into a specific institutionalized discourse before they were transformed into literary tales for children of the European upper classes. For instance, Heide Göttner-Abendroth has demonstrated convincingly in *Die Göttin und ihr Heros*[18] that the matriarchal worldview and motifs of the original folktales underwent successive stages of "patriarchalization." That is, by the time the oral folktales, originally stamped somewhat by matriarchal mythology, circulated in the Middle Ages, they had been transformed in different ways: the goddess became a witch, an evil fairy, or a stepmother; the active, young princess was changed into an active hero; matrilineal marriage and family ties became patrilineal; the essence of the symbols, based on matriarchal rites, was depleted and made benign; and the pattern of action that concerned maturation and integration was gradually recast to stress domination and wealth.

As a pagan or non-Christian art form, one that was variable depending on the natural condition or social situation that was its reference, the folktale developed a partiality for everything metallic and mineral and conceived of a world that was solid and imperishable. Such a set and highly structured world can be linked to notions of medieval patriarchalism, monarchy, and absolutism in the fifteenth, sixteenth, and seventeenth centuries. The world of the folktale is inhabited largely by kings, queens, princes, princesses, soldiers, peasants, animals, and supernatural creatures (witches, fairies, elves, dwarfs, goblins, giants)—rarely by members of the bourgeoisie or the church—and there are no machines, signs of industrialization, or elaborate descriptions of commerce and town life. In other words, the main characters and concerns of a monarchistic, patriarchal, and feudal society are presented, and the focus is on class struggle and competition for power among the aristocrats themselves and between the peasantry and aristocracy. Hence, the central theme of all the folktales of this particular precapitalist period: "might makes right."[19] He who has power can exercise his will, right wrongs, become ennobled, amass money and land, and win women as prizes and social prestige. Tenèze was correct when she placed her finger on power and oppression as the key concerns of the folktales, and this is why the people, largely peasants, were predominantly attracted to the tale and became its prime carriers: the oral folktales were those symbolic acts in which they enunciated their aspirations and projected the magic possibility in an assortment of imaginative ways so that anyone could become a knight in shining armor or a lovely princess. They also presented the stark realities of power politics without disguising the violence and brutality of everyday life. Starvation and abandonment of children, rape, corporeal punishment, ruthless exploitation—these are some of the conditions that are at the root of the folktale, conditions that were so overwhelming that they demanded symbolic abstraction.[20]

As Lüthi has shown,[21] the folktale's manner of portrayal is direct, clear, paratactical, and one-dimensional in its narrative perspective, and this narrative position reflects the limitations of feudal life where alternatives to one's situation were extremely limited. So it is in the folktale. Despite magical transformation, there is no mention of another world. Only one side of the characters and living conditions is described. *Everything is confined to a realm without morals*, where class and power determine power relations. Hence, the magic and miraculous serve to rupture the feudal confines and represent metaphorically the conscious and unconscious desires of the lower classes to seize power. In the process, power takes on a moral quality. The fact that the people as carriers of the tales do not *explicitly* seek a total revolution of social relations does not minimize the utopian aspect in the *imaginative* portrayal of class conflict. Whatever the outcomes of the tales are—and for the most part, they are happy ends and "exemplary" in that they affirm a more just feudal order with democratizing elements—the impulse and critique of the "magic" are rooted in a historically explicable desire to overcome oppression and change society.

In the seventeenth century, children of all classes listened to these tales. The peasants did not exclude children when stories were told around the hearth, and lower-class wet nurses and governesses related the same tales to children of the upper classes. Moreover, people of all classes told all types of tales and absorbed them. "Folk" must be understood as "inclusive" not exclusive. The folktale was the staple of what was to become the literary fairy tale for children. Before this could occur, however, it was necessary to prescribe the form and manner in which the tales would be adapted and used to entertain and instruct children. The adaptation of folk material, an act of symbolic appropriation, was a recodification of the material to make it suitable for the discursive requirements of French court society and bourgeois salons. The first writers of fairy tales had to demonstrate the social value of the genre before literary fairy tales could be printed—for adults and children alike. The morality and ethics of a male-dominated Christian civil order had to become part and parcel of the literary fairy tale. This was a given, and it was with this rule in mind, whether one agreed with it or not, that the early French writers of fairy tales began writing—and acted symbolically.

Throughout the Middle Ages children were gradually regarded as a separate age group with a special set of characteristics, and it was considered most important to advance the cause of civilité with explicit and implicit rules of pedagogization so that the manners and mores of the young would reflect the social power, prestige, and hierarchy of the ruling classes. Thus it became vital to bring about socialization through fairy tales and the internalization of specific values and notions of gender. We must remember that the fairy tale for children originated in a period of absolutism when French culture was setting standards of civilité for the rest of Europe. Exquisite care was thus taken to cultivate a discourse on the civilization process through the fairy tale for the benefit of well-raised children. In this regard fairy tales for children were no different from the rest of the literature (fables, primers, picture books, sermons, didactic stories, etc.) that conveyed a model of the exemplary child that was to be borne in mind while reading. Fairy tales and children's literature were written with the purpose of socializing children to meet definite normative expectations at home and in the public sphere. The behavioral standards were expressly codified in books on manners and civility. This means that the individual symbolic act of writing the literary fairy tale expressed a certain level of social consciousness and conscience that was related to the standard mode of socialization at that time.

In her discussion of the origins of the literary fairy tale for children in Europe, Denise Escarpit has made it clear that the purpose of the tale from the beginning was to instruct and amuse; that is, to make moral lessons and social strictures palatable. "It was a utilitarian moralism that taught how to 'act in a proper way'; that is, to insert oneself into society docilely but astutely, without disrupting society and also without creating trouble for oneself. One thing is quite clear: there was a threefold manipulation by the author—a manipulation that served a cultural and personal politics, a manipulation of a social kind that presented a certain image of society, and a moralistic manipulation that adhered to the code of bourgeois moralism at the end of the seventeenth century. It was this possibility of multiple manipulation that constituted the power of the tale. According to how the tale was cloaked, it could assume very diverse forms that were functions of social and cultural imperatives at the time. And, in the same way, according to social and cultural imperatives, the tale experienced periods of favor and disfavor. This is the reason why it was transformed into an erotic tale, a philosophical one, or a pedagogical moral tale. It was the latter that directed itself to children."[22]

There is obviously a danger in seeing the fairy tale written for children too much in terms of manipulation. If this were its central role or function, one would have to speak about the genre as a conspiracy. As I have endeavored to demonstrate, however, the literary fairy tale for children, as it began to constitute itself as genre, became more an institutionalized discourse with manipulation as one of its components. This *discourse* had and continues to have many levels to it: the writers of fairy tales for children entered into a dialogue on values and manners with the folktale, with contemporary writers of fairy tales, with the prevailing social code, with implicit adult and young readers, and with unimplied audiences. The shape of the fairy-tale discourse, of the configurations within the tales, was molded and bound by the European civilizing process that was undergoing profound changes in the sixteenth, seventeenth, and eighteenth centuries. The profundity of the literary fairy tale for children, its magic, and its appeal are marked by these changes, for it is one of the cornerstones of our bourgeois heritage. As such, it revolutionized the institution of literature at that time while abiding by its rules. Perrault saw it as modern, as making history, history in the making through innovative symbolic acts.

To write a social history of the literary fairy tale for children in relation to the Western civilizing process is an immense task—and it is not the project of this book. However, I do want to try to provide a framework for such a social history by investigating the contours of the fairy-tale discourse on civilization. My focus in the initial chapters is on the major *classical* writers in Europe and America from the seventeenth to the twentieth century, mainly on Giovan Francesco Straparola, Giambattista Basile, Charles Perrault, Jacob and Wilhelm Grimm, Hans Christian Andersen, George MacDonald, Oscar Wilde, and L. Frank Baum. These writers—and it is noteworthy that they are mainly male— are significant because they helped evolve, expand, and reform the discourse and have thus been rewarded with "classical" status in our cultural heritage. The reasons for their "classicity" vary, for their symbolic acts were made either to legitimize or to criticize the course of the Western civilizing process. Some even converted the fairy-tale discourse to subvert it. The subversion through symbolical innovation and involution is amply demonstrated in the last three chapters, which deal with the struggle for domination over the fairy-tale discourse during the Weimar and Nazi periods in Germany, the postwar attempts in the West at large to create liberating tales for children, and the effects that Disney's films have had on the fairy-tale discourse.

My concern is largely with the fairy-tale discourse as a dynamic part of the historical civilizing process, with each symbolic act viewed as an intervention in socialization in the public sphere. To have a fairy tale published is like a symbolic public announcement, an intercession on behalf of oneself, of children, of civilization. It is a historical statement. History is conceived of here not as chronology but rather as absence and rupture—in need of a text. The symbolic act of writing a fairy tale or producing a fairy tale as play or film is problematized by the asking of questions that link the fairy tale to society and our political unconscious. How and why did certain authors try to influence children or adult images of children through the fairy tale? How did these authors react to the prescribed fairy-tale discourse and intervene to alter it according to their needs and social tendencies? My own critical text is obviously an endeavor to make the *absent cause* of history speak for itself, and I avowedly seek a political understanding of our notion of classicism and classical fairy tales, the process of selection, elimination, and reward. The fairy tales we have come to revere as classical are not ageless, universal, and beautiful in and of themselves, and they are not the best therapy in the world for children. They are historical prescriptions, internalized, potent, explosive, and we acknowledge the power they hold over our lives by mystifying them.

2

THE ORIGINS OF THE FAIRY TALE IN ITALY: STRAPAROLA AND BASILE

Although the French writers of the 1690s such as Marie-Catherine d'Aulnoy, Charles Perrault, Catherine Bernard, Marie-Jeanne Lhéritier, Henriette Julie de Murat, Charlotte-Rose de la Force, Jean de Mailly, Eustache Le Noble, and others were chiefly responsible for the establishment of the fairy tale as a literary genre in Europe, they were not as original as one would think, nor were they the innovators of the genre. In fact, the Italian writers Giovan Francesco Straparola and Giambattista Basile played a highly significant role in the rise of the literary fairy tale in Europe, and their tales had a profound influence on the French. This is one of the best kept secrets in the history of the fairy tale, and it is a secret that is well worth unlocking because it reveals just how closely tied the literary fairy tale as genre is to the spread of the civilizing process throughout Europe.

The rise of the literary fairy tale as a short narrative form stemmed from the literary activity that flourished in Florence during the fourteenth century and led to the production of various collections of *novelle* in Italian and Latin under the influence of Boccaccio's *Decamerone*. The *novella*, also called *conto*, was a short tale that adhered to principles of unity of time and action and clear narrative plot. The focus was on surprising events of *everyday* life, and the tales (influenced by oral wonder tales, fairy tales, *fabliaux*, chivalric romances, epic poetry, and fables) were intended for the amusement and instruction of the readers. Before Boccaccio had turned his hand to writing his tales, the most famous collection had been the *Novellino* written by an anonymous Tuscan author in the thirteenth century. But it was Boccaccio who set a model for all future writers of this genre with his frame narrative and subtle and sophisticated style. It was Boccaccio who expanded the range of topics of the novella and created unforgettable characters that led to numerous imitations by writers such as Ser Giovanni Fiorentino, Giovanni Sercambi, Franco Sachetti, Piovano Arlotto, and Matteo Bandello, to name but a few.

It was undoubtedly because of Boccaccio's example, the growth of literacy and publishing in Venice, and the great interest in the novella that Straparola came to publish his collection *Le piacevoli notti* (1550 and 1553) in two volumes. Straparola is a fascinating figure because he was the first European writer to adapt many tales from the oral tradition, and he created approximately fourteen literary fairy tales in his collection of seventy-four novelle. He is also a mysterious figure because we know next to nothing about him. Straparola was born probably about 1480 in Carvaggio, but there are no records that confirm anything about his life, and even his surname "Straparola," which means the loquacious one, may have been a pseudonym. We have information only from the first volume of *Le piacevoli notti* that he was born in Carvaggio and that he was the author of another work, *Opera nova de Zoan Francesco Straparola da Caravazo* (1508), a collection of sonnets and poems, published in Venice. Also, we are not certain of his death in 1557. Most likely he had moved to Venice as a young man, and it is clear from his collection of novelle, which he called *favole*, that he was very well educated and that he must have lived in Venice for some time. He knew Latin and various Italian dialects, and his references to other literary works and understanding of literary forms indicate that he was well versed in the humanities. Whoever Straparola may have been, his *Le piacevoli notti* had great success: it was reprinted twenty-five times from 1553–1613 and translated into French in 1560 and 1580 and into German in 1791. It was also at one time banned by the pope.

The allure of his work can be attributed to several factors: his use of erotic and obscene riddles, his mastery of polite Italian used by the narrators in the frame narrative, his introduction of plain earthy language into the stories, the critical view of the power struggles in Italian society and lack of moralistic preaching, his inclusion of fourteen unusual fairy tales into the collection, and his interest in magic, unpredictable events, duplicity, and the supernatural. Similar to Boccaccio, Straparola exhibited an irreverence for authorities, and the frame narrative reveals a political tension and somewhat ironic if not pessimistic outlook on the possibilities of living a harmonious happy ever after life.

In the opening of the book that sets the frame for all the *favole*, Straparola depicts how Ottoviano Maria Sforza, the bishop-elect of Lodi (most likely the real Sforza, who died in 1540), was forced to leave Milan because of political plots against him. He takes his daughter, Signora Lucretia, a widow, with him, and because her husband had died in 1523, it can be assumed that the setting for *Le piacevoli notti* is approximately some time between 1523 and 1540. The bishop and his daughter flee first to Lodi, then to Venice, and finally settle on the island of Murano. They gather a small group of congenial people around them: ten gracious ladies, two matronly women, and four educated and distinguished gentlemen. Since it is the time of Carnival, Lucretia proposes that the company take turns telling stories during the two weeks before Lent, and consequently, there are thirteen nights in which stories are told, amounting to seventy-four tales in all.

To a certain extent, the fictional company on the island of Murano can be regarded as an ideal representation of how people can relate to one another and comment in pleasing and instructive ways about all types of experience. The stories created by Straparola are literary fairy tales, revised oral tales, anecdotes, erotic stories, buffo tales of popular Italian life, didactic anecdotes, fables, and tales based on the works of writers who preceded him, such as Boccaccio, Franco Sacchetti, Ser Giovanni Forentino, Giovanni Sercambi, and others. In the fairy tales, as well as in most of the other narratives, Straparola focuses on power and fortune. Without luck (magic, fairies, miracles) the hero cannot succeed in his mission, and without knowing how to use the power of magic or taking advantage of a fortuitous event or gift, the hero cannot succeed. Though wicked people are punished, it is clear that standards of civility are set only by the people in power. Actually, most civil standards and proper norms are rarely upheld. Thus, in "Galeotto," a tale imitated by Mme d'Aulnoy in "Le Prince Marcassin" and Mme de Murat in "Le Roy Porc," the animal prince can kill his brides at will, and in "Tebaldo," which may have influenced Perrault's "Peau d'Ane," a father can seek to sleep with his daughter at will. The majority of the tales center on active male protagonists who are "heroic" mainly because they know how to exploit opportunities that bring them wealth, power, and money. Straparola begins most of his tales in small towns or cities in Italy and sends his protagonists off to other countries and realms and, of course, into woods or onto the sea. His protagonists are adventurers, and there is a sense that the fairy tales have been gathered from far and wide and not just from the region of Venice.

If Straparola did indeed spend most of his life in Venice—and we cannot be certain about this—it would not be by chance that the tales that he read and heard came to this port city from other regions in Europe and other countries. Venice was a thriving and wealthy city in the sixteenth century, and Straparola would have had contact with foreigners from all over Italy, Europe, and the Orient. Or he would have had news about them. This real news formed the basis of the *fiabe* (fairy tales) in his collection, and it is a collection that also was fairly well disseminated in Europe. But its significance for the development of the literary fairy tale in Europe has generally been neglected. Of course, he alone did not trigger the development, but there are clear signs that his tales circulated throughout Europe and had a considerable influence among educated writers: Basile, who later spent some time in Venice, was apparently familiar with his book, and it is obvious that Mme d'Aulnoy, Mme de Murat, Charles Perrault, Eustache Le Noble, and Jean de Mailly knew his tales in some version, and through them the tales spread to Germany and eventually influenced the Brothers Grimm, who wrote about Straparola and Basile.[1] In short, Straparola helped initiate the genre of the literary fairy tale in Europe, and though it would be misleading to talk about a diachronic history of the literary fairy tale with a chain reaction that begins with Straparola, leads to Basile and then to the French writers of the 1690s, and culminates in the work of the Brothers Grimm, I want to suggest that they do form a historical frame in which the parameters of the early literary fairy tale were set, and within that frame there was an institutionalization of what we now call fairy-tale characters, topoi, motifs, metaphors, and plots. Their conventionalization enabled numerous writers (and storytellers in the oral tradition) to experiment and produce highly original fairy tales at the same time. In Italy, Straparola's work was particularly innovative because the oral folktale had rarely been adapted as a literary fairy tale in the vernacular. Straparola was writing at a time when Latin was still the dominant print language, and he was using Tuscan Italian and some dialect to appeal to a growing audience of middle-class readers. Also his perspective with regard to the corruption and immorality of the times reflects his concern in bringing about a change in morals, manners, and customs. There was no standard civilizing process in Italy during his times, although there were numerous books about courtly manners and the proper education of the aristocracy, some with references to specific principalities in Italy, others that concerned European society. The French were the progenitors of a more general and effective civilizing process in the sixteenth century. But literacy in Italy, that is, the significance of becoming literate, was part of the process, and the publication, distribution, and reading of Straparola's fairy tales were part of the nascent civilizing process in Italy. In particular, he demonstrated how both oral and literary fairy tales could be shaped in metaphorical form to address delicate issues pertaining to the power of tyrannical princes, justice, and proper comportment. Given the reading practices of his day, many of his tales must have been read aloud, and he himself (with his strange name associated with loquacity) may have been a storyteller of some kind. Writers were also tellers in the sixteenth century, for the split between oral and literary narrators was never as great as we imagine it to be, and their familiarity with the folklore of their respective societies played a role in their literary representations in the fairy tale. Basile's work is a case in point.

We know a great deal about Basile, in contrast to the little we know about Straparola. Born in a small village near Naples about 1575, he came from a middle-class family, and in 1603 he left Naples and traveled north, eventually settling in Venice, where he earned his living as a soldier and began writing poetry. By 1608 he returned to the region of Naples and held various positions as administrator and governor in different principalities and courts while pursuing a career as poet and writer until his death in 1632. Though he became well known for his poems, odes, eclogues, and dramas, written in Italian, and he helped organize court spectacles, his fame today is a result of his astounding collection of fifty fairy tales written in Neapolitan dialect, *Lo cunto de li cunti* (The Tale of Tales, 1634–36), also known as the *Pentamerone* (The Pentameron), published posthumously thanks to the efforts of his sister Adriana, a famous opera singer.

There is no clear proof that Basile knew Straparola's tales, but it is more than likely he was acquainted with them in some form, especially since he had spent about three years in Venice, where Straparola's tales had been published and had been popular. However important Straparola might have been for Basile's conception of his fairy tales, he was a pale light in comparison with the fiery imaginative Basile. Not only did the Neapolitan author draw on an abundance of literary and historical sources to create his uproarious ironic tales but he also was acquainted with the folklore of a vast region around Naples and was familiar with Oriental tales, as was Straparola. His command of the Neopolitan dialect is extraordinary, for he managed to combine an elevated Baroque form of the dialect with vulgar expressions, metaphors, idioms, and brilliant proverbs, many of which he created himself. The frame narrative (following Boccaccio, of course) is fascinating in and of itself. His "tale of tales" sets the stage for forty-nine marvelous stories. In this frame tale, Zoza, the daughter of the King of Vallepelosa, cannot laugh, and her father is so concerned about her happiness that he invites people from all over to try to make her laugh. Yet nobody can succeed, until an old woman, who attempts to sop up oil in front of the palace, has her jug broken by a mischievous court page. The ensuing argument between the old woman and the page, each hurling coarse and vulgar epithets at one another, is so delightful that Zoza bursts into laughter. However, this laughter does not make the old woman happy, and she curses Zoza by exclaiming, "Begone, and may you never find even the shadow of a husband unless you take the Prince of Camporotondo!"[2] To her dismay, Zoza learns that this prince named Tadeo is under the spell of a wicked fairy and is in a tomb. He can be wakened and liberated only by a woman who fills a pitcher hanging on a nearby wall with her tears.

In need of help, Zoza visits three different fairies and receives a walnut, a chestnut, and a hazelnut as gifts. Then she goes to Tadeo's tomb and weeps into the pitcher for two days. When the pitcher is almost full, she falls asleep because she is tired from all the crying. While she is sleeping, however, a slave girl steals the pitcher, fills it, wakes Tadeo, and takes the credit for bringing him back to life. Consequently, Tadeo marries her, and she becomes pregnant. But Zoza, whose happiness depends on Tadeo, is not about to concede the prince to a slave girl. She rents a house across from Tadeo's palace and manages to attract the attention of Tadeo. In response, the slave girl threatens to beat the baby if Tadeo spends any time with Zoza, who now uses another tactic to gain entrance into Tadeo's palace. On three different occasions she opens the nuts. One contains a little dwarf, who sings; the next contains twelve chickens made of gold; and the third contains a doll that spins gold. The slave girl demands these fascinating objects, and Tadeo sends for them, offering Zoza whatever she wants. To his surprise, Zoza gives the objects as gifts. Yet the final one, the doll, stirs an uncontrollable passion in the slave girl to hear stories during her pregnancy, and she threatens Tadeo again: unless women come to tell her tales, she will kill their unborn baby. So, Tadeo invites ten women from the rabble known for their storytelling. The women spend the day chattering and gossiping, and after the evening meal, one tale is told by each one of the ten for five nights. Finally, on the last day, Zoza is invited to tell the last tale, and she recounts what happened to her. The slave girl tries to stop her, but Tadeo insists that Zoza be allowed to tell the tale to the end. When he realizes that Zoza's tale is true, Tadeo has the pregnant slave girl buried alive, and he marries Zoza to bring the tale of tales to a "happy" conclusion.

Unlike the narratives by Boccaccio and Straparola, Basile's tales, which are told during banquets with music, games, and dance, are entirely fairy tales, revised apparently from the oral tradition and told by lower-class figures. There are constant local references to Naples and the surrounding area and to social customs, political intrigues, and family conflicts. Basile was an astute social commentator, who despaired of the corruption in the courts that he served, and he was obviously taken with the country folk, their surprising antics, and their need and drive for change and the acquisition of better living conditions.

Similar to Straparola, Basile shared a concern with power, civility, and transformation and was fascinated by the wheel of fortune and how Lady Fortuna, often in the form of a mysterious *fata* (fairy, linked to fate), intervened in people's lives to provide them with the opportunity to advance in society or to gain some measure of happiness. Of course, he also depicted how Lady Fortuna could devastate people and cause destruction. Again, like Straparola, he was not overly optimistic about establishing social equality and harmonious communities. Conflict reigns in his tales in which a usually demure Cinderella chops off the head of her stepmother and a discreet princess virtually liquidates a seducer in a battle of the sexes. Nevertheless, his tales exude mirth because of the manner in which he turns language inside out and creates a catnivalesque atmosphere.[3] Just as the frame tale leads to the exposure of the stealthy slave girl to her deadly detriment, all the narratives seek to reveal the contradictory nature in which all members of society pretend to comport themselves according to lofty standards but will stoop as low as they must to achieve wealth and happiness. Basile takes great delight in minimizing the differences between coarse peasants and high aristocrats, and certainly if his tales had been written and published in Italian, they would have found their way to the Church's Index of Prohibited Books.

Remarkable as it may seem, Basile's tales were, in fact, reprinted several times in the seventeenth century, despite the difficulty people might have had reading the Neapolitan dialect, and, through translations into Italian and then into French, they became fairly well known in Italy and France during the seventeenth and eighteenth centuries. It is apparent that Mlle Lhéritier was very familiar with his tales, and three of hers, "L'Adroite Princesse" ("The Discreet Princess"), "Les Enchantements de l'éloquence" ("The Enchantments of Eloquence"), and "Ricdin-Ricdon," depend heavily on three of his stories, "Sapia Liccarda," "Le Tre Fate" ("The Three Fairies"), and "Le Sette Cotennine" ("The Seven Pieces of Bacon Rind"). In fact, the Italian influence in France during the 1690s was much more profound than scholars have suspected. At least six of Mme d'Aulnoy's fairy tales can be traced to Straparola's *fiabe*; two of Mme de Murat's tales owe a great debt to Straparola; and three of Mailly's tales and two of Le Noble's are very imitative of Straparola's works. Even Antoine Galland's "Histoire de deux soeurs jalouses de leur cadette" ("The Jealous Sisters and Their Cadette") in *Les Milles et une nuit* (*One Thousand and One Nights*) appears to have been stamped by Straparola's "Ancilotto." Finally, almost all of Perrault's tales have models in the collections of Straparola and Basile, especially "Le Maître Chat ou le chat botté" ("Puss in Boots") and "Cendrillon" ("Cinderella"). Familiarity with the Italian tales was certainly there.[4] What is significant and fascinating is the manner in which French writers began about 1690 to be attracted to folktales and fairy tales and to create a vogue of writing that was to last approximately a century and firmly institutionalize the fairy tale as a literary genre throughout Europe and North America.

Perhaps I should say French women writers or, to be even more specific, Mme d'Aulnoy, because she and they almost single-handedly transformed the Italian and Oriental tales as well as oral tales into marvelous fairy tales that were serious commentaries on court life and cultural struggles at the end of the eighteenth century in Versailles and Paris.[5] Like Straparola and Basile, the French writers were deeply concerned about the civilizing process in their respective societies and the power struggles among members of their own class and the contradictions between social classes. For the most part, the French writers set their fairy tales in frame narratives following Straparola and Basile so that their tales became conversation pieces told to inform readers in a pleasurable way about marvelous disputes that were in fact embedded in the reality of their times. Many of the tales emanated from the French salons in which the French writers recounted their tales. When the individual French tales are compared with their Italian predecessors, it is apparent that the changes and transformations that the French authors made were determined by their reactions to the French mores and social codes. In this respect the French tales are interventions in the debates about the role of women, the nature of *tendresse*, and the proper exercise of power and justice at French courts.[6] Moreover, they reflect the cultural wars of the times begun by Nicolas Boileau and Perrault in the "Querelles des anciens et des modernes" ("Quarrels of the Ancients and the Moderns") that also included major debates about the role of women.[7] Whether consciously or unconsciously, the French writers modernized the folklore of their times as well as the Italian literary tales that had influenced them with a view toward having them comment on the civilizing process as it took shape in France. In this respect, they lay the grounds for the modernization of the fairy tale in Europe that was to have great ramifications in Germany and later in England and North America. But this rise of the French fairy tale to such preeminence, we should not forget, was part of a historical continuum that received its start in Italy.

When we, therefore, speak about the influence of the Italians on the French writers of the 1690s, it is not necessary to ascertain and prove exactly which specific Italian tale a French writer knew, adapted, or appropriated, even though this knowledge is helpful. Rather, it is more important to discuss how the French writers learned from the Italians to use a narrative strategy that enabled them to intervene in the civilizing process and allowed them to publish and publicize subversive views that questioned the power of hegemonic groups. Before, however, I explain how Straparola and Basile set examples of intervention in the civilizing process, I want to say a few words about Norbert Elias's work concerning this process and amplify his ideas with some notions borrowed from Pierre Bourdieu.

In his pioneer work *Über den Prozeß der Zivilisation* (*The Civilizing Process*), which was first published in 1939 but did not have an impact in Europe until it was rediscovered in 1977, Elias used the ancien régime of Louis XIV as an example to develop a theoretical model to explain how nation-states form structures that produce long-term processes to maintain power, governance, and subsistence, and one of the most important processes was the civilizing process that incorporated all groups of people into an interdependent network dominated by hegemonic groups through the inculcation of norms, customs, rules, etiquette, and cultural codes. Elias argued that there are four elementary functions that must be fulfilled if people are to survive interdependently as a society or state: (1) the economic function that allows for the provision of food and other basic necessities of life; (2) the function of conflict management that establishes control of violence within a group and control of violence in the relationship between different survival groups; (3) the function of knowledge that fosters domination and mediation so that the fear of nature can be overcome and understanding between different groups of people can be negotiated; and (4) the function of the civilizing process that requires individual adaptation to a social pattern of self-restraint or a civilizing process based on initiation rites, peer pressure, group pressure, social codes, and legislation.[8]

The rise of the state, whether it may be the city-state in Italy during the fifteenth, sixteenth, and seventeenth centuries or later the nation-state of France in the seventeenth century, depended more and more on specific modes and norms of self-restraint that reinforced the power of the ruling classes. The shifts in the control and use of power bring about changes in the civilizing process as a result of a reciprocal attunement of needs and satisfactions of the functionaries, specialists of all kinds, and dominant groups to keep power among themselves. By examining how groups are formed in relation to power, Elias asserts that one can grasp how society developed and changed. That is, one can grasp how the civilizing process works. "Human groups specialized for the means of violence, orientation, capital accumulation and investment, and organizing other groups of people, were able, at one time or another, to establish themselves as controllers of the central monopolies of a state and thus, alone or in partnership, to perform ruling functions in their society. Recurrent power conflicts within or between states, whether between competing establishments or between established and outsiders—in other words, hegemonial and survival struggles of various kinds—formed one of the strongest, perhaps the strongest, driving force in the development of societies."[9]

One aspect of the civilizing process that Elias neglected to treat was gender formation and conflict that Pierre Bourdieu illuminates so brilliantly in his book *Masculine Domination*. Bourdieu maintains that "the social world constructs the body as a sexually defined reality and as the depository of sexually defining principles of vision and division. This embodied social programme of perception is applied to all the things of the world and firstly to the body itself, in its biological reality. It is this programme which constructs the difference between the biological sexes in conformity with the principles of a mythic vision of the world rooted in arbitrary relationship of domination of men over women, itself inscribed, with the division of labour, in the reality of the social order."[10]

The process of masculine domination is, of course, much older than the civilizing process and thus inherent in it. That is, whatever conflicts and struggles for power are played out in the civilizing process involve the manner in which men reinforce their authority and force and the manner in which women confront and expose the arbitrary rule of men. To be civil in any society, to be counted as a civilian, one must understand and follow social codes that are not of one's making and that determine to a large degree one's sexual identity and social status.

Fairy tales—and one could add the oral folktales as well—always have been concerned with sex roles, social class, and power. Both Straparola and Basile were astute observers of how the civilizing process functioned and was being corroded in the different Italian principalities through wars, family conflicts, and transformation of trade and commerce in the sixteenth and seventeenth centuries. They were apparently drawn to the fairy tale because it offered them a mode of writing, a narrative strategy and discourse, to address their concerns about the deformation of the civilizing process and the transmission of norms of behavior that involved the management of violence and self-restraint. It is not by chance that Straparola sets his frame around a powerful duke fleeing for his life and taking refuge in Venice. It is not by chance that Basile sets his frame around a conflict between two women in a court society in which the prince is a feeble and naive bystander of events that he does not fully comprehend. It is also not by chance that the majority of the tales told in Straparola's frame are spoken by elegant ladies, and in Basile's frame they all are told by gifted female storytellers from the lower classes. In each case, the perspective is from the dominated sex, from down under, from a subversive point of view that exposes the darkness of court societies and the absurd and arbitrary ways men use power to enforce what they consider to be the proper gender roles and social codes of their civilizing processes. Commenting on Basile's Lo cunto de li cunti, Michele Rak maintains that "the work was prepared anticipating its method of use in view of diversion (pastime or intrattenimento) and the practices of courtly conversation with its genres and theatrical, comical, and deviant registers within the limits of a social situation previewed in the index of current customs and its manners. The work is one of the Baroque links in the tradition of the European story that stems from the Medieval vigils around the hearth to the fairy tales of the French salon of the seventeenth century."[11] This tendency to reflect on and use courtly conversation and storytelling within the civilizing process is also very apparent in Straparola's work, but because conditions for the formation and institutionalization of a literary fairy-tale genre were not yet ripe in Italy, the works of Straparola and Basile could take hold, so to speak, only at the end of the seventeenth century in France.

Many of the French writers of the 1690s, when the fairy tale did become institutionalized as a genre in Europe, were women, who often used frames of conversation in their collections to tell their tales. They wrote many more tales than the men, who generally dispensed with the frames. Yet both the men and women were deeply invested in the conflicts of the civilizing process in France that was centered at King Louis XIV's court. Almost all were attached to the court in some way. Since most were aware of how Straparola and Basile effectively used folktales and fairy tales to criticize so-called courtly behavior, immorality, and arbitrary violence without suffering from papal or ducal censorship, they were drawn to the genre and wrote subversively to question the mores, customs, habits, and use of power during their own time.

Given the different cultures and different times the Italian and French tales were written, the tales reflect on the particular civilizing processes of their states in very specific ways. But they do have one thing in common: they lay bare the contradictions of the civilizing process, reveal how power works for those who are opportunistic and well situated, and propose modes of self-restraint in keeping with the civilizing process. Moreover, they often use irony, sarcasm, and farce to make a mockery of the abuse of power and to indicate possibilities for change. Certainly none of the Italian and French writers were radicals in their day. Straparola was probably from the educated middle classes and familiar with courtly customs, as was Basile, while the French writers were mainly from the aristocratic class with the exception of Perrault, who was from the *haute bourgeoisie* and as close to the court as one could get. But they were all discontent and questioned the regimes of their times. What better way to do this without being punished than through the fairy tale? But what exactly were their strategies?

Because it would take a book to explore all their tales, I want to cite a few examples to suggest how the Italians and French cultivated oral and literary tales to express their critical sentiments about the civilizing process. In partic-ular, I want to deal with discursive sets of recognizable tale types that were evidently common in both the oral and literary traditions of the late medieval and Renaissance periods. They emanated from oral traditions and circulated by word of mouth and through print to communicate notions of self-restraint and behavior necessary for social survival. Since the tales in a particular set repeated and changed motifs and characters in the familiar plots, they formed recognizable discourses that became relevant in socialization and civilizing processes.

The first set of tales concerns a prince born as a beast of some kind; the second set deals with a vulgar fisherman, a fool, who exposes the frailties of a court society; the third set is about a young woman who disguises herself as a knight to reform a court; and the fourth set centers on a cunning cat who shows how clothes make the man and how superficial kings and their followers are. In all of these tales, the writers deal with a *lack* or weakness in court society that needs to be filled or cured through proper comportment. There are, of course, other ways to interpret these tales, but it appears to me that the Italian and French writers are asking key questions that deal with *civilité* and the civilizing process. What virtues are necessary for members of the ruling class to bring about an ideal kingdom? What type of behavior must a young man or woman exhibit to rise in society or reform society so that there is just rule? Implicit in the fairy tales is a critique of a court society that lacks kindness, graciousness, humility, wisdom, tenderness, and justice, qualities necessary to advance the cause of civilité.

Straparola, d'Aulnoy, and de Murat each wrote a fairy tale—"Galeotto, re d'Anglia, ha un figliuolo" ("The Pig Prince," 1550), "Le prince Marcassin" ("The Wild Boar," 1698), and "Le roy porc" ("The Pig King," 1699), respectively—that depicted the problems caused by a beastly prince whose coarse ways expose the amorality and brutality of the court. But the revelation of the problems also allows the authors to propose ways to civilize the prince so that the court will become more humane and moral. The plot of all three fairy tales can easily be summarized: a desperate, seemingly infertile queen wishes for a son, no matter what form he might take. The fairies grant her wish, and she gives birth to either a pig or a boar. When the prince reaches maturity, he wants to marry, and despite the queen's shock and embarrassment, she grants the wish and provides prospective brides for him. However, each time he weds one, he brutally kills his young wife when she does not accept his beastly ways. Only his third bride is patient and self-effacing enough to put up with his crude manners and nasty ways. Thus he is saved by her virtuous behavior and transformed into a handsome prince. That is, her modesty, devotion, and self-control lead to his humane transformation.

There is a long oral and literary tradition of beast–bridegroom tales that can be traced back to the *Pancatranta* (300 CE), a collection of Indian didactic fables and stories in Sanskrit, up through Apuleius's Latin romance *The Golden Ass* (second-century CE), and that reflected on how men might be humanized or civilized to become integrated in a social group. The value of the female was determined by her virtues or how, through her behavior, she could bring about the integration. What is interesting in Straparola's tale is that, from a male perspective, the responsibility for his transformation is placed on poor young women, who are obliged to prove that they will suffer his coarse and crude manners. Otherwise, they will be and are killed. Only the third daughter, who can endure the pig prince's stench and filth, is spared and, in turn, helps bring about the prince's transformation. If there is any standard of civility in Straparola's tale, it is determined by arbitrary male rule that can be modified only by the self-abnegation of a woman. In d'Aulnoy's "Le prince Marcassin" and de Murat's "Le roy porc," two long and elaborate narratives, there is an apparent shift in emphasis, for both writers stress the civilizing power of the fairies, who aid a young woman so that she can change a brute into a tender lover. The beastlike prince is not allowed to kill anyone. Instead, he must suffer in compliance with the commands of the fairies, who charge a princess with the task of humanizing him. Clearly, the French women writers did not want to recognize the power of Louis XIV or the Catholic Church, for their tales are all secular and the narratives are devised so that the sentiments of aristocratic women will be fulfilled. Although the fairies can be somewhat arbitrary, their acts support and constitute standards of comportment that differ vastly with the amorality of the Italian courts and with the reigning principles in their own times. Violence and violation are critiqued and adumbrated in the tales by d'Aulnoy and de Murat, who clearly speak on behalf of humiliated women in a humble and firm voice.

In another group of tales involving a poor and somewhat foolish and humiliated fisherman, who wishes that a supercilious princess become pregnant, the civilizing effect of the fairies in both the Italian and the French tales is also stressed. In the tales—"Pietro the Fool" by Straparola, "Peruonto" by Basile, and "The Dolphin" by Madame d'Aulnoy—the fisherman is always a fool, who is blessed by either a magic fish or fairies, and once it is discovered that he may have impregnated the princess through magic, the king banishes his daughter and the fool from his kingdom. He sets them in a barrel with little to eat and sends them out into the sea. Miraculously, they survive, land on an island, and transform it into a magnificent kingdom. Later, the king, regretting his actions, lands on the island by chance and is taught a lesson in civility by his daughter. In Straparola's tale, both Pietro and the princess undergo a transformation—she is only twelve when she becomes pregnant, and he is a fool. Thanks to the magic fish, both are turned into mature, gracious young people, and everyone learns humility. In Basile's tale, the simpleton Peruonto is described in lavish detail at the beginning of the tale:

> A worthy woman of Casoria called Ceccarella had a son called Peruonto, who was the most disgraceful, the most stupid, and the most terrific blockhead that nature had ever produced. That is why the poor woman's heart turned darker than a dustcloth, and why she cursed more than a thousand times that day when her knees had opened the door to that birdbrain, who was not even worth a dog's bowels. But no matter how much the unfortunate woman might open her mouth and scream, the lazybones did not give a shit and would not do a simple damn favor for her.[12]

It is by luck or *fortuna* that he will be able to change his life: he does a favor for three sons of a fairy, and they bestow magic power on him that enables him to obtain whatever he desires. However, the ending of this tale is much more ironic than Straparola's, for Peruonto and his wife beg for the king's pardon after amazing him with their wealth and grandeur. Neither Straparola nor Basile believes that one can earn a high position in court through merit. It is through chance and *fortuna* that one is transformed and gains power to protect oneself from the violence of the dominant class. In contrast, d'Aulnoy and the

French writers of fairy tales set out prescribed values necessary for the forging of *civilité*, generally among members of the ruling class. In d'Aulnoy's tale "The Dolphin," the protagonist Alidor is a prince with a good heart, but he is so ugly that he feels ashamed and leaves his father's kingdom. When he travels to the court of the King of the Woods, he falls in love with the beautiful princess Livorette, who mocks him because of his ugliness. Fortunately, while fishing, he catches a dolphin that grants him magic powers because Alidor kindly lets him go free. Soon after, Alidor courts Livorette as a canary, but he accidentally insults an evil fairy named Grognette who wants to make him and Livorette suffer. So, Grognette makes Livorette pregnant, and after she gives birth to a son, she is banished with Alidor in human form and sent out to sea in a barrel. However, the dolphin helps them establish a utopian reign on an island: "the inhabitants of the island provided them with every pleasure possible. Their rivers were full of fish, their forests, of game, their orchards, of fruit, their fields, of wheat, their meadows, of grass, their wells, of gold and silver. There were no wars and no lawsuits. It was a land where youth, health, beauty, wit, books, pure water, and good wine abounded, and where snuffboxes were inexhaustible! And Livorette was as much in love with Alidor as Alidor with Livorette."[13]

It is in this ideal kingdom, counterposed to the real realm of King Louis XIV, that Livorette is reconciled with her parents, again thanks to the good dolphin and the fairies, for it is through the feminine magic touch only that standards of civility can be maintained. Everyone must curb their violent feelings and grasp what it means to be humiliated.

In another group of tales that deal with princesses disguised as knights, Straparola, Basile, d'Aulnoy, and de Murat ponder questions that deal with the reformation of a court that is either sick and corrupt or under attack by barbarous forces hostile to civilization. In each tale, a young valorous princess must disguise herself as a knight and represent her father because he has no male offspring and is too old to help the king. (Incidentally, there is a clear influence of the Arthurian knights in these tales.) When she arrives at the king's court, she becomes involved in intrigues and exposes the corruption in the court. Her noble behavior is held up as an example of *civilité*, and her marriage with the king brings about the restoration of just rule. In Straparola's "Constanza/Constanzo," the disguised princess manages to capture a satyr threatening the court, and in turn, the satyr reveals that the king's wife had many lovers. Consequently, the king has his wife and her lovers burned in a large fire, and then he marries Constanza. In Basile's "The Three Crowns," Basile changes the plot somewhat by having a princess named Marchetta flee from an arranged marriage. After she helps an ogress, she is given men's clothing and a magic ring. A king finds her in the woods and brings her back to his castle as his page. Unfortunately for Marchetta, the queen falls in love with her, thinking she is a young man, and then demands that she be burned at the stake when Marchetta rejects her advances. Fortunately, she can use the ogress's magic ring to reveal the truth, and the queen is thrown into the sea. In d'Aulnoy's "Belle-Belle; or the Chevalier Fortuné," Belle-Belle meets seven extraordinary men who help her defeat the king's enemy. This time it is the king's sister who is angered by Fortuné's unwillingness to have an affair with her. She deceives her brother the king by pretending Fortuné has assaulted her and demands that she be burned at the stake. However, when Fortuné's clothes are ripped off, the executioners and people realize she is a woman and could not have attacked the king's sister. So, she is saved and then marries the king. Basile's tale ended with the ironic moral, "God will heed/A ship in need." D'Aulnoy's tale ends with the following:

> Belle-Belle's change saved her innocent soul,
> And struck her royal persecutor down.
> Heaven protects the innocent and plays its role
> By defeating vice and rewarding virtue with a crown.[14]

It is virtue that also plays a key role in Mme de Murat's "The Savage," based, it seems, on both Straparola's and Basile's tales. Here a princess named Constantine flees an arranged marriage and eventually marries the king of Sicily, thanks to a savage who turns out to be an enchanted prince.

De Murat's and d'Aulnoy's tales are very long and intricate and contain courtly discourses about proper manners and virtues that tend to extol tender and natural love, women, and fairies as the forces that bring about harmony and the reformation of a court. In contrast, Charles Perrault, the most famous fairy-tale writer from this period, suggests in such a tale as "Puss in Boots" that the civilizing process may always be flawed and that women may be nothing but appendages in the process. Straparola wrote the first literary version known, and in his tale "Constantino Fortunato," the cat turns out to be a fairy who helps a bumbling peasant deceive a greedy king by having him exchange his tattered clothes for royal garments and pass as a rich nobleman. The theme of "clothes make the man" is the most obvious one in this tale, and it is also central to Basile's "Cagliuoso." Like Straparola, Basile seeks to reveal how superficial and pretentious court society is. However, he goes one step further: his magic female cat who helps the crude peasant Cagliuoso become a king is so maltreated by Cagliuoso at the end that she runs away. No doubt, Cagliuoso will become as corrupt and ungracious as his father-in-law. Perrault transforms this theme somewhat by turning the cat into a master male cat for the first time, and it is the cat, representative of the opportunistic haute bourgeoisie in Paris, who becomes the hero of the tale. It is the cunning cat who arranges everything, refines the peasant, kills an ogre, and is rewarded with a high position at the end of the tale. What is implied here as a critique of so-called *civilité* in Louis XIV's times is that not only must one have the right clothes, manners, and pretensions to succeed in court society but also one must kill and be duplicitous.

As we can see, Straparola and Basile set examples for the French writers of fairy tales by focusing on violent conflicts that demanded some kind of self-restraint and resolution in accordance with the civilizing process of their times. Their ideological perspectives and narrative strategies varied in light of the social and political problems depicted in their tales. What is most significant is that the French writers apparently realized that their tales could be adapted, cultivated, and used to articulate their views on *civilité* at the end of the seventeenth century when Louis XIV's reign was in crisis. The vast potential of the fairy tale was mined and developed as a metaphorical discourse and narrative strategy to comment on the French civilizing process, and as forms of literacy in Europe took greater hold in this historical process in all social classes, so, too, did the literary fairy tale ground itself as genre. Not only is it still employed as a means of civilizing children and adults in the twenty-first century, but its influence has expanded through radio, film, theater, opera, and the Internet to communicate and debate notions of gender, comportment, and violence management. Perhaps the social classes, the means of communication and diversion (entertainment), and the use of power are much different in the twenty-first century than they were during the Renaissance, but as two recent popular fairy-tale films titled *Shrek* (2002) and *Shrek 2* (2004) have demonstrated, there are still rich rulers who act like celebrities, abuse the poor, pretend to uphold standards of *civilité*, and rejoice in their abuse of power and hypocrisy. Times may have seemed to change, but thanks to the creation of the fairy tale by Straparola and Basile, we can still rely on its narrative strategy to see how dangerous it is to think that we live in a more civilized and better world than the realms of the past.

3

SETTING STANDARDS FOR CIVILIZATION THROUGH FAIRY TALES: CHARLES PERRAULT AND THE SUBVERSIVE ROLE OF WOMEN WRITERS

In the case of those cultures which I have named "archaic," there is, in contrast to our own culture, a much clearer awareness extant that we can only always *be* that what we are when, at the same time, we are what we are *not*, that we can only know who we are when we have experienced our limits and thus have surpassed them, as Hegel might say.

This does not mean, however, that we are to drive the stakes of our limits further and further into the wilderness, that we are perpetually to root out, cultivate, and categorize that which is "outside" us. Rather this means that we ourselves are to become wild in order not to *place ourselves at the mercy* of our own wildness, in order to gain thereby an awareness of ourselves as tame, as cultural creatures.

—Hans Peter Duerr, *Traumzeit* (1978)

I

Published in 1697, Charles Perrault's Histoires ou contes du temps passé appeared at a time when there was a major shift in social norms and manners. As Philippe Ariès notes,

Although demographic conditions did not greatly change between the thirteenth and seventeenth centuries, and although child mortality remained at
a very high level, a new sensibility granted these fragile, threatened creatures
a characteristic which the world had hitherto failed to recognize in them: as
if it were only then that the common conscience had discovered that the
child's soul too was immortal. There can be no doubt that the importance
accorded to the child's personality was linked to the growing influence of
Christianity on life and manners.[1]

Thus, it is not by chance that Perrault and the women writers of the 1690s
created their fairy tales for the most part to express their views about young
people and to prepare them for roles that they idealistically believed they
should play in society. Since the fairy tales of Perrault and the women writers
of the salons were created at the point in history when more and more
European writers began composing explicitly for children as separate entities
and when standards were first being set for the development of modern children's literature, their works must be viewed as part of a larger social phenomenon. In fact, they were responsible for a veritable deluge of literary fairy tales
in the eighteenth century that was to take a more definite shape in children's
literature and popular chapbooks in the nineteenth century throughout
Europe and North America.

To be sure, the majority of the tales still courted favor primarily with
adults, but there was an overwhelming tendency in these fairy stories to
provide models of behavior for the rearing and schooling of upper-class children. In fact, the literary fairy tales differed remarkably from their precursors,
the oral folktales and the Italian literary tales, by the manner in which they
portrayed children and appealed to them as a possibly distinct audience. The
fairy tales were cultivated to ensure that young people would be properly
groomed for their social functions. Many were adapted from the Italian tales
of Straparola and Basile and from the oral tales of nurses, governesses, and
servants of the lower classes. They were all carefully refined to be told in
salons and courtly circles and later published to address a larger public.
Indeed the 1690s experienced a tremendous vogue of writing and circulating
literary fairy tales for adults and young people.[2] When Marie-Catherine
d'Aulnoy included the remarkable, dystopian fairy tale "The Island of
Happiness" in her novel *Histoire d'Hippolyte, Comte de Duglas* in 1790, she was not
aware that she was about to set a trend in France.[3] Within five years, the literary
fairy tale became the talk of the literary salons, or what had been the talk in
these salons now came to print: her tales were followed by Mlle Marie-Jeanne
Lhéritier's *Oeuvres Meslées* (1695); Mlle Catherine Bernard's *Inès de Cordoue*
(1695), a novel that included "Les Enchantements de l'Eloquence" and
"Riquet à la houppe"; Mlle Charlotte-Rose Caumont de la Force's *Les Contes des*

Contes (1797); Perrault's Histoires ou contes du temps passé (1697); Mme d'Aulnoy's Les Contes des fées, four volumes (1697–98); Chevalier de Mailly's Les Illustres Fées, contes galans (1698); Mme Henriette Julie de Murat's Contes de fées (1798); Paul-François Nodot's Histoire de Mélusine (1698); Jean de Prechac's Contes moins contes que les autres (1698); Mme Durand's La Comtesse de Mortane (1699); Mme de Murat's Histoires sublimes et allégoriques (1699); Eustache Le Noble's Le Gage touché (1700); Mme Louise d'Auneuil's La Tiranie des fées détruite (1702); and Mme Durand's Les Petits Soupers de l'année 1699 (1702).

Not only did bourgeois and aristocratic writers explore and exploit the treasures of French folklore but, as I discussed in the previous chapter, they also borrowed from the Italian literary tradition, especially from the works by Giovan Francesco Straparola (Le piacevoli notti, 1550 and 1553) and Giambattista Basile (Lo cunto de li cunti, 1634–36), and they began to translate Oriental fairy tales, which had a tremendous influence. In 1704 Antoine Galland published part of the Thousand and One Nights, and in 1707 Petit de Lacroix edited a collection of Persian fairy tales under the title A Thousand and One Days. There were innumerable talented writers in the eighteenth century who either experimented ingeniously with the fairy-tale genre or simply imitated the examples set by Perrault, d'Aulnoy, de Murat, Lhéritier, and Prechac at the end of the seventeenth century.[4] Among the more unique and interesting writers were Gabrielle-Suzanne de Villeneuve (Contes marins ou la Jeune Amériquaine, 1740–43), Jacques Cazotte (Mille et une fadaise, contes à dormer debout, 1742), Claude-Philippe de Caylus (Le Prince Courtebotte et la Princesse Zibeline, 1741–43), Jeanne-Marie Leprince de Beaumont (Magasin des enfans, 1757), and Charles Duclos (Acajou et Ziphile, 1762). Even Jean-Jacques Rousseau wrote a tale titled "La Reine Fantastique" in 1758. The fairy-tale vogue eventually culminated in Charles-Joseph de Mayer's remarkable collection of the major literary fairy tales published in the seventeenth and eighteenth centuries. He printed them in forty-one volumes as Le Cabinet des fées ou Collection choisie des contes des fées et autres contes merveilleux (1785–89).

The fairy-tale boom subsided significantly with the outbreak of the French Revolution, when the interests of the lower classes were made more manifest, and the result was a shift in sociocultural perspective. However, the French literary fairy tales did continue to exercise a powerful influence in Germany. Certainly Mozart's The Magic Flute (1791) emanated from this tradition, and such writers as Christoph Martin Wieland, Johann Karl August Musäus, Johann Wolfgang von Goethe, Ludwig Tieck, Novalis, Clemens Brentano, Joseph von Eichendorff, Friedrich de la Motte Fouquè, Adelbert von Chamisso, E.T.A. Hoffmann, and the Brothers Grimm were all beneficiaries of the French vogue in one form or another. In general the rise of the French literary fairy tale at the end of the seventeenth century can be regarded as the source of the flowering of fairy tales in Europe and America in the nineteenth century.

More specifically, I am talking about a literary heritage that was first intended for the upper classes and gradually spread to lower social echelons, and I am concerned here with these fairy tales as they became more and more directed toward children to set exemplary standards of behavior in the civilizing process.

In France the development of those fairy tales that were to form the genre for children of breeding was initiated first by aristocratic and educated ladies and some male writers like Perrault and Mailly, who forged a discourse about manners, laws, and customs through the new genre of the fairy tale. There were two major tendencies among French fairy-tale writers: either they took the genre seriously and endeavored to incorporate ideas, norms, and values in the narrative structure that they considered worthy of emulation for both the child and the adult reader or they parodied the genre, especially in the eighteenth century, because they considered it trivial and associated magic and the miraculous with the superstitions of the lower classes who were not to be taken seriously anyway. Both sets of writers demonstrated remarkable finesse and literally transformed conversational tales from the French salons and the common folktale into "high" art. To be sure, one could speak of authors who did in fact trivialize the fairy-tale genre by grossly imitating the more skilled writers just to become a social or what we would call today a commercial success. Yet whatever their purpose of writing a fairy tale was, all the authors employed the tale to engage in an ongoing institutionalized discourse about mores and manners in the seventeenth and eighteenth centuries.

Perrault's own contribution to the development of the literary fairy tale for children is an unusual one, because he is often given credit for creating the vogue when it was really the talented female writers who founded the genre and played a more dynamic role in establishing the fairy tale to subvert the more classical genres. However, Perrault, as a member of the Académie Française, has been given more attention in Western civilization for a complex of reasons, and two reasons concern the fact that he was a male writer with an established name and that he was a more polished and acceptable writer than the female writers of fairy tales—and also all the other men. Though he was not as innovative as the ladies, his tales have had a greater long-term influence: he is often regarded as being responsible for shaping folklore into an exquisite literary form and endowing it with an earnest and moral purpose to influence the behavior of adults and children in a tasteful way. At the same time he set stringent standards of comportment that were intended to regulate and limit the nature of children's development and regulate the sexual relations and social comportment of young adults. This intent to "civilize" readers is also evident in the works of Lhéritier, d'Aulnoy, de la Force, de Murat, Leprince de Beaumont, and others: they sought to socialize their readers to inhibit them. In the specific case of the women writers, they also sought to subvert the male code and replace it with a more liberal one favorable to the predilections of educated women, who wanted more power to determine their lives. This is not to argue that Perrault and the women writers had nefarious plans and conspired to fill children's heads with false illusions by writing their fairy tales. For example, despite his ironic attitude toward folklore and his double intention of writing for children and adults with moral fervor and charm, Perrault was most sincere in his intentions to improve the minds and manners of young people. In the preface to the *Contes en Vers* (1695), he argued that people of good taste have recognized the substantial value of the tales. "They have noticed that these trifles [the tales] were not mere trifles, that they contained a useful moral, and that the playful narrative surrounding them had been chosen only to allow the stories to penetrate the mind more pleasantly and in such a manner to instruct and amuse at the same time."[5] Perrault compared his tales with those of his forebears,

> who always took care that their tales contained a praiseworthy and instructive moral. Virtue is rewarded everywhere, and vice is always punished. They all tend to reveal the advantage in being honest, patient, prudent, industrious, obedient and the evil that can befall them if they are not that way. Sometimes the fairies give a gift to a young girl who answers them with civility, and with each word that she speaks, a diamond or a pearl falls from her mouth. And another girl who answers them brutally has a frog or a toad fall from her mouth. Sometimes there are children who become great lords for having obeyed their father or mother, or others who experience terrible misfortune for having been vicious and disobedient. No matter how frivolous and bizarre all these fables are in their adventures, it is certain that they arouse a desire in children to resemble those whom they see become happy and at the same time a fear of the misfortunes that befall wicked characters because of their wickedness. Is it not praiseworthy of fathers and mothers when their children are still not capable of appreciating solid truths stripped of all ornaments to make them love these truths, and, as it were, to make them swallow them by enveloping them in charming narratives which correspond to the weakness of their age? It is incredible how avariciously innocent souls whose natural rectitude has not yet been corrupted receive these hidden instructions.[6]

This argument was repeated in the 1697 dedication in the *Histoires ou contes du temps passé*,[7] and later, in the dedication to the 1729 English translation of Perrault's tales, Robert Samber continued the didactic tradition by stressing their educational and moral value:

> It was however objected, that some of them were very low and childish, especially the first. It is very true, and therein consists their Excellency. They

therefore who made this as an Objection, did not seem very well to understand what they said; they should have reflected they are designed for children: And yet the Author hath so ingeniously and masterly contrived them,
that they insensibly grow up, gradually one after another, in Strength and
Beauty, both as to their Narration and Moral, and are told with such a
Naiveté, and natural innocent Simplicity, that not only children, but those of
Maturity, will also find in them uncommon Pleasure and Delight.[8]

During the course of history, Perrault's tales and those of the women writers
succeeded admirably in their cultural mission: contemporary fairy tales
have been greatly informed by the aesthetics and ideology of seventeenth-
and eighteenth-century French fairy tales that have become part and
parcel of a general civilizing process in the West. There is a direct line from
the Perrault fairy tale of court society to the Walt Disney cinematic fairy tale
of the culture industry. Obviously, many samples of the French fairy-tale
vogue have not survived the test of time and have been replaced by
more adequate modern-day equivalents. But, for the most part, the writers
of the French vogue prepared the way for a social institutionalization of
the fairy tale and stamped the very unreflective and uncritical manner in
which we read and receive fairy tales to the present. What we praise as our
classical fairy-tale heritage, however, has a "dark" side to it that I should like
to discuss in terms of the modern Western civilizing process. To penetrate this
dark side of fairy tales in relation to their socializing function for children, I
want to elaborate more than I did in the first chapter on the notions of civilization developed by Norbert Elias in his two-volume study *The Civilizing
Process* as they pertain to Perrault.[9] Then I want to examine Perrault's major
tales and some written by the neglected female writers in light of their
contradictory and subversive contribution to the education of children
through literature.

My foremost concern is how fairy tales operate ideologically to indoctri-
nate children so that they will conform to dominant social standards that are
not necessarily established in their behalf. Here I should like to make it clear
that the ideology carried by the "classical" literary fairy tales since the seventeenth century and their ideological impact on children are difficult to
pinpoint in a specific scientific way. Given the constant changes in the classical tales, the socioliterary variables in different countries, the differences in
the translations, and the relative nature of reception since the seventeenth
century, one must pay close attention to the sociopsychological mechanisms
through which ideology exercises an influence on readers of fairy tales.
Therefore, it is advisable to uncover paradigmatic patterns, which may correspond to social configurations, to shed light on the way ideology works. As
Christian Zimmer remarks,

> To grapple with ideology is to grapple with a phantom since ideology has neither a body nor a face. It has neither origin nor base which one could recast to provide the battle against it with a precise and well-defined object. Ideology only manifests itself under the form of fluid, of the diffuse, of permanent polymorphism and acts through infiltration, insinuation and impregnation. . . . Ideology does not have a real language and especially not one of violence. Its total lack of aggression, its capacity to transform itself into everything, its infinite malleability, permits it to assume the mask of innocence and neutrality. And above all, as I have said, to blend itself with reality itself. Finally, its most supreme ruse is to delimit a kind of preserved *secteur* which it has called amusement (*divertissement*) and which it has cut off from reality by decree—always *menaced* as such by subversion . . . (moreover it acts on two levels: that of daily life and that of the lapse of the daily, the dream, the imaginary). Amusement is thus a direct creation of ideology. It is always alienation in power. To amuse oneself is to disarm oneself.[10]

At its point of origin, the literary fairy tale for children was designed both to divert as amusement and to instruct ideologically as a means to mold the inner nature of young people. Like the ideology of amusement that it embraces, the classical fairy tale of Perrault was, and still is, considered harmless and entertaining. Yet, considered as one of the vital socializing elements in Western civilization, the literary fairy tale has always been more a subject of concern and debate than we tend to realize. In fact, as childhood assumed a more precious and distinct state of experience during the nineteenth and twentieth centuries, the social forces dominating education constantly checked and investigated to see if the "standard" fairy tale maintained an "ideology of harmlessness"; that is, discreet inquiry and censorship have always been employed to guarantee that fairy tales were more or less constructed to follow the classical pattern and to reinforce the dominant social codes within the home and school. It is impossible and foolish to speak about a one-dimensional literary plot formed by the classical fairy tale and conservative guardians of culture. Yet it is important to examine the complex patterns that have historically emerged in the civilizing process to trace how harmful or contradictory the literary fairy tale with all its utopian verve has been, even though it has enjoyed a celebrated place in our hearts.

II

Norbert Elias's remarkable sociohistorical study of the civilizing process is most useful for illuminating the dark socializing side of the classical fairy tales because he stresses the interrelationship between the sociogenetic evolution of society and the psychogenetic makeup of human beings:

> Even in civilized society no human being comes into the world civilized, and . . . the individual civilizing process that he compulsorily undergoes is a function of the social civilizing process. Therefore, the structure of the child's effects and consciousness no doubt bears a certain resemblance to that of "uncivilized" peoples, and the same applies to the psychological stratum in grown-ups which, with the advance of civilization, is subjected to more or less heavy censorship and consequently finds an outlet in dreams, for example. But since in our society each human being is exposed from the first moment of life to the influence and the molding of civilized grown-ups, he must indeed pass through a civilizing process in order to reach the standard attained by his society in the course of its history, but not through the individual historical phases of the social civilizing process.[11]

Elias demonstrates that the major sociopolitical shift in favor of absolutism and religious orthodoxy in the latter part of the seventeenth century determined modern Western attitudes toward civilization. The decentralized societies of the Middle Ages ceded to more centralized and regulated nation-states and principalities that abandoned lax notions of *courteoisie* (soon to be called barbaric) for more stringent notions of *civilité*, partly introduced and reinforced by the bourgeoisie, at least in France and England.

It is important to understand the cultural and political input of large *secteurs* of the bourgeoisie in France if we are to grasp Perrault's role in "civilizing" the folktale and some of the Italian literary tales and transforming them into the literary fairy tale for upper-class adults and children. The French aristocracy of the sixteenth and seventeenth centuries displayed a unique capacity to adopt and use the best elements from other classes. The nobility provided access for a select group of reliable people of the third estate to its circles, which were expanded as the need arose to secure aristocratic rule throughout the nation, and Perrault was among the fortunate members of the *haute bourgeoisie* to be honored by the court.[12] He was a high, royal civil servant, one of the first members of the Académie Française, a respected polemicist, and a significant figure in literary salons. Moreover, he endorsed the expansive political wars of Louis XIV and believed in the exalted mission of the French absolutist regime to "civilize" Europe and the rest of the world. Perrault supported the "manifest destiny" of seventeenth-century France not only as a public representative of the court but also privately in his family, and he was also one of the first writers of fairy tales who explicitly sought to "colonize" the internal and external development of adults and children in the mutual interests of a bourgeois–aristocratic elite.

The interaction between the French nobility and bourgeoisie must be carefully studied to grasp the sociogenetic import of literary fairy tales for children in Western culture. Elias makes this connection clear:

> Both the courtly bourgeoisie and the courtly aristocracy spoke the same language, read the same books, and had, with particular gradations, the same manners. And when the social and economical disproportionalities burst the institutional framework of the ancien régime, when the bourgeoisie became a nation, much of what had originally been the specific and distinctive social character of the courtly aristocracy and then also of the courtly-bourgeois groups, became, in an ever widening movement and doubtless with some modification, the national character. Stylistic conventions, the forms of social intercourse, effect-molding, esteem for courtesy, the importance of good speech and conversation, articulateness of language and much else—all this is first formed in France within courtly society, then slowly changes, in a continuous diffusion, from a social into a national character.[13]

By the time Perrault had begun writing his fairy tales, the major crises of the Reformation period that had been manifested drastically in the massive witch hunts between 1490 and 1650 had been temporarily resolved, and they resulted in greater rationalization and regulation of social and spiritual life. This civilizing process coincided with an increase in socioeconomic power by the bourgeoisie, particularly in France and England, so that the transformed social, religious, and political views represented a blend of bourgeois–aristocratic interests. The *homme civilisé* was the former *homme courteois*, whose polite manners and style of speech were altered to include bourgeois qualities of honesty, diligence, responsibility, and asceticism. To increase its influence and assume more political control, the French bourgeoisie was confronted with a twofold task: to adapt courtly models in a manner that would allow greater laissez-faire for the expansion and consolidation of bourgeois interests and to appropriate folk customs and the most industrious, virtuous, and profitable components of the lower classes to strengthen the economic and cultural power of the bourgeoisie. In this regard the French bourgeoisie was indeed a middle or mediating class, although its ultimate goal was to become self-sufficient and to make the national interests identical with its own.

Literary socialization was one way of disseminating its values and interests and of subliminally strengthening its hold on the civilizing process. Because childhood had become more distinguished as a separate phase of growth and was considered as the crucial base for the future development of the individual character, special attention was now paid to children's manners, clothes, books, toys, and general education. Numerous books, pamphlets, and brochures appeared in the sixteenth and seventeenth centuries that dealt with table manners, natural functions, bedroom etiquette, sexual relations, and correct speech.[14] The most classic example was Erasmus of Rotterdam's *De Civiltate morum puerilum* (*On Civility in Children*, 1530). Also important were the works of Giovanni della Casa (*Galateo*, 1558), C. Calviac (*Civilité*, 1560), Antoine de Courtin (*Nouveau traité de civilité*, 1672), François de Callières (*De la science du monde des connoissances utiles à la conduite de la vie*, 1717), and LaSalle (*Les Règles de la bienséance et de la civilité chrétienne*, 1729). It was impossible for a member of the aristocratic or bourgeois class to escape the influence of such manuals that became part of the informal and formal schooling of all upper-class children. These same views were disseminated to the peasantry through the cheap pamphlets of the *Bibliothèque Bleue*. Coercion exerted by members of high society to act according to new precepts of good behavior increased so that the codes of dress and manner became extremely stringent and hierarchical by the end of the seventeenth century. Though not conspired, the rational purpose of such social pressure was to bring about an internalization of social norms and mores so that they would appear as second nature or habit, what Pierre Bourdieu described as a *habitus* in his important book *La Distinction*.[15] Yet self-control was actual social control, and it was a mark of social distinction not to "let go of oneself" or to "lose one's senses" in public. As Elias noted, the system of standardization and social conditioning had assumed fairly concrete contours with multilevel controls by the mid-seventeenth century:

> There is a more or less limited courtly circle which first stamps the models only for the needs of its own social situation and in conformity with the psychological condition corresponding to it. But clearly the structure and development of French society as a whole gradually makes ever broader strata willing and anxious to adopt the models developed above them: they spread, also very gradually, throughout the whole of society, certainly not without undergoing some modification in the process.[16]

As French society became more regulated and as efforts were made to bring about a homogeneous state, the pressures placed on children to conform to role models became more severe. In keeping with rigid social standards that denounced open forms of sexual behavior, table manners, dress, and natural functioning as "barbaric" and "uncivilized"—that is, ways that had been commonly accepted by the upper classes prior to the sixteenth century—it became important to cultivate feelings of shame and to arouse anxiety in children when they did not conform to a more inhibiting way of social conduct. Restraint and renunciation of instinctual gratification were part of a socioreligious code that illuminated the proper way to shape human drives and ideas so that children would learn docilely to serve church and state. Perhaps one of the main reasons for the rise of a "state of childhood" by the end of the seventeenth century was the rise of a greater discrepancy between adult and child as the civilizing process became geared more instrumentally to dominate nature. The entire period from 1480 to 1650 can be seen as a historical transition in which the Catholic Church and the reform movement of Protestantism combined efforts with the support of the rising mercantile and industrial classes to rationalize society and literally to exterminate social deviates who were associated with the devil, such as female witches, male werewolves, Jews, and gypsies. In particular, women were linked to the potentially uncontrollable natural instincts,[17] and as the image of the innocent, naive child susceptible to wild natural forces arose, the necessity to control and shelter children became more pronounced. Social nonconformism and deviation had to be punished brutally in the name of civility and Christianity. Hundreds of thousands of people, according to H.R. Trevor-Roper,[18] were executed to arouse fear and anxiety, while new models of male and female behavior were created to exalt a more ascetic way of life. The standards of conduct, discipline, and punishment,[19] formed in the name of absolutist Christian rulers, helped create divisions that were to operate in favor of the rising bourgeois industrial and mercantile classes. To make the overwhelming number of subjects in a given nation-state or principality pliable and serviceable, tests to control human instincts were first made among the members of the upper classes and then spread to the lower classes. Thus, using the knife and fork as instrumental and dignified tools for eating, sitting straight at the table, using hierarchical forms of serving, maintaining a certain posture while speaking or moving in a prescribed way,[20] repressing one's bodily functions, and wearing special dress signifying one's social class were all measures taken in the fifteenth and sixteenth centuries that were meant to transform positive pleasure comportments that had been formerly accepted and regarded as harmless into negative manners that caused displeasure, revulsion, and distaste in the seventeenth century.

Elias notes, "Precisely by this increased social proscription of many impulses, by their 'repression' from the surface of social life and of consciousness, the distance between the personality structure and behavior of adults and children is necessarily increased."[21] In other words, by the end of the seventeenth century, childhood became identified as a state of "natural innocence" and potentially corruptible, and the civilizing of children—social indoctrination through anxiety provoking effects and positive reinforcement—operated on all levels in manners, speech, sex, literature, and play. Instincts were to be trained and controlled for their sociopolitical use value. The supervised rearing of children was to lead to the *homme civilisé*.

Civilité is the code word that can provide the key to understanding how Perrault's tales and those of other French writers assumed a unique and powerful role within the French socialization process. Moreover, they incorporated standards of comportment for children and adults that have been adopted in our own time and are still of actual interest and concern. Let us, therefore, now turn to Perrault's prose tales to grasp what he meant by civilité and to question the underlying moral assumption of civilization in the classical fairy tales.

III

If we regard the eight prose fairy tales in Histoires ou contes du temps passé as providing behavioral patterns and models for children, then they can be divided into two distinct groups based on gender. "Sleeping Beauty," "Little Red Riding Hood," "Blue Beard," "The Fairies," and "Cinderella" are aimed directly at females; "Puss in Boots," "Ricky of the Tuft," and "Little Tom Thumb" address males. By focusing on the exemplary qualities, which distinguish the heroines from the heroes, we shall see how carefully Perrault wove notions of civilité into the fabric of his tales.

In "Sleeping Beauty," the princess is actually endowed with the following "gifts" by the fairies: beauty, the temper of an angel, grace, the ability to dance perfectly, the voice of a nightingale, and musicality. In other words, she is bred to become the ideal aristocratic lady. Furthermore, she is expected to be passive and patient for a hundred years until a prince rescues and resuscitates her. Her manner of speech is such that she charms the prince, and he marries her. Then she must demonstrate even more patience when the ogress takes her children from her. Such docility and self-abandonment are rewarded in the end when the prince returns to set things right. Perrault then added a verse moral, which sings a hymn of praise to patience.

"Little Red Riding Hood," the only warning tale of the volume, which ends on an unhappy note, still provides a model of behavior for girls. By giving expression to her fancy, Little Red Riding Hood brings about both her grandmother's downfall and her own. Thus, by negative example, the reader learns what a good girl should be like. In fact, the moral tells us that young girls, who are pretty, well bred, and courteous, should never talk to strangers or let themselves go. Otherwise, they will be violated and swallowed by wolves. In other words, they must exercise control over their sexual and natural drives or else their own sexuality will devour them, in the form of a dangerous wolf.

In "Blue Beard" the message is almost the same except that the wife of Blue Beard is saved because she realizes her error and says her prayers. Here the heroine is beautiful and well bred but too curious. Again the moral explains that it is a sin for a woman to be curious and imaginative and that women must exercise self-control. This message is softened by a second moral, which ironically implies that the relationship between men and women has changed: men are no longer the monsters they used to be, and women have more power. Nevertheless, the female role is dictated by conditions that demand humility and self-discipline.

In "The Fairies" one daughter is played off against the other. The youngest is beautiful, gentle, and sweet, and she works hard in the household. She never utters a complaint. The other is disagreeable, arrogant, and lazy. Because the younger exhibits the proper polite manners in helping a poor village dame, she is given a gift: with every word she utters, a flower or precious stone falls from her lips. She is eventually rewarded with a prince, while her sister is banished from the house and dies. The moral celebrates kindness.

Just as the daughter in "The Fairies" is an industrious, self-effacing house-keeper, so too is Cinderella, who also has her negative counterparts. In the fairy tale named after her, Cinderella is described as sweet, gentle, and diligent. Later, when she is properly dressed as a type of fashion queen, she is also the most beautiful woman in the world. Her "excellent" qualities are recognized by the prince, who marries her, and the moral praises the *bonne grace* of Cinderella, which accounts for her winning ways.

Perrault's fairy tales, which "elevate" heroines, reveal that he had a distinctly limited view of women. His ideal *"femme civilisée"* of upper-class society, the composite female, is beautiful, polite, graceful, industrious, and properly groomed and knows how to control herself at all times. If she fails the obedience test, she is punished, as in Red Riding Hood's case, but this girl's fate is exceptional and belongs to a particular genre of warning tales, which I shall discuss later in more detail. The task confronted by Perrault's model female is to show reserve and patience; that is, she must be passive until the right man comes along to recognize her virtues and marry her. She lives only through the male and for marriage. The male acts, the female waits. She must cloak her instinctual drives in polite speech, correct manners, and elegant clothes. If she is allowed to reveal anything, it is to demonstrate how submissive she can be.

In commenting on how Perrault portrays women in his tales, Lilyane Mourey explains,

> The concept of "morality" assumes here a very particular value mixed with irony and satire. Perrault argues for the total submission of the woman to her husband. Feminine coquetry (which is only the privilege of the dominant class) disturbs and upsets him: it could be the sign of female independence. It opens the way for the amorous conquest which endangers one of the fundamental values of society—the couple, the family. As we have seen, the heroines of the tales are very pretty, loyal, dedicated to their household chores, modest and docile and sometimes a little stupid insofar as it is true

that stupidity is almost a quality in women for Perrault. Intelligence could be dangerous. In his mind as in that of many men (and women) beauty is an attribute of woman, just as intelligence is the attribute of man.[22]

Of course, Perrault's disposition was totally different in his fairy tales that focused on male protagonists. In "Puss in Boots" the actual hero of the story is Puss, who needs the proper implements (a pair of boots and a pouch) to serve his master. The cat is the epitome of the educated bourgeois secretary who serves his master with complete devotion and diligence. He has such correct manners and wit that he can impress the king, and he uses his intelligence to dispose of an ogre and arrange a royal marriage for his low-born master. Thus, he can end his career by becoming a *grand seigneur*. Perrault provides us with a double moral here: one stresses the importance of possessing *industrie et savoir faire*, whereas the other extols the virtues of dress, countenance, and youth to win the heart of a princess.

In "Ricky of the Tuft" we learn again that it is not so much beauty and modesty that counts for men but brains and ambition. Prince Ricky is ugly and misshapen, but he has an abundance of intelligence and the power to bestow the same degree of intelligence on the person he loves best. As the tale would have it, Ricky meets a stupid beautiful princess who promises to marry him in a year if he endows her with brains. After she enjoys her new brains for a year, she wants to break her engagement, but Ricky's polite manners and ability lead her to believe that she now has the power to make him appear handsome. Mind wins over matter, and both short morals underline the virtue of good sense.

Certainly good sense and wit play a major role in "Little Tom Thumb," too. Here the tiny hero, the youngest of seven sons, is described as kind and smart. Of all the brothers, he is the most prudent and most shrewd. Consequently he assumes leadership when the brothers are abandoned in the woods without food and money. He tricks the ogre and ogress, saves his brothers, and gains a fortune because he can outsmart everyone. Despite his size—and the moral emphasizes this—Tom Thumb demonstrates that brains are better to have than brawn.

The composite male hero of Perrault's tale is strikingly different from the composite female. None of the heroes is particularly good looking, but they all have remarkable minds, courage, and deft manners. Moreover, they all are ambitious and work their way up the social ladder: the cat becomes a *grand seigneur*; the prince acquires a beautiful princess to increase his social prestige; and Tom Thumb becomes a rich and respected courtier. Unlike the fairy tales dealing with women where the primary goal is marriage, these tales demonstrate that social success and achievement are more important than winning a wife. In other words, women are incidental to the fates of the male characters, whereas men endow the lives of women with purpose. The heroes are active, pursue their goals by using their minds, and exhibit a high degree of civility. If anything, their virtues reflect on the courtly bourgeoisie during King Louis XIV's reign, if not on Perrault's very own character.

By examining the major features and behavior of Perrault's male and female protagonists, we can clearly see that he sought to portray ideal types to reinforce the standards of the civilizing process set by upper-class French society. Not only did Perrault inform his plots with normative patterns of behavior to describe an exemplary social constellation but he also employed a distinct bourgeois–aristocratic manner of speech that was purposely contrived to demonstrate the proper way to converse with eloquence and civility. Polite conventions, eloquent phrases, and rationalities were employed to distinguish the characters as having high social rank and proper breeding. In addition Perrault used formal description to show the exemplary nature of his protagonists. For instance, Cinderella's transformation from "slutty maid" to "virtuous princess," accomplished by the fairy godmother, was in part an exercise in fashion design. Perrault wanted to display what superior people should wear and how they should carry themselves. "All the ladies paid close attention to her hairdo and clothes with the intention of resembling her on the morrow provided that they could find materials just as beautiful and tailors just as talented."[23] Cinderella displays all the graces expected from a refined, aristocratic young lady. Moreover, she has perfect control over her feelings and movements. She does not disgrace her sisters but treats them with dignity. Her composure is most admirable, and, when it comes time to depart, she demonstrates great self-discipline tempered with politeness.

Perrault's narrative style matches the decor, characters, and virtues that he describes. Each fairy tale exudes a polished baroque air with Cartesian reasoning.[24] As stylist, Perrault cultivated a simple, frank, and graceful style, which incorporated the eloquent turns of high French practiced in court society and bourgeois circles. His ironic sense of humor allowed him to distance himself from the magical world and to poke fun at certain incidents, especially in the verse morals, and yet he could still plead a case for civilized behavior: he took these stories seriously as examples of modern literature in his debate about *les Anciens et les Modernes* with Nicolas Boileau. In this respect he also took care to provide a blend of bourgeois–aristocratic standards to demonstrate how modern fairy tales could be used for morally and ideologically acceptable purposes.

More than he realized, Perrault was responsible for the literary "bour-geoisification" of the oral folktale,[25] and he paved the way for founding a children's literature that would be useful for introducing manners to children of breeding. If we examine the origins of the eight prose tales in *Histoires ou contes du temps passé*, we can trace most of the motifs to oral folktales that circulated in Perrault's time and to literary works by Straparola, Basile, and French writers, who had already adapted folk material. In other words, Perrault amalgamated folk and literary motifs and shaped them in a unique way to present his particular bourgeois view of social manners. In doing this Perrault shifted the narrative perspective of the popular folktale genre from that of the peasantry to that of the bourgeois–aristocratic elite. This may not seem so significant at first, but, viewed in terms of the socialization of children, it had major consequences on the way children came to perceive their own status, sexuality, social roles, manners, and politics through the fairy tale, and it explains why middle-class families began readily repeating and reading the tales to their children in the nineteenth and twentieth centuries. As we have already seen in the case of the heroes and heroines, the shifting of the narrative perspective was not a mere stylistic refining of uncouth expression and social views but a substantial transformation of the manner in which society or reality was to be depicted. In terms of the literary fairy-tale genre for children, Perrault radically changed familiar folktale characters, settings, and plots to correspond to a civilizing process aimed at regulating the inner and outer nature of children. As already demonstrated in the works of Ariès and Elias, the rearing of children was designed more and more to convey prescriptions and prohibitions, and Perrault shaped the tales to deprive the "folk" of its say in the matter and at the same time to establish a social codex or manual by which young people were expected to abide. Just how crucial Perrault's shifting of the narrative perspective was for the socialization of children can be traced in each individual tale. Let us look at two that are most revealing: "Little Red Riding Hood" and "Cinderella."

Until the 1950s it was generally believed that Perrault did not use an oral folktale as the basis for his literary rendition of "Little Red Riding Hood." However, the research efforts of Paul Delarue, Marianne Rumpf, and Marc Soriano[26] have proved conclusively that Perrault must have been acquainted with an oral tale widely known in France that runs more or less as follows:

A little peasant girl goes to visit her grandmother carrying freshly baked bread and butter. On her way she meets a werewolf who asks her where she is going and which path she is taking, the one of needles or the one of pins. He takes the shorter path, arrives at the grandmother's house, eats her, and puts part of her flesh in a bin and her blood in a bottle. Then the little girl arrives. The werewolf disguised as the grandmother gives her the flesh to eat and the blood to drink. A crow scolds her for doing this. The werewolf tells her to throw each article of clothing into the fire since she will not be needing her clothes anymore. She gets into bed and asks ritual questions, the first one concerned with how hairy the werewolf's body is. When the werewolf finally reveals that he intends to eat her, she alertly replies that she has to relieve herself outside. He tells her to do it in the bed. She insists that she must do it outside. So the werewolf ties a piece of rope around her leg and allows her to go outside to take care of her natural functions. However, she ties the rope around a tree and runs home. The deceived werewolf follows in hot pursuit but fails to catch her.

This tale, which has a long French tradition, was told most likely from the seventeenth century up to the present. It became prominent in the seventeenth century because of the widespread superstitious belief in werewolves[27] and the great witch hunt. There were numerous notorious cases of werewolf trials, and thousands of men and women were persecuted and exterminated because they were charged with being werewolves.[28] The tale about the girl without a red cap and name and with a werewolf was also popular in the region where Perrault's family had lived, and it is more than likely that he was influenced by some version of the folktale when he wrote his unique literary story. Of course, he felt impelled to make many drastic changes, and Paul Delarue maintains,

> The common elements that are lacking in the literary story are precisely those which would have shocked the society of his period by their cruelness (the flesh and blood of the grandmother tasted by the child), their puerility (Road of Pins, Road of Needles), and their impropriety (question of the girl on the hairy body of the grandmother). And it seems plausible that Perrault eliminated them while he kept in the tale a folk flavor and freshness which make it an imperishable masterpiece.[29]

Although there is no doubt that Perrault took care not to offend the tastes of upper-class society, it is debatable whether he really retained the folk qualities, for he totally corrupted the perspective and import of the warning tale.

Instead of really warning girls against the dangers of predators in forests, the tale warns girls against their own natural desires, which they must tame. The brave little peasant girl, who can fend for herself and shows qualities of courage and cleverness, is transformed into a delicate bourgeois type, who is helpless, naive, and culpable, if not stupid. In the folktale the little girl displays a natural, relaxed attitude toward her body and sex and meets the challenge of a would-be seducer. In Perrault's literary fairy tale Little Red Riding Hood is chastised because she is innocently disposed toward nature in the form of the wolf and woods, and she is *raped* or punished because she is guilty of not controlling her natural inclinations.

Guilt was never a question in the original folktale. The little girl, who meets a werewolf and drinks the blood and eats the flesh of her grandmother, acts out an initiation ritual that has two aspects to it: the pattern of the ritual reflected a specific French peasant tradition and a general "archaic" belief. In those regions of France, where the tale was popular, the tale was related to the needlework apprenticeship, which young peasant girls underwent, and designated the arrival of puberty and initiation into society.[30] The girl proves that she is mature and strong enough to *replace* the grandmother. This specific tradition is connected to the general archaic belief about witches and wolves as crucial for self-understanding. Hans Peter Duerr points out:

> In the archaic mentality, the fence, the hedge, which separated the realm of wilderness from that of civilization did not represent limits which were unsurpassable. On the contrary, this fence was even torn down at certain times. People who wanted to live within the fence *with awareness* had to leave this enclosure at least once in their lifetime. They had to have roamed the woods as wolves or "wild persons." That is, to put it in more modern terms: they had to have experienced the wildness in themselves, their *animal nature*. For their "cultural nature" was only one side of their being, bound by fate to the animallike *fylgja*, which became visible to those people who went beyond the fence and abandoned themselves to their "second face."[31]

In facing the werewolf and temporarily abandoning herself to him, the little girl sees the animal side of herself. She crosses the border between civilization and wilderness and goes beyond the dividing line to face death to live. Her return home is a move forward as a whole person. She is a wo/man, self-aware, and ready to integrate herself in society *with awareness*.

Such a symbolical ritual expressed in the original folktale about a strong young woman must have confused and irritated Perrault. His hostility toward the pagan folk tradition and fear of women were exhibited in all his tales. In "Cinderella" we should recall that the different oral folk versions emanated from a matriarchal tradition that depicted the struggles of a young woman (aided by her dead mother as the conserver of society) to regain her stature and rights within society.[32] After Cinderella is humiliated, forced to put on rags, and compelled to perform hard labor, she does not turn her cheek but rebels and struggles to offset her disadvantages. (For instance, in Basile's "Cat Cinderella" [1634], which emanates from a folk tradition, the young protagonist does not hesitate to kill a stepmother and embarrass her father to get her way.) In doing so she *actively* seeks help and uses her wits to attain her goal, which is not marriage but recognition. She is not clothed in baroque manner, and she does not wear a glass slipper, which could easily break. Rather, she is dressed in a way that will reveal her true identity. The recovering of the lost leather slipper and the marriage with the prince are symbolically an affirmation of her strong independent character. In Perrault's literary fairy tale, Cinderella is changed to demonstrate how submissive and industrious she is.

Only because she minds her manners is she rescued by a fairy godmother and a prince. Perrault ridicules the folk version while projecting another model of passive femininity, which was to be taken seriously by the audience for which he was writing.

Lilyane Mourey aptly remarks,

> Perrault's suppressions, omissions or additions to the folk tales allow us to conclude that he did not see his task as restoring them in their authenticity. Those stories which he found interesting and amusing became above all the privileged places where the man, the politician, and the academician could put his ideas and his fantasies to work in a leisurely way and sometimes to make caricatures. For it is this tone which the moralities assume at times and which emerges from one moment to the next in the tales. This explains why Perrault selected only a small number from the ensemble of the folktale repertory. He retained the tales which "pleased" him, which "attracted" him for infinite and complex reasons because they offered him the possibility to develop (or to indicate at the very least) some of his preoccupations and some of his feelings on a literary, political, and social level. Since women were at the center of his reflections, Perrault spontaneously chose the tales which show the situation of women. The ideal "virtues" of a woman such as Perrault conceived them—beauty, sweetness, kindness, obedience to the husband, dedication to the maintenance of the home, lack of coquetry, and loyalty—are indissolubly linked with one another and reinforce one another in contrast to the behavior of women whom Perrault denounces, women of the aristocracy and *haute bourgeoisie* with whom he came in contact as reputable civil servant, academician, and *homme de cour*.[33]

IV

Perrault's social views on manners and morality were not always shared by the other French writers of fairy tales. Yet despite differences in intention and style, it is significant for the development of the fairy tale for children that there was general agreement in the ideological and aesthetical tendency among them. Here the crucial factor to consider is the social standard to which all French writers subscribed: the literary fairy tale was to be used as a vehicle to discuss proper breeding and behavior exemplified by models drawn from the practice in court society and bourgeois circles and the theoretical writings on manners. Each author distinguished himself or herself by the refined and original contribution he or she made to this discussion. The center of concern was civility, and the fairy-tale discourse reflected variations on this theme and became increasingly moralistic as children were regarded as the major audience.

It is almost impossible to examine the manifold ways in which the other significant French writers, especially the women, employed the literary fairy tale to set standards for civilization. Yet it is possible to compare different works as representative of the general manner in which traditional motifs were cultivated to express upper-class notions of behavior. Therefore, I want to take one major theme that has received almost uniform treatment up through the present to discuss the underlying reasons why it assumed what one could call a "classical" fairy-tale form. The theme centers on "beauty and the beast," and the specific tales that I discuss will enable us to see the close connections between psychogenetic and sociogenetic civilizing factors as they became embodied by symbolic configurations within the development of the fairy-tale discourse and gave rise to the most widely known version of "Beauty and the Beast." I discuss only the most prominent tales: Perrault's "Ricky of the Tuft" (1696); Mlle Bernard's "Ricky of the Tuft" as related in her novel *Inès de Cordoue* (1696); Madame d'Aulnoy's "Le Mouton" ("The Ram," 1697), "La Grenouille bienfaisante" ("The Beneficent Frog," 1697), and "Serpentin Vert" ("The Green Serpent," 1697); Madame de Villeneuve's "Beauty and the Beast" (1740); and Madame Leprince de Beaumont's "Beauty and the Beast" (1756).

Most critics who have analyzed the beauty and the beast cycle have emphasized its positive aspects, particularly those who have studied the psychological implications. For instance, Bruno Bettelheim asserted that "Beauty and the Beast"

> foreshadows by centuries the Freudian view that sex must be experienced by the child as disgusting as long as his sexual longings are attached to his parent, because only through such a negative attitude toward sex can the incest taboo, and with it the stability of the human family, remain secure. But once detached from the parent and directed to a partner of more suitable age, in normal development, sexual longings no longer seem beastly—to the contrary, they are experienced as beautiful.[34]

And Jacques Barchilon seconded this thesis in his comprehensive essay on this subject:

> Not to be afraid of the beast is to make it disappear. This means abandoning infantile fantasies, becoming a woman and accepting a reality which is much more tangible and satisfying than dreams. Beauty matures. She accepts the sexual reality of the beast with lucidity. Thereby, she gets rid of her taboos and infantile fears.[35]

All this sounds very convincing from a contemporary pseudo-Freudian perspective. The analyses, however, are unhistorical and too glib. The pseudo-Freudian approach to literature suggests that children are born with basic fears, anxieties, and wishes. But if we examine the development of the individual and family in different societies in relation to the civilizing process, we can see that instinctual drives are conditioned and largely determined through interaction and interplay with the social environment. Human sexuality has not been static, and, as Michel Foucault, Norbert Elias, and Jos Van Ussel have demonstrated about the historical development of sexuality,[36] there was an important shift in European attitudes in the sixteenth and seventeenth centuries so that the open display of sex and bodily functions gradually became curtailed. Restriction and revulsion toward frank sexual behavior replaced open acceptance of sexual and bodily functions. The roles of males and females became more rigidly defined: men became more closely associated with reason, temperance, activism, and sovereign order; females became more identified with irrationality, whimsy, passivity, and subversive deviance.

From a historical psychological point of view, one that endeavors to trace the connections between the psychogenetic and sociogenetic factors, the fairy tale assumes great importance because it reveals how social mores and values were induced in part through literature and constituted determinants in the rearing of an individual child. The beauty and the beast tales were not and are not important in the civilizing process because they enabled and enable children and adults to overcome "natural" psychic conflicts and to accept their innate sexuality. On the contrary, they were and are important because they set standards for sexual and social conduct that complied with inhibiting forms of socialization and were to be internalized by the readers and auditors of the tales. Though the narrative perspective may vary, the starting point for the discourse on manners through fairy tales affirms the dominant Christian absolutist view regarding the regulation of inner and outer nature in favor of male hegemony and rationalized industry.

If we compare those oral folktales about the animal bridegroom, which stem from matriarchal societies, with those literary fairy tales about beauty and the beast at the end of the seventeenth century, it becomes evident that the transformations in the portrayal of sexual configurations and cultural patterns were connected to significant changes within the civilization process. As Heide Göttner-Abendroth shows, the man is

> a wild, roving beast (wolf, bear, horse, raven, swan) in most of the animal bridegroom tales, and this condition represents his homelessness and undomesticity. That is, in the eyes of the matriarchal woman, who created a cultivated environment for herself, he has never developed beyond the condition of a predatory animal that roams the woods. He is still covered by fur or feathers, while she wears human clothes which she herself has made. The male condition as human is not yet extant, or it is one of "death," which

is the meaning of the state of "enchantment" as beast. The transformation into an animal is likened to death and is the male condition, and it is worse than that of the female because it does not mean initiation into a higher form of life. Rather the male has not yet reached the cultural level of the human (= woman). It is up to the woman to bring him salvation by making human clothes for him and accepting him into her house as a domesticated inhabitant.[37]

The symbolical cultural pattern of matriarchy, which designated the female as initiator of human action and integration, experienced constant changes over the course of centuries in both the oral and the literary tradition. The result was that, by the end of the seventeenth century, the original female bringer of salvation could find her own "true" salvation only by sacrificing herself to a man in his house or castle, symbolical of submission to patriarchal rule.

As the most famous and perhaps the most talented fairy-tale writer at the end of the seventeenth century, Perrault continued the patriarchal cycling of beauty and the beast in a form that was to be emulated by many other writers of his time. Although he did not employ an animal bridegroom in his tale "Ricky of the Tuft," we do know that he based his story partly on Apuleius's "Cupid and Psyche" of the second century and Straparola's tale "Re Porco" ("King Pig") of the sixteenth century to demonstrate the superiority of male intelligence over feminine beauty.[38] What needs to be stressed about Perrault's tale is his insistence that the female cannot behave civilly or live happily without the male to temper her. Even when given the power of reason or, rather, particularly when given the power of reason, the female is dangerous. Perrault's princess wants to break her promise to the hideous Ricky because she realizes that she can win the favors of a more handsome man and perhaps be more satisfied. Thus, Ricky must exercise all the powers of his superior reason to convince her rationally that she now has it within her "discretion and good qualities of her soul and mind"[39] to regard him in a more pleasing light: the beast is really true nobility. In sum, Perrault's tale presents a "civilized" version of the taming of the shrew whereby the female must learn to deny her sexual urges and subordinate her wishes and drives to please the reasonable male who knows what is best for her. Though ugly and misshapen, he endows her life with the spiritual discipline and dignity it would otherwise lack.

If we examine this fairy tale in its historical context, then it becomes evident why it fits sociologically and psychologically into the civilizing process. First, younger women of bourgeois and aristocratic circles were constantly being forced into marriages of convenience with elderly men, who were not always physically appealing or likeable. Second, women had become equated with potential witchlike figures by the end of the seventeenth century, so control of their alleged sexual powers of seduction was linked by church and state to control of diabolical forces.[40] Third, open sexuality had become a clandestine affair; that is, it was to be hidden and privatized because the church had ordained sex without marriage a sin and repulsive. As we know, a properly groomed child was to learn to fear and find sex disgusting. Finally, instead of projecting the female's fear of sexuality, the tale depicts Perrault's own fear of women and perhaps of his own sexual drives, which he disguised so that he could accept them in a more "civilized" form. From his fears and desires he shaped the configurations of the fairy tale to engender an aesthetic–ideological constellation of dependable and temperate male governance over whimsical female naiveté.

Perrault's projection of the "beauty and beast" constellation must be linked to the peculiar and dubious views he held on sexuality and manners. However, he was not idiosyncratic. In fact, his opinions were shared by many of his peers, and furthermore, they were fervently endorsed by many a literary lady, though they tended to question many of the gender stereotypes he depicted. The very year before Perrault published his tale, Mlle Bernard included a different version of "Riquet à la Houppe" in her novel *Inès de Cordoue*. A relative of Corneille and Fontenelle, and a respected writer in her own right, Mlle Bernard was well known and associated in the same circles as Perrault, and there is some speculation as to whether she influenced him. That is, however, somewhat irrelevant because the topic had already become a subject of social and cultural discourse. La Fontaine published his version of the classical story of "Psyche and Cupid" in 1669. In 1670 Molière and Corneille used the story as the basis for a tragic ballet in five acts first performed at court in 1670 and subsequently in public in 1671. What is significant is that both Mlle Bernard and Perrault employed the same literary constellation to engage in a discourse on manners that was to become part of the fairy-tale heritage for children. Moreover, Mlle Bernard appears to have identified with the oppressed heroine and thus questions notions of male hegemony.[41]

Her plot differs in a unique and fascinating way from Perrault's. The story begins as follows:

> A great nobleman of Grenada, who possessed all the riches worthy of his birth, was grieved by a domestic tragedy which poisoned everything consti-tuting his fortune. His only daughter, born with all the traits which make for beauty, was so stupid that her beauty itself only rendered her more disagree-able. Her actions were without grace. Her figure, though slender, was heavy because it lacked a soul in its body.[42]

The task set by the narrative concerns the acquisition of a "soul" or "reason" for Mama, which is the name given to the princess. One day she encounters a hideous creature, Ricky of the Tuft, who is king of the gnomes. Because he is aware of her difficulties, he offers her intelligence if she will marry him after a year. Obviously she accepts, not realizing that she will fall in love with a young man named Arada. After a year has elapsed, her relationship with Arada makes her unwilling to marry Ricky, who, despite his beastly appearance, is a gentleman and gives her a choice: either she can return to her father's kingdom where she will resume being stupid or she can retain her acquired intelligence and live with him in his splendid underground kingdom as queen of the gnomes. She decides to marry him, and her intelligence increases to the point that she can easily continue her clandestine affair with Arada. When Ricky discovers this, he punishes her by making her stupid during the day and intelligent during the night. She responds by continuing her affair in the evening. Finally, Ricky takes his vengeance by transforming Arada into his twin, and the queen must spend the rest of her life unable to make a distinction between husband and lover. In fact, she must learn to accept the reasonable rule of ugliness.

In many respects Mlle Bernard is harsher in her treatment of the female figure and more severe in insisting on proper forms of civilizing young people than Perrault. The princess becomes wily, deceitful, and sexual once she has the brains to match her beauty. She can hardly be tamed. Ricky's superiority resides in the power of his mind to transform things. He is fair in his treatment of her, and he acts vengefully after it becomes apparent to him that his wife can be domesticated only when deprived of free will. The message delivered by this tale states unequivocally that women must be placed under constant surveillance even when they are endowed with reason to temper their appetites: they are potentially destructive and may be harmful to civil order. But the tale also can be read as a critique of the way in which men ruthlessly punished women if they dared to think and fulfill their own desires. A strong woman was a dangerous woman for men, and Bernard reflects on the potentiality of women who learn to use their brains to obtain objects of their own desire.

Madame d'Aulnoy elaborates on this topic in one of her beauty and the beast tales titled "The Ram." Here Merveilleuse, the youngest daughter of a king, must flee the court under threat of death because the king wrongly thinks that she is insolent. Lost in a forest she encounters a talking ram, a prince, who had been transformed into an animal by the evil fairy Ragotte. He provides asylum for Merveilleuse in grand and civil fashion. Gradually she learns to love the beast and intends to wait five years when his sentence of enchantment will end and he can resume human form. However, she learns that her sister is to be married and desires to attend the wedding celebration. The ram gives her permission to visit her home, providing that she promises to return. Otherwise, he will perish. She gives him her word and returns. Yet when her second sister marries, she goes home again, and the joyous reconciliation with her father makes her forget the ram, who dies as a result of her neglect, and his death causes her the "greatest misery"[43] at her happiest moment.

D'Aulnoy depicts both the negative and the positive power of beauty. When docile and obedient, it can benefit male nobility. On the other hand, when it loses control over itself, beauty can destroy domestic tranquility and masculine dignity. The well-groomed lady must never forget her self-sacrificing and submissive function in her relationship with a lord, no matter how ugly he may be. What is interesting in all of d'Aulnoy's tales, however, is that the absolute power over men and women resides in fairies, not in the church or the state. And the fairies determine what the quality of beauty means. It is a mark of social distinction when a beautiful lady is willing to abandon herself to a monster to save other people, especially if she is compassionate and sincere. This is evident in d'Aulnoy's fairy tale "The Beneficent Frog," in which Princess Moufette reveals her constancy through her readiness to be eaten by a dragon. Of course, she is saved by her fiancé Prince Moufy, and the dragon, too, turns out to be a noble lord, who exhibits fine manners when his bestial shell disappears.

D'Aulnoy's most classic statement on the beauty and beast theme is in "The Green Serpent." Not only does she have her heroine Laidronette read the story about "Psyche and Cupid" to learn a lesson but she also masterly weaves motifs from such other tales as "Sleeping Beauty" into the plot to create a marvelous model of prudence for young women. Laidronette has many adventures and learns to deal with her ugliness and overcome her imprudent curiosity. For her good sense and behavior she is rewarded by the good fairy Protectrice in a double manner: first, she is transformed into a beautiful woman and given the name Queen Discrete, then she is allowed to sacrifice herself for the Green Serpent, who is transformed into a noble prince, the saved as savior.

All d'Aulnoy's fairy tales provide moral lessons, and the ones that involve beauty and the beast reiterate the message of Perrault's tales. The woman must be constantly chastised for her curiosity, unreliability, and whimsy. True beauty depends on prudence and discretion, which are figuratively depicted by the heroine either sacrificing herself to a male beast or submitting to his commands and wishes because he has a noble soul and civil manners. The hidden message in all these tales is a dictum that the women of d'Aulnoy's time, including d'Aulnoy,[44] had to obey or else face degradation and ostracism: control your natural inclinations and submit to the fate that male social standards decree. Civility meant enduring the anguish of self-denial because men sought to rationalize their fear of women, sexuality, and equality by establishing regulations that deprived women and other oppressed groups of self-expression and independence. There are many subversive signs in d'Aulnoy's works, such as "Finette Cendron," "The White Cat," and "The Wild Boar," and also in tales by de la Force ("The Good Woman" and "Persinette") and de Murat ("The Palace of Revenge" and "The Pig King") that reveal how they sought to criticize arbitrary male behavior, but, for the most part, they compromised themselves under great social pressure. Indeed, the sad state of the dark side of the classical fairy tales is that women writers often felt compelled to give more expression to male needs and hegemony than to their own.

The two most classic examples of this self-abnegation are the fairy tales titled "La Belle et la Bête" by Mme de Villeneuve and Mme Leprince de Beaumont, published in 1740 and 1756, respectively. It is important to note that both these writers came after the more innovative phase of fairy-tale writing by women and that they tended to be more conservative and pedagogical than the early writers. The basic plot in their beauty and beast tales is the same in both versions, which are didactic discourses on manners, morals, and social class. The general narrative line depicts the fortunes of a very rich merchant whose children (six boys and six girls in Villeneuve's story and three boys and three girls in Beaumont's) become spoiled and arrogant because of the family's accumulation of wealth. Indeed, with the exception of Beauty, all the children aspire beyond their class. Hence, this eminently nouveau riche, bourgeois family must be taught a lesson. The merchant loses his money and social prestige, and the children are compelled to adjust to hard work on a country estate, which is the only property left to the family's name. The boys are diligent, but the daughters resent the fact that they must perform menial chores and cannot wear fancy clothes and attend balls. They remain haughty, arrogant, and vain. Only Beauty, the youngest, exhibits modesty and self-sacrificial tendencies. In addition, she displays how industrious and good-tempered she can be during these trying times. When her father takes a trip to recoup the family fortune and finds himself in danger of losing his life because he transgresses against the beast (i.e., nobility), Beauty as model of humility and obedience saves her father by agreeing to live with the monster. Later, impressed by the civil treatment and noble nature of the beast (appearances are obviously deceiving; that is, male aristocrats may look like beasts, but they have gentle hearts and kind manners), she develops a great affection for him. Yet it is only after she visits her family and almost causes the beast's death by her long departure that she realizes she loves him and is willing to marry him. Suddenly he is transformed into a handsome prince and explains that he had been condemned to remain a beast until a beautiful, virtuous virgin should consent to wed him. As usual, marriage is the ultimate reward for a good girl's behavior, whereas the man not only acquires a bride but also has his rights and property restored to him as a sovereign. In other words, his virility is confirmed and no longer placed in jeopardy.

Generally speaking the longer version of "Beauty and the Beast" by Mme de Villeneuve is either ignored or considered irrelevant when compared with the more concise rendition by Mme Leprince de Beaumont, which is more popular and often considered superior. Each tale is, however, fascinating in its own right, and a comparison between the two will demonstrate how consciously both authors cultivated their tales to participate in the discourse about the civilizing process. At the outset it is important to stress that Mme Leprince de Beaumont wrote her fairy tale sixteen years after the appearance of Mme de Villeneuve's version and that it was purposely shortened and made more moralistic so that it could better serve to improve the manners of upper-class youngsters when it was published in her *Magasin des enfans, ou dialogues entre une sage gouvernante et plusieurs de ses élèves de la première distinction*. In 1758 a German translation appeared, titled *Der Frau Maria le Prince de Beaumont Lehren der Tugend und Weisheit für die Jugend*, and three years later an English version was printed in *The Young Misses Magazine*. Since then it has served as the primary model for most modern beauty and the beast adaptations in the Western world, including Jean Cocteau's famous black-and-white film *La Belle et la Bête* (1946) and the Disney Studio's even more famous animated film *Beauty and the Beast* (1990) and all its sequels.

Whereas Mme Leprince de Beaumont represented a social perspective on breeding that was very much open to the alliance of the bourgeoisie and aristocracy (thus guaranteeing its future success), Mme de Villeneuve was more rigid in delineating class behavior and propriety. Her tale, which exceeded three hundred pages in its original publication in *La Jeune Amériquaine et les contes marins*, was directed largely at adults and contained elaborate descriptions of the beast's court and remarkable psychological digressions in the form of dreams. There are also several points in the plot and contents that diverge from Mme Leprince de Beaumont's tale. Beauty's sisters are described in a negative way as indolent, petty, and jealous, but they are not punished or used as exact counterparts, because it turns out they do not come from the same social class. The beast asks Beauty not simply to marry him but to sleep with him. She refuses, and his discreet manner of respecting her wishes makes a great impression on her. Moreover, he appears to her in dreams and wins her spiritual love. When she finally does consent to sleep with him, they do not have sexual intercourse, for that would be contrary to the decorum of their social standing that called for the consecration of marriage. Besides, there is an important anticlimax here. The beast's queen mother arrives with the good fairy. The beast is transformed into a handsome prince, but then his mother protests against the *mésalliance*, even though Beauty is most virtuous. There is a long discussion between the good fairy, the mother, Beauty, and the prince as to whether the daughter of a merchant, no matter how chaste, prudent, modest, and obedient, is worthy enough to become the wife of a prince of royal blood. The problem is eventually solved when the fairy reveals that Beauty is in actuality of noble blood and was given to the merchant to be raised for her own safekeeping. Revealed in all her majesty, Beauty now bestows her blessings on the members of her adopted bourgeois family (including her nasty stepsisters) and rewards them with money, position, and proper mates.

The constellation is altered somewhat in Mme Leprince de Beaumont's tale. She is actually more rigorous and demanding on a moral and ethical scale. She approves of the alliance between the bourgeoisie and aristocracy but then demands even stricter adherence to the dominant social code. She makes her views known through stark contrasts and pithy descriptions of proper behavior.[45] Beauty is designed to conform in the perfect bourgeois, virtuous fashion, and the Beast embodies all the genteel and dignified characteristics of the nobility. Here he asks not that Beauty sleep with him but that she become his wife. When she finally accepts, the beautiful fairy presents the handsome prince to her in this manner: "Come and receive the reward for your good choice. You've preferred virtue over beauty and wit, and you deserve to find these qualities combined in one and the same person. You're going to become a great queen, and I hope that a throne will not destroy your virtuous qualities."[46] In contrast, her sisters are transformed into statues and placed by the gates to the royal couple's estate to warn against the evils of maliciousness and envy.

Social deviates, such as the sisters, are brutally punished, and it is even possible to interpret the fortunes of the merchant's clan as a test of a bourgeois family in danger of overstepping the bounds of propriety. The rational expectations of the narrative perspective call for an internalization of the Christian–rationalistic normative pattern to foster social notions of aesthetics and virtues that all children were to accept, especially young girls. Mme Leprince de Beaumont spent approximately twenty years as a governess in London, where she taught young girls and wrote prolifically on the subject of manners. In addition to "Beauty and the Beast," she wrote other fairy tales such as "Prince Spirituel," similar to "Ricky of the Tuft," and numerous stories that preached feminine submissiveness. As Barchilon remarks, "This feminine submissiveness undoubtedly demands an explanation. Mme Leprince de Beaumont addressed an audience of young girls in pre-puberty and always took care to insist on this note of submissiveness. She wanted to prepare them for 'life' that is for marriage ordained according to the normally accepted bourgeois conventions."[47]

There is a distinct cultural pattern that emerges when we examine the treatment of the beauty and beast theme from Perrault and Mlle Bernard to

Mme Leprince de Beaumont or from 1696 to 1756. What began as a fairy-tale discourse on manners with examples set for adults and children developed into a fairy-tale sermon primarily for children. There is no more room for critical discourse after Mme de Villeneuve's version of "Beauty and the Beast": a distinct constellation becomes fixed as a classical set of rules and behavior for proper boys and girls in Mme Leprince Beaumont's tale. Temperance and rationality reign in the end. The mark of beauty for a female is to be found in her submission, obedience, humility, industry, and patience; the mark of manliness is to be found in a man's self-control, politeness, reason, and perseverance. Moreover, as the configurations were developed individually in each beauty and the beast tale in relation to the civilizing process, it became clear that the female character could assume her "civil" form only if she were willing to sacrifice herself for a beastlike male. By denying herself, she could obtain what all women supposedly wanted and want—namely, marriage in the form of male domination. The male character could assume his "civil" form only when socially deviant forces were tamed and when the female was not a threat but actually charmed or tranquilized by his rationality. It is interesting that the woman has the power to save or destroy the man who always represents civility and rationality. The male protagonist is *never* responsible for the world being out of joint. Each tale depicts him as a victim (generally transfigured by a wicked female fairy) and a model of bourgeois *raisonnement*.

Yet, as we have seen, there is a dark side to this bourgeois *raisonnement* as it manifests itself in the civilizing process and in the origins of the literary fairy-tale tradition for children in Western culture. In the case of "Beauty and the Beast" the classical constellation was carried in different forms by Charles Lamb's poetical version in 1811 and by the Brothers Grimm in their 1812 and 1815 editions of *Household Tales*: "The Singing, Springing Lark," "The Frog Prince," "King of the Golden Mountain," "Bearskin," and "Snow White and Rosebud." The nineteenth century saw a proliferation of "Beauty and the Beast" narratives as a broadsheet, abridged, moralistic tale for the masses, picture books, and drama. It reached its "classical" high point in Sir Arthur Quiller-Couch's adaptation. In the twentieth century there have been countless beauty and the beast stories, plays, operas, musicals, films, and TV programs, as well as feminist revisions that pick up on the subversive resistance that can be detected in some of the women's tales of the French vogue. We continue to celebrate the charm and grace of "Beauty and the Beast" and others similar to it that have come down to us in our literary heritage. We continue to enjoy this harmless pastime of telling classical fairy tales to our children, not realizing the possible harm of harmlessness.

4

WHO'S AFRAID OF THE BROTHERS GRIMM? SOCIALIZATION AND POLITICIZATION THROUGH FAIRY TALES

The wolf, now piously old and good,
When again he met Red Riding Hood
Spoke: "Incredible, my dear child,
What kinds of stories are spread—they're wild.

As though there were, so the lie is told,
A dark murder affair of old.
The Brothers Grimm are the ones to blame.
Confess! It wasn't half as bad as they claim."

Little Red Riding Hood saw the wolf's bite
And stammered: "You're right, quite right."
Whereupon the wolf, heaving many a sigh,
Gave kind regards to Granny and waved good bye.
                    —Rudolf Otto Wiemer, *The Old Wolf* (1976)

More than two hundred years ago, the Brothers Grimm began collecting original folktales in Germany and stylized them into potent literary fairy tales.

Since then these tales have exercised a profound influence on children and adults alike throughout the Western world. Indeed, whatever form fairy tales in general have taken since the original publication of the Grimms' narratives in 1812, the Brothers Grimm have been continually looking over our shoulders and making their presence felt. For most people this has not been so disturbing. However, during the past thirty-five years there has been a growing radical trend to overthrow the Grimms' benevolent rule in fairy-tale land by writers who believe that the Grimms' stories contribute to the creation of a false consciousness and reinforce an authoritarian socialization process. This trend has appropriately been set by writers in the very homeland of the Grimms, where literary revolutions have always been more common than real political ones.[1]

During the post-1945 period West German writers[2] and critics gradually came to regard the Grimms' fairy tales and those of Hans Christian Andersen, Ludwig Bechstein, and their imitators as "secret agents" of an education establishment that indoctrinates children to learn fixed roles and functions within bourgeois society, thus curtailing their free development.[3] This attack on the conservatism of the "classical" fairy tales was mounted in the 1960s, when numerous writers began using them as models to write innovative, emancipatory tales, more critical of changing conditions in advanced technological societies based on capitalist production and social relations. What became apparent to these writers and critics was that the Grimms' tales, though ingenious and perhaps socially relevant in their own times, contained sexist and racist attitudes and served a socialization process that placed great emphasis on passivity, industry, and self-sacrifice for girls and on activity, competition, and accumulation of wealth for boys. Therefore, contemporary West German writers moved in a different, more progressive direction by parodying and revising the fairy tales of the eighteenth and nineteenth centuries, especially those of the Grimms.

For the most part, the classical fairy tales have been reutilized or what the Germans call umfunktioniert: the function of the tales has been literally turned around so that the perspective, style, and motifs of the narratives expose contradictions in capitalist society and awaken children to other alternatives for pursuing their goals and developing autonomy. The reutilized tales function against conformation to the standard socialization process and are meant to function for a different, more just society that can be gleaned from the redirected socialization process symbolized in the new tales. The quality and radicalism of these new tales vary from author to author[4] and from generation to generation, especially if we take into consideration that East Germans had a different attitude toward the Grimms' tales and that East and West Germany are now united. It may even be that many of the writers were and are misguided, despite their good intentions. Nevertheless, during the 1960s and onward, West German writers raised pertinent questions about the sociopolitical function of fairy tales, and just this question raising alone is significant. Essentially they reflect on and seek to understand how the messages in fairy tales tend to repress and constrain children rather than set them free to make their own choices. They assume that the Grimms' fairy tales have been fully accepted in all Western societies and have ostensibly been used or misused in furthering the development of human beings—to make them more functional within the capitalist system and to prescribe choice. If one shares a critique of capitalist society, what then should be changed in the Grimms' tales to suggest other possibilities? What sociogenetic structural process forms the fairy tales and informs the mode by which the human character is socialized in capitalist society?

Before looking at the literary endeavors made by West German writers to answer these questions, it is important to discuss the nature of the Grimms' fairy tales and the notion of socialization through fairy tales. Not only have creative writers been at work to reutilize the fairy tales but there also has been a host of progressive critics who have uncovered important historical data about the Grimms' tales and have explored the role that these stories have played in the socialization process.

I

Until the 1970s it was generally assumed that the Brothers Grimm collected their oral folktales mainly from peasants and day laborers and that they merely altered and refined the tales while remaining true to their perspective and meaning. Both assumptions have been proved false.[5] The Grimms gathered their tales primarily from petit bourgeois or educated middle-class people, who had already introduced bourgeois notions into their versions. In all cases the Grimms did more than simply change and improve the style of the tales: they expanded them and made substantial changes in characters and meaning. Moreover, they excluded many other well-known tales from their collection, and their entire process of selection reflected the bias of their philosophical and political point of view. Essentially, the Brothers Grimm contributed to the literary "bourgeoisification" of oral tales that had belonged to the peasantry and lower classes and had been informed by the interests and aspirations of these groups. This is not to say that they purposely sought to betray the heritage of the common people in Germany. On the contrary, their intentions were honorable: they wanted the rich cultural tradition of the common people to be used and accepted by the rising middle classes. It is for this reason that they spent their lives conducting research on myths, customs, and the language of the German people. They wanted to foster the development of a strong national bourgeoisie by unraveling the ties to Germanic traditions and social rites and by drawing on related lore from France and central and northern Europe. Wherever possible, they sought to link the beliefs and behavior of characters in the folktales to the cultivation of bourgeois norms.

> It was into this nineteenth century where a bourgeois sense for family had been developed that the Grimms' fairy tales made their entrance: as the book read to children by mothers and grandmothers and as reading for the children themselves. The Grimms countered the pedagogical doubts from the beginning with the argument that the fairy-tale book was written both for children and for adults, but not for the badly educated. . . . The enormous amount of editions and international circulation of the Grimms' fairy tales as literary fairy tales can also be explained by their bourgeois circle of consumers. Here is where the circle closes. Aside from the questionable nature of the "ancient Germanic" or even "pure Hessian" character of the collection, we must consider and admire the genial talents of the Brothers, who were able to fuse random and heterogeneous material transmitted over many years into the harmonious totality of the *Children and Household Tales*. They were thus able to bring about a work which was both "bourgeois" and "German" and fully corresponded to the scientific temper and emotional taste of their times. The general room for identification provided for the bourgeoisie completely encompassed the virtues of a national way of thinking and German folk spirit, and the Grimms' *Children and Household Tales* contained all this in the most superb way. Its success as a book cannot be explained without knowledge of the social history of the nineteenth century.[6]

The sources of the tales were European, old Germanic, and bourgeois. The audience was a growing middle-class one. The Grimms saw a mission in the tales and were bourgeois missionaries. And, although they never preached or sought to convert in a crass manner, they did modify the tales much more than we have been led to believe. Their collection went through seven editions during their own lifetime and was constantly enlarged and revised. Wilhelm Grimm, the more conservative of the two brothers, did most of the revisions, and it is commonly known that he endeavored to clean up the tales and make them more respectable for bourgeois children—even though the original publication was not expressly intended for children. The Grimms collected the tales not only to "do a service to the history of poetry and mythology" but also to write a book that could provide pleasure and learning.[7] They called their edition of 1819 an *Erziehungsbuch* (an educational book) and discussed the manner in which they made the stories more pure, truthful, and just. In the process they carefully eliminated those passages that they thought would be harmful for children's eyes.[8] This became a consistent pattern in the revisions after 1819. Once the tales had seen the light of print and once they were deemed appropriate for middle-class audiences, Wilhelm consistently tried to meet audience expectations. And the reading audience of Germany was becoming more *Biedermeier* or Victorian in its morals and ethics. As a moral sanitation man, Wilhelm set high standards, and his example has been followed by numerous "educators," who have watered down and cleaned up the tales from the nineteenth century up to the present.

Thanks to the 1975 republication of the neglected 1810 handwritten manuscript side by side with the published edition of the tales of 1812 by Heinz Rölleke, we can grasp the full import of the sanitation process in relation to socialization. We can see how each and every oral tale was conscientiously and, at times, drastically changed by the Grimms. For our purposes I want to comment on three tales to show how different types of changes relate to gradual shifts in the norms and socialization process reflecting the interests of the bourgeoisie. Let us begin with the opening of "The Frog Prince" and compare the 1810 manuscript with the editions of 1812 and 1857.

1810 Manuscript

The king's daughter went into the woods and sat down next to a cool well. Then she took a golden ball and began playing with it until it suddenly rolled down into the well. She watched it fall to the bottom from the edge of the well and was very sad. Suddenly a frog stuck his head out of the water and said: "Why are you complaining so?" "Oh, you nasty frog, you can't help me at all. My golden ball has fallen into the well." Then the frog said: "If you take me home with you, I'll fetch your golden ball for you."[9]

1812 Edition

Once upon a time there was a king's daughter who went into the woods and sat down next to a cool well. She had a golden ball with her that was her most cherished toy. She threw it high into the air and caught it and enjoyed this very much. One time the ball went high into the air. She had already stretched out her hand and curled her fingers to catch the ball when it fell by her side onto the ground and rolled and rolled right into the water.

The king's daughter looked at it in horror. The well was so deep that it was impossible to see the bottom. She began to cry miserably and complain: "Oh! I would give anything if only I could have my ball again! My clothes, my jewels, my pearls and whatever I could find in the world." While she was complaining, a frog stuck his head out of the water and said: "Princess, why are you lamenting so pitifully?" "Oh," she said, "you nasty frog, you can't help me! My golden ball has fallen into the well." The frog said: "I won't demand your pearls, your jewels, and your clothes, but if you accept me as your companion, and if you let me sit next to you at your table and eat from your golden plate and sleep in your bed, and if you cherish and love me, then I'll fetch your ball for you."[10]

1857 Edition

In olden times when making wishes still helped, there lived a king whose daughters were all beautiful, but the youngest was so beautiful that the sun itself, who has seen so much, was astonished by her beauty each time it lit upon her face. Near the royal castle there was a great dark wood, and in the wood under an old linden tree there was a well. And when the day was quite hot, the king's daughter would go into the woods and sit by the edge of the cool well. And if she was bored, she would take a golden ball and throw it up and catch it again, and this was the game she liked to play most.

Now it happened one day that the golden ball, instead of falling back into the little hand of the princess when she had tossed it up high, fell to the ground by her side and rolled into the water. The king's daughter followed it with her eyes, but it disappeared. The well was deep, so deep that the bottom could not be seen. Then she began to cry, and she cried louder and louder and could not console herself at all. And as she was lamenting, someone called to her. "What is disturbing you, princess? Your tears would melt a heart of stone." And when she looked to see where the voice came from there was nothing but a frog stretching his thick ugly head out of the water. "Oh, is it you, old waddler?" she said. "I'm crying because my golden ball has fallen into the well." "Be quiet and stop crying," the frog answered. "I can help you, but what will you give me if I fetch your ball again?" "Whatever you like, dear frog," she said. "My clothes, my pearls and jewels, and even the golden crown that I'm wearing." "I don't like your clothes, your pearls and jewels and your golden crown, but if you love me and let me be your companion and playmate, let me sit at your table next to you, eat from your golden plate and drink from your cup, and sleep in your bed, if you promise me this, then I shall dive down and fetch your golden ball for you again."[11]

Comparison

By comparing these three versions we can see how "The Frog Prince" became more and more embroidered in a short course of time—and this did not occur merely for stylistic reasons. In the original folktale of 1810, the setting is simple and totally lacking in frills. There is no castle. The incident appears to take place on a large estate. The king's daughter could well be a peasant's daughter or any girl who goes to a well, finds a ball, loses it, and agrees to take the frog home if he finds the ball for her. He has no other desire but to sleep with her. There is no beating around the bush in the rest of the narrative.

It is explicitly sexual and alludes to a universal initiation and marital ritual (derived from primitive matriarchal societies), and in one other version, the princess does not throw the frog against the wall but kisses it as in the "Beauty and Beast" tales. Mutual sexual recognition and acceptance bring about the prince's salvation. In both the 1812 and 1857 versions the princess provides more of an identification basis for a bourgeois child, for she is unique, somewhat spoiled, and very wealthy. She thinks in terms of monetary payment and basically treats the frog as though he were a member of a lower caste—an attitude not apparent in the original version. The ornate description serves to cover or eliminate the sexual frankness of the original tale. Here the frog wants to be a companion and playmate. Sex must first be sweetened up and made to appear harmless because its true form is repulsive. The girl obeys the father, but like all good bourgeois children she rejects the sexual advances of the frog, and for this she is rewarded. In fact, all three versions suggest a type of patriarchal socialization for young girls that has been severely criticized and questioned by progressive educators today, but the final version is most consistent in its *capacity* to combine feudal folk notions of sexuality, obedience, and sexual roles with bourgeois norms and comportment. The changes in the versions reveal social transitions and class differences that attest to their dependency on the gradual ascendancy of bourgeois codes and tastes.

Even the earlier French *haute bourgeois* values had to be altered by the Grimms to fit their more upright, nineteenth-century, middle-class perspective and sense of decency. Let us compare the beginning of Perrault's "Le Petit Chaperon Rouge" with the Grimms' 1812 "Rotkäppchen," because the French version was their actual source.

"Le Petit Chaperon Rouge" (1697)

Once upon a time there was a little village girl, the prettiest that was ever seen. Her mother doted on her, and her grandmother doted even more. This good woman made a little red hood for her, and it became the girl so well that everyone called her Little Red Riding Hood.

One day her mother, having baked some biscuits, said to Little Red Riding Hood: "Go and see how your grandmother is feeling; someone told me that she was ill. Take her some biscuits and this little pot of butter." Little Red Riding Hood departed immediately for the house of her grandmother, who lived in another village.[12]

"Rotkäppchen" (1812)

Once upon a time there was a small sweet maid. Whoever laid eyes on her loved her. But it was her grandmother who loved her most. She never had enough to give the child. One time she gave her a present, a small hood made out of velvet, and since it became her so well, and since she did not want to wear anything but this, she was simply called Little Red Riding Hood. One day her mother said to her: "Come, Red Riding Hood, take this piece of cake and bottle of wine and bring it to grandmother. She is sick and weak. This will nourish her. Be nice and good and give her my regards. Be orderly on your way and don't veer from the path, otherwise you'll fall and break the glass. Then your sick grandmother will have nothing."[13]

Comparison

In their article on Perrault's "Little Red Riding Hood," Carole and D.T. Hanks Jr. commented on the "sanitization" process of the Grimms and later editors of this tale. "Perrault's tale provides a classic example of the bowdlerizing which all too often afflicts children's literature. Derived from the German version, 'Rotkäppchen' (Grimm No. 26), American versions of the tale have been sanitized to the point where the erotic element disappears and the tragic ending becomes comic. This approach emasculates a powerful story, one which unrevised is a metaphor for the maturing process."[14] The word *emasculates* is an unfortunate choice to describe what happened to Perrault's tale (and the original folktales), because it was the rise of authoritarian patriarchal societies that was responsible for fear of sexuality and stringent sexual codes. Second, Perrault's tale was written not only for children but also for an educated upper-class audience that included children.[15] The development of children's literature, as we know, was late, and it only gradually assumed a vital role in the general socialization process of the eighteenth and nineteenth centuries. Therefore, Perrault's early tale had to be made more suitable for children by the Grimms and had to reinforce a more conservative bourgeois sense of morality. This moralistic impulse is most apparent in the changes the Grimms made at the very beginning of the tale. Little Red Riding Hood is no longer a simple village maid but the epitome of innocence. It is not enough, however, to be innocent. The girl must learn to fear her own curiosity and sensuality. So the narrative purpose corresponds to the socialization for young girls at that time: if you do not walk the straight path through the sensual temptations of the dark forest, if you are not orderly and moral (*sittsam*),[16] then you will be swallowed by the wolf; that is, the devil or sexually starved males. Typically the savior and rebirth motif is represented by a male hunter, a father figure devoid of sexuality. Here again the revisions in word choice, tone, and content cannot be understood unless one grasps the substance of education and socialization in the first half of the nineteenth century.

Let us take one more example, a short section from the Grimms' 1810 and 1812 versions of "Snow White."

1810 Manuscript

When Snow White awoke the next morning, they asked her how she happened to get there. And she told them everything, how her mother the queen had left her alone in the woods and went away. The dwarfs took pity on her and persuaded her to remain with them and do the cooking for them when they went to the mines. However, she was to beware of the queen and not let anyone in the house.[17]

1812 Edition

When Snow White awoke, they asked her who she was and how she happened to get in the house. Then she told them how her mother wanted to have her put to death, but that the hunter spared her life, and how she had run the entire day and finally arrived at their house. So the dwarfs took pity on her and said: "If you keep our house for us, and cook, sew, make the beds, wash and knit, and keep everything tidy and clean, you may stay with us, and you will have everything you want. In the evening, when we come home, dinner must be ready. During the day we are in the mines and dig for gold, so you will be alone. Beware of the queen and let no one in the house."[18]

Comparison

These passages again reveal how the Grimms had an entirely different socialization process in mind when they altered the folktales. Snow White is given instructions that are more commensurate with the duties of a bourgeois girl, and the tasks that she performs are implicitly part of her moral obligation. Morals are used to justify a division of labor and the separation of the sexes. Here, too, the growing notion that the woman's role was in the home and that the home was a shelter for innocence and children belonged more to a conception of women, work, and child rearing in bourgeois circles than to the ideas of the peasantry and aristocracy. Certainly, the growing proletarian class in the nineteenth century could not think of keeping wives and children at home, for they had to work long hours in the factories. Snow White was indeed a new kind of princess in the making and was constantly remade. In the 1810 version the father comes with doctors to save his daughter. Then he arranges a marriage for her daughter and punishes the wicked queen. In the margin of their manuscript, the Grimms remarked, "This ending is not quite right and is lacking something."[19] Their own finishing touches could be topped only by the prudish changes made by that twentieth-century sanitation man, Walt Disney.

Aside from situating the compilation of folktales and grasping the literary transformations within a sociohistorical framework, we must investigate the pervasive influence that the Grimms have had in the socialization process of respective countries. We know that the Grimms' collection (especially the 1857 final edition) has been the second-most popular and widely circulated book in Germany for more than a century, second only to the Bible. We also know that the tales and similar stories are the cultural bread and butter of most children from infancy until ten years of age. Studies in Germany show that there is a fairy-tale reading age between six and ten.[20] Otherwise the tales have already been read or told to the children by adults before they are six. Incidentally, this process of transmission means that certain groups of adults are constantly rereading and retelling the tales throughout their lives. Ever since the rise of the mass media, the Grimms' tales (generally in their most prudish and prudent version) have been broadcast by radio; filmed; recorded for records, tapes, and video; used as motifs for advertisements; and commercialized in every manner and form imaginable. Depending on the country and relative reception, these particular tales have exercised a grip on our minds and imagination from infancy into adulthood, and, though they cannot be held accountable for negative features in advanced technological societies, it is time—as many West German writers believe—to evaluate how they impart values and norms to children that may actually hinder their growth, rather than help them to come to terms with their existential condition and mature autonomously, as Bruno Bettelheim and others maintain.[21]

Here we must consider the socialization of reading fairy tales with the primary focus on those developed by the Brothers Grimm. In discussing socialization I shall be relying on a general notion of culture that is defined by the mode through which human beings objectify themselves, come together, and relate to one another in history and materialize their ideas, intentions, and solutions, in the sense of making them more concrete. By concrete I also mean to imply that there are forms people create and use to make their ideas, intentions, and solutions take root in a visible, audible, and generally perceptible manner so that they become an actual part of people's daily lives. Thus, culture is viewed as a historical process of human objectification, and the level and quality of a national culture depends on the socialization developed by human beings to integrate young members into the society and to reinforce the norms and values that legitimize the sociopolitical systems and that guarantee some sort of continuity in society.[22]

Reading as internalization, or, technically speaking, as resubjectification, has always functioned in socialization processes, whether it be the conscious or unconscious "understanding" of signs, symbols, and letters. In modern times, that is, since the Enlightenment and rise of the bourgeoisie, reading has been the passport into certain brackets of society and the measure by which one functions and maintains a certain place in the hierarchy.[23] The reading of printed fairy tales in the nineteenth century was a socially exclusive process:

it was conducted mainly in bourgeois circles and nurseries, and members of the lower classes who learned how to read were not only acquiring a skill but also acquiring a value system and social status, depending on their conformity to norms controlled by bourgeois interests. The social function of reading is not to be understood in a mechanistic or reductive way; that is, that reading was solely a safeguard for bourgeois hegemony and allowed only for singular interpretations. Certainly the introduction of reading to the lower classes opened up new horizons for them and gave them more power. Also the production of books allowed for a variety of viewpoints often contrary to the ruling forces in society. In some respects reading can function explosively like a dream and serve to challenge socialization and constraints. But, unlike the dream, it is practically impossible to determine what direct effect a fairy tale will have on an individual reader in terms of validating his or her own existence. Still, the tale does provide and reflect on the cultural boundaries within which the reader measures and validates his or her own identity. We tend to forget the sociohistorical frameworks of control when we talk about reading and especially the reading of fairy tales. Both socialization and reading reflect and are informed by power struggles and ideology in a given society or culture. To become literate means to learn how to operate within the laws of literacy that are class determined. The Grimms' fairy tales not only were products of the struggles of the common people to make themselves heard in oral folktales—symbolically representing their needs and wishes—but also became literary products of the German bourgeois quest for identity and power. To this extent, the norms and value system that the Grimms cultivated within the tales point to an objectified, standard way of living that was intended and came to legitimate the general bourgeois standard of living and work, not only in Germany but throughout the Western world.

In all there were fifty-one tales in the original manuscript of 1810. Some were omitted in the 1812 book publication, and those that were included were all extensively changed and stylized by the Grimms to meet middle-class taste. This process of conscious alteration for social and aesthetic reasons was continued until 1857. The philological research by Rölleke and others in the 1970s and 1980s that have stressed and documented this are not merely significant for what they tell us about the Grimms' method of work or the relation of the tales to late feudal and early bourgeois society in Germany. They have greater ramifications for the development of the literary fairy tales in general, especially in view of socialization through reading and the meaning of literacy.

II

First of all, through understanding the subjective selection process and adaptation methods of the Grimms, we can begin to study other collections of folktales that have been published in the nineteenth and twentieth centuries and analyze similar transcription methods in light of education and socialization. Recent attention has been paid to the role of the narrator of the tales in folklore research, but the role of the collector and transcriber is also significant, for we have seen how consciously and unconsciously the Grimms integrated into the tales their worldviews and those of their intended audience as well. The relationship of the collector to audience is additionally significant because printed and transcribed folktales were not meant to be reinserted into circulation as books for the original audience. As Rudolf Schenda demonstrated in *Volk ohne Buch*,[24] the lower classes did not and could not use books because of their lack of money and training. Their tradition was an oral one. The nineteenth-century and early twentieth-century transcription of folktales was primarily for the educated classes, young and old. The reception of the tales influenced the purpose and style of the collectors. This remains true up through the present.

As I have noted, psychologists have explored the relationship between dream and fairy-tale production, and moreover they have endeavored to explore the special role that fairy tales have played in socialization. One of the most succinct and sober analyses of why the fairy tale in particular attracts children and functions so well in the socialization process has been made by Emanuel K. Schwartz. He argues,

> The struggle between what is perceived as the "good parent" and the "bad parent" is one of the big problems of childhood. In the fairy tale the bad mother is commonly seen as the witch (phallic mother). The great man, the father figure (Oedipus), represents the hero, or the hero-to-be, the prototype, for the young protagonist of the fairy tale. The process of social and psychological change, characteristic of the fairy tale, is childishly pursued, and magic is used to effect changes. On the other hand, experience with having to struggle for the gratification and the fulfillment of wishes results in a social adherence to and the development of an understanding of social norms and social conformities. This does not mean, however, that the reinforcement of an awareness of socialization results in submissiveness; but a certain amount of common sense, which goes into conforming with the social mores, is a realistic necessity for children and adults alike.[25]

To a certain extent, Schwartz minimizes the inherent dangers in such narratives as the Grimms' fairy tales, which function to legitimize certain repressive standards of action and make them acceptable for children. Reading as a physical and mental process involves identification before an internalization of norms and values can commence, and identification for a child comes easily in a Grimms' fairy tale. There is hardly one that does not announce who the protagonist is, and he or she commands our identification almost immediately by being the youngest, the most oppressed, the wronged, the smallest, the most naive, the weakest, the most innocent, and so on. Thus, direct identification of a child with the major protagonist begins the process of socialization through reading.

Although it is extremely difficult to determine exactly what a child will absorb on an unconscious level, the patterns of most Grimms' fairy tales draw conscious attention to prescribed values and models. As children read or are read to, they follow a social path, learn role orientation, and acquire norms and values. The pattern of most Grimms' fairy tales involves a struggle for power, survival, and autonomy. Though there are marked differences among the tales, I can suggest an overall pattern that will make it clear why and how they become functional in the bourgeois socialization process.

Initially the young protagonist must leave home or the family because power relations have been disturbed. Either the protagonist is wronged or a change in social relations forces the protagonist to depart from home. A task is imposed, and a hidden command of the tale must be fulfilled. The question that most of the Grimms' tales ask is, How can one learn—what must one do to use one's powers rightly to be accepted in society or re-create society in keeping with the norms of the status quo? The wandering protagonist always leaves home to reconstitute home. Along the way the male hero becomes handsome and learns to be active, competitive, industrious, cunning, and acquisitive. His goal is money, power, and a woman (also associated with chattel). His jurisdiction is the open world. His happiness depends on the just use of power. The female hero learns to be passive, obedient, self-sacrificing, hardworking, patient, and straight-laced. Her goal is wealth, jewels, and a man to protect her property rights. Her jurisdiction is the home or castle. Her happiness depends on conformity to patriarchal rule. Sexual activity is generally postponed until after marriage. Often the tales imply a postponement of gratification until the necessary skills, power, and wealth are acquired.

For a child growing up in a capitalist society in the nineteenth and twentieth centuries, the socialization process carried by the pattern and norms in a Grimms' fairy tale functioned and still functions to make such a society more acceptable to the child. Friction and points of conflict are minimized, for the fairy tale legitimates bourgeois society by seemingly granting upward mobility and the possibility for autonomy. All the Grimms' tales contain an elaborate set of signs and codes. If there is a wrong signaled in a Grimms' fairy tale—and there is always somebody being wronged or a relation disturbed—then it involves breaking an inviolate code that is the basis of benevolent patriarchal rule. Acceptable norms are constituted by the behavior of a protagonist whose happy end indicates the possibility for resolution of the conflicts according to the code. Even in such tales as "How Six Made Their

Way through the World," "Bremen Town Musicians," "Clever Gretel," and "The Blue Light," in which the downtrodden protagonists overthrow oppressors, the social relations and work ethos are not fundamentally altered but reconstituted in a manner that allows for more latitude in the hierarchical social system—something that was desired incidentally by a German bourgeoisie incapable of making revolutions but most capable of making compromises at the expense of the peasantry. Lower-class members become members of the ruling elite, but this occurs because the ruling classes need such values that were being cultivated by the bourgeoisie—thrift, industry, patience, obedience, and so forth. Basically, the narrative patterns imply that skills and qualities are to be developed and used so that one can compete for a high place in the hierarchy based on private property, wealth, and power. Both command and report[26] of the Grimms' fairy tales emphasize a *process* of socialization through reading that leads to internalizing the basic nineteenth-century bourgeois norms, values, and power relationships, which take their departure from feudal society.

For example, let us consider "The Table, the Ass and the Stick" to see how functional it is in terms of male socialization. It was first incorporated into the expanded edition of the Grimms' tales in 1819 and deals mainly with lower middle-class characters, focuses on males, and is the basis for a discussion about a reutilized tale by F.K. Waechter. All the incidents concern master–slave relationships. Three sons are in charge of a goat, who rebels against them by lying and causing all three to be banished by their father, a tailor. After the banishment of the sons, the tailor discovers that the goat has lied. So he shaves her, and she runs away. In the meantime, each one of the sons works diligently in a petit bourgeois trade as joiner, miller, and turner. They are rewarded with gifts by their masters, but the two eldest have their gifts stolen from them by the landlord of a tavern. They embarrass the father and bring shame on the family when they try to show off their gifts, which the landlord had replaced with false ones. It is up to the third son to outsmart the landlord, bring about a family reunion, and restore the good name of the family in the community through exhibiting its wealth and power. The father retires as a wealthy man, and we also learn that a busy bee has duly punished the goat.

Though the father wrongs the boys, his authority to rule remains unquestioned throughout the narrative, and we are not to question it. The blame for disturbing the seemingly natural relationship between father and sons is placed on liars and deceivers, the goat and the landlord. They seek power and wealth through devious means. The elaborated code of the tale holds that the only way to acquire wealth and power is through diligence, perseverance, and honesty. The goal of the sons is submission to the father and maintenance of the family's good name. The story enjoins the reader to accept the norms and values of a patriarchal master–slave relationship and private property relations. In general, there is nothing wrong with emphasizing the qualities of "diligence, perseverance, and honesty" in a socialization process, but we are talking about socialization through a story that upholds as positive goals patriarchal domination and the accumulation of wealth and power for private benefit.

In almost all the Grimms' fairy tales, male domination and master–slave relationships are rationalized so long as the rulers are benevolent and use their power justly. If tyrants and parents are challenged, they relent or are replaced, but the property relationships and patriarchy are not transformed. In "The Table, the Ass and the Stick" there is a series of master–slave relationships: father–son, patriarchal family–goat, master–apprentice, and landlord–son. The sons and other characters are socialized to please the masters. They work to produce wealth and power for the father, who retires in the end because the sons have accumulated wealth in the proper, diligent fashion according to the Protestant Ethic. The goat and landlord are punished for different reasons: the goat is punished because she resented the master–slave relationship, and the landlord is punished because, as a false father, he violated the rules of private property. Although this remarkable fairy tale allows for many other interpretations, viewed in light of its function in the bourgeois socialization process, we can begin to understand why numerous West German writers began looking askance at the Brothers Grimm during the rise of the antiauthoritarian movement of the late 1960s.

III

Actually the reutilization and transformation of the Grimms' tales were not the inventions of West German writers or were they so new.[27] There was a strong radical tradition of rewriting folktales and fairy tales for children that began in the late nineteenth century and blossomed during the Weimar period, until the Nazis put an end to such experimentation. This tradition was revived during the 1960s, when such writers as Hermynia Zur Mühlen, Lisa Tetzner, Edwin Hoernle, and Walter Benjamin[28] were rediscovered and when the antiauthoritarian movement and the Left began to focus on children and socialization. One of the results of the general radical critique of capitalism and education in West Germany was the attempt to build a genuine, noncommercial children's public sphere that might counter the exploitative and legitimizing mechanisms of the dominant bourgeois public sphere. To provide cultural tools and means to reutilize the present public sphere for children, groups of people with a progressive bent tried to offset the racism, sexism, and authoritarian messages in children's books, games, theaters, TV, and schools by creating different kinds of emancipatory messages and cultural objects with and for children.

In children's literature, and specifically in the area of fairy tales, several publishing houses played an active role in introducing reutilized fairy tales created to politicize the children's public sphere, where children and adults cooperated and conceived more concrete, democratic forms of play and work in keeping with the needs and wishes of a participating community.[29] Obviously the rise of a broad left-oriented audience toward the end of the 1960s encouraged many big publishers to direct their efforts to this market for profit, but not all the books were published by giant companies or solely for profit. And, at the beginning of the twenty-first century, when the so-called New Left is no longer so new or as vocal as it was during the late 1960s, there are still numerous publishing houses, large and small, that are directing their efforts toward the publication of countercultural or reutilized fairy-tale books and children's literature. My discussion will limit itself and focus on the reutilized Grimms' tales published by Rowohlt, Basis, Schlot, and Beltz and Gelberg during the 1970s and 1980s. In particular I shall endeavor to demonstrate how these fairy tales reflected possibilities for a different social-ization process from standard children's books and, to a certain extent, how some of the ideas, plots, and practices in the tales have been realized in the children's public sphere and education.

In 1972 the large Rowohlt Verlag, under the general editorship of Uwe Wandrey, established a book series for children titled *rororo rotfuchs*. An impres-sive series was developed and contained a wide range of progressive chil-dren's stories, histories, autobiographies, handbooks, and fairy tales for young people between the ages of four and eighteen. Here I want to concen-trate on two of the earlier and best efforts to reutilize old fairy tales.

Friedrich Karl Waechter, illustrator and writer,[30] has written and drawn numerous politicized fairy tales and fairy-tale plays for children. One of his first books, *Tischlein deck dich und Knüppel aus dem Sack* (*Table Be Covered and Stick out of the Sack*, 1972), is a radical rendition of the Grimms' "The Table, the Ass and the Stick." His story takes place a long time ago in a small town named Breitenrode. (From the pictures the time can be estimated to be the early twentieth century.) Fat Jakob Bock, who owns a large lumber mill and most of the town, exploits his workers as much as he can. When a young carpenter named Philip invents a magic table that on command continually spreads as much food as one can eat, Bock (the name means ram in German) takes over the invention and incorporates it, because it was done on company time. He promises Philip his daughter Caroline if he now invents a "stick out of the sack"—the power Bock needs to guard his property. Philip is given the title of inventor and put to work as a white-collar worker, separating him from his friends, the other carpenters, who had helped him build the magic table. At first Philip and his friends are not sure why Bock wants the stick, but an elf named Xram (Marx spelled backward) enlightens them. They decide to work together on this invention and to keep control over it. But, when it is finished, Bock obtains it and plants the magic table as stolen property in the house of Sebastien, a troublemaker, who always wants to organize the workers around their own needs. Bock accuses Sebastien of stealing the table and asserts that he needs the stick to punish thieves like Sebastien and to protect his property. However, Philip exposes Bock as the real thief, and the greedy man is chased from the town. Then the workers celebrate as Philip announces that the magic table will be owned by everyone in the town, while Xram hides the stick. The final picture shows men, women, children, dogs, cats, and other animals at a huge picnic, sharing the fruits of the magic table while Bock departs.

Like the narrative, Waechter's drawings were intended to invert the socialization process in West Germany at that time. The story line is primarily concerned with private property relations, and it begins traditionally with the master–slave relationship. The ostensible command of the tale—"obey the boss and you'll cash in on the profits"—is gradually turned into another command—"freedom and happiness can be attained only through collective action and sharing." The narrative flow of the tale confirms this reversed command, and the reading process becomes a learning process about socialization in capitalist society. Philip experiences how the fruits of collective labor expended by himself and his friends are expropriated by Bock. With the magical help of Xram (i.e., the insights of Marx) the workers learn to take control over their own labor and to share the fruits equally among themselves. Here the master–slave relationship is concretely banished, and the new work and social relationships are based on cooperation and collective ownership of the means of production. The virtues of Philip and the workers—diligence, perseverance, imagination, honesty—are used in a struggle to overcome male domination rooted in private property relations. Socialization is seen as a struggle for self-autonomy against exploitative market and labor conditions.

In Andreas and Angela Hopf's *Der Feuerdrache Minimax* (*The Fire Dragon Minimax*, 1973), also an illustrated political fairy tale,[31] the authors use a unique process to depict the outsider position of children and strange-looking creatures and also the need for the outsider to be incorporated within the community if the community is to develop. The Hopfs superimpose red drawings of Minimax and the little girl Hilde onto etchings of medieval settings and characters.[32] The imposition and juxtaposition of red figures on black-and-white prints keep the reader's focus on contrast and differences. The narrative is a simple reutilization of numerous motifs that commonly appear in the Grimms' tales and associate dragons, wolves, and other animals with forces of destruction endangering the status quo. *The Fire Dragon Minimax* demonstrates how the status quo must be questioned and challenged.

The story takes place during the Middle Ages in the walled town of Gimpelfingen. While sharpening his sword, the knight causes sparks to fly, and the town catches fire. There is massive destruction, and the dragon is immediately blamed for the fire, but Hilde, who had fled the flames, encounters Minimax, who had been bathing in the river when the fire began. So she knows that he could not have caused the fire. In fact, he helps extinguish part of the fire and then carries Hilde to his cave, because he prefers to roast potatoes with his flames and sleep for long hours rather than burn down towns. The knight pretends to fight in the interests of the town and accuses Minimax of starting the fire and kidnapping Hilde. He dons his armor and goes in search of the dragon, but he is no contest for Minimax, who overwhelms him. The knight expects the dragon to kill him, but Minimax tells him instead to take Hilde home because her parents might be worried about her. Again the knight lies to the townspeople and tells them that he has rescued Hilde and killed the dragon. Hilde tries to convince the people that he is lying, but she is believed by only a handful of people, who fortunately decide to see if Minimax is alive or dead. After finding him, they realize the truth and bring Minimax back to town. This causes the knight to flee in fear. Minimax is welcomed by the townspeople, and he helps them rebuild the town. Thereafter, he remains in the town, roasts potatoes for the children, or takes them on rides in the sky. Hilde is his favorite, and he flies highest with her and often tells her fairy tales about dragons.

Obviously the Hopfs are concerned with racism and militarism in this tale. The dragon represents the weird-looking alien figure, who acts differently from the "normal" people. And the Hopfs show how the strange and different creature is often used by people in power as a scapegoat to distract attention from the real enemy; namely, the people in power. In contrast to the dominant master–slave relationship established in the medieval community, the friendship of Hilde and the dragon is based on mutual recognition. Their relationship is opposed to the dominant power relationship of male patriarchy in the town. In terms of problems in today's late capitalist society, the tale also relates to feminism and the prevention of cruelty to animals. The activism of Hilde on behalf of the dragon sets norms of behavior for young girls, when she asserts herself and uses her talents for the benefit of oppressed creatures in the community. As in Waechter's politicized fairy tale, the textual symbols of goal-oriented behavior are aimed at cooperation and collectivism, not domination and private control.

The publishing house that was the most outspoken on behalf of such general socialist goals in children's culture during the 1970s was Basis Verlag in West Berlin. Working in a collective manner, the people in this group produced a number of excellent studies on fairy tales and children's literature,[33] as well as a series of different types of books for young readers. Here I want to remark on just one of their fairy-tale experiments titled *Zwei Korken für Schlienz* (*Two Corks for Schlienz*, 1972) by Johannes Merkel based on the Grimms' tale "How Six Made Their Way through the World." The reutilized fairy tale deals with housing difficulties in large cities, and the text is accompanied by amusing photos with superimposed drawings. Four young people with extraordinary powers seek to organize tenants to fight against an exploitative landlord. Ultimately, they fail, but in the process they learn, along with the readers, to recognize their mistakes. The open ending suggests that the four will resume their struggle in the near future—this time without false illusions.

Most of the tales in *Janosch erzählt Grimm's Märchen* (*Janosch Tells Grimm's Fairy Tales,* 1972) are intended to smash false illusions, too, but it is not so apparent that Janosch has a socialist goal in mind; that is, that he envisions collective living and sharing as a means to eliminate the evils in the world.[34] He is mainly concerned with the form and contents of fifty Grimms' tales that he wants to parody to the point of bursting their seams. He retells them in a caustic manner using modern slang, idiomatic expressions, and pointed references to deplorable living conditions in affluent societies. Each tale endeavors to undo the socialization of a Grimms' tale by inverting plots and characters and adding new incidents. Such inversion does not necessarily amount to a happier or more emancipatory view of the world. If Janosch is liberating, it is because he is so humanely candid, often cynical, and disrespectful of conditioned and established modes of thinking and behavior. For instance, in "The Frog Prince" it is the frog who loses his ball and is pursued by a girl. The frog is forced by his father to accept the annoying girl in the subterranean water palace. Her pestering, however, becomes too much for him, and he suffocates her. This causes her transformation into a frog princess, whereupon she marries the frog prince and explains to him how she had been captured by human beings and had changed herself into an ugly girl to escape malicious treatment by humans. Her ugliness prevented other humans from marrying her and allowed her to return to her true form.

Such an inversion makes a mockery of the Grimms' tale and perhaps makes the reader aware of the potential threat that humans pose to nature and the animal world. This point can be argued. But what is clear from the story is that Janosch fractures the social framework of audience expectations, whether or not the readers are familiar with the original Grimms' tales. The numerous illustrations by Janosch are just as upsetting, and the tales derive their power by not conforming to the socialization of reading the Grimms' tales as harmless stories. His anarchistic, somewhat cynical rejection of the Grimms and the norms they represent is related to his rejection of the hypocritical values of the new rich in postwar Germany created by a so-called economic miracle. For instance, in "Puss 'n' Boots," a marvelous cat exposes his young master Hans to the emptiness and meaninglessness of high society. When Hans experiences how rich people place more stock in objects than in the lives of other people, he decides to abandon his dreams of wealth and success and to lead a carefree life on a modest scale with the cat. This is not to say that the cat or Hans are model characters or point to models for creating a new society. They are symbols of refusal, and by depicting such refusal, Janosch seeks to defend a "questioning spirit," totally lacking in the Grimms' tales and very much alive in his provocative revisions, where everything depends on a critical new viewpoint.

One of Janosch's major supporters of revisions was Hans-Joachim Gelberg, who was one of the most important proponents for the reutilization of the Grimms' tales and the creation of more politicized and critical stories for children and adults. Gelberg edited special yearbooks, which included various types of experimental fairy tales and received prestigious awards in West Germany,[35] for Gelberg pointed in new directions for a children's literature that refuses to be infantile and condescending. In addition to the yearbooks, Gelberg published a significant volume of contemporary fairy tales titled *Neues vom Rumpelstilzchen und andere Haus-Märchen von 43 Autoren* (1976).[36] Because there are fifty-eight different fairy tales and poems, it is difficult to present a detailed discussion of the reutilization techniques in regard to socialization in the tales. Generally speaking, the direction is the same: a wholesale rethinking and reconceptualization of traditional fairy-tale motifs to question standard reading and rearing processes. Since the title of the book features "Rumpelstiltskin" and the motto of the book—"No, I would rather have something living than all the treasures of the world"—is taken from his tale, I shall deal with the two versions of "Rumpelstiltskin" by Rosemarie Künzler and Irmela Brender,[37] because they represent the basic critical attitude of most of the authors.

Both Künzler and Brender shorten the tale drastically and take different approaches to the main characters. Künzler begins by stressing the boastful nature of the miller, who gets his daughter into a terrible fix. She is bossed around by the king and then by some little man who promises to help her by using extortion. When the little man eventually barters for her first-born child, the miller's daughter is shocked into her senses. She screams and tells the little man that he is crazy and that she will never marry the horrid king or ever give her child away. The angry little man stamps so hard that he causes the door of the room to spring open, and the miller's daughter runs out into the wide world and is saved. This version is a succinct critique of male exploitation and domination of women. The miller's daughter allows herself to be pushed around until she has an awakening. Like Janosch, Künzler projects the refusal to conform to socialization as the first step toward actual emancipation.

Brender's version is different. She questions the justice in the Grimms' tale from Rumpelstiltskin's point of view, for she has always felt that the poor fellow has been treated unfairly. After all, what he wanted most was something living; in other words, some human contact. She explains that Rumpelstiltskin did not need money, because he was capable of producing gold any time he wanted it. He was also willing to work hard and save the life of the miller's daughter. Therefore, the miller's daughter could have been more understanding and compassionate. Brender does not suggest that the miller's daughter should have given away the child, but as the young queen, she could have invited Rumpelstiltskin to live with the royal family. This way Rumpelstiltskin would have found the human companionship he needed, and everyone would have been content. The way things end in the Grimms' version is for Brender totally unjust. Her technique is a play with possibilities to open up rigid social relations and concern about private possession. Through critical reflection her narrative shifts the goal of the Grimms' story from gold and power to justice and more humane relations based on mutual consideration and cooperation.

Both Künzler and Brender seek a humanization of the socialization process by transforming the tales and criticizing commodity exchange and male domination, and they incorporate a feminist perspective that is at the very basis of an entire book titled *Märchen für tapfere Mädchen (Fairy Tales for Girls with Spunk*, 1978) by Doris Lerche, illustrator, and O.F. Gmelin, writer.[38] They use two fictitious girls named Trolla and Svea and a boy named Bror from the North to narrate different types of fairy tales that purposely seek to offset our conditioned notions of sexual roles and socialization. For instance, the very beginning of "Little Red Cap" indicates a markedly different perspective from the Grimms' version: "There was once a fearless girl."[39] She is not afraid of the wolf, and, even though she is swallowed by him in her grandmother's bed, she keeps her wits about her, takes out a knife, cuts herself a hole in his stomach while he sleeps, and rescues herself and granny. In Gmelin's rendition of "Hans and Gretel," the poor parents are not the enemies of the children; rather poverty is the source of trouble. To help the parents, the children go into the woods in search for food and eventually they become lost. Then they encounter a woman who is no longer a witch but an outcast who has learned to live by the brutal rule of the land set by others. Hans and Gretel overcome the obstacles that she places in their quest for food, but they do not punish her. They are more concerned about reestablishing strong bonds of cooperation and love with their parents. The children return home without a treasure, and the ending leaves the fate of the family open.

IV

The open endings of many of the reutilized fairy tales from West Germany of the 1970s indicate that the future for such fairy tales may also be precarious.

Given the social import and the direct political tendency of the tales to contradict and criticize the dominant socialization process in Germany, these tales were not used widely in schools, and their distribution was limited more to groups partial to the tales among the educated classes in West Germany. They were also attacked by the conservative press because of their "falsifications" and alleged harmfulness to children. Nevertheless, the production of such tales did not abate in the 1980s and 1990s, and such continuous publication may reflect something about the diminishing appeal of the Grimms' tales and the needs of young and adult readers to relate to fantastic projections that are connected more to the concrete conditions of their own reality.

Folktales and fairy tales have always been dependent on customs, rituals, and values in the particular socialization process of a social system. They have always symbolically depicted the nature of power relationships within a given society. Thus, they are strong indicators of the level of civilization, that is, the essential quality of a culture and social order. The effectiveness of emancipatory and reutilized tales has depended not only on the tales but also on the manner in which they have been received and their use and distribution in society. The fact that West German writers argued and continue to argue that it is time for the Brothers Grimm to stop looking over their shoulders may augur positive changes for part of the socialization process. At the very least, they compel us to reconsider where socialization through the reading of the Grimms' tales has led us.

5

HANS CHRISTIAN ANDERSEN
AND THE DISCOURSE OF
THE DOMINATED

Andersen visited me here several years ago. He seemed to me like a
tailor. This is the way he really looks. He is a haggard man with a
hollow, sunken face, and his demeanor betrays an anxious, devout
type of behavior that kings love. This is the reason why they give
Andersen such a brilliant reception. He is the perfect representation
of all poets, just the way kings want them to be.

—Heinrich Heine (1851)[1]

If the Brothers Grimm were the first writers in the nineteenth century to
distinguish themselves by remolding oral folktales explicitly for a bourgeois
socialization process, then Hans Christian Andersen completed their mission
so to speak and created a canon of literary fairy tales for children and adults
between 1835 and 1874 in praise of essentialist ideology. By infusing his
tales with general notions of the Protestant Ethic and essentialist ideas of
natural biological order, Andersen was able to receive the bourgeois seal of
good housekeeping. From the dominant class point of view his tales were
deemed useful and worthy enough for rearing children of all classes, and
they became a literary staple in Western culture. Niels Kofoed underlined that
Andersen had basically one tale to tell, not unlike the Horatio Alger myth, and
he repeated it so persuasively and charmingly that it was embraced by the
imagination of nineteenth-century readers:

Andersen, identifying with Aladdin, made his tale a *leitmotif* in the drama of his own life. When people would mock him for his peculiar appearance, he would clench his fists in his pockets saying: I am going to prove that I am not the simpleton that they take me for! Just wait! Some day they will stand up and bow to the triumphant poet—the genius of the world, who will be seated on Parnassus beside Homer, Dante, Shakespeare and Goethe. Andersen told this tale time and again. . . . In Andersen's novels and in his tales and stories he repeated and varied the theme of his life numerous times, developing it and enlarging on it, turning it into a universal song about poetry being of common interest to all mankind. He even considered the fairy-tale genre to be the underlying structure of all good novels and the universal genre of a coming global civilization.[2]

Fortunately for Andersen he appeared on the scene when the original middle-class prejudice against imaginative fairy tales was receding. In fact, there was gradual recognition that fantasy could be employed for the utilitarian needs of the bourgeoisie, and Andersen proved to be a most humble servant in this cause.

But what was at the heart of Andersen's mode of service? In what capacity did his tales serve children and adults in Europe and America? What is the connection between Andersen's achievement as a fairy-tale writer, his servile demeanor, and our cultural appreciation of his tales? It seems to me that these questions have to be posed even more critically if we are to understand the underlying reasons behind Andersen's rise to fame and general acceptance in the nineteenth century. In fact, they are crucial if we want to grasp the continual reception, service, and use of the tales in the twenty-first century, particularly in regard to socialization through literature and film.

Despite the fact that Andersen wrote a great deal about himself and his tales and was followed by scholars who have investigated every nook and cranny of his life and work, there have been very few attempts to study his tales ideologically and to analyze their function in the acculturation process. This is all the more surprising when one considers that they were written with a plump didactic purpose and were overloaded with references to normative behavior and ideal political standards. Indeed, the discourse of his narratives has a distinct ideological bias peculiarly marred by his ambivalent feelings toward his social origins and the dominant classes in Denmark that controlled his fortunes. It is this "marred ambivalence" that is subsumed in his tales and lends them their dynamic tension. Desirous of indicating the way to salvation through emulation of the upper classes and of paying reverence to the Protestant Ethic, Andersen also showed that this path was filled with suffering, humiliation, and torture—and that it could even lead to crucifixion. It is because of his ambivalent attitude, particularly toward the dominance of essentialist ideology, that his tales have retained their basic appeal up through the present day. But before we reevaluate this appeal as constituted by the socializing elements of the tales, we must first turn to reconsider Andersen in light of the class conflict and conditions of social assimilation in his day.

I

The son of a poor cobbler and a washerwoman, Andersen was embarrassed by his proletarian background and grew to insist on notions of natural nobility. Once he became a successful writer, he rarely mingled with the lower classes. If anything, the opposite was the case: he was known to ingratiate himself by making paper cuts and performing for his dinner, so to speak, before upper-class families whom he visited in Copenhagen and throughout all of Europe. Indeed, he successfully opened doors that had been shut in his face when he had first arrived in Copenhagen and made himself welcome by learning how to alter his bearing to please his so-called superiors. However, his success then and now cannot be attributed to his opportunism and conformism. That is, he cannot simply be dismissed as a class renegade who catered to the aesthetic and ideological interests of the dominant classes. His case is much more complex, for in many respects his tales were innovative narratives that explored the limits of assimilation in a closed social order to which he aspired. Despite all the recognition and acceptance by the nobility and bourgeoisie in the Western world, Andersen never felt himself to be a full-fledged member of any group. He was the outsider, the loner, who constantly traveled in his mature years, and his wanderings were symptomatic (as the wanderers and birds in his tales) of a man who hated to be dominated though he loved the dominant class.

As Elias Bredsdorff, one of the more astute biographers of Andersen, maintained,

> Speaking in modern terms Andersen was a man born in the "Lumpenproletariat" but completely devoid of class "consciousness." In his novels and tales he often expresses an unambiguous sympathy for "the underdog," especially for people who have been deprived of their chance of success because of their humble origins, and he pours scorn on haughty people who pride themselves on their noble birth or their wealth and who despise others for belonging to, or having their origin in, the lower classes. But in his private life Andersen accepted the system of absolutism and its inherent class structure, regarded royalty with awe and admiration and found a special pleasure in being accepted by and associating with kings, dukes and princes, and the nobility at home and abroad.[3]

Though Andersen's sympathy did lay with the downtrodden and disenfranchised in his tales, it was not as unambiguous as Bredsdorff would have
us believe, for Andersen's fawning servility to the upper classes also manifested itself in his fiction. In fact, as I have maintained, the ambivalent feelings
about both his origins and the nobility constitute the appeal of the tales.
Andersen prided himself on his "innate" gifts as poet (Digter), and he devoutly
believed that certain biologically determined people were chosen by divine
providence to rise above others. This belief was his rationalization for aspiring
toward recognition and acceptance by the upper classes. And here an important distinction must be made. More than anything else Andersen sought the
blessing and recognition of Jonas Collin and the other members of this
respectable, wealthy, patriarchal family as well as other people from the
educated bureaucratic class in Denmark, like Henriette Wulff. In other words,
Andersen endeavored to appeal to the Danish bourgeois elite that was cultivated in the arts, adept at commerce and administration, and quick to replace
the feudal caste of aristocrats as the leaders of Denmark.

The relationship to Jonas Collin was crucial in his development, for Collin
took him in hand, when he came to Copenhagen, and practically adopted
him as a son. At first he tried to make a respectable bourgeois citizen out of
the ambitious poet but gradually relented and supported Andersen's artistic
undertakings. In due course Andersen's primary audience came to be the
Collin family and people with similar attitudes. All his artistic efforts
throughout his life were aimed at pleasing them. For instance, on Collin's
birthday in 1845 he wrote the following:

> You know that my greatest vanity, or call it rather joy, consists in making you
> realize that I am worthy of you. All the kind of appreciation I get makes me
> think of you. I am truly popular, truly appreciated abroad, I am famous—all
> right, you're smiling. But the cream of the nations fly towards me, I find
> myself accepted in all families, the greatest compliments are paid to me by
> princes and by the most gifted of men. You should see the way people in
> so-called High Society gather round me. Oh, no one at home thinks of this
> among the many who entirely ignore me and might be happy to enjoy even a
> drop of the homage paid to me. My writings must have greater value than
> the Danes will allow for. Heiberg has been translated too, but no one speaks
> of his work, and it would have been strange if the Danes were the only ones
> to be able to make judgments in this world. You must know, you my beloved
> father must understand that you did not misjudge me when you accepted
> me as your son, when you helped and protected me.[4]

Just as important as his relationship to the father Collin was his relationship to his "adopted" brother Edvard, who served as Andersen's superego and

most severe critic. Not only did Edvard edit Andersen's manuscripts and scold him for writing too fast and too much to gain fame, but also he set standards of propriety for the writer through his cool reserve, social composure, and businesslike efficiency. In his person Edvard Collin, a Danish legal administrator like his father, represented everything Andersen desired to become, and Andersen developed a strong homoerotic attachment to Edvard, which remained visibly powerful during his life. In 1838 Andersen wrote a revealing letter that indicates just how deep his feelings for Edvard were:

> I'm longing for you, indeed, at this moment I'm longing for you as if you were a lovely Calabrian girl with dark blue eyes and a glance of passionate flames. I've never had a brother, but if I had I could not have loved him the way I love you, and yet—you do not reciprocate my feelings! This affects me painfully or maybe this is in fact what binds me even more firmly to you. My soul is proud, the soul of a prince cannot be prouder. I have clung to you, I have—bastare! which is a good Italian verb to be translated in Copenhagen as "shut up!" . . . Oh, I wish to God that you were poor and I rich, distinguished, a nobleman. In that case I should initiate you into the mysteries, and you would appreciate me more than you do now. Oh! If there is an eternal life, as indeed there must be, then we shall truly understand and appreciate one another. Then I shall no longer be the poor person in need of kind interest and friends, then we shall be equal.[5]

The fact is that Andersen never felt himself equal to any of the Collins and that he measured his worth by the standards they set. Their letters to him prescribe humility, moderation, asceticism, decorum, economy of mind and soul, devotion to God, and loyalty to Denmark. On the one hand, the Collins family provided Andersen with a home, and on the other, their criticism and sobriety made him feel insecure. They were too classical and refined, too "grammatically" correct, and he knew he could never achieve full recognition as Digter in their minds. Yet that realization did not stop him from trying to prove his moral worth and aesthetic talents to them in his tales and novels. This is not to suggest that all or even most of the fairy tales are totally informed by Andersen's relationship to the Collins. However, to understand their vital aspect—the ideological formation in relationship to the linguistic and semantic discourse—we must grasp how Andersen approached and worked through notions of social domination.

Here Noëlle Bisseret's study Education, Class Language and Ideology is most useful for my purposes, because she endeavors to understand the historical origins of essentialist ideology and concepts of natural aptitudes that figure prominently in Andersen's tales. According to her definition,

> Essentialist ideology, which originates along with the establishment of those structures constituting class societies, is a denial of the historical relations of an economic, political, juridical and ideological order which preside over the establishment of labile power relationships. Essentialist ideology bases all social hierarchy on the transcendental principle of a natural biological order (which took over from a divine principle at the end of the eighteenth century). A difference in essence among human beings supposedly predetermines the diversity of a psychic and mental phenomena ("intelligence," "language," etc.) and thus the place of an individual in a social order considered as immutable.[6]

By analyzing how the concepts of aptitude and disposition were used to designate a contingent reality in the late feudal period, Bisseret is able to show a transformation in meaning to legitimize the emerging power of the bourgeoisie in the nineteenth century: aptitude becomes an essential hereditary feature and is employed to justify social inequalities. In other words, the principle of equality developed by the bourgeoisie was gradually employed as a socializing agent to demonstrate that there are certain select people in a free market system, people with innate talents who are destined to succeed and rule because they "possess or own" the essential qualities of intelligence, diligence, and responsibility.

We must remember that the nineteenth century was the period in which the interest in biology, eugenics, and race became exceedingly strong.[7] Not only did Charles Darwin and Herbert Spencer elaborate their theories at this time but Arthur de Gobineau wrote his *Essai sur l'inégalité des races humaines* (1852) and Francis Galton wrote *Hereditary Genius* (1869) to give a seemingly scientific veneer to the middle-class social selection process. Throughout the Western world a more solidified bourgeois public sphere was establishing itself and replacing feudal systems, as was clearly the case in Denmark.[8] Along with the new institutions designed for rationalization and maximization of profit, a panoptic principle of control, discipline, and punishment was introduced into the institutions of socialization geared to enforce the interests and to guarantee the domination of the propertied classes. This is fully demonstrated in Michel Foucault's valuable study *Discipline and Punish*,[9] which supports Bisseret's thesis of how the ideological concept of attitudes became the "scientific" warrant of a social organization that it justified.

> The ideology of natural inequalities conceived and promoted by a social class at a time when it took economic, and later on political, power gradually turned into a scientific truth, borrowing from craniometry, then from anthropometry, biology, genetics, psychology, and sociology (the scientific practice of which it sometimes oriented); the elements enabling it to substantiate its

assertions. And by this very means, it was able to impose itself upon all the social groups which believed in the values presiding over the birth of aptitude as an ideology: namely Progress and Science. It now appears that well beyond the controversies, which oppose the different established groups, this general ideology directs the whole conception of selection and educational guidance: the educational system aims at selecting and training an "elite," which by its competence, merit, and aptitude is destined for high functions, the responsibility of which entails certain social and economic advantages.[10]

If we look at the case of Andersen in light of Bisseret's thesis at this point, two factors are crucial for his personal conception of an essentialist ideology. First, Denmark was a tiny country with a tightly knit bureaucratic feudal structure that was rapidly undergoing a transformation into a bourgeois-dominated society. There were fewer than 1,200,000 people in the country, and 120,000 in Copenhagen. Among the educated bourgeoisie and nobility everyone knew everyone else who was of importance, and, though the country depended on the bourgeois bureaucratic administrators and commercial investors, the king and his advisors made most of the significant decisions up until the early 1840s, when constitutive assemblies representing the combined interests of industry, commerce, and agriculture began assuming more control. Essentially, as Bredsdorff aptly states, "in Danish society of the early nineteenth century it was almost impossible to break through class barriers. Almost the only exceptions were a few individuals with unusual artistic gifts: Bertel Thorvaldsen, Fru Heiberg and Hans Christian Andersen. And even they had occasionally to be put in their place and reminded of their low origin."[11] Here it is difficult to talk about a real breakthrough. Throughout his life Andersen was obliged to act as a dominated subject within the dominant social circles, despite his fame and recognition as a writer.

Even to reach this point—and this is the second crucial factor—he had to be strictly supervised, for admission to the upper echelons had to be earned and constantly proved. And, Andersen appeared to be a "security risk" at first. Thus, when he came to Copenhagen in 1819 from the lower-class and provincial milieu of Odense, he had to be corrected by his betters so that he could cultivate proper speech, behavior, and decorum. Then for polishing he was also sent to elite private schools in Slagelse and Helsingör at a late age from 1822 to 1827 to receive a thorough formal and classical education. The aim of this education was to curb and control Andersen, especially his flamboyant imagination, not to help him achieve a relative amount of autonomy.

Jonas Collin's purpose in rescuing Andersen and sending him to a grammar school was not to make a great writer out of him but to enable him to become a useful member of the community in a social class higher than the one into which he was born. The grammar-school system was devised to teach boys to learn properly, to mould them into the desired finished products, to make them grow up to be like their fathers.[12]

As Bredsdorff remarks, the system was not so thorough that Andersen was completely reshaped and stamped for complete approval. But it left its indelible marks. What Andersen was to title *The Fairy Tale of My Life*—his autobiography, a remarkable mythopoeic projection of his life[13]—was in actuality a process of self-denial cultivated as individual genius with God-given talents. As I have pointed out, Andersen was ashamed of his family background and did his utmost to avoid talking or writing about it. When he did, he invariably distorted the truth. For him, home was the Collin family, but home, as Andersen knew quite well, was unattainable because of social differences.

It was through his writings and literary achievement that Andersen was able to veil his self-denial and present it as a distinct form of individualism. At the beginning of the nineteenth century in Denmark there was a literary swing from the universality of classicism to the romantic cult of genius and individuality, and Andersen benefited from this greatly. As a voracious reader, Andersen consumed all the German romantic writers of fairy tales along with Shakespeare, Scott, Irving, and other writers who exemplified his ideal of individualism. Most important for his formation in Denmark, as I have already remarked, the romantic movement was

accompanied by what is known as the Aladdin motif, after the idea which Oehlenschläger expressed in his play *Aladdin*. This deals with the theory that certain people are chosen by nature, or God, or the gods, to achieve greatness, and that nothing can succeed in stopping them, however weak and ill-suited they may otherwise seem. . . . The twin themes of former national greatness and of the possibility of being chosen to be great, despite all appearances, assumed a special significance for Denmark after 1814. Romantic–patriotic drama dealing with the heroic past appealed to a population looking for an escape from the sordid present, and served as a source of inspiration for many years. At the same time the Aladdin conception also took on new proportions: it was not only of use as a literary theme, but it could be applied to individuals—Oehlenschläger felt that he himself exemplified it, as did Hans Christian Andersen—and it was also possible to apply it to a country.[14]

Andersen as Aladdin. Andersen's life as a fairy tale. There is something schizophrenic in pretending that one is a fairy-tale character in reality, and Andersen was indeed troubled by nervous disorders and psychic disturbances throughout his life. As I have already discussed, Andersen developed a very peculiar religious and philosophical belief system based on notions of Hans Christian Ørsted, articulated in *The Spirit of Nature*, to temper his compulsive drive for success and thirst for admiration. To justify his schizophrenic existence, he adopted the Danish physicist Hans Christian Ørsted's ideas from *The Spirit of Nature* and combined them with his animistic belief in Christianity.[15] Both Andersen and Ørsted were followers of the theory of intelligent design. Therefore, if the great Creator controlled the workings of the world, genius was a divine and natural gift and would be rewarded regardless of birth. Power was located in the hands of God, and only before Him did one have to bow. However, Andersen did in fact submit more to a temporal social system and had to rationalize this submission adequately enough so that he could live with himself. In doing so, he inserted himself into a sociohistorical nexus of the dominated, denying his origins and needs to receive applause, money, comfort, and space to write about social contradictions that he had difficulty resolving for himself. Such a situation meant a life of self-doubt and anxiety for Andersen.

Again Bisseret is useful in helping us understand the sociopsychological impact on such ego formation and perspectives:

> Dominant in imagination (who am I?), dominated in reality (what am I?), the ego lacks cohesion, hence the contradiction and incoherence of the practices. Dominated-class children think in terms of aptitudes, tastes and interests because at each step in their education their success has progressively convinced them that they are not "less than nothing" intellectually; but at the same time they profoundly doubt themselves. This doubt is certainly not unrelated to the split, discontinuous aspects of their orientations, as measured by the standards of a parsimonious and fleeting time. Their day-to-day projects which lead them into dead ends or which build up gaps in knowledge which are inhibitory for their educational future, reinforce their doubts as to their capacities.[16]

In the particular case of Andersen, the self-doubts were productive insofar as he constantly felt the need to prove himself, to show that his aptitude and disposition were noble and that he belonged to the elect. This is apparent in the referential system built into most of his tales, which are discourses of the dominated. In analyzing such discourse, Bisseret makes the following point:

> The relationship to his social being simultaneously lived and conceived by each agent is based on unconscious knowledge. What is designated as the "subject" (the "I") in the social discourse is the social being of the dominant. Thus in defining his identity the dominated cannot polarize the comparison

between the self/the others on his "me" in the way the dominant does. . . . There cannot be a cohesion except on the side of power. Perhaps the dominated ignore that less than the dominant, as is clear through their accounts. Indeed, the more the practices of the speaker are the practices of power, the more the situation in which he places himself in the conceptual field is the mythical place where power disappears to the benefit of a purely abstract creativity. On the other hand, the more the speaker is subjected to power, the more he situates himself to the very place where power is concretely exercised.[17]

Though Bisseret's ideas about the dominated and dominant in regard to essentialist ideology are concerned with linguistic forms in everyday speech, they also apply to modes of narration used by writers of fiction. For instance, Andersen mixed popular language or folk linguistic forms with formal classical speech in creating his tales, and this stylistic synthesis not only endowed the stories with an unusual tone but also reflected Andersen's efforts to unify an identity that dominant discourse kept dissociating. Andersen also endeavored to ennoble and synthesize folk motifs with the literary motifs of romantic fairy tales, particularly those of Hoffmann, Tieck, Chamisso, Eichendorff, and Fouqué. His stylization of lower-class folk motifs was similar to his personal attempt to rise in society: they were aimed at meeting the standards of "high art" set by the middle classes. As Bengt Holbek points out in regard to Andersen's use of folktales, "He heard them in one milieu and told them in another. He had to make adjustments, one of which was that he had to disguise or obliterate all traces of overt sexuality; such matters were not then deemed fitting entertainment for the children of the bourgeoisie."[18] The self-censorship was done in accordance with the principles of domination, but it was also undermined by Andersen's own metaphorical language that exposed his contradictions. In sum, Andersen's linguistic forms and stylized motifs reveal the structure of relationships as they were being formed and solidified around emerging bourgeois domination in the nineteenth century.

With a few exceptions, most of the 156 fairy tales written by Andersen contain no "I," that is, the "I" is sublimated through the third person, and the narrative discourse becomes dominated by constant reference to the location of power. The identification of the third-person narrator with the underdog or dominated in the tales is consequently misleading. On one level, this occurs, but the narrator's voice always seeks approval and identification with a higher force. Here, too, the figures representing dominance or nobility are not always at the seat of power. Submission to power beyond the aristocracy constituted and constitutes the real appeal of Andersen's tales for middle-class audiences: Andersen placed power in divine providence, which invariably acted in the name of bourgeois essentialist ideology. No other writer of literary fairy tales in the early nineteenth century introduced so many Christian notions of God, the Protestant Ethic, and bourgeois enterprise in his narratives as Andersen did. All his tales make explicit or implicit reference to a miraculous Christian power that rules firmly but justly over His subjects. Such patriarchal power would appear to represent a feudal organization, but the dominant value system represented by providential action and the plots of the tales is thoroughly bourgeois and justifies essentialist notions of aptitude and disposition. Just as aristocratic power was being transformed in Denmark, so Andersen reflected on the meaning of such transformation in his tales.

There are also clear strains of social Darwinism in Andersen's tales mixed with the Aladdin motif. In fact, survival of the fittest is the message of the very first tale, "The Tinderbox," which he wrote for the publication of his anthology. However, the fittest is not always the strongest but the chosen protagonist who proves himself or herself worthy of serving a dominant value system. This does not mean that Andersen constantly preached one message in all his tales. As a whole, written from 1835 to 1874, they represent the creative process of a dominated ego endeavoring to establish a unified self while confronted with a dominant discourse, which dissociated this identity. The fictional efforts are variations on a theme of how to achieve approbation, assimilation, and integration in a social system that does not allow for real acceptance or recognition if one comes from the lower classes. In many respects Andersen is like a Humpty-Dumpty figure who had a great fall when he realized as he grew up that entrance into the educated elite of Denmark did not mean acceptance and totality. Nor could all the king's men and horses put him back together when he perceived the inequalities and was humiliated. So his fairy tales are variegated and sublimated efforts to achieve wholeness, to gain vengeance, and to depict the reality of class struggle. The dominated voice, however, remains constant in its reference to real power.

Obviously there are other themes than power and domination in the tales and other valid approaches to them, but I believe that the widespread, continuous reception of Andersen's fairy tales in Western culture can best be explained by understanding how the discourse of the dominated functions in the narratives. Ideologically speaking Andersen furthered bourgeois notions of the self-made man or the Horatio Alger myth, which was becoming very popular in America and elsewhere, while reinforcing a belief in the existing power structure that meant domination and exploitation of the lower classes. Indeed, Andersen's fame in America and England in the nineteenth century was somewhat meteoric. This is why we must look more closely at the tales to analyze how they embody the dreams of social rise and individual happiness that further a powerful, all-encompassing bourgeois selection process furthering domination of the mind and fantasy.

II

Most scholars of Andersen's tales note that he initially published his tales for children and gradually shifted his attention to adults. Actually, he always wrote for adults, and his tales began to exclude children as readers after 1850. The first booklets called Eventyr, fortalte for Børn (Fairy Tales Told for Children) were published as insets in books for adults in 1837. Gradually the booklets became books for children with illustrations by Vilhelm Pedersen. Then changes were made in the titles to Eventyr (Fairy Tales), Nye Eventyr (New Fairy Tales), Historier (Stories), and finally by 1850, Eventyr og Historier (Fairy Tales and Stories). The evolution of his style and interests are reflected in the titles of the volumes and his shift of focus. Andersen began first by transforming tales from the oral tradition and adapting them for bourgeois children and adults. By the early 1840s he very rarely used recognizable folktales as his subject matter but created more and more his very own fairy tales by animating plants, animals, and things—something that he had done from the very beginning. But now the preponderance of the tales dealt with animals and objects in narratives that resembled fables and parables but were mixed with motifs from fairy tales. Finally, after 1850 his tales were no longer addressed to children and included legends, philosophical ruminations, supernatural stories, and historical commentaries. As Finn Hauberg Mortensen comments,

> Like all great artists Andersen struggled first and foremost with himself by continually widening the bounds of his expressive abilities. This is exemplified in his unrequited love of the theater and in his attempts to expand the shorter prose of the fairy tale to epic compositions. Today many of these attempts are forgotten because there was a limit to what could be successful—even for Andersen. The core of his mastery of the fairy tale, however, lies in his lucid detailed observations, in his ability to perceive the odd aspects of existence, and in the tightly composed world of the short prose works which, in a concise oral language, reveal the schism in the uniform bourgeois culture within which, and against which, tales are written.[19]

Although Mortensen argues that each one of Andersen's tales should be analyzed and interpreted carefully as a separate work of art instead of being grouped together and examined as representative of a common or typical Andersen tale, he does see common threads that connect the disparate narratives. One of the most important is the manner in which Andersen revealed "the schism in the uniform bourgeois culture" that he almost obsequiously sought to repair throughout his life. The most common thread is his discourse of the dominated, and I want to examine several tales, "The Traveling

Companion" (1837), "The Nightingale" (1843), "The Ugly Duckling" (1843), "The Shepherdess and the Chimney Sweep" (1845), "Everything in Its Right Place" (1853), "The Pixy and the Grocer" (1853), and "The Gardener and His Master" (1871), to demonstrate how Andersen consistently rationalized the power of dominant groups that distressed and disturbed him. These tales are important because they cover the spectrum of his productive life and reveal how he put his extraordinary talent to use by inventing a variety of approaches to questions that involved the significance of providence, the essence of geniality, the role of the artist, the treatment of women, and the system of patronage.

"The Traveling Companion" is a good example of how Andersen carefully reshaped oral folktales to suit the religious tastes of a bourgeois readership and to foster his notion of essentialist ideology. It is also a tale that puts women in their proper place and exalts a lowly hero, who is a devout believer in divine providence. In 1830 he wrote an earlier version, "The Dead Man. A Tale from Funen," which was the first tale that he ever published, but he was not satisfied with it and rewrote it seven years later as "The Traveling Companion." The material for the tale was well known not only in Denmark but throughout Europe. The Brothers Grimm published a version titled "The Grateful Dead Man and the Princess Rescued from Slavery" in their annotations of 1856, and there were many other variants in circulation before Andersen and the Grimms dealt with this tale type. In fact, folklorists have traced its history to an oral tradition that existed in the second-century BC and formed part of the apocryphal book of Tobit.[20] Antti Aarne and Stith Thompson categorized the different variants under the numbers AT 505–508 *The Grateful Dead*[21] and provided the basic motifs for the tale: the hero comes upon a dead man whose corpse is lying in the open and is being disgraced because the dead man has not paid his debts. The hero shows compassion and pays the debts by giving away all the money he has in his possession. He continues on his way and meets an old man, servant, or fox, who agrees to help him, provided that he will share his winnings. Now the young man travels with a companion who helps him rescue a princess or helps him free her from a spell. In the end the helper reveals himself as the dead man whose debts the hero had paid and then disappears. In many Scandinavian versions the princess is in league with a troll, who has enchanted her. The hero chops off the head of the troll, and then the princess is whipped with birch switches and bathed three times with milk, sour milk, and sweet milk so that she is purified and can marry the hero.

It is not certain what version Andersen knew, but it is more than likely that he was familiar with a Scandinavian pagan tale, which he completely transformed into a sentimental romantic tale that celebrates the power of God, for the protagonist is helpless without divine power. The message is overt and repeated several times so that Johannes, the hero, appears to be pathetic. Indeed, at the outset he is an orphan, who has just buried his father, and when he looks up at the sun, it reveals to him that his father is begging God to help him so that everything will go well for him. Then Johannes responds, "I will always try to be good. . . . Then I, too, will go to heaven when I die and see my father again. I will have so much to tell him, and he will teach me about all the beautiful things in heaven, as he taught me about all that is beautiful here on earth. Oh, how wonderful it will be!" (p. 41). And it is indeed wonderful. Johannes sets out into the marvelous world, and when he spends a night in a church, he discovers two wicked men who are about to desecrate a dead man in a coffin because he has not paid his debts. Johannes intervenes and gives the men fifty marks, his entire inheritance. Then he declares, "I can get along without money, I am strong and God will help me" (p. 43). He continues on his way, and when he leaves a forest, a stranger, who becomes his traveling companion, joins him. This stranger is not your ordinary companion, for he helps people in need with a magic salve and receives payment from them—birch switches from an old woman and an old sword from a theater director. In addition, he cuts off the wings of a dead swan with his newly acquired sword. Finally Johannes and the stranger arrive at a city where they hear about a beautiful but terrifying princess. She had proclaimed that whoever proposes to her could win her hand in marriage only if he answered three questions. However, if he failed, he would lose his head, and numerous men had already lost their heads. When Johannes hears this, he exclaims, "What a horrible princess. . . . She should be switched, that is what she deserves. If I were the old king I would beat her until I drew blood" (p. 48). However, as soon as he sees her, he falls helplessly in love with her and decides to propose to her. Everyone tries to dissuade him, but he is stubborn. The night before his test, he falls asleep at the inn, and the stranger attaches the swan's wings to his back, makes himself invisible, and follows the princess, who flies through the air, to the troll's castle. Along the way he beats her with the birch switches, and once there, he learns the answer to her first question and tells it to Johannes, who uses it the next day to save his life. The stranger helps Johannes two more times and cuts off the troll's head. Then he instructs the young man to dip the princess in a tub and dunk her under water three times to rid her of the evil spell. "Johannes prayed to God as he pushed her under the third time; and instantly she changed into the most beautiful princess. She was even lovelier than before; and she thanked him, with tears in her eyes, for having broken the evil spell" (p. 55). Now that the stranger's job is done, he reveals himself as the dead debtor and disappears. Johannes marries the princess and soon takes over the kingdom.

On the surface, it seems that Andersen's rewriting of the oral folktale about the grateful debtor is a quaint, charming narrative filled with humorous description and solemn appeals to God Almighty that were appropriate for young Danish children and adult readers. Yet there are some disturbing aspects that need to be addressed because they are repeated time and again in his other tales and reveal how Andersen was prompt to submit his heroes to high authorities like God and to demean female characters, even though his heroes might worship them. There are clear submissive and misogynistic tones in many of his tales. Women must be put in their place, and all places are ordained either by royalty or by divine powers.

Bengt Holbek, one of the leading Danish folklorists of the twentieth century, has incisively pointed out how Andersen changed a folktale from a tale focused on male oppression to one that actually celebrates domination. "The main event of 'The Travelling-Companion,' " Holbek comments, "is of course the confrontation with the princess who demands to have three questions answered on pain of death. This is where my analysis of folktales leads me to the conclusion that Andersen does not understand what they really are about; or if he understands it he conceals it in such a way as to make it exceedingly difficult for modern people to understand. At this point, it should be emphasized that in traditional peasant communities, magic tales were principally entertainment for adult people. When they are transplanted to the world of the children of the bourgeoisie, some extremely important aspects are lost as I shall try to explain."[22]

What Holbek explains is that the troll was more than likely a symbolic representation of her father, and that the riddle she poses is an expression of an illicit emotional attachment to her father. In other words, the tale, like other well-known folktales such as "The Maiden without Hands," reflects the dilemma of a young woman who is being oppressed by her father or is under her father's spell. The task of the hero is to replace the father, not to win his approval, as is the case in Andersen's tale. Whether one accepts Holbek's interpretation of the folktale as one that deals with incest, it is clear that Andersen's tale is a whitewash and that the narrative structure and themes deal with the maintenance of virtue and virginity in service to a higher authority. The stranger does all the difficult work in the tale. Johannes's mission in life is to show God how clean, innocent, and pure he is. The princess, who is beaten for her so-called bad behavior, is dipped into a tub until she becomes a white swan. Once she is turned into a virgin again, she and her pure husband can marry. But what has Johannes done to deserve her? What is his accomplishment as a hero? Departing from Holbek's thesis somewhat, is it possible that the princess was having an illicit affair with an outsider, a man, whom she desired? Are her father and the court trying to limit her desire? Johannes acts in the name of virtue by basically following the orders of the stranger, who acts allegedly in God's name. Johannes is essentially good and deserving of reward because he complies with commands from above. If Johannes is to be a model protagonist for young readers, and not only for the young, we must bear in mind that he does nothing but help a dead man and moves through the world as a naive bumpkin, who resembles Joseph von Eichendorff's simpleton in *Aus dem Leben eines Taugenichts* (*From the Life of a Ne'er-Do-Well*, 1826), a work that Andersen knew. Johannes has his life legislated for him, and thus he is readily accepted by court society, for he will carry out the laws of domination that satisfy the requisites of a king.

In almost all of Andersen's early tales, he focuses on lower-class or disenfranchised protagonists, who work their way up and into society. Their rise is predicated on their proper behavior that must correspond to a higher power, which elects and tests the hero. Though respect is shown for feudal patriarchy, the correct normative behavior reflects the values of the bourgeoisie. If the hero comes from the lower classes, he or she must be humbled if not humiliated at one point to test obedience. Thereafter, the natural aptitude of a successful individual will be unveiled through diligence, perseverance, and adherence to an ethical system that legitimizes bourgeois domination. Let me be more specific by focusing on what I consider some other popular tales written after 1837, such as "The Nightingale," "The Ugly Duckling," and "The Shepherdess and the Chimney Sweep."

There are two important factors to bear in mind when considering the reception of these tales in the nineteenth century and the present in regard to the narrative discourse of the dominated. First, as a member of the dominated class, Andersen could experience only dissociation despite entrance into upper-class circles. Obviously this was because he measured his success as a person and artist by standards that were not of his own social group's making. That ultimate power that judged his efforts and the destiny of his heroes depended on the organization of hierarchical relations at a time of sociopolitical transformation that was to leave Denmark and most of Europe under the control of the bourgeoisie. This shift in power led Andersen to identify with the emerging middle-class elite, but he did not depict the poor and disenfranchised in a negative way. On the contrary, Andersen assumed a humble, philanthropic stance—the fortunate and gifted are obliged morally and ethically to help the less fortunate. The dominated voice of all his narratives does not condemn his former social class, rather Andersen loses contact with it by denying the rebellious urges of his class within himself and making compromises that affirmed the rightful domination of the middle-class ethic.

A second factor to consider is the fundamental ambiguity of the dominated discourse in Andersen's tales: this discourse cannot represent the interests of the dominated class; it can only rationalize the power of the dominant class so that this power becomes legitimate and acceptable to those who are powerless. As I have noted before, Andersen depersonalizes his tales by using the third-person stance that appears to universalize his voice. However, this self-denial is a recourse of the dominated, who always carry references and appeal to those forces that control their lives. In Andersen's case he mystifies power and makes it appear divine. It is striking, as I have already stressed, when one compares Andersen to other fairy-tale writers of his time, how he constantly appeals to God and the Protestant Ethic to justify and sanction the actions and results of his tales. Ironically, to have a soul in Andersen's tales one must sell one's soul either to the aristocracy or to the bourgeoisie, something he clearly knew and felt. In any case it was the middle-class moral and social code that guaranteed the success of his protagonists, guaranteed his own social success, and ultimately guaranteed the successful reception of a select number of his tales to the present, canonical tales chosen consciously and unconsciously to maintain ideological notions that serve principles of domination.

This does not mean that Andersen was always self-denigrating in his tales. He often attacked greed and false pride. What is interesting is that vice is generally associated with the pretentious aristocracy and hardly ever with bourgeois characters. Generally speaking, Andersen celebrated the chosen few from the lower classes who naturally rise to fame, and he punished "over-reachers" from the lower echelons or "overbearing people" from the upper classes. Decorum and balance became articles of faith in his philosophical scheme of things. Knowing one's place and duty is to form the principle of cognition. For instance, in "The Swineherd," he delights in depicting the poor manners of a princess who has lost her sense of propriety. Andersen had already parodied the artificiality and pretentiousness of the nobility in "The Tinderbox" and "The Emperor's Clothes." Similar to the "taming of the shrew" motif in the folktale "King Thrushbeard," Andersen has the dominant figure of the fickle, proud princess humiliated by the dominated figure of the prince disguised as swineherd. However, there is no happy end here, for the humor assumes a deadly seriousness when the prince rejects the princess after accomplishing his aim: "'I have come to despise you,' said the prince. 'You did not want an honest prince. You did not appreciate the rose of the nightingale, but you could kiss a swineherd for the sake of a toy. Farewell!' " (p. 197).

The oppositions are clear: honesty versus falseness, genuine beauty (rose/nightingale) versus manufactured beauty (toys), nobility of the soul versus soulless nobility. Moreover, as in many instances, the "evil" protagonist is a woman who has lost control of her passions. Indirectly Andersen argues that the nobility must adapt to the value system of the emerging bourgeoisie or be locked out of the kingdom of happiness. Without appreciating the beauty and power of genuine leaders—the prince is essentially middle class—the monarchy will collapse.

This theme is at the heart of "The Nightingale," which can also be considered a sophisticated treatise about art, genius, and the role of the artist. The plot involves a series of transformations in power relations and service. First the Chinese emperor, a benevolent patriarch, has the nightingale brought to his castle from the forest. When the chief courtier finds the nightingale, he exclaims, "I had not imagined it would look like that. It looks so common! I think it has lost its color from shyness and out of embarrassment at seeing so many noble people at one time" (p. 205). Because the common-looking bird (an obvious reference to Andersen) possesses an inimitable artistic genius, he is engaged to serve the emperor. The first phase of the dominant–dominated relationship based on bonded servitude is changed into neglect when the emperor is given a jeweled mechanical bird that never tires of singing. So the nightingale escapes and returns to the forest, and eventually the mechanical bird breaks down. Five years later the emperor falls sick and appears to be dying. Out of his own choice the nightingale returns to him and chases death from his window. Here the relationship of servitude is resumed with the exception that the nightingale has assumed a different market value: he agrees to be the emperor's songbird forever as long as he can come and go as he pleases. Feudalism has been replaced by a free market system, yet the bird/artist is willing to serve loyally and keep the autocrat in power. "And my song shall make you happy and make you thoughtful. I shall sing not only of the good and of the evil that happen around you, and yet are hidden from you. For a little songbird flies far. I visit the poor fisherman's cottage and the peasant's hut, far away from your palace and your court. I love your heart more than your crown, and I feel that the crown has a fragrance of something holy about it. I will come! I will sing for you!" (p. 211). In fact, the nightingale's song is indispensable for the emperor's survival. Andersen appears to be making the argument that genuine poetry (livspoesi, the poetry of life) is uniquely in touch with the real life of the common people and is also the source of the emperor's life.

As we know, Andersen depended on the patronage of the King of Denmark and other upper-class donors, but he never felt esteemed enough, and he disliked the strings attached to the money given to him. Instead of breaking with such patronage, however, the dominated voice of this discourse seeks to set new limits that continue servitude in marketable conditions more tolerable for the servant. Andersen reaffirms the essentialist ideology of this period and reveals how gifted "common" individuals are the pillars of power—naturally in service to the state. Unfortunately, he never bothered to ask why "genius" cannot stand on its own and perhaps unite with like-minded people.

In "The Ugly Duckling" genius also assumes a most awe-inspiring shape, but it cannot fly on its own. This tale has generally been interpreted as a parable of Andersen's own success story because the naturally gifted underdog survives a period of ugliness to reveal its innate beauty. Yet more attention should be placed on the servility of genius and beautiful creatures. Though Andersen continually located real power in social conditions that allowed for the emergence of bourgeois hegemony, he often argued—true to conditions in Denmark—that power was to be dispensed in servitude to appreciative rulers, and naturally these benevolent rulers were supposed to recognize the interests of the bourgeoisie. As we have seen in "The Nightingale," the artist returns to serve royalty after the emperor neglects him. In "The Ugly Duckling," the baby swan is literally chased by coarse lower-class animals from the hen yard. His innate beauty cannot be recognized by such crude specimens, and only after he survives numerous ordeals does he realize his essential greatness. But his self-realization is ambivalent, for right before he perceives his true nature, he wants to kill himself: "I shall fly over to them, those royal birds! And they can hack me to death because I, who am so ugly, dare to approach them! What difference does it make! It is better to be killed by them than to be bitten by the other ducks, and pecked by the hens, and kicked by the girl who tends the henyard; or to suffer through the winter" (pp. 223–24).

Andersen expresses a clear disdain for the common people's lot and explicitly states that to be humiliated by the upper class is worth more than the trials and tribulations one must suffer among the lower classes. And, again, Andersen espouses bourgeois essentialist philosophy when he saves the swan and declares as narrator, "It does not matter that one has been born in the henyard as long as one has lain in a swan's egg" (p. 224). The fine line between eugenics and racism fades in this story where the once-upon-a-time dominated swan reveals himself to be a tame but noble member of a superior race. The swan goes not to "home" but to a beautiful garden where he is admired by children, adults, and nature. It appears as though the swan has finally come into his own, but, as usual, there is a hidden reference of power. The swan measures himself by the values and aesthetics set by the "royal" swans and by the proper well-behaved children and people in the beautiful garden. The swans and the beautiful garden are placed in opposition to the ducks and the hen yard. In appealing to the noble sentiments of a refined audience and his readers, Andersen reflected a distinct class bias if not classical racist tendencies.

This is also the case in "The Shepherdess and the Chimney Sweep," which is a defense of pure love and a flight from sexuality. Similar to "The Ugly Duckling," this humorous but sad tale depicts the journey into the world by the shepherdess and the chimney sweep because they are afraid their pure love will be contaminated by an amazing carved figure, "a man with a long beard, who had little horns sticking out of his forehead and the legs of a goat" (p. 297). The narrator indicates that the shepherdess and the chimney sweep, who are made of porcelain, belong together, while Mr. Goat-Legged Commanding-General-Private-War-Sergeant is made of mahogany and is thus unacceptable as a husband for the shepherdess, despite the fact that he has the approval of the Chinese mandarin, her grandfather, another porcelain figure. Why the chimney sweep does not stand his ground and fight for the shepherdess is unclear. At one point he suggests that he and the shepherdess jump into the potpourri jar and throw salt in the mandarin's eyes. But ultimately he complies with the shepherdess's wish to flee the world of the parlor where arranged marriages appear to be common and to go out into the wide world. When confronted by this world, however, she becomes frightened and demands to be taken back to the security of the parlor. Upon their return, they find that the porcelain Chinese mandarin had fallen off the table in pursuit of them and had broken into three pieces. The shepherdess exclaims, "How horrible! . . . Old Grandfather is broken and it's all our fault! I shan't live through it!" (p. 300). But the chimney sweep responds, "He can be put together again. . . . Don't carry on so! . . . All he needs is to be glued and have a rivet put in his neck, and he'll be able to say as many nasty things as he ever did" (p. 300). Indeed, the Chinese mandarin is repaired, but because he cannot nod his head, he cannot give his consent anymore to the threatening goat-legged figure to marry the shepherdess. So, the narrator informs us that "the two young porcelain lovers stayed together. They blessed the rivet in Grandfather's neck and loved each other until they broke" (p. 301).

The ending to the tale is somewhat bittersweet, and the union of the shepherdess and the chimney sweep is brought about and secured only after the Chinese mandarin is restored to his rightful place, albeit with limited power. The flight from oppression becomes a flight back to submission. Even the chimney sweep recognizes this when he says they could have saved themselves a lot of trouble by staying put. They feel sorry for their oppressor, even though his accident inadvertently prevented the shepherdess from the sexual threat of the dark goat figure. Fortunately, their love can remain pure. The racist implications are not as strong in this tale as they are in "The Ugly Duckling," but it is clear that the goat figure as sexual Pan is a dark threat to their innocent state of being. The narrator appears to mock them in the ambivalent ending, for their wholeness cannot last forever. False harmony tops off real disharmony like a varnish.

III

What saves Andersen's tales from simply becoming sentimental homilies (which many of them are) was his extraordinary understanding of how class struggle affected the lives of people in his times, and some tales even contain a forthright criticism of abusive domination, though his critique was always balanced by admiration for the upper classes and a fear of poverty. For instance, there are some exceptional tales that suggest a more rebellious position. Indeed, the dominated discourse is not homogenous or univocal, though it constantly refers to bourgeois power and never seeks to defy it. In 1853, shortly after the revolutionary period of 1848–50 in Europe, Andersen reflected on the thwarted rebellions in a number of tales, and they are worth discussing because they show more clearly how Andersen wavered when he subjected himself to bourgeois and aristocratic domination.

In "Everything in Its Right Place" (1853) the arrogant aristocratic owner of a manor takes pleasure in pushing a goose girl off a bridge. The peddler, who watches this scene and saves the girl, curses the master by exclaiming "everything in its right place" (p. 417). Sure enough, the aristocrat drinks and gambles away the manor in the next six years. The new owner is none other than the peddler, and, of course, he takes the goose girl for his bride and the Bible as his guide. The family prospers for the next hundred years with its motto "everything in its right place." At this point the narrator introduces us to a parson's son, who is tutoring the humble daughter of the now wealthy ennobled house. This idealistic tutor discusses the differences between the nobility and bourgeoisie and surprises the modest baroness by stating,

> "I know it is the fashion of the day—and many a poet dances to that tune to say that everything aristocratic is stupid and bad. They claim that only among the poor—and the lower you descend the better—does pure gold glitter. But that is not my opinion; I think it is wrong, absolutely false reasoning. Among the highest classes one can often observe the most elevated traits. . . . But where nobility has gone to a man's head and he behaves like an Arabian horse that rears and kicks, just because his blood is pure and he has a degree, there nobility has degenerated. When noblemen sniff the air in a room because a plain citizen has been there and say, 'It smells of the street,' why then Thespis should exhibit them to the just ridicule of satire."
> (pp. 420–21)

This degradation is, indeed, what occurs. A cavalier tries to mock the tutor at a music soirée, and the tutor plays a melody on a simple willow flute that suddenly creates a storm with the wind howling "everything in its right place!" In the house and throughout the countryside the wind tosses people about, and social class positions are reversed until the flute cracks and everyone returns to their former place. After this scare, Andersen still warns that "eventually everything is put in its right place. Eternity is long, a lot longer than this story" (p. 423). Such a revolutionary tone was uncharacteristic of Andersen, but given the mood of the times, he was prompted time and again in the early 1850s to voice his critique of the upper classes and question not only aristocratic but also bourgeois hegemony.

In "The Pixy and the Grocer" (1853) a little imp lives in a grocer's store and receives a free bowl of porridge and butter each Christmas. The grocer also rents out the garret to a poor student who would rather buy a book of poetry and eat bread for supper instead of cheese. The pixy visits the student in the garret to punish him for calling the grocer a boor with no feeling for poetry. Once in the garret, however, the pixy discovers the beauty and magic of poetry and almost decides to move in with the student. Almost, for he remembers that the student does not have much food and cannot give him porridge with butter. So he continues to visit the garret from time to time. Then one night a fire on the street threatens to spread to the grocer's house. The grocer and his wife grab their gold and bonds and run out of the house. The student remains calm while the pixy tries to save the most valuable thing in the house—the book of poetry. "Now he finally understood his heart's desire, where his loyalty belonged! But when the fire in the house across the street had been put out, then he thought about it again. 'I will share myself between them,' he said, 'for I cannot leave the grocer altogether. I must stay there for the sake of the porridge.' " "That was quite human," the dominated narrator concludes, "after all, we, too, go to the grocer for the porridge's sake" (p. 427).

This tale is much more ambivalent in its attitude toward domination than is "Everything in Its Right Place," which is open-ended and allows for the possibility of future revolutions. Here, Andersen writes more about himself and his own contradictions at the time of an impending upheaval (i.e., fire = revolution). Faced with a choice, the pixy/Andersen leans toward poetry or the lower classes and idealism. But, when the fire subsides, he makes his usual compromise, for he knows where his bread is buttered and where power resides. The narrative discourse is ironic, somewhat self-critical, but ultimately rationalizing. Since everyone falls in line with the dominant forces that provide food, why shouldn't the pixy? Who is he to be courageous or different? Nothing more is said about the student nor is there any mention of those who do not make compromises. Andersen makes it appear that servility is most human and understandable. Rarely does he suggest that it is just as human to rebel against inequality and injustice out of need as it is to bow to arbitrary domination.

The tales of 1853 demonstrate how Andersen was not unaware of possibilities for radical change and questioned the conditions of bourgeois–aristocratic hegemony. In one of his most remarkable tales, "The Gardener and His Master," written toward the very end of his life in 1871, he sums up his views on servitude, domination, and aptitude in his typically terse, ambivalent manner. The plot is simple and familiar. A haughty aristocrat has an excellent plain gardener who tends his estate outside of Copenhagen. The master, however, never trusts the advice of the gardener or appreciates what he produces. He and his wife believe that the fruits and flowers grown by other gardeners are better, and when they constantly discover, to their chagrin, that their very own gardener's work is considered the best by the royal families, they hope he won't think too much of himself. Then, the storyteller Andersen comments, "He didn't; but the fame was a spur, he wanted to be one of the best gardeners in the country. Every year he tried to improve some of the vegetables and fruits, and often he was successful. It was not always appreciated. He would be told that the pears and apples were good but not as good as the ones last year. The melons were excellent but not quite up to the standard of the first ones he had grown" (p. 1018).

The gardener must constantly prove himself, and one of his great achievements is his use of an area to plant "all the typical common plants of Denmark, gathered from forests and fields" (p. 1020), which flourish because of his nursing care and devotion. So, in the end, the owners of the castle must be proud of the gardener because the whole world beat the drums for his success. "But they weren't really proud of it. They felt that they were the owners and that they could dismiss Larsen if they wanted to. They didn't, for they were decent people, and there are lots of their kind, which is fortunate for the Larsens" (p. 1021).

In other words, Andersen himself had been fortunate, or at least this was the way he ironically viewed his career at the end of his life. Yet there is something pathetically sad about this story, given the fact that Andersen wrote it at the end of his life and continued to feel unappreciated in Denmark. The gardener Larsen is obviously the storyteller Andersen, and the garden with all its produce is the collection of fairy tales that he kept cultivating and improving throughout his life. The owners of the garden are Andersen's patrons and may be associated with the Collin family and other upper-class readers in Denmark. We must remember that it was generally known that the Collin family could never come to recognize Andersen as a *Digter* but thought of him as a fine popular writer. Andersen, whose vanity was immense and unquenchable, was extremely sensitive to criticism, and he petulantly and consistently complained that he felt undervalued in Denmark whereas other European countries recognized his genius. Such treatment at home despite the fact he considered himself a most loyal servant, whether real or projected, became symbolized in this tale. The reference to the "common plants," which the gardener cultivates, pertains to the folk motifs and everyday objects he employed and enriched so they would bloom aesthetically on their own soil. Andersen boasts that he, the gardener, has made Denmark famous, for pictures are taken of this garden and circulated throughout the world. Yet it is within the confines of servitude and patronage that the gardener works, and the dominated voice of the narrator, even though ironic, rationalizes the humiliating ways in which his masters treat Larsen: they are "decent" people. But, one must wonder—and the tension of the discourse compels us to do so—that, if the gardener is superb and brilliant, why doesn't he rebel and quit his job? Why does the gardener suffer such humiliation and domination? Why doesn't he emigrate?

Andersen pondered these questions often and presented them in many of his tales, but he rarely suggested alternatives or rebellion. Rather he placed safety before idealism and chose moral compromise over moral outrage, individual comfort and achievement over collective struggle and united goals. He aimed for identification with the power establishment that humiliates subjects rather than opposition to autocracy to put an end to exploitation through power. The defects in Andersen's ideological perspective are not enumerated here to insist that he should have learned to accept squalor and the disadvantages of poverty and struggle or that he should have become a radical like Heine and live in exile. They are important because they are the telling marks in the historical reception of his tales. Both the happy and sad endings of his narratives imply that there is an absolute or a divine, harmonious power and that unity of an essentialist ego and salvation are possible under such power. Such a projection, however, was actually that of a frustrated and torn artist who was obliged to compensate for an existence that lacked harmonious proportions and autonomous power. Andersen's life was one based on servility, and his tales were endeavors to justify a false consciousness: literary exercises in the legitimation of a social order to which he subscribed.

Whether the discourse of such a dominated writer be a monologue with himself or dialogue with an audience who partakes of his ideology, he still can never feel at peace with himself. It is thus the restlessness and the dissatisfaction of the dominated artist that imbue his work ultimately with the qualitative substance of what he seeks to relate. Ironically, the power of Andersen's fairy tales for him and for his readers has very little to do with the power he respected. It emanates from the missing gaps, the lapses, which are felt when the compromises are made under compulsion, for Andersen always painted happiness as adjusting to domination no matter how chosen one was. Clearly, then, Andersen's genius, despite his servility, rested in his inability to prevent himself from loathing all that he admired.

6

INVERTING AND SUBVERTING THE WORLD WITH HOPE: THE FAIRY TALES OF GEORGE MACDONALD, OSCAR WILDE, AND L. FRANK BAUM

The only form in which the future presents itself to us is that of possibility, while the imperative, the "should," tells us which of these possibilities we should choose. As regards knowledge, the future—in so far as we are not concerned with the purely organized and rationalized part of it—presents itself as an impenetrable medium, an unyielding wall. And when our attempts to see through it are repulsed, we first become aware of the necessity of willfully choosing our course and, in close connection with it, the need for an imperative (a utopia) to drive us onward. Only when we know what are the interests and imperatives involved are we in a position to inquire into the possibilities of the present situation, and thus to gain our first insights into history.
—Karl Mannheim, *Ideology and Utopia* (1936)

I

Toward the latter part of the nineteenth century the discourse on proper socialization through fairy tales received a jolt. Whereas Perrault, the Grimms, Andersen, some imitators like Benjamin Tabert, Felix Summerly, Gustav Holting, Ludwig Bechstein, and a host of other writers legitimized the normative standards of civilité through their symbolic constructs, configurations, and plots of their tales, a new trend became visible in the Anglo-Saxon world, namely, in Great Britain and the United States, which reflected sharp criticism of traditional child rearing and the rationalized means of discipline and punishment employed to make children into good and responsible citizens.

There is a tendency on the part of some literary critics to assume that the fairy tale for children went completely underground during the first half of the nineteenth century because it was considered too pleasurable and entertaining and not instructive and pious enough for young souls. Yet these critics tend to neglect the tremendous popularity of fairy-tale broadsheets, chapbooks, and the continual favorable reception of Perrault, the Grimms, and Andersen in England, America, and on the Continent. They also forget that the basic discourse of the classical fairy tale was not contrary to the civilizing purposes of the bourgeoisie. Perhaps it is true that publication of fairy tales was limited and curtailed in comparison to later years and that the selection and censorship of the tales were severe. In other words, the fairy-tale discourse was controlled by the same sociopolitical tendencies that contributed toward strengthening bourgeois domination of the public sphere in the first half of the nineteenth century.[1] Reason and morality were used to perpetuate and conserve the material gains of the rising middle classes. This conservatism, however, was not to last.

By the 1860s, if not earlier, literary conservatism in children's book publishing was challenged by a new wave of innovative fairy tales, as Brian Alderson amply shows in his essay "Tracts, Rewards and Fairies."[2] He points to John Ruskin's "King of the Golden River" (1851), the reissue of the Grimms' German Popular Stories (1868) with Ruskin's introduction, and William Allingham's In Fairy Land (1870) as significant breakthroughs in the fairy-tale discourse. There was, in fact, a "munificent productiveness" in fairy tales that can be gleaned in Jonathan Cott's fine collection Beyond the Looking Glass.[3] In discussing the extraordinary works of fantasy and fairy tale, specifically in England, Cott notes,

> Writing fairy tales for children had become an acceptable literary activity. Not only had Thackeray, Ruskin, Dickens, and Christina Rossetti done so, but Victorian children's book writers were generally less involved than "adult" literary writers in the contemporary debates concerning "moral aesthetics" engaged in by Tennyson, Ruskin, Arnold, Buchanan, and Pater. In some way the Victorian writers for children had transcended the age-old debate concerning the purposes of "literature" (instruction vs. delight) as well as the equivalent moral tract vs. fairy story argument regarding children's literature. Children's literature of this period almost always had a moral or

religious basis, but it was often just this conflict between morality and invention (or morality and eroticism in Christina Rossetti's *Goblin Market*) that created some of the era's greatest works.[4]

It is difficult to pinpoint exactly when and where the fairy-tale discourse underwent a profound change, who the chief instigators were, and why this began primarily in England. Certainly the development of a strong proletarian class, industrialization, urbanization, educational reform acts, evangelism, and the struggles against those forces that caused poverty and exploitation led to social and cultural upheavals that affected the fairy-tale works of Dickens, Ruskin, Thackeray, Lewis Carroll, Charles Kingsley, Andrew Lang, William Morris, the neo-Raphaelites, and numerous other well-known authors. However, the truly "classical" fairy-tale writers, who not only made a mark on their own times but also have continued to speak to us today, were George MacDonald, Oscar Wilde, and L. Frank Baum, the American offspring of the British movement. They were the ones who used the fairy tale as a radical mirror to reflect what was wrong with the general discourse on manners, mores, and norms in society, and they commented on this by altering the specific discourse on civilization in the fairy-tale genre.

No longer was the fairy tale to be like the mirror, mirror on the wall reflecting the cosmetic bourgeois standards of beauty and virtue that appeared to be unadulterated and pure. The fairy tale and the mirror cracked into sharp-edged, radical parts by the end of the nineteenth century. This was true for all the tales, those written for children as well as for adults. There was more social dynamite in the contents of the tales, also more subtlety and art. Commenting on the essence of fairy tales, Michel Butor once compared fairyland to a "world inverted," an exemplary world, a criticism of ossified reality. "It does not remain side by side with the latter; it reacts upon it; it suggests that we transform it, that we reinstate what is out of place."[5] On the one hand, this is an extremely broad and naive statement because we know how the literary fairy tales of Perrault, the Grimms, and Andersen offer a pseudocriticism of real social conditions to guarantee that children of all classes will mind their manners and preserve the status quo—all to the advantage of those who control the dominant discourse. On the other hand, Butor has a keen eye for the subversive potentiality within the fairy-tale genre: he perceives how *certain* fairy tales can disrupt the normative structure and affirmative discourse of the classical fairy-tale tradition that are locked into the bourgeois public sphere. In particular, experimental fairy tales for children are endowed with a subversive potential, but the degree of their "subversiveness" must be qualified.

In her illuminating study of fantasy as the literature of subversion, Rosemary Jackson argues,

> Each fantastic text functions differently, depending upon its particular histor-
> ical placing, and its different ideological, political and economic determi-
> nants, but the most subversive fantasies are those which attempt to *transform*
> the relations of the imaginary and the symbolic. They try to set up
> possibilities for radical cultural transformation by making fluid the relations
> between these realms, suggesting, or projecting, the dissolution of the
> symbolic through violent reversal or rejection of the process of the subject's
> formation.[6]

Jackson views the subversive capacity of fairy tales with some reserve
because they belong more to the literature of the marvelous and tend to
discourage reader participation: instead of transgressing the values of the
"real" world, they interrogate them only retrospectively or allegorically. In
other words, by conceptualizing other worlds and alternatives, presenting
ideals, fairy tales do not problematize reality or open up space without or
outside cultural order. The metaphors are too coherent.[7]

Though the distinctions Jackson draws between fairy tales and fantastic
narratives are helpful, she clings too much to a static model of the fairy tale,
neglects the radical transformations of the fairy-tale genre, and thus over-
looks the close connections to the mode of the fantastic. For instance, Jackson
maintains that it is not by chance that the fantastic tended to become a genre
in its own right in the nineteenth century in opposition to conventionalized
mimesis: "Subverting this unitary vision, the fantastic introduces confusion
and alternatives; in the nineteenth century this meant an opposition to bourgeois ideology upheld through the 'realistic' novel."[8] Such subversion was
also under way within the fairy-tale discourse during the nineteenth century
and was directed at adults and children. The major breakthrough had been
made by the German romantics, who dissolved reader expectations by transforming familiar topoi and motifs into mysterious, symbolic landscapes that
lured readers to question the former secure worlds of conservative fairy tales
and the very real world of their immediate surroundings. It is true, as Jackson
demonstrates, that most fairy tales, even the experimental ones, re-present
the world as an "exemplification of a possibility to be avoided or embraced."[9]
Yet this imaginary projection does not lessen the subversive potential of the
author's symbolic act and the work's constellation. The question of subversion concerns degree and the challenge to reader expectations. Certainly, for
children, the historical shift in fairy-tale discourse must be related to a
longing by adult writers to open up and subvert traditional socialization by
posing infinite textual possibilities for the subjects/readers to define themselves against the background of finite choices proposed by society.

Historically viewed, the first movement of the subversion began at the very
moment when the literary fairy tale ironically started to find *acceptance* in the

well-kept nurseries, schools, and libraries of nineteenth-century Europe and America and when publishers sought to make their profit by pushing them on the thriving market for children consumers. Many writers of fairy tales catered to the market and the publishers, but the more critical ones recognized that the utopian kernel in the original folktales—the lust for change and the wish for better living conditions—had been appropriated and cultivated in the classical literary fairy tales to give rise to false hopes. As part of the household, the tales of Perrault, the Grimms, Andersen, and disciples exercised a stranglehold on the topoi of fairy-tale discourse, and more and more writers like MacDonald, Wilde, and Baum sought to break this grip. To be sure, they were in the minority, and they did not upset the literary conventions of accepted fairy-tale narration. Yet they did invert and subvert the real world and classical schemes of Perrault, the Grimms, and Andersen. They expanded the fairy-tale discourse on civilization to conceive alternative worlds and styles of life. This departure from the traditional mode prepared the way for even greater experimentation with fairy tales for children in the twentieth century, and numerous authors began cultivating what might be termed the "art of subversion" within the fairy-tale discourse.

As is often the case with innovators, even with the most radical, MacDonald, Wilde, and Baum have become known as classical fairy-tale writers. Their classicism, however, is qualitatively different from that of Perrault, the Grimms, and Andersen, and it is most important that we distinguish their singular contributions to the genre because they represent a turning point in the fairy-tale discourse on civilization and set examples for contemporaries and later innovators. All three, MacDonald, Wilde, and Baum, refused to comply with the standard notions of sexuality and sex roles and questioned the restrictions placed on the imagination of children. Moreover, they generally told their stories from the perspective of the oppressed lower classes and added a dimension to their dissatisfaction that resisted the compromises that Andersen had proposed for his protagonists. MacDonald, Wilde, and Baum bring out the need for the alteration and restructuring of social relations by questioning the arbitrariness of authoritarian rule and the profit motives of rulers. Neither one of the writers is revolutionary in the sense that they called for "violent overthrows" of the government, but it is their intense discontent with domination and the dominant discourse that propelled them to invert and subvert the world with hope in their tales.

If we examine their key works in the history of the literary fairy tale for children, we can see that they were consciously inserting themselves into the discourse on civilization in the process of change. They furthered this change with their socially symbolic acts, and each one made a unique historical contribution in behalf of children to undo what they ostensibly considered damage done to children through the traditional fairy-tale discourse.

II

George MacDonald's life was filled with struggles against social conservatism, religious orthodoxy, and commercial capitalism.[10] Though the types of socioreligious changes he desired were never realized in his day, he never lost his hope and zest for reform: the beastliness of civilization was to be countered by uncovering and perfecting the divine qualities of humankind— despite the corrupting influences of society.

Raised on a large farm in a rural district of Scotland, MacDonald believed that hard work and diligence would pave the way to success. As a teenager he organized and became president of the local temperance society, and it appeared that his devotion to the clean-cut life would reap benefits. In 1840 he won a scholarship to the University of Aberdeen to pursue his studies, mainly in science. It appears, however, that his first long contact with city life almost brought about his ruin. He drank and pursued women rather than his studies, and in 1842 he was compelled to leave the university for some time. This proved to be one of the turning points in his life. He spent several months working in the library of a nobleman's mansion and discovered German romanticism, classical English poetry, and medieval romances. He also fell in love with the daughter of the house but was spurned because of his lower social status. When he was able to return to the university, he brought with him a distinct hatred for rich aristocrats and a passionate love for literature, especially romanticism.

After receiving a degree in chemistry and physics, he spent the next three years as a private tutor in London and apparently did a great deal of soul-searching, for he decided to become a minister. In 1848 he enrolled in Highbury College, a Congregational Divinity School in London, and he also announced his engagement to Louisa Powell, who would become his wife and companion in 1853 for the rest of his life, undoubtedly the model for many of his admirable female protagonists in his literary works. By the time he graduated from divinity school in 1850 and was ready to assume his first ministry in Sussex, he was brought down by tuberculosis, the disease that haunted his family. It caused the death of his father and some of his own children. From this point on he was beset with physical difficulties and suffered from other ailments such as eczema throughout his life. The struggles against physical diseases actually strengthened his spiritual beliefs and moral character. During his convalescence he wrote a long dramatic poem, which was the first manifestation of his nonconformist mystical inclinations. He did not hesitate to incorporate his unusual views about God, nature, epiphany, and the perfection of humankind in his sermons and other writings. In 1851 he published a translation of *Twelve Spiritual Songs of Novalis* and began voicing his heterodox views about salvation from the pulpit. Such frankness and intensity were not appreciated by his congregation, and he was forced to resign his position in 1853 and begin his career as writer. Yet MacDonald's personal religious mission did not change.

No matter what form his writing took, MacDonald was bent on spreading his socioreligious convictions to large audiences. Indeed, he wrote more than forty volumes of prose and poetry and became one of the most successful novelists and popular lecturers of his day. Like Dickens, he wanted to expose the deplorable material conditions and unjust social relations in England during the period of industrialization. Building the empire meant breaking the backs of common people, and he demanded reforms. However, he never argued for a radical transformation of the hierarchical structure of society and government. Influenced by his agrarian upbringing, his politics were more inclined to take the form of safeguarding the natural rights and autonomy of individuals whose own responsibility was to create the moral and ethical fiber of good government. As Richard H. Reis remarks,

> This is not to say that MacDonald was insensitive to the problems of the working class. Although he did not recognize the existence of the industrial mass-proletariat, he was convinced that the individual artisan—the shoemaker, blacksmith, carpenter, mason—was the backbone of the English and social economic system. No doubt he was influenced by the social theories of Ruskin and William Morris, who longed for the vanished day of the individual workman's dignity before he was engulfed by mass production and wage slavery; for MacDonald's scattered suggestions toward Utopia are usually built along the lines of medieval feudalism.[11]

It is interesting to note that MacDonald's social and political views generally took a more conventional form in his realistic novels than in his fairy tales for children. Writing in the fantastic mode apparently freed him to explore personal and social problems to a degree that fostered his radicalism and innovation. It is generally acknowledged that MacDonald's major historical contribution to literature is in the area of fantasy and children's literature. In particular the fairy tale nurtured his religious mysticism and fundamental beliefs in the dignity of men and women whose mutual needs and talents could be developed only in a community that was not based on exploitation and profit making. Since MacDonald felt that dreams were like religious epiphanies and that fairy tales were symbolically related to dreams, he endowed their symbolic constellations with social-religious values to convey messages without sermonizing in a laborious manner.

Between 1864 and 1883 MacDonald made his views known to children in various ways. He edited a magazine titled *Good Words for the Young* (1868–72), in which several fairy tales appeared, including his most famous one, "The Light

Princess." He published four book-length fairy tales: *At the Back of the North Wind* (1871), *The Princess and the Goblin* (1872), *A Double Story* (1874–75) also known as *The Lost Princess*, and *The Princess and Curdie* (1883). In addition he incorporated some fairy tales in novels such as *Adela Cathcart* (1864) and published them collectively, as in *Dealings with Fairies* (1867), or individually as separate books. In each case MacDonald consciously sought to enter into the fairy-tale discourse on manners, norms, and values and to transform it. More than the perspectives of any of the classical writers before him, MacDonald's perspective on the socialization of children contradicted the accepted version of discipline and punishment of the British civilizing process. Indeed, the patterns and configurations of his tales clearly display a tendency to negate the institutionalized and established forms of raising children.

As a Christian mystic, MacDonald believed in the perfection of humankind and maintained that each individual could achieve a supreme state in this world. MacDonald preached not just "divine individualism" but the necessity to develop compassion for other human beings and nature. Implicit in most of his fairy tales is a notion of utopia: the utopian impulse can be realized in the here and now if one is receptive to God who makes his will known through all earthly creation. "Nature is brimful of symbolic and analogic parallels to the goings and comings; the growth and changes of the highest nature in man."[12] In MacDonald's mind, there is no *fixed* path to perfection, the equivalent of union with God. Each individual must learn to recognize divine qualities in the immediate surroundings and in himself or herself. Through such an epiphany the individual will act according to a conscience that bespeaks God's will. MacDonald placed great significance on developing the creative potential of human beings, and he regarded daydreams, dreams, and mystical experiences as means toward a union with the divine spirit. "All dreams are not false; some dreams are truer than the plainest facts. Fact at best is but a garment of truth, which has ten thousand changes of raiment woven on the same loom. Let the dreamer only do the truth of his dream and one day he will realize all that was worth realizing it."[13] Like Novalis, MacDonald felt strongly that the fantastic elements of life and fiction were hieroglyphics of the divine essence. Learning to become a human being in the fullest sense of the term meant becoming a creative artist. The true individual was a self-made autonomous artwork, and MacDonald's fairy tales for children sought to stimulate young readers to recognize their special creative talents so that they could religiously begin their own artful enterprise.

If we compare MacDonald's fairy tales with many of the prudish and pious ones of his day—including those by Hans Christian Andersen—we see that he was arguing against the conventional rules of pedagogy and strict Christian upbringing. He shunned upper-class dictums of an authoritarian nature, and his fairy tales shift and expand attitudes toward children by moving God from a transcendental place to within the child: the divine is to be discovered inside and through the imagination. Such a different perspective on socializing children demanded a reformulation of the norms, values, and social relations and the use of fantasy to mirror the ossification of English social and religious standards. To grasp MacDonald's utopian critique conveyed through his fairy tales, I want to deal with three of his more prominent shorter pieces, "The Light Princess" (1864), "The Golden Key" (1867), and "The Day Boy and the Night Girl" (1879), and two of his major longer narratives, The Princess and the Goblin (1872) and The Princess and Curdie (1883). The pattern in all of these fairy tales is similar. There is never one hero, rather there are always male and female protagonists, who learn to follow their deep inclinations, respect each other's needs and talents, and share each other's visions. Together they overcome sinister forces that want to deprive them of possible happiness and the realization of an ideal community. In contrast to all his poems, novels, and essays, MacDonald forgoes the pathos and the rhetoric of sermonizing in the name of God. Though his Christian mysticism may be behind the ideological perspective of each narrative, his very use of unique and bizarre fairy-tale symbols imbue his stories with a touch of the unorthodox. The moral rebel in MacDonald led to a playful experimentation with conventions to undermine them and illuminate new directions for moral and social behavior.

"The Light Princess" (1864) like his tale "Little Daylight" (1867) is a parody of "Sleeping Beauty" and "Rapunzel," and, for that matter, it reflects MacDonald's disrespectful attitude toward traditional folktales and fairy tales. MacDonald realized that the symbolism of most of the traditional tales points to a dead end and prevents children from glimpsing their special relationship to the divine within and beyond them. It is striking that he sees his point of departure for the fairy-tale discourse not in the works of the Grimms or Andersen but largely in those of the German romantics, particularly the fascinating stories of Novalis. Certainly the three tales in Novalis's Heinrich von Ofterdingen with their utopian motifs and religious-erotic development of young couples had a great impact on him. In "The Light Princess" MacDonald follows Novalis's tendency to turn an ordered world topsy-turvy so that the conventional social order and relations could be parodied and the possibility of creating new modes of behavior and values could be perceived and designated.

The plot of "The Light Princess," a story still in wide circulation today, is well known. A king and queen are without child. When they eventually have one, they insult the king's own sister, Princess Makemnoit, a witch by trade, by not inviting her to the christening. As is to be expected, the insulted witch casts a spell on the baby daughter by destroying her gravity. The princess soars and floats when she wants to walk and is difficult to control because she is light bodied. When she becomes seventeen, she learns the pleasure of swimming, gains a sense of gravity, and also meets a young prince, who is willing to sacrifice himself so she can pursue her passion for water. Only by using himself as a plug to stop the water in the lake from disappearing (another spell cast by the witch) will she have enough water to swim. When it dawns on her that the prince is dying for her, she tries to save him, breaks the spell by bursting into a passion of tears, and finds her gravity.

The irreverent tone of the story places in question not only the convention of traditional fairy tales but also the very style of aristocratic life. For instance, the king is a banal figure, a "little king with a great throne, like many other kings."[14] The royal metaphysicians, Hum-Dru and Kopy-Keck, are fools. Even the typical prince is mocked.[15] MacDonald winks his eye and debunks aristocratic language and codes, and yet there is a serious side to the light comedy. From the beginning, after the bewitchment, the princess, the court, and the implied reader of the tale are faced with a problem: how to provide gravity for the princess who does not have her feet on the ground and could cause continual havoc in the kingdom. The major theme of the tale concerns social integration, but—and this is significant—gravity (social responsibility and compassion) cannot be imposed or learned abstractly. It is gained through passion and experience, and it is also liberating. Once the princess touches water, she develops a veritable passion for it because she can control her own movements, and she can share her pleasure with the prince. Moreover, she overcomes her egocentrism by realizing her pleasure is not worth the death of a beloved human being. Through her relation to the prince, who is self-sacrificing and tender in the mold of traditional fairy-tale females, she develops social empathy, and her learning to walk after the spell is broken, though painful, can be equated to the difficult acceptance of social responsibility.

Of course, one can argue that MacDonald leaves the aristocratic social structure unchanged—a system that harbors authoritarianism—and that the princess seems to achieve her gravity or identity through the male hero. These were clearly his ideological preferences and weaknesses from a political point of view. I should point out, however, that MacDonald was more interested in the reformation of social character and was convinced that all social change emanated from the development of personal integrity not necessarily through political restructuring and upheaval. This belief is why he stressed ethical choice and action through intense quests and experience. Moreover, in "The Light Princess" his female protagonist does not become dependent on the prince, who is a "softy." Rather she gains certain qualities through her relationship with him, just as he benefits from the encounter. There is more sensitive interaction between two unique individuals than traditional role-playing at the end of the tale, a special configuration that MacDonald was to develop in all his narratives.

For instance, in "The Golden Key" the young boy Mossy goes in pursuit of treasure at the end of the rainbow only to learn that the real riches in life are those experiences that amount to self-knowledge. In part he learns this from Tangle, a maltreated thirteen-year-old girl, who runs away from home out of fear. Both are brought together in the middle of fairyland by the mysterious grandmother (a kind of mother nature), and she instills in them courage so that they bravely embark on a quest for the keyhole of the golden key, which had already been found by Mossy at the end of the rainbow. On their way they become separated and undergo various experiences with the old men of the sea, earth, and fire. Eventually, after enduring all kinds of trials, they are reunited before the country whence the shadows fall. Ageless they move toward their conception of paradise.

At the basis of MacDonald's utopia is the perfect social and sexual relationship. Mossy and Tangle are companions. As we the readers become lost in this highly symbolic and complex tale, we are compelled to read and interpret the symbols and to become receptive to nature and the challenges of life. Mossy and Tangle have their own unique adventures and impressions while seeking the keyhole (another obvious voyage of sexual exploration).[16] Their mystical and sensual experiences form the bedrock of their growth. Their diligence is rewarded not through material riches but through entrance to another world that promises the fulfillment of their intuitions.

This pattern of self-exploration—symbolic trips toward inner realms that can help create understanding of other people and the outside world—is depicted in a variety of intriguing ways in MacDonald's other tales, "The Carasoyn," "Little Daylight," and "Cross Purposes." The fairy tale, however, that is by far MacDonald's most unusual portrayal of mutual respect and interdependence between men and women is the provocative narrative of "The Day Boy and the Night Girl" (1879). MacDonald creates a witch named Watho, who has a wolf in her mind, and her uncontrollable appetite to know everything leads her to experiment indiscriminately with human beings. She invites two ladies named Aurora and Vesper to her castle, and she uses her magical powers to have them give birth to children. After the births the two women flee the witch in dread. Watho keeps the boy Photogen and the girl Nycteris in separate parts of the castle and exposes one only to darkness and the other only to light. In fact they each develop a respective fear of their opposites, night and day. It is only later during their adolescence that the two of them chance to meet and discover that Watho's means of raising them has crippled them. Therefore, Nycteris offers to be Photogen's eyes in darkness while she teaches him to see, and there is an amusing scene in which MacDonald addresses the entire problem of regimentation and sex-role conditioning:

> He wished she would not make him keep opening his eyes to look at things he could not see; and every other moment would start and grasp tight hold of her, as some fresh pang of terror shot into him.

"Come, come, dear!" said Nycteris, "you must not go on this way. You must be a brave girl, and—"

"A girl!" shouted Photogen, and started to his feet in wrath. "If you were a man, I should kill you."

"A man?" repeated Nycteris. "What is that? How could I be that? We are both girls—are we not?"

"No, I am not a girl," he answered; "—although," he added, changing his tone, and casting himself on the ground at her feet, "I have given you too good reason to call me one."

"Oh, I see!" returned Nycteris. "No, of course!—You can't be a girl: girls are not afraid—without reason. I understand now: it is because you are not a girl that you are so frightened."

Photogen twisted and writhed upon the grass.[17]

This delightful reversal is only one aspect of MacDonald's endeavor in this narrative to depict what he calls "the arrogance of all male creatures until they have been taught by the other kind."[18] In the course of events Nycteris and Photogen realize that they have a great deal to learn from each other, and this realization gives them the power to overcome the witch. Their relationship becomes a synthesis in which light can be found in darkness and darkness in light.

This fairy tale is perhaps MacDonald's most outspoken statement on child rearing. Watho's castle, personality, and treatment of the children assume symbolic forms of school, rigid teacher, and arbitrary programming, respectively. Against this system MacDonald pits the painful but meaningful exploration of two human beings who gradually recognize that their essence and autonomy depend on the interdependence of all things. Photogen and Nycteris come to revere the totality of nature by developing a receptivity to what they fear most. The confrontation with fear, however, enables them to see anew, to rethink and refeel their surroundings so that they gain ultimate pleasure from their senses and begin building a world commensurate with their ideals. MacDonald shuns Victorian prudery, as he did in almost all his fairy tales, and projects the symbolic sexual play and intercourse that can prepare the way for a wholesome union of the sexes.

MacDonald believed firmly that individuals could be "civilized" in a natural way to attain a devout reverence for the nature and needs of all living creatures, but he also had grave doubts as to whether people as a whole, that is, society, could attain the level of "civilization" that separate individuals could. Here his notion of civilization was in direct contradiction to the class-bound civilization process of England, and his two book-length fairy tales, *The Princess and the Goblin* and *The Princess and Curdie*, demonstrate to what extent he went against the Victorian grain. In the first narrative the Princess Irene is plagued by goblins who want to kidnap her and destroy her father's kingdom. She is protected by her omniscient and mysterious grandmother, who endows her with the fortitude and sensitivity necessary to cope with her enemies. Furthermore, she is aided by a brave miner's son named Curdie, who literally undermines the sinister plans of the goblins and puts an end to their kingdom. In the sequel, Curdie is in danger of becoming a "beastly character," until he is summoned by the majestic grandmother. He then realizes that he was on the verge of becoming decrepit, and the grandmother sends him on a mission to help the father of Princess Irene because he is being poisoned by corrupt officials. On his way to the city of Gwyntystorm, Curdie organizes a squadron of forty-nine strange creatures and misfits, who ironically return order and justice to the community. Curdie marries Princess Irene, but they have no children. When they die, the people choose a new king who is interested mainly in mining for gold, and the people become corrupt and dissolute once again. Their self-destructive tendencies lead to the destruction and disappearance of the city.

Not a very happy end for a fairy tale, and one must ask why MacDonald wrote such a book in 1883, his very last one for children. Had he become pessimistic? Or was this a warning to children? Was this MacDonald's way to keep the utopian impulse alive in his readers by pointing to the dangers of slumbering—not keeping one's creative sensitivities active in a religious way? There are indications that the two narratives taken as a whole expressed MacDonald's sober optimism: humanity must raise itself from a beastly state to form the utopian society and must constantly exercise creative and moral powers to pursue the ideal society. Otherwise, there will be a return to barbarianism.

MacDonald appears to have been greatly influenced by Novalis's and E.T.A. Hoffmann's notions of love and Atlantis in *Heinrich von Ofterdingen* and *The Golden Pot*, respectively. Both the German romantics have a woman incarnate a mystical concept of Eros, and she becomes the mediator between the profane and the sacred. In pursuit of her love the protagonist discovers his own powers and identity, and only then is he able to create a compassionate relationship with all forms of life—utopia becomes attainable, but only momentarily. Novalis has his Atlantis disappear in one tale, and Hoffmann sends his hero Anselmus to Atlantis, which is beyond the reach of the narrator and his readers. Implicit was critique of a mundane society too immersed in pettiness and routine to appreciate the divine nature of life and art.

It is obvious that this was MacDonald's perspective, too. Writing about late nineteenth-century England, he deplored the materialistic behavior of the majority of people and the corruption of government. The relationship between Curdie and the princess is intended to be exemplary and provocative for young readers. In fact, MacDonald depicts the experiences and growth of the two protagonists to mirror all that was wrong in English society. Princess Irene's communion with the other world—her mystical and creative powers—is distrusted by her governess and everyone around her. To a large extent, her behavior and views are the opposite of how children in Victorian England were socialized to behave. Even Curdie is suspicious of her and expresses doubts about her sanity and character until the very end of the first book. These doubts continue in the sequel, and because of them it seems that Curdie might become an ordinary, crass miner, insensitive to other people and the world around him. However, his love and admiration for the tiny princess is such that a spark of his great potential is still alive, and, through his imagination, he comes to symbolize all that *should be* but *could not be*—the coal miner/king's efforts on behalf of humanity are lost on a society in quest of power and wealth.

MacDonald never ceased deploring the evils of social influences that interfered with the natural and sublime endeavors of human beings to become perfect. Early in his life he grasped the importance of the German romantics' aesthetic critique of philistine society, and he drew out the mystical religious essence while still defending the powers of the imagination and creative artist. At the point where he entered the fairy-tale discourse for children in England, he could not help but be influenced by social reform movements and the ideas of Dickens and Ruskin. From 1864 to 1882 he made a major effort to expand the discourse of fairy tales and to shift the perspective from the legitimatizing voice to one critical of the civilizing process. His works were just the beginning: fairy tales were about to acquire a new quality of conscious social protest.

III

Though no two men could be more dissimilar in personality and conviction than George MacDonald and Oscar Wilde, there are striking similarities in their lives that account for a common endeavor to reformulate the terms of the civilizing process through the fairy tale in Victorian England. Both were born outside established English society—MacDonald was born in Scotland, and Wilde was born in Ireland, two countries noted for their indigenous and unique folklore and anti-English politics. Both were influenced by the social reform movement of their times and directly by artistic innovators with a political conscience such as John Ruskin and William Morris. Both hated hypocrisy and stodgy English upper-class conventions, and they sought to use their art to express religious views directly opposed to the Anglican Church. As we have seen, the form MacDonald's critique of society assumed in his fairy tales was influenced by his Christian mysticism; Wilde's was stamped by an unusual commitment to Christian socialism that celebrated individualism and art. Ironically, Wilde the aesthete was more radical in what he preached through his compelling fairy tales than was MacDonald the Christian reformer.

Wilde's fascinating life, art, and unfortunate end have been explored in depth by numerous scholars and critics—and the books pro and con Wilde keep coming.[19] Yet very few have dealt at length on the subject of his fairy tales, which are perhaps his best-known works. Not only have they sold in the millions in different languages but they also have been adapted in various ways for stage, screen, radio, and the record industry. Ironically, these unconventional tales have achieved classical status, and because they are bound up with his rebellious life, we should consider certain aspects of his development as a writer to understand why he sought to transform the fairy-tale discourse and followed MacDonald's example, though he was never directly influenced by the Scotsman. If anything, both were moved by the same spirit—to change the anachronistic contents and style of fairy tales that did not pertain to the social and political realities of modern England.

As is well known, both Wilde's father William and his mother Jane Francesca Elgee were social celebrities and writers who led eccentric lives in Dublin. His father was noted for his discoveries in medicine and archaeology and his exploits with women. His mother achieved fame as poetess, writer, and patriotic defender of the rights of the Irish. From the time he was two years old, Wilde participated at all meals with his parents and guests, and this participation is obviously the reason why he developed into such a skillful and polished raconteur. Yet more important for his social and aesthetic views is the fact that Wilde was given the opportunity to witness how refined people played with social conventions to mock conformity, and he learned to explore alternatives to stifling forms of socialization at a very early age. As a consequence, he employed his extraordinary rhetorical and creative skills both to gain attention and to keep the world at a distance. In Dublin, where high society lived on smut and scandal, Wilde learned to assume poses and dedicate himself to his studies and art for the main purpose of survival.

After winning numerous awards at Trinity College, he went to Magdalen College at Oxford in 1874. There he came under the influence of Ruskin and Pater, who stimulated him in two directions that were not necessarily as opposite as many critics like to believe. Ruskin drew Wilde's attention to social questions and the connections between art and concrete practical life, whereas Pater demonstrated how private experience is essential for grasping the beautiful and profound nature of the external world. Ultimately, Wilde synthesized the notions of these two brilliant scholars to form his own social concept of aesthetics, and in some respects his own personality was symbolically most representative of this concept: Wilde was always bent on transforming himself into a work of art.

At Oxford he became more daring and lavish in his dress, postures, conversation, writings, and deeds. Most of his contemporaries as well as critics who have written on his life have dismissed his dandyism as egocentric behavior and snobbism. Yet there can be no doubt that he took his posturing and artful conversation seriously and came to perceive himself consciously and subconsciously as a type of artistic creation. As Philippe Jullian remarked, Wilde was fond of saying, "To get into society nowadays one has either to feed people or shock people—that is all."[20] His years at Oxford were like an apprenticeship, except that he was his own teacher and learned to cultivate the bizarre and extraordinary. When he entered London society in 1878, Wilde began to make a fashion out of being preposterous while showing how society was even more preposterous in its ways. In a certain sense he became a late rendition of the court fool who was always pardoned for mirroring the foibles of aristocratic society despite his shocking truth. George Woodcock points out, "In the course of two decades as a public figure in the London salons, he found out that the aristocrats did not even justify their wealth and privileges by displaying virtue or serving any social purpose, and he quickly came to despise the majority of them. In his plays they become the most grotesque figures, the Lady Bracknells and Lord Cavershams; upper-class stupidity is pilloried in his elderly parliamentarian aristocrats, and calculating vulgarity in his dowagers and duchesses."[21]

At bottom Wilde's carefully calculated conversation and display were based on a contempt of the people whom he also admired. In this sense he was much different from another writer of fairy tales who loved and flirted with social prominence, the submissive Hans Christian Andersen. Like Andersen, Wilde felt himself more noble and worthy of respect than the nobility. Unlike Andersen, however, he refused to kowtow to contemptible social conventions and authority, for he wanted to be accepted by society as unacceptable. That was his calling card, and the more he was accepted by society, the more he sought to break the norms and test the repressive tolerance of a cruel system of class justice.

From 1878 until the publication of *The Happy Prince and Other Tales* in 1888, Wilde was still in the process of learning his art, but this time his experiences were not contained within the halls of the university. He was exposed to social conditions in London, America, and the Continent and exchanged critical views on art and literature with the best writers of his day. His own poetry, criticism, lectures, and editorial work began to flower, and the appearance of his fairy tales signaled the advent of his great creative period: *The Soul of Man under Socialism* (1891), *The House of Pomegranates* (1891), *The Picture of Dorian Gray* (1891), *Lady Windermere's Fan* (1892), *A Woman of No Importance* (1893), *The Ideal Husband* (1895), and *The Importance of Being Earnest* (1895). As Wilde became more innovative in his writing, he became more and more daring and intolerable in his personal and social life. Though he took pains to protect his family, he professed his homosexuality in the face of social recrimination and almost demanded that his art be idolized. Strangely, his art was a means for both establishing his individualism and maintaining distance from a demeaning society from which he expected great, if not excessive, admiration.

It is most fitting that the volume *The Happy Prince and Other Tales* should be the work that was to launch his great creative period, for it reveals how highly disturbed Wilde was by the way society conditioned and punished young people if they did not conform to the proper rules. Late in his life he wrote about the cruel treatment of juvenile delinquents that he witnessed in prison.[22] Yet he had always been sensitive to the authoritarian schooling and church rigidity that most English children were expected to tolerate. His tales are imbued with a Christian socialist notion of humanism, and they contradict the civilizing process as it was practiced in England. To achieve the effect he desired, Wilde broke with the apologetics of classical fairy tales and the puerile Victorian stories to mirror social problems in Victorian England with a glimmer of hope—with a utopian impulse for change. As Isobel Murray points out,

> The gently Christian tone of "The Happy Prince"—and of "The Young King," written shortly after, and the quasi-biblical language do combine the fairy-tale mode with the shattering problems of Victorian poetry, privilege, and art, as Tennyson had most schematically outlined these in *The Palace of Art*.... Themes that recur in Andersen certainly occur in Wilde. "The Nightingale" is a parable about nature, art, and artifice which was bound to appeal to Wilde, and "The Neighboring Families" is similar in appeal. And Wilde probably learned from Andersen the witty, deflating touches which grace the stories, but never, even in "The Selfish Giant," is he betrayed into such depths of sentimentality as Andersen. He takes witty talking animals and objects and uses them as frames for stories, as in "The Devoted Friend," but he avoids Andersen's cloying moments, and generally transcends him.[23]

Perhaps a better word than *transcendence* to describe Wilde's underlying purpose in writing his tales is *subversion*. He clearly wanted to subvert the messages conveyed by Andersen's tales, but more important his poetic style recalled the rhythms and language of the Bible to counter the stringent Christian code. His interpretation of Christianity demonstrated the malpractice of the Church and questioned the compromising way Church leaders used Christianity to curb the pleasure instincts and to rationalize a socioeconomic system of exploitation. Wilde's "scriptural" tales were composed to enter into the discourse of the fairy-tale tradition and to shift its direction in a radical way. Key for understanding the socioaesthetic tendency of the tales is his essay *The Soul of Man under Socialism*, written in 1891.

Wilde had already conceived some of his central anarchistic ideas and notions of individualism in his significant essay "Chuang Tzu" on Taoism. *The Soul of Man under Socialism* brings together his disparate views on socialism in response to a speech given by George Bernard Shaw on Fabian socialism, and its importance rests not in its theoretical contribution to the cause of socialism but in the way it lends understanding to the unique socioaesthetics of Wilde. One of his favorite sayings contended that it does not take much to make humans into socialists, but to make socialism human is a great task. This is the central idea of his essay, which depends on Christ as its theoretical construct, and all his fairy tales evince the same sentiments. The major reason why Wilde argues for socialism is that it will lead to individualism in a humanitarian sense. At first he attacks private property and the philanthropy of the rich for preventing the rise of socialism. "The true perfection of man lies not in what man has, but in what man is. Private property has crushed true Individualism, and set up an Individualism that is false. It has debarred one part of the community from being individual by putting them on the wrong road, and encumbering them. Indeed, so completely has man's personality been absorbed by his possessions that the English law has always treated offenses against his person, and property is still the test of complete citizenship."[24] However, it is not only the elimination of private property but also the consequent development of an antiauthoritarian attitude, particularly among the poor, that is necessary for socialism. Christ is held up as the model of a person "who is perfectly and absolutely himself,"[25] and, if people become Christlike, there will be no need for government. With socialism, the perfection of individualism, there will be no crime, and machines will free people to be creative. "A map of the world that does not include Utopia, is not worth even glancing at, for it leaves out the one country at which Humanity is always landing. And when Humanity lands there, it looks out, and seeing a better country, sets sail. Progress is the realisation of Utopia."[26] Wilde has a vested interest in speaking for socialism because its advent will further the cause of art, which "is the most intense mode of Individualism that the world has known."[27]

In the struggle for better living conditions, people have been conditioned too much to accept pain, and here Christ's suffering has been regarded and misused as a goal in itself, "for it is through joy that the Individualism of the future will develop itself. Christ made no attempt to reconstruct society, and consequently the Individualism that he preached to man could be realised only through pain or in solitude. The ideals we owe to Christ are the ideals of a man who resists society absolutely. But man is naturally social."[28] What is significant here—and this is central for understanding the fairy tales—is that, on the one hand, Christ is upheld as a model of antiauthoritarianism and humanism but that, on the other hand, he must be transcended through a common struggle of joy toward socialism. In contrast to Christ, "the modern world has schemes. It proposes to do away with poverty and the suffering that it entails. It desires to get rid of pain, and the suffering that pain entails. It trusts to Socialism and Science as its methods. What it aims at is an Individualism expressing itself through joy."[29] Paradoxically the individual struggle against society is not enough for the creation of individualism, which entails a collective building of paradise on earth.

To a certain extent, Wilde was criticizing himself when he discussed the shortcomings of Christ with whom he obviously identified. The fact that he portrayed so many Christlike protagonists in his fairy tales did not mean that he wanted to propagate the Christian way as the path toward salvation or that he felt obliged to indulge himself in Christian moralizing for the sake of children, as some critics have mistakenly argued. Though Christlike behavior is laudable, it is not radical enough, and suffering is not acceptable as the recourse to a social system of domination that appears to be unchangeable. Actually, Wilde used the figure of Christ to show the need to subvert the traditional Christian message. *The Happy Prince* is a good example of how he placed the Christlike figure in a context aimed at altering classical fairy-tale discourse and at provoking readers to contemplate social change.

High above the city on a tall column sits the lead statue of the dead prince who appears magnificent because he is ornamented with sapphires, rubies, and gold. Everyone admires him, especially the town councillors, because he is so beautiful and appears to be the model of happiness that he once was. However, this happiness was based on ignorance, for he never realized how much his people suffered. It is only after his death that he grasps their suffering. The prince resolves to make up for his past negligence and egocentrism by bidding a devoted swallow to distribute the jewels from the statue to a poor seamstress, an artist, and a match girl. Eventually the swallow dies because of exposure to the cold winter, and the statue is melted because it is no longer beautiful and useful to the mayor and councillors, who would like to have statues made of themselves.

It is obvious from this brief summary that the "crucified" prince is Christlike and the swallow is a kind of apostle. Their humane actions are exemplary. The prince overcomes an art for art sake's position and thereby reveals the social essence of all beauty. The swallow forgets about the fickle love he had for a reed and develops a compassion for the poor through his bond of love for the prince. The ideological perspective of the story contains both sympathy and critique of the prince, and thus Wilde is able to stress the great disparities in English society by ironically making the dead prince's pedestal so high that he can realize how miserable the common people are and how responsible he is for their misery; that is, as the major representative of the ruling class. Yet—and this is the major point of Wilde's story—the individual actions of a Christlike person are not enough to put an end to poverty, injustice, and exploitation. Though the prince and bird may be blessed by God in the end, the mayor and town councillors remain in control of the city. These vain buffoons will certainly rule for their own benefit, and the philanthropic actions of the prince will go for naught.

The power of Wilde's story emanates from the unresolved tensions. The fabric of society is not changed. Nobody learns from the good deeds of the prince except perhaps the readers of the tale whom Wilde intended to provoke. In other words, the real beauty of the prince goes unnoticed because the town councillors and the people are too accustomed to identifying beauty with material wealth and splendor. Wilde suggests that the beauty of the prince cannot be appreciated in a capitalist society that favors greed and pomp. He does not preach the overthrow of these conditions. Rather his reverence for the prince is conveyed by rhythms and metaphors suggestive of a religious parable, and he makes his point by contrasting the prince with the town officials.

There is a discourse on manners and values in *The Happy Prince* that shows how deeply troubled Wilde was by the hypocrisy of the English upper class and bourgeoisie. All his fairy tales were artistic endeavors to expose their wanton and cruel ways by juxtaposing Christlike figures to the norms reinforced by the civilizing process—and I should stress that Wilde took care to show that the Christ figure, too, had shortcomings. This figure was Wilde's aesthetic artifact, employed in his stories as a device to reveal social conflicts and contradictions. While the rejection of society along with compassion for the poor is upheld as humane and beautiful, Wilde wants us to become more aware of what constitutes the mechanisms of ugly action such as domination and exploitation. It is first by perceiving how the civilizing process contributes to degradation of human beings that one can begin to struggle against it.

For instance, in the initial tale of *The House of Pomegranates* Wilde continued to elaborate the theme presented in *The Happy Prince* by depicting the workings of society more clearly. Here, in "The Young King," a goatherd is jolted one day when he is told that he is the only heir (the illegitimate son of the king's daughter) of his royal grandfather, who is about to die. He is swept from nature to the city and must make preparations for his coronation after a period of mourning. However, he has visions very much like the epiphanies in MacDonald's tales—religious illuminations—that open the young king's eyes so that he can see that beauty in his society is based on the abuse of workers. Since he will have no part of this, he decides to ride to his coronation in his former garb as goatherd, with a wild briar as his crown. Wilde reverses the notion of "clothes make the people" and transforms the mock motif in Andersen's "The Emperor's Clothes" into a radical ideological statement.[30] The king as Christlike beggar opposes social conventions, the Church, and the nobility. When a priest tries to dissuade him from his actions, he asks, "Shall Joy wear what Grief has fashioned?"[31] The king epitomizes the individual who refuses to compromise until the people learn to see that society must change. His beggarly appearance is ennobled and becomes radiant in the eyes of his onlookers because he has found the social essence of beauty.

In contrast to the happy prince, who was ultimately crucified despite (or perhaps because of) his philanthropic measures, the young king points a way to utopia by setting a model of behavior that he hopes everyone will recognize and follow. Basically he demonstrates that the beautiful appearance of the civilized world serves merely to conceal barbaric working conditions. His rejection of robe, crown, and scepter is a rejection of private property, ornamentation, and unjust power. By refusing to be parasitic, and by dressing in his original clothes, he becomes both an individual and an equal among men. The beauty of his deed derives from a compassion for humankind and a realization that his own potential depends on whether people are truly free. Though the social antagonisms remain unresolved at the end, Wilde went beyond The Happy Prince by making his Christ figure into a symbol of joy intent on paving the way to utopia.

Actually most of Wilde's tales are not as optimistic as this one and follow more the pattern of The Happy Prince to compel readers to question why social relations do not give rise to a better world. "The Nightingale and the Rose," "The Devoted Friend," "The Remarkable Rocket," "The Star Child," and "The Fisherman and His Soul" generally depict how hypocritical social conventions and double standards serve to maintain unjust rule. The result is pain and suffering, and the plots of the tales deny a happy end because property relations and social character are not altered. The highest personal state one can achieve under such conditions is crucifixion. Wilde's style, the mode that he chose to present his views of religion, art, and civilization, involved a subtle reutilization of biblical language and traditional fairy-tale motifs. That is, he transformed the style and themes of the Bible and classical fairy tales and put them to new use to convey his notions of Christian socialism.

For instance, "The Star Child" is a reversal of Andersen's "The Ugly Duckling" and incorporates motifs of the birth of Christ.[32] Whereas Andersen sees beauty as connected to the duckling's outward grace as a swan and subservience to the aristocracy of the swans, Wilde's ideological position implicitly mocked Andersen while presenting a more complex notion of beauty. For Wilde, beauty was based on a joyous recognition that misery can be overcome by opposing abusive power and private property. In "The Star Child" a beautiful boy who is proud, cruel, and selfish must learn that his fortunate appearance does not give him the right to maltreat less fortunate people. He is made ugly and placed in their position. After years of wandering and helping others, he regains his beauty, which is more striking because it is spiritual, and he is recognized as a king who rules his people with justice and mercy. However, Wilde is not content to leave us with a notion that all's well that ends well for one person. The biblical tone that closes the story reads like a warning: "Yet ruled he not long, so great had been his suffering, and so bitter the fire of his testing, for after the space of three years he died. And he who came after him ruled evilly."[33] Unlike Andersen, Wilde constantly insisted on the need to rid society of domination if the essence of beauty is to manifest itself.

In "The Fisherman and His Soul," Wilde again reversed an Andersen story. This time it was "The Little Mermaid," and instead of having a mermaid mutilate and mortify herself to acquire a soul, Wilde had a fisherman fall in love with a mermaid and discard his soul. However, his soul, representative of his superego and social convention, is jealous and seeks revenge. It drives the fisherman to do evil deeds, but the fisherman's love for the mermaid is so strong that he succeeds in turning his back on church and society and becomes united with her at death. The fisherman's nonconformity is symbolically a refusal to comply with the interests of the priest and merchants. Love is a liberating experience and allows him to become one with himself without the interference of a soul. Wilde ironically extols the life of a man who refuses a soul and thus considers him a saint. The reverential tone and religious imagery serve to denounce the hypocrisy of orthodox Christian practice that rationalized suffering in the name of the rich.

As we have seen, most of Wilde's tales end provocatively with Christlike figures dying, and the reader is compelled to question why such remarkable protagonists could not fulfill themselves within society. The provocation emanates from Wilde's utopian impulse, which was more positively developed in only two tales: "The Young King" and "The Selfish Giant." The latter tale, one of Wilde's most popular, is perhaps his most consummate statement on capitalist property relations and the need to restructure society along socialist lines. There are three stages to the tale. The first stage involves the eviction of the children from the garden. The giant as landholder opposes the children as collective. The second stage is the epiphany. The selfish giant suffers because he cannot share his wealth. His heart melts when he realizes how his selfishness makes a young boy miserable. The final stage is the transformation of his garden into a paradise for the children. He shares his property with everyone and shares their joy as well. In this latter phase the giant searches for the little boy whom he had helped but does not find him until the moment before his death. It is then that he realizes the boy is the incarnation of Christ, who leads the giant to paradise. This ending can be interpreted in various ways. Obviously it is related to Wilde's homosexuality, and he depicted the love for the boy as a form of liberation. On another level, this love is the type of humane compassion that Wilde felt was necessary for the building of socialism. Finally, the giant's pursuit and union with Christ is the pursuit of Christ within us, and as we know from his essay on *The Soul of Man under Socialism*, this type of joyous individualism can flower only in the progress made toward utopia.

Like MacDonald, Wilde was careful not to portray the contours of utopia because he was so familiar with the sordid conditions in Victorian England and realized that there would be a long struggle before we would even begin to catch a glimpse of real social utopia. This was the reason why he, like MacDonald, placed so much stress on reversing the process of socialization or civilization in his fairy-tale discourse. The building of a moral and aesthetic sensibility for social action was at the root of both writers' fairy tales. Whereas MacDonald wanted his protagonists mainly to rectify wrongs, Wilde insisted that his heroes try to grasp the roots of existence to change society. The patterns in most of their fairy tales are remarkably similar and reflect on socialization in England. Generally speaking, a young ignorant and innocent protagonist experiences an awakening through a dream or vision. At this point the protagonist sees what ails society, and his or her actions tend to go against the status quo of society. The configurative action of the heroes implied a critique of the civilization process and a notion of utopia that reflected on the actual social ossification in England. Given the social disparities and grim conditions in England at the end of the nineteenth century, it is no wonder that MacDonald and Wilde opted to stress the potential for human perfection rather than social perfection. If anyone was going to paint the possibilities for a modern utopia in fairy tales, a "naive" American had to be the one to do it.

IV

It is to L. Frank Baum's credit that he spent nearly twenty years of his adult life portraying a fairy-tale utopia with strong socialist and matriarchal notions to express his disenchantment with America, if not with the course of Western civilization in general. Baum was cut from the same mold as MacDonald and Wilde. Dreamer, idealist, reformer, he was a man who believed firmly in human perfection but who did not believe that perfect humanity could be attained through conformity to a society that allowed common people to be degraded. Like MacDonald and Wilde, he followed in the footsteps of Ruskin and Morris by instilling his art with social purpose. Between 1888 and 1901 there were more than sixty utopian novels published in the United States, and Baum, an avid reader, was particularly fond of Edward Bellamy's *Looking Backward* (1888) and Morris's *News from Nowhere* (1891).[34] Yet instead of using romance on which to base his conception of utopia, he chose the classical fairy tale. Most important is that he felt it incumbent on himself to "Americanize" this predominantly European literary genre, and in doing so he opened up new frontiers for the fairy-tale discourse on civilization and paved the way for later writers to experiment even more with the potential of *sequel* fairy tales to present radical alternatives to social reality.

There are very few book-length utopian fairy tales like *The Wonderful Wizard of Oz* that have managed to stay popular as a classic. This may, in fact, be due to the ingenuous manner in which it illuminates a way out of the gray world around us and awakens our creative energies, suggesting that we can become what we want to become without compromising our dreams. Right from its appearance in 1900, *The Wonderful Wizard of Oz* with those remarkable illustrations by W.W. Denslow captivated young American readers, and it was soon to charm adults as a musical play in 1902. Thereafter, the thirteen sequels along with the original book enchanted children and adults alike throughout the world. By 1939 it was made into a semianimated musical film with memorable performances by Judy Garland, Bert Lahr, Ray Bolger, and Jack Haley, and the fairy tale's classicism was thus guaranteed film immortality by MGM.[35] The melody of "somewhere over the rainbow way up high, there's a land that I dreamed of" continues to instill hope in millions of viewers who are led to believe that the experience of a trip to Oz may help them transform conditions at home. In this respect the film, though it changed many incidents, retained the utopian impulse of the book. Book and film celebrate the need for utopia. Yet there is a tragic side to Baum's concept of Oz that the film (but few critics) have explored in depth: the book and its sequels emanate from the sensitivity of a naive writer who was disturbed by the Gilded Age, which glossed over the desperate economic plight of farmers and workers, especially in the Midwest. And the film, too, arose *against* the background of the great economic Depression of the 1930s.

Baum was not a philosopher and did not seek to expound great worldviews in *The Wonderful Wizard of Oz*. If anything, he was astonishingly if not painfully ingenuous, good-hearted, and trusting. His writing reflects an unusual propensity for inventiveness and candor. He thrived on puns, the burlesque, and the preposterous. His style and message were direct and lucid: he hated violence and exploitation with a humane passion. There is very little subtlety in the plots of his books, and his characters, though unusual, rarely develop in a complex way. Such simplicity might make for boring reading (and does in some of the sequels), but there is a profound and scintillating vision of America conveyed through his charming fairy tales, and this critical insight endows them with extraordinary power. The frank, candid narratives are disarming and leave one's imagination dangerously open to subversive ideas. A trip to Oz is not escape, because one is forced to become aware of what is absent in America and in the world at large. It is interesting that Baum initially felt that the gaps in Dorothy's gray dull life could be filled after one short trip to Oz. The more he became disappointed with the American way of life, however, the more he allowed Dorothy to spend time and enjoy herself in Oz. By Book Six, *The Emerald City* (1908), he had her turn her back on Kansas and "home" for good. Home became Oz, a self-imposed exile from America. A strange act. Was it the closing of the American frontier and the limitations of American society that drove Baum to compel Dorothy to remain in Oz? Just what was it that Baum saw in the American "civilizing process" that forced him to make Oz invisible to the outside world for its own self-protection?

The course that Baum's own life took can help explain in part the nature of his discourse on civilization and utopia in the Oz books. His unique fall; his downward social mobility from the upper class; his experiences as actor, salesman, storekeeper, and journalist; his travels from East Coast to West Coast all provided him with an elementary basis for understanding and sympathizing with the plight of the common people in America during the Gilded Age—a period of massive economic expansion and crises. We must bear in mind that the self-proclaimed "nonpolitical" Baum had an unusually perceptive political viewpoint that owed a great deal to utopian writings, American populism, and the suffragette movement. It is always intriguing to read the imaginative works of a writer who claims that he had very little to do with politics and yet made this the very core of his work. It is in such naiveté that one often finds the keenest political insights into the contradictions of the times.

Baum was born symbolically with a heart defect in 1856 in upstate New York.[36] His father Benjamin Ward Baum was a wealthy oil executive and could afford to provide his son with the necessary care and protection that might allow him to lead a fairly normal life. Nevertheless, Baum lived with the fear that he might have an attack and die at any moment, and this fear was the basis for his deep regard and zest for all forms of life and also for his avoidance of conflict and violence. Educated at home on a fifteen-acre estate outside Syracuse, Baum could explore the farm and the nearby woods to his heart's content. He took a particular delight in chickens, which he bred, and he spent a great deal of time reading when not taking private lessons. It is interesting to note that he absorbed himself in the tales of Grimm and Andersen but disliked their violence, cruelty, and sadness. Baum was bent on seeing the brighter side of life, for he never knew how much more time he would have to appreciate the world around him.

Sent to the Peekskill Military Academy in 1868 because his parents wanted to bring their son the dreamer down to earth, he lasted fewer than two years because he hated the corporal punishment and discipline of the institution. Thereafter, he completed his education at home with private tutors, and Dickens became one of his favorite authors. By 1873 Baum was ready to try his hand at journalism and took a job as cub reporter for the New York World. Soon he became involved with other newspaper projects, and in 1875 he began managing a printing shop in Bradford, Pennsylvania, where he established the newspaper the New Era. Because his father owned some opera houses and theaters in New York and Pennsylvania, Baum began to manage them, and he became absorbed in the theater as writer and actor. His first real success was the Irish musical comedy The Maid of Arran (1881), and this play encouraged him to make theater his career. Because of his naiveté, however, he was bound for a rocky road. In many instances his father (almost like a fairy godfather) had already provided assistance and connections or bailed him out when Baum's trust in people was abused. This is not to say that Baum was the spoiled rich boy who constantly needed a doting father. On the contrary, Baum was a tireless inventor, extremely gifted and versatile as musician, writer, and manual worker.

There was no doubt that, in 1881, he was a young man on the rise, and, when he met Maud Gage that same year, it seemed that success was staring him in the eyes. Maud was the daughter of Matilda Gage, who collaborated with Susan B. Anthony and Elizabeth Cady Stanton to write the four-volume History of Woman Suffrage and who was famous for her own work Woman, Church and State. Needless to say, Maud, who was educated at Cornell, came from a different social environment than Baum, and yet they appeared to complement each other, she with her sober social ideas, and he with his boundless idealism and imagination. They were going to need both sobriety and idealism after their marriage in 1882 because a series of accidents and tragic events was about to send them on a course of downward social mobility.

In 1884 Baum lost his shares in an opera-house chain through bad management and fire. He then opened up a small company to sell crude oil products in conjunction with his father's business. However, his father's firm was failing because some employees were defrauding accounts. By the time Benjamin Baum died in 1887, the business had collapsed, and the oil fortune had all but vanished.

Like many Americans at this time Baum turned West toward new frontiers and moved to Aberdeen, South Dakota, with Maud and their first of three sons. He opened up a variety store called Baum's Bazaar, but because he continually gave credit to the poor customers, especially farmers, and spent a lot of time telling stories to youngsters who frequented the store, he was forced to close in 1890. This was at the height of a severe economic depression, and Baum was witness to the way in which farmers were exploited by bankers and businessmen alike. Foreclosure and poverty were common conditions in South Dakota, and Baum wrote about them in the *Aberdeen Saturday Pioneer*, which he edited for one year. Then in 1891 he moved with his family (there were now three sons) to Chicago, where he had a series of jobs as reporter for the *Chicago Evening Post* and then worked as traveling salesman for a china and glassware firm. During the first six years in Chicago, he actually took part in a populist demonstration, and his sympathies were clearly with social reform groups that were highly active and radical at that time. However, his main worry was surviving and supporting his family. In 1897 fatigue and nasal hemorrhages, which were signs of a stressed heart, caused him to retire as a salesman, and he assumed the editorship of the *Show Window*, the first magazine in America to be published for window decorators. At the same time, encouraged by his mother-in-law Matilda Gage, who thought highly of his bedtime stories for his sons, he began producing children's books: *Mother Goose in Prose* (1897), *My Candalabara's Glare* (1898), and *Father Goose* (1899). All were successful, but it was the publication of *The Wonderful Wizard of Oz* in 1900 that enabled him to resign his position as editor of the *Show Window* and to dedicate himself to writing and the theater. Actually Baum never intended to write a series of Oz books. He followed *The Wonderful Wizard of Oz* with *Dot and Tot of Merryland* and *Baum's American Fairy Tales* in 1901, *The Life and Adventures of Santa Claus* in 1902, and *The Enchanted Island of Yew* in 1903. It was not until 1904 that he published a sequel, *The Marvelous Land of Oz*, and the reasons were mixed. First, there had been a large demand for a sequel to *The Wonderful Wizard of Oz* by readers of all ages, and the success of the musical adaptation in 1902 stimulated even more interest in Oz. Second, Baum had run into financial difficulty because of his theatrical ventures, and he knew that a sequel with dramatic possibilities would provide him with the funds he needed. Thus, he developed a curious relationship to the Oz books: it was his pot of luck to which he could turn when he needed money, and it was the means through which he had contact with hundreds if not thousands of readers who wrote and gave him suggestions for characters, incidents, and plots.

When Baum made a decision in 1909 to move to Hollywood permanently and try his hand at films—he was always ready for new experiments and fantastic projects and even thought of constructing an "Ozland" on an island off the coast of California—he tried to bring an end to the Oz books with *The Emerald City of Oz* in 1910. However, his film company failed, and he declared personal bankruptcy in 1911. Soon thereafter, in 1913, he resumed publication of the Oz series with *The Patchwork Girl of Oz*. From then on, most of the works he wrote in California were concerned with utopian projections, and it appeared that they could take on concrete form only in Oz. This was only appropriate, for it was through the Oz books that he gained the feeling of bringing joy to innumerable readers who shared his utopian fantasy. And, as he became progressively ill because of his weak heart—he suffered laming facial attacks in 1914 and became bedridden in 1917—he turned more and more to Oz as a source of comfort. All this was in his house "Ozcot," right near Hollywood where Walt Disney was to establish his studio years later. California was ideal for Baum's resting place, the final frontier. It was almost as if he had been driven from the East Coast to the West Coast in search of a better America knowing all the while, his dark secret, that it would never come. It was difficult to admit this, and perhaps this is why he endeavored until his death in 1919 to give hope to his readers that there may be another way of pursuing the American dream than the way it was being pursued in reality with vengeance.

There have been a number of fine and thorough studies of Baum's works, and there is even an international society and Baum journal dedicated to keeping his spirit alive. Yet few of the essays written on Baum's Oz books have placed them in the historical context of a fairy-tale discourse, and very few have written about the tragic undertones of his writing. I should like to do both by emphasizing a distinction between *The Wonderful Wizard of Oz* and the five books that followed, paying close attention to *The Emerald City of Oz*. As is well known, Baum wrote the Oz fairy tales in three phases, and the first two are highly significant because he initially wanted Dorothy to return home and face the gray music of Kansas. In the second phase he kept shipping her back and forth between Oz and Kansas until he decided that Dorothy and her aunt and uncle would never be happy in America. The last phase—the eight sequels written in California—is interesting because it concerns Baum's desire to complete the picture of utopia and to work through certain problems. In all his works the civilization of Oz is opposed to the American civilization, and we must understand how and why his critique of American socialization and values became so severe that he placed Dorothy in permanent exile.

One of the most revealing studies of the original Oz fairy tale is Henry M. Littlefield's essay "The Wizard of Oz: Parable on Populism,"[37] in which he convincingly demonstrates that the book reflects the impoverished state of farmers in South Dakota, the depression and strikes of the 1890s, the war with Spain, and Baum's democratic populism. His major thesis is that Baum "delineated a Midwesterner's vibrant and ironic portrait of this country as it entered the twentieth century . . . throughout the story Baum poses a central thought: the American desire for symbols of fulfillment is illusory. Real needs lie elsewhere."[38] The allegorical parallels that Littlefield draws are instructive. Led by naive innocence and protected by goodwill (Dorothy), the farmer (scarecrow), the laborer (tin woodsman), and the politician (lion) approach the mystic holder of national power (wizard) to ask for personal fulfillment only to learn that they must ultimately provide for it by themselves.

Littlefield's thesis must be qualified and expanded. To begin with, Baum was by no means a midwesterner, and his ideological perspective should be clarified if we are to grasp the essence of his discourse on American civilization through the fairy tale. By the time he began writing the Oz fairy tales, Baum had become "declassed"; that is, he had fallen from the upper classes and had experienced the trauma of downward social mobility. Moreover, his political consciousness had been awakened through his mother-in-law's and wife's feminism, the farmers' struggles in the Midwest, and the populist movement. His portrait of America was that of an upper-class easterner, whose social expectations had been betrayed and who "betrayed" his class by seeking to delude children of false illusions about America as a land of opportunity.

Such deep concern in American reality led Baum to transform and "Americanize" the classical fairy-tale pattern and motifs found in the Grimm and Andersen narratives. Generally, the hero has three encounters of various kinds to reach a type of peripeteia and then another three encounters to achieve a goal. The encounters are most often with friends or qualities that the hero needs so he or she can overcome obstacles and evil. In The Wonderful Wizard of Oz, the gray landscape is immediately recognizable as American, and Dorothy is clearly as American as apple pie. What's more, she is an orphan who expresses great compassion for downtrodden eccentrics on her journey through Oz. The scarecrow, tin woodsman, and lion are recognizable American types, and Baum employs traditional fairy-tale convention to synthesize their qualities through a *female* figure. His purpose is to bring loners and outcasts together to depict just how capable they are. Implicit is the notion that common people do not need managers or middlemen to run their affairs, that the latent creative potential in each simple person need only be awakened and encouraged to develop. Baum's major characters in The Wonderful Wizard of Oz are noncompetitive and nonexploitative. They desire neither money nor success. They have little regard for formal schooling or irrelevant social conventions. They respect differences among all creatures and seek the opportunity to fill a gap in their lives. In depicting their behavior, Baum develops a discourse on manners and norms that contradicts the standard discourse in the tales of Grimm and Andersen and questions the actual civilizing process in America.

Perhaps it was because he was petrified by what he witnessed in South Dakota and Chicago that Baum sought to subvert the American socialization process based on competition and achievement. There is no doubt that he wanted to educate readers to the fact that individualism could be achieved in other ways—through tenderness, goodwill, and cooperation. To be smart, compassionate, and courageous is to have qualities that can be put to use to overcome alienation. The colors and ambience of Oz are part of an atmosphere that allows for creativity and harmony along with a sense of social responsibility. Dorothy sees and feels this. She is "wizened" by her trip through Oz, and Baum knows that she is stronger and can face the drabness of Kansas. This is why he closes the book in America: Dorothy has a utopian spark in her that was to keep her alive in gray surroundings.

In his next four books, *The Marvelous Land of Oz* (1904), *Ozma of Oz* (1907), *Dorothy and the Wizard in Oz* (1908), and *The Road to Oz* (1909), Baum elaborated his concept of utopia and explored its social relations in contrast to America. In *The Marvelous Land of Oz*, Baum seemingly mocked the woman's suffragette movement, and yet the hero of his fairy tale turns out to be a heroine, very much representative of feminine ideals. Many American librarians have yet to forgive Baum for a kind of transvestite act—he turned the male Tip into a female so she could resume her proper form and become Ozma of Oz, the gracious and just ruler.[39] For whatever psychological reasons, whether it was because he had always desired to have a daughter, whether it was because he could never have a close relationship with his mother, or whether it was because he sought the approval of his wife Maud, Baum extolled feminine qualities as prerequisites for the foundation of utopia. In *Ozma of Oz* Dorothy and Ozma have their first encounter with the Nome King, who represents materialist greed and the lust for power for the sake of power. His defeat only brings out his sinister desire for revenge. In *Dorothy and the Wizard in Oz* the ageless six-year-old girl is reunited with the wizard, and they are rescued by Ozma from underground creatures who have neither heart nor humane ideals. Here the wizard returns to Oz for good, the first of a series of moves from America to Oz. In *The Road to Oz* Dorothy meets the Shaggy Man, who possesses a love magnet, and he tells Dorothy that money makes people proud and haughty and that he doesn't want to be proud and haughty. All he wants is to have people love him, which they will do as long as he owns the Love Magnet. This may be necessary in America, land of strife and alienation, but once he lands in Oz, the Shaggy Man learns that he does not need possessions or magic to gain what he seeks. Ozma tells him that people in Oz are loved for themselves alone, for their kindness to one another, and for their own good deeds. Thus, the Shaggy Man decides, like the wizard, to remain in Oz, where he is accepted and loved for what he is.

By the time Baum came to write *The Emerald City of Oz* in 1910, he had developed precise principles for his utopia, and he formulated them at the beginning of this book:

Each man/woman, no matter what he or she produced for the good of the community, was supplied by the neighbors with goods and clothing and a house and furniture and ornaments and games. If by chance the supply ever ran short, more was taken from the great storehouses of the Ruler, which were afterward filled up again when there was more of any article than the people needed.

Everyone worked half the time and played half the time, and the people enjoyed the work as much as they did the play, because it is good to be occupied and have something to do.

There were no cruel overseers set to watch them, and no one to rebuke them or find fault with them. So each one was proud to do all he could for his friends and neighbors, and was glad when they would accept the things he produced.

Oz being a fairy country, the people were, of course, fairy people; but that does not mean that all of them were very unlike the people of our own world. There were all sorts of queer characters among them, but not a single one who was evil, or who possessed a selfish or violent nature. They were peaceful, kind-hearted, loving and merry, and every inhabitant adored the beautiful girl who ruled them, and delighted to obey her every command.[40]

Baum's socialist utopia is a strange one because it is governed by a princess named Ozma, but there is no real hierarchy or ruling class in Oz. Ozma the hermaphrodite is a symbol of matriarchy and guarantees the development of socialist humanism in Oz by regulating magic, especially by banning black magic. Not only does she welcome the downtrodden Aunt Em and Uncle Henry, who had been maltreated by bankers and had become fully isolated in America, but she also protects Oz against the revengeful Nome King through a strategy of nonviolence. *The Emerald City of Oz* is aesthetically the most innovative and thematically the most radical of Baum's fairy tales. The narrative is based on a twofold plot with dialectical scenes that infuse the action with dramatic suspense. While Dorothy endeavors to "recivilize" Aunt Em and Uncle Henry by showing them the wonders of their new home, the Nome King amasses a large army and attempts to destroy Oz. Baum draws a parallel between the bankers, who are merciless and crush old farmers who can no longer be employed because of bad health, and the Nome King and his allies, the Whimsies, Growleywogs, and Phanfasms, who want to enslave people to attain wealth and power. Each step Aunt Em and Uncle Henry take to realize and appreciate the liberating principles and environment of Oz is matched by a step taken by the Nome King to undermine the utopian civilization. The narrative perspective leads the reader to identify with the cause of Oz, and Baum demonstrates insight and ingenuity in the way he has Ozma save Oz and guarantee its eternal existence. Because he was against violence of any kind, Baum invented a fountain with water of oblivion. One sip of the water makes one forget everything, especially one's evil intentions, and Ozma's enemies are led to taste, forget, and return to their homes outside Oz. Baum did not preach a Christian turning of the cheek. Rather he was more aware that, if one uses the same methods as one's enemies, one can easily become like them. To become cutthroat and militant like the gnomes and bankers would have tarnished the spirit and principles of Oz, and so the endeavor to be different and humanitarian at the same time engenders a greater sense of creativity and humanity in Ozma and her friends. Yet because of this conflict with enemies, Ozma decides to make Oz invisible and unapproachable by outsiders because they mean tragedy for utopia. From Baum's ideological viewpoint he grasped that technology in the hands of capitalist entrepreneurs would mean the doom of utopian developments like Oz. By making this land invisible, Baum was saying that the chances for the realization of utopia in America had been cancelled and forfeited. The American dream had no chance against the real American world of finance, which manipulated and exploited the dream for its own ends.

In one of the most incisive essays about the Oz books, Gore Vidal[41] agrees with Marius Bewley[42] that the tension between technology and pastoralism is one of the things that the Oz books are about, whether Baum was aware of it or not.

> In Oz he presents the pastoral dream of Jefferson (the slaves have been replaced by magic and good will); and into this Eden he introduces forbidden knowledge in the form of black magic (the machine) which good magic (the values of pastoral society) must overwhelm.
>
> It is Bewley's view that because "the Ozites are much aware of the scientific nature of magic, Ozma wisely limited the practice of magic." As a result, controlled magic enhances the society just as controlled industrialization could enhance (and perhaps even salvage) a society like ours. Unfortunately, the Nome King has governed the United States for more than a century; and he shows no sign of wanting to abdictate. Meanwhile, the life of the many is definitely nome-ish and the environment has been, perhaps, irreparably damaged. To the extent that Baum makes his readers aware that our country's "practical" arrangements are inferior to those of Oz, he is a truly subversive writer.[43]

As I have endeavored to demonstrate, Baum was not alone in developing an "art of subversion" through the fairy tale. With the rise of industrialization and the rationalized exploitation of the working classes came different social reform movements and improved methods of education that people used to expose the contradictions in the civilizing process of so-called advanced technological countries. Generally speaking, most writers of fairy tales in England and America of the nineteenth century continued to use the form to mollify and apologize for broken promises of a better life as working conditions and social relations became more stressful and alienating. However, as we have seen, there was a small but powerful oppositional group of fairy-tale writers like Dickens, Ruskin, MacDonald, Wilde, and Baum, to name but a few, who transformed the fairy-tale discourse on mores and manners through a political perspective that placed both the classical fairy tales and society in question. There was also a new and larger reading audience composed of young people from the working and petit bourgeois classes who were the targets of both traditional and oppositional fairy-tale writers. And, of course, upper-class children were consistently included as part of the intended general audience.

What is important to know about the reform-minded fairy-tale writers is that they saw the possibility of providing a new kind of political consciousness that might lend more social confirmation to the relatively "new" readers of the lower classes and that might make the privileged readers aware of their true social responsibility. It is clear that there is a shift in the ideology of the narrative perspective away from that of Perrault, the Grimms, and Andersen in the late 1800s: another world is glimpsed through the ideological lens of writers who refused to legitimate the views of the upper classes in England and America and who devised aesthetical configurations to convey socialist utopian impulses. In essence, the literary fairy tale was becoming more and more a political weapon used to challenge or capture the minds and sensibilities of the young. This had always been the case, more or less, but the genre in its classical form and substance had used magic and metaphor to repress the desires and needs of the readers. The new classical fairy tales of MacDonald, Wilde, and Baum were part of a process of social liberation. Their art was a subversive symbolic act intended to illuminate concrete utopias waiting to be realized once the authoritarian rule of the Nome King could be overcome.

7

THE BATTLE OVER FAIRY-TALE DISCOURSE: FAMILY, FRICTION, AND SOCIALIZATION IN THE WEIMAR REPUBLIC AND NAZI GERMANY

Mildew
More than ever before, people are living with it. Children are not raised without it. They carry it with them or suffer until they themselves are like the father. Even the person who does not listen picks up the discussions of commonplace people. What remains is the sitting around the kitchen table, the gossip, the visit, the artificial laughter and the genuine poison which they spread among one another. Even the person who does not inhale is greeted by the confining stale air. It penetrates to the young man below and to the beautiful people above. Remains good and quiet here, good and mute there.

—Ernst Bloch, *Erbschaft dieser Zeit* (1934)

Given the significant attempts in recent years to grasp the essential features of Weimar and Nazi culture and the crucial links between these two phases of German history, it is remarkable that very little attention has been paid to fairy tales.[1] I use the word *remarkable* for good reasons. Unlike any country in the Western world, with the possible exception of Great Britain, Germany has incorporated folktales and fairy tales in its literary socialization process so that they play a most formative role in cultivating aesthetic taste and value systems. In fact, it is generally impossible to think about folktales and fairy tales without first thinking about the Grimms and Germany. Though it is not wise to attribute too much influence to any one cultural product in the formation of national customs and consciousness, there is no doubt that folktales and fairy tales participated heavily in the creation of beliefs and norms and symbolically reflected changes in the social orders of Germany. As we know, fairy tales in particular were used consciously and unconsciously during the rise of the bourgeoisie to indicate socially acceptable roles for children and to provide them with culture, the German version of *civilité*.

The very fact that the Nazis recognized the necessity to create a policy with regard to folktales and fairy tales demonstrated a general awareness about their cultural impact on children and adults. Even before the Nazis arrived on the scene, there were debates among members of the educated class in Germany about negative and positive effects of folktales and fairy tales, especially for children. These debates began during the eighteenth-century Enlightenment and have lasted until the present. As public disputes, they can be considered an extension of the fairy-tale discourse in the commensurate institution of criticism, and they deal with the effect that the tales have on the psyche of children and consequently on their social attitudes, behavior, and creativity. Since it is extremely difficult to measure such an effect, the different perspectives are significant mainly insofar as the *positions themselves* reveal ideological and social views about literature and child rearing in a given historical epoch. In the case of Weimar and Nazi Germany, there is much that can be learned about the family, socialization, and cultural attitudes by studying the cultural production of fairy tales and their use in the public sphere. In view of the fact that this topic is a vast one, I want to limit myself to the question of family behavioral patterns and the ideology of competition and domination.

The Weimar and Nazi periods are extremely important in the general development of the fairy-tale genre in the Western world at large. As we have seen, the discourse on civilization through the fairy tale for children in the Western world was expanded, inverted, and subverted toward the end of the nineteenth century. This resulted in a fierce public struggle over the discourse at the beginning of the twentieth century, and nowhere was it so strikingly apparent as it was in Germany that the fairy-tale discourse was bound up with the civilizing process. This was because of the tremendous social and political upheavals that polarized the society and compelled writers to assume clear-cut ideological positions in their symbolic acts. We can draw parallels to other countries at this time, and the analogies can help us perceive the broadly similar contours of the fairy tale for children in the West as well as the unevenness and particularity of cultural developments. As my chosen focal point in this chapter, the German literary fairy tales enable us to grasp the course that the civilizing process in the Western world was taking, and, as a case study, it is interesting to see how they broke even more from the classical fairy-tale patterns to discuss domination and barbarism. The vital attempt to find an antidote to the "mildew" in Germany—Bloch's metaphor for those atavistic attitudes that the Nazis used to create their empire—reinvigorated the fairy-tale discourse in Weimar Germany and then succumbed to the poison of the 1930s. Since the concerns of the fairy tale for children and the fairy tale for adults were so close in Weimar and Nazi Germany, I shall try to show in this chapter how they formed a pervasive battle over fairy-tale discourse in which the future of civilization was often implied to be at stake. This battle was also being waged by fairy-tale writers in other Western countries, and it is with an awareness of the total literary war, whose history is yet to be written, that Germany can help us grasp the points of historical gaps to be filled as critical text.

I

The significance of the classical fairy tale for children in Germany at the onset of the twentieth century can be measured to a large extent by the voluminous attention paid to the tale by scholars of different disciplines.[2] By "classical" I am referring to the standard popular works of the Grimms, Andersen, and Bechstein, which were the major reference point in German debates and discussions and often regarded as folktales. In the field of psychology, the most important works were written by Charlotte Bühler, *Das Märchen und die Phantasie des Kindes* (*The Fairy Tale and the Imagination of the Child*, 1919), Hans Hr. Busse, *Das literarische Verständnis der werktätigen Jugend zwischen 14 und 18* (*The Literary Comprehension of Working Youth between 14 and 18*, 1923), and Erwin Müller, *Psychologie des deutschen Volksmärchens* (*Psychology of the German Folk Tale*, 1928). Along with the interest of the Freudian and Jungian schools in dreams and their relationship to fairy tales, these studies pointed to the general importance of fairy tales in helping children develop full personalities, and they defended their positive virtues for role development and maturation within the socialization process. The sociological and pedagogical studies, Wilhelm Ledermann's *Das Märchen in Schule und Haus* (*The Fairy Tale in School and Home*, 1926) and Reinhard Nolte's *Analyse der freien Märchenproduktion* (*Analysis of the Free Production of Fairy Tales*, 1931), documented the widespread popularity and use of the classical fairy tales and supported the findings of Bühler, Busse, and others.[3] Walter A. Berendsohn endeavored to make clear-cut distinctions between the fairy tale and other short forms of narrative prose in *Grundformen volkstümlicher Erzählkunst in den Kinder- und Hausmärchen der Brüder Grimm* (*Basic Forms of the Popular Art of Narration in the Household Tales*, 1922). Researchers of a conservative folklore tradition sought to trace the symbolical figures of the classical fairy tales and folktales to Nordic religions and myths. Here the work of Karl von Spiess, *Das deutsche*

Volksmärchen (*The German Folk Tale*, 1925), Georg Schott, *Weissagung und Erfüllung im deutschen Volksmärchen* (*Prophecy and Fulfillment in the German Folk Tale*, 1925), and Werner von Bülow, *Märchendeutungen durch Runen. Geheimsprache der deutschen Märchen* (*The Meanings of Fairy Tales through Runes: The Secret Language of German Fairy Tales*, 1925) helped prepare the way for one-sided fascist studies and formative anthropological works in the field of folklore. Finally, Edwin Hoernle dealt at length with the reception and use of fairy tales from a Marxist point of view in *Die Arbeit in den Kommunistischen Kindergruppen* (*Work in the Communist Children's Groups*, 1923), which was developed in a more sophisticated way by Ernst Bloch[4] and Walter Benjamin[5] in the 1930s.

The heated discussion about the value and effects of the classical fairy tale during the Weimar period must be seen within the context of a debate concerning the function of children's books in the socialization process unleashed earlier by Heinrich Wolgast's book *Das Elend unserer Jugendliteratur. Ein Beitrag zur künstlerischen Erziehung der Jugend* (*The Misery of Our Literature for the Young: A Contribution to the Artistic Education of Youth*, 1896). Wolgast, a left-liberal, who sympathized with the Social Democratic Party,[6] helped found an organization called the *Jugendschriftenbewegung*, which sought to clean up books for children and young people and raise aesthetic standards. In the 1920s his position was best represented by Herman L. Köster, author of *Geschichte der deutschen Jugendliteratur in Monographien* (*History of the German Literature for Youth in Monographs*, written in 1906 and revised in 1927). As cofounder of the *Jugendschriftenbewegung*, Köster and others worked in the 1920s to keep the artistic standards of children's literature high and morally decent. Their basic ideological position, however, allowed more and more for chauvinistic and militaristic books and other illustrated volumes that implicitly reinforced the value system of the conservative wing of the bourgeoisie.

In opposition to this conservative trend in the *Jugendschriftenbewegung*, which was eventually taken over by the Nazis under the leadership of Severin Rüttgers, there was a strong movement led by communists, radicals, and progressives to politicize children's literature openly and thereby to raise the artistic and ideological quality of literature for young people. Because the classical fairy tale was used so prominently to help children adapt to expected roles in the bourgeois socialization process, it is not by chance that this genre was one of the first that socialists sought to revise and reutilize. In 1923 Edwin Hoernle argued,

> Just in general we must learn again how to tell stories, those fantastic, artless stories as they were heard in pre-capitalist times in spinning rooms of the peasants and in homes of the artisans. The thoughts and emotions of the masses are mirrored here most simply and therefore are most clear. Capitalism with its destruction of the family and its mechanization of working

human beings annihilated this old "popular art" (Volkskunst) of telling tales. The proletariat will create the new fairy tales in which workers' struggles, their lives, and their ideas are reflected and correspond to the degree to which they demonstrate how they can become human time and again, and how they can build up new educational societies in place of the decrepit old ones. It makes no sense to complain that we do not have suitable fairy tales for our children. Professional writers will not create them. Fairy tales do not originate from the desk. The real fairy tale originates unconsciously, collectively in the course of longer time-spans, and the work of the writer consists mainly in refining and rounding out the material at hand. The new proletarian and industrial fairy tale will come as soon as the proletariat has created a place in which the fairy tales will be told, not read aloud, and will be composed orally, not repeated. Then machines, tools, boilers, trains, ships, telegraphs and telephones, mine shafts and chemical tubes will become alive and begin to speak just as previously the wolf or the water kettle in the folk tales of the peasantry and petit bourgeois spoke.[7]

As we know, this prediction by Hoernle has not become entirely true, but the production of progressive, socialistically oriented fairy tales did begin, and it began much sooner than he even realized. There were already clear socialist strains in literary fairy tales for children throughout Europe and America by the end of the nineteenth century. Still, it was not until the end of World War I that a barrage of demonstrable communist and socialist fairy tales for children began appearing. In Germany Hermynia Zur Mühlen started writing political fairy tales for children in 1921 with *Was Peterchens Freunde erzählen* (*What Little Peter's Friends Tell*), and she followed this with other collections, such as *Das Schloss der Wahrheit* (*The Castle of Truth*, 1924) and *Es war einmal, . . . und es wird sein* (*Once Upon a Time . . . And It Will Come to Be*, 1930). In addition, Ernst Friedrich gathered some interesting political tales by Berta Lask, Carl Ewald, and Robert Grötzsch in *Proletarischer Kindergarten* (*Proletarian Kindergarten*, 1921), while Bruno Schönlank's *Grossstadt-Märchen* (*Big City Fairy Tales*, 1923), Walter Eschbach's *Märchen der Wirklichkeit* (*Fairy Tales of Reality*, 1923), Heinrich Schulz's *Von Menschlein, Tierlein und Dinglein* (*Little People, Animals and Things*, 1925), Cläre Meyer-Lugau's *Das geheimnisvolle Land* (*The Mysterious Country*, 1925), and Lisa Tetzner's *Hans Urian* (1931) demonstrated how fairy tales could be used to explain social contradictions to children in a highly illuminating way. However, the movement to radicalize fairy tales really never took root among children and adults in the Weimar Republic. The classical fairy tales of the Grimms, Andersen, and Bechstein reigned supreme and were imitated by a host of mediocre writers who fostered a canon of condescending, morally didactic tales that were used basically to sweeten the lives of children like candy for consumption. Moreover, the classical fairy tale was now disseminated through radio and film, and this distribution made its impact even greater on children of all classes. The mildew was no longer spread just by everyday talk but also transmitted by the mass media. Modern technology in support of anachronistic ideology.

When the Nazis took power in 1933, there was a gradual change in the production of fairy tales for children. First, of course, the socialist experiments were banned. Second, writers were less and less encouraged to write fairy tales. The folktales were considered to be holy or sacred Aryan relics. Therefore, the classical fairy tales of the Grimms, Andersen, and Bechstein were promoted as ideal on recommended reading lists for children along with those of Musäus, whereas the romantic fairy tales and other *Kunstmärchen* were to be avoided. What was now stressed and came to be part of a policy in regard to fairy tales was a cleansing policy to recover the pure Aryan tradition of the folktale. As Christa Kamenetsky points out,

> The National Socialist conception of folk, community, peasant, and folklore differed substantially from that which emerged from even the most nationalistic writings of Herder, the Brothers Grimm, Arndt, Goerres, or Jahn, as it combined some romantic notions with the ideological orientation of the Third Reich. The "fighting folk community," standing "in a single column" behind the Führer in unity and unquestioning loyalty, had but little to do with the rural folk community of an idyllic village. The innocent folktale was transformed into an ideological weapon meant to serve the building of the Thousand Year Reich. Thus, Party official Alfred Eyd announced in 1935, "the German folktale shall become a most valuable means for us in the racial and political education of the young."[8]

This did not mean a new folktale or fairy-tale tradition was to be created (the way sought by socialists and communists). If one examines the folktale and fairy-tale collections and the production during the fascist period, it is actually remarkable how little was actually done to change the format of the books. One cannot speak of a folktale in the strict sense of the word because most of the tales collected and published for children were the classical fairy tales of the Grimms, Andersen, and Bechstein. The illustrations were also influenced to a large extent by nineteenth-century artists (Rackham, Dulac, Doré) or were imitated idyllic peasant scenes. In other words, there was no massive attempt to rewrite the tales stressing their Aryan features or to paint pictures with Nordic types. There was, however, an enormous effort made by educators, party functionaries, and literary critics to revamp the interpretation of the tales in accordance with Nazi ideology and to use these interpretations in socializing children. In addition, there were numerous articles and debates about fairy-tale films for children in the official party journal, *Film und*

Bild.[9] Josef Prestel's remarks about the Nordic qualities of the classical fairy tale can give us an idea about the general tendencies of the fascist reinterpretation of the tales and how they were put to use:

> In heroic racist sense, new light is also shed on the role of the king's daughter in the fairy tale. She is the highest reward for the hero. Whoever risks his life will be rewarded in life. Whom does the king's daughter choose? The fearless one, the good-hearted, the loyal one, even if he is a herdsman or hunter. He brings with him the best qualities "from the folk." He enters the circle of the courtiers victoriously. The powerful qualities from the folk unite with the bearer of a noble race: the king's daughter as the reward of the hero is the symbol for the improvement of the species, of the high racist idea, of the perpetuation of the race, "and so they are still living today." . . . The fairy tale provides in palpable images the reflection of the moral world radiated by the certainty of salvation associated with the child's optimism. Yes, it is made specifically to exhibit the virtues of the folk: loyalty, steadfastness, perseverance, fearless courage in the case of male heroes, a sense of sacrifice, humble dedication and sympathy in the case of female heroes.[10]

Aside from obvious anti-Semitic explications of such tales as "The Jew in the Thorn" or the association of thievery and cheating with Jews, most of the National Socialist interpretations stressed the struggle between two worlds: the pure Aryan world versus the contaminated alien world. Thus, G. Grenz could interpret "Cinderella" in the following way:

> And so these worlds fight against each other, and it appears that deceit and falsehood triumph. But nature does not let itself be cheated and deceived. It opens itself up to the pure person and the devoted. It reveals its help to him! It fuses the suitable specimens of a species together, and in this way it perfects the natural laws with relentless logical consistency. And the prince finds the genuine, worthy bride because his unspoiled instinct leads him, because the voice of his blood tells him that she is the right one.[11]

If the classical fairy tale was used throughout the fascist period to give children a sense of their Nordic heritage and race and to provide them with notions of feudal community and heroic roles with which they were to identify, the tales also allowed children and young people to escape. That is, the books were not always read in the presence of Party teachers and functionaries, and since many tales were not dressed with explicit political symbols or rewritten to preach the glories of the Third Reich, they could be used by children and adults to compensate for the political bombardment in their daily life. According to one historian of children's literature, the fairy tales became more and more popular toward the end of World War II because they were a kind of refuge from the bitter reality of the war and ideological warfare.[12] Still, the dominant social function of the classical fairy tale tended to further the illusion that the Nazis were recreating a folk community in keeping with the unfulfilled needs of the German people, who, under the leadership of Hitler, could now rise up, struggle, and reclaim their worthy position in the world.

As we have seen, there was hardly any change in the production of the classical fairy tales in the Weimar and Nazi periods, but there were definite changes in the strategic employment and interpretation of the tales in the public sphere. With regard to the literary fairy tale for adults, the changes during these two periods were much greater. The literary fairy tale as a variation of the folktale had developed a long tradition of commenting and reflecting on social reality in a critical fashion through the play on and ingenious use of symbols, motifs, and plots. From the eighteenth century to the Weimar period, German fairy-tale writers had become famous if not notorious for their subversive skills. Depending on the particular author's political and philosophical viewpoint, the fairy tale was put to use as a socially symbolic act in a variety of ways. Therefore, it is perfectly logical that Hartmut Geerken in his collection of expressionist fairy tales *Die goldene Bombe*[13] set up the following categories to describe early twentieth-century experimentation with the tale: (1) God is dead—the human being in the cosmos; (2) magic—black humor; (3) knight's moves—satires—grotesque; (4) astral aspects; (5) the Satanic in the double bed; (6) social political; (7) the old tale; and (8) Dada. His work brings together the tales of such different writers as Hans Arp, Hugo Ball, Bertolt Brecht, Theodor Däubler, Albert Ehrenstein, Hans von Flesch-Brunningen, Oskar Maria Graf, Victor Hadwiger, Franz Held, Georg Heym, Jacob von Hoddis, Franz Kafka, Klabund, Fritz Lamp, Kurd Lasswitz, Gustav Meyrink, Carlo Mierendorff, Alfred Mombert, Mynona, Oskar Panizza, Hans Reimann, Paul Scheebart, Hans Schiebhelbuth, Kurt Schwitters, Reinhard Johannes Sorge, and Otto Stoessl. A good many of these names are practically unknown today, yet these writers were well known in their own day and represented an important avant-garde tradition in the arts that reflected great social changes at the beginning of the twentieth century. The collection of the tales dating from 1900 to 1930 reveals a continuity with the way the romantics used the fairy tales to project their dissatisfaction with the existing state of things in a highly complex symbolical mode. In commenting on the general tendency of the expressionist fairy tale, Christoph Eykmann states,

> The fairy tale in its veiled form often has the capacity to make what is meant more effective than the direct polemical assertion. One could almost expect that the typical expressionist could conceive his utopian ideal image of a

more pure world better in the fairy tale than in any other literary form. But—just as in the non-fairy-tale literature of expressionism—the emphasis is placed almost exclusively on the aspect of criticism of the existing state of things and not on the anticipatory conception of the way things should be. To be sure, the goal in Scheebart's fairy tales is a better human world. However, it is thwarted by the forces of nature. In Hadwiger's tale, the representative of this better world, the giant, becomes the victim of a base reality. In Ehrenstein's tale "The Guilt," humanity destroys itself. The way out of the stagnate social world succeeds only through death.[14]

As Eykmann admits, this overwhelming pessimism is not dominant in most of the fairy tales but connected to the essential quality of the fairy tales written during the Weimar period. Unlike the romantics, who conceived new utopian worlds out of the breakdown of a social order reflected in their tales, fairy-tale writers for adults between 1919 and 1933 did not or could not posit utopian solutions. They developed another characteristic feature that evolved from the romantic fairy tale during the transition from feudalism to capitalism, namely, the ambivalence of protagonists caught between changing social orders, desirous of creating new structures, but torn between the old and the new. If we consider some of the other disparate fairy-tale products of the Weimar period not collected by Geerken, then the open-endedness of the tales mirroring disturbed relations and ambivalence appears to be the central feature of the works. Hesse's "Strange News from Another Planet," "The Poet," and other fairy tales printed in 1919 project a longing for harmony and peace that was barely obtainable at that time in society, neither for his heroes nor for his readers. Thomas Mann's monumental *Magic Mountain* (1924), cast totally in the mold of the romantic fairy tale, depicts a floundering hero wallowing in mud at the end of his ironic narrative. Ödön von Horváth's *Sportmärchen* (*Sport Fairy Tales*, 1924) and his other tales written at this time show the shallowness of petit bourgeois life and the uselessness of inherited traditions: his characters become caricatures of themselves, imprisoned by their own banal forms of speaking and thinking. Oskar Maria Graf sets the scenes of his fairy tales in *Licht und Schatten* (*Light and Shadow*, 1927) as though they were fragmented communities that must be pieced together again by people who have been ripped apart themselves. In two fairy tales composed in 1929, Bertolt Brecht touches on the lack of communication in worlds turned topsy-turvy. Even in the more conservative writings of Hermann Stehr and Hans Friedrich Blunck during the 1920s there is an implicit quest for community, for the restoration of a world with virtue that will refurbish humanity on the verge of despair.

Though the artistic structures and contents of the fairy tales varied, there were two givens that were generally operative in Weimar writing: the old folktale and classical fairy-tale forms were useful only insofar as they provided models of anachronism that had to be superseded in configurations closely related to Weimar social reality; and the configurations and protagonists had nothing to do with an idyllic folk community of the past but symbolized the breakdown of human relations in the capitalist world and thus revealed the negative trends of mechanization, automatization, and commodity fetishism. Given the fascist optimism and doctrinaire stress on a new world order, it is quite apparent why the new literary fairy tale of Weimar did not and could not thrive in Nazi Germany.

Most of the progressive fairy-tale writers fled Nazi Germany, and if they continued to produce fairy tales at all, then they were not distributed and circulated in the fatherland. Whatever tales were allowed to circulate, such as those of Blunck, Stehr, Hesse, and Wilhelm Matthiessen, did not contradict the folk ideology of the National Socialists but could be used to further the Nazi orientation toward purity, loyalty, maternal sacrifice, and male courage. Thus, the critical tradition of the romantic fairy tale was deprived of a public and made to appear nefarious. Christa Kamenetsky points to a speech on "The Romantic Fairy Tale," prepared by Dr. Albert Krebs in the early 1930s, as an example of how the Nazis opposed the literary fairy tale:

> Krebs was the author of various school readers and anthologies, and his books were recommended by the editors of the educational journal Die Volksschule, issued by the National Socialist Teachers' Association. In line with recent trends, he called attention to the "healthy and organic" world view of the folktale, contrasting it sharply with the "artificial and decadent view" of the literary fairy tale. The literary fairy tale, as an expression of the early Romantic writers, was the product of a baroque and distorted perception of reality, he said, and it should be kept off the children's book shelves.[15]

Not only were the romantic fairy tales to be banned from children but they also were reevaluated for adults and declared inferior to the classical tales. As a result of the folk ideology and the disregard of the literary fairy tale, considered alien to folk culture, few fairy tales of any consequence were produced by profascist writers, and few German writers dared to use the literary genre to express their dissatisfaction with the existing state of things. Gerhart Hauptmann wrote his highly esoteric "Das Märchen," imitative of Goethe's tale, in 1939, which contained a political statement of discontent. Ernst Wiechert wrote fairy tales toward the end of the war with a gun under a nearby pillow. These tales, which had antifascist features, were published only after the Nazi world order had collapsed. Fortunately, this collapse allowed German writers gradually to resume their experimentation with the literary fairy tale, and, to a certain degree, Hoernle's hope for a flowering of radically new fairy tales with modern paraphernalia and socialist ideas was given a second chance, but this post-war development, too, is faced with a dominant fairy-tale discourse that looks at radical utopianism askance.

II

Given the fact that classical fairy tales were the most widespread stories known to children and adults in Weimar and Nazi Germany and used extensively in the socialization process, it is important that we consider the patterns and normative roles portrayed in these tales and analyze their possible ideological implications. The results may help us understand more about the social and cultural tendencies in these two periods of German history and their effect on the fairy-tale discourse in general. Since classical fairy tales were not written during this period but used in a particular political way to educate both children and adults, it is necessary to compare and contrast their function as exemplary cultural products with the literary fairy-tale experiments, which were, if anything, provocative and disquieting. Here the new and innovative forms may reveal what changes in the civilizing process were under way and may still be under way in our time. As usual, we shall see that the issues of power and domination are crucial for the interpretation and reception of fairy tales as they pertain to the family and socialization.

In his essay "Familie und Natur im Märchen" ("Family and Nature in the Fairy Tale"), Max Lüthi asserts that the family plays a predominant role in the magic folktale (Zaubermärchen).[16] It is not the extended family (Grossfamilie), as is commonly believed, but the small or nuclear family (Kleinfamilie) that is central to the fairy tale. According to Lüthi, the concentration on the small family provides the simple and comprehensible framework of the tale. Within this structure it is not harmony that characterizes familial relations but rather tension, argument, and conflict. Lüthi makes the following major points:

1. The child is often endangered by parents who want to give the child away or who are compelled to do this by evil stepmothers, brothers, and sisters, who are jealous of the child or by a hunter or servant who is commanded to kill the child.

2. Most fairy tales do not concern children but the young individual who generally breaks with the family and leaves home at the outset of the tale. The major theme concerns the maturation of the individual. This maturation is not fostered by the family and social milieu. The young person must rely on nature and his or her own gifts to discover happiness.

3. Marriage is the goal in most fairy tales, but it is not the subject matter. Like the royal realm it is symbolic. Both male and female protagonists strive for this goal, and often the family itself causes difficulties.

4. The antagonists in the fairy tale are more often humans and members of one's own family than animals.

In sum, the danger in the intimate circle and the safety in nature and the universe are special forms of interdependence and isolation in which the basic pattern of the fairy tale's image of humankind can be seen. And the intensification of familial tensions to the point of death is not to be interpreted merely from the psychological and anthropological side. Such intensification is characteristic of the entire style of the fairy tale, which seeks to move to extremes all over in the portrayal of beauty and reward as well as in the portrayal of crime and punishment. In addition, the readiness for sacrifice, the capacity to suffer, and the perseverance of the sister who saves her brothers and of the wife who seeks the husband are intensified and become unreal (and are at the same time transposed so that they become visible). Here, too, there are strong tensions and exertion, but of a positive kind. The power of love in familial relations is not completely concealed in the fairy tale. It also appears in great intensity. And, when reality is dark, possibility remains light, and the royal marriage radiates as goal.[17]

Lüthi's hypotheses are helpful but also misleading if we are to comprehend the overall meaning of the depiction of the family in the classical fairy tale. Before I deal with Lüthi's findings in detail, I would like to consider Eleasar Meletinsky's remarks about marriage in the classical fairy tale.

One of the forms with a social function was the marital "exchange," and the result was the social consolidation of the tribes. It was with this that the exchange of all values began. In this way the "marital exchange" originates in myth. In the fairy tale, where the matter no longer concerns the welfare of the tribe but rather individual happiness, the marital "exchange" removes itself more and more from its "communicative function" and assumes a new meaning. Indeed, for the individual it means a particular "miraculous" escape from exposed social conflicts which are embodied by forms of daily relations in the fairy tale. (It must be noted that the family in the fairy tale is to a great degree an extended family [Grossfamilie], that is, it typifies the patriarchal community of the semi-gentile type.) . . . The basic contradictions (the types of life-death, etc.) accede to lively social conflicts which are generally revealed in the family sphere. The mediation is expressed in the way the hero flees the conflict and moves to a higher social status. This change of social status originates as a result of marriage with the king's son, the merchant, or the king's daughter, depending on who the protagonist is. Thus, in the fairy tale the "marriage" becomes the means of mediation for a person to emancipate him or herself from basic social relations.[18]

Meletinsky, who combines Claude Lévi-Strauss's findings with his own research, contradicts Lüthi in regard to two significant points. First, he correctly associates the family in classical fairy tales with the patriarchal extended family. Second, he indicates how marriage is not simply the goal of most fairy tales but, as *mediation*, the way all characters relate to one another and, as such, marriage determines the normative actions of the protagonists and plots. Moreover, Meletinsky's anthropological method points to a more substantial approach toward comprehending the significance of family and familial relations in fairy tales than does Lüthi's literary descriptive method. The role of the family in the classical fairy tale cannot be evaluated merely by noting the characters, motifs, and ontological dilemmas. Rather we must analyze the configurations and constellations formed through the interaction of characters representing familial types who stress certain values and world-views. In the specific case of the classical fairy tale, we must try to grasp the sociogenetic references of the family conflicts and patterns in relation to the ideology and social function maintained by the family in the tale.

Neither Lüthi nor Meletinsky is concerned with the reception of the classical fairy tale in a specific historical epoch, and neither one operates with a clearly defined notion of family and socialization. Thus, their studies are limited in that they explain what occurs among family members without exploring the underlying sociohistorical origins and implications of the tales. They also remain within the general discipline of folklore and regard the *Zaubermärchen* as a folktale. In our present study we must go beyond their work if we are to learn how fairy tales with their images of family and ideology of competition and domination functioned in the socialization process of Weimar and Nazi Germany.

As we know, the *Zaubermärchen* studied by Lüthi and Meletinsky had already become classical literary fairy tales as a result of the work of the Grimms and their disciples in the nineteenth century. The original primitive and feudal components were reworked and adapted to the bourgeois value system that was in ascendance at this time. In sum, the classical fairy tale as recorded by the Grimms and later by other researchers and also adapted by writers like Bechstein contained a mixture of elements from pre-Christian periods, feudalism, and early capitalism, but the terms of the language and normative patterns as selected, recorded, altered, and published were heavily influenced by the bourgeois civilizing process. What then does this mean when we talk about the family and socialization in classical fairy tales, particularly of the Grimms' vintage?

Here I want to operate with certain assumptions developed by Mark Poster in *Critical Theory of the Family*.[19] Poster's study is significant in that he endeavors to define the family not according to size but with regard to issues connected to emotional patterns. For him, the family has a function within the socialization process, but, as an institution, it is primarily the social location where psychic structure is most decisively prominent.

> The family is here conceptualized as an emotional structure, with relative autonomy, which constitutes hierarchies of age and sex in psychological forms. The family is conceived as a system of love objects. Child-rearing patterns are theorized as interactional processes, focusing on the first three stages of development (oral, anal and genital). In these interactions, a pattern of authority and love is instituted by the adults forming a background to the strategies for raising children. Finally, a pattern of identification can be discerned which cements the bonds between adults and children. When these categories are studied in detail, a concrete family structure becomes intelligible.[20]

Poster also adds, "While the family generates a psychological pattern of internalized age and sex hierarchies, it also participates in larger social institutions. The types of this participation must be made intelligible."[21]

If we bear in mind Poster's ideas, particularly those concerning emotional patterns and interactional processes, we get a more differentiated picture of the family in the classical fairy tale than the one suggested by Lüthi and Meletinsky. To demonstrate what this image or picture might signify, I want to take the fourteen most popular fairy tales for children in Germany listed by Charlotte Bühler in 1919[22] to examine interaction, familial relations, and bonds and their ideological meanings as they pertain to domination and competition. The tales in question are "Little Red Riding Hood," "The Wolf and the Seven Kids," "Sleeping Beauty," "Hansel and Gretel," "Snow White," "Mother Holle," "Cinderella," "Brother and Sister," "The Goose Maid," "The Frog Prince," "The Master Thief," "King Thrushbeard," "Jorinde and Joringel," and "The King of the Golden Mountain." At times I shall refer to other Grimms' tales with the assumption that they were also widely known. Significant is that the basic type of the popular Grimms' fairy tale was the *Zaubermärchen* and not the *Schwankmärchen* (anecdotal tale), which tended to be more socially critical. In other words, social reception tended to be conservative.

The milieu of the fairy tales reflects feudal agrarian conditions, and the characters are either of the nobility, peasantry, or third estate (*burgher*). In other words three social types of families are depicted with distinctions made according to power, money, and sex. Though all family members are rarely present, each household gives indication that it is large. We must remember that servants and close relatives belonged to the extended family. Even the animals (such as the goat) have seven children or more, and most of the tales work with three, seven, or twelve children and suggest that it is a sin to be without children. In other words, fertility and large families are esteemed in the fairy tale. At the head of the extended family is an authoritarian male, who makes most of the decisions ("Sleeping Beauty," "The Frog Prince," "King Thrushbeard," and "King of the Golden Mountain"). If the mother, queen, or fairy godmother appears in a more active role than the male, she still acts in favor of a patriarchal society. Whether she be good or evil, her actions lead a young woman to seek salvation in marriage with a prince ("Cinderella," "The Goose Maid," and "Snow White"). To prove her worth, the young girl must display through her actions such qualities as modesty, industriousness, humility, honesty, diligence, and virginity. Moreover, she must be self-effacing and self-denying. The young man is generally more active and must demonstrate such characteristics as strength, courage, wisdom, loyalty, and, at times, a killing instinct ("King of the Golden Mountain"). In all the social classes, the young male and female protagonists may have conflicts with their original family, but they do not reject the institution of the patriarchal family. They move away from their family, interact with outsiders to show their value, an exchange value, so that they can be considered worthy to contract a marriage or to be accepted in a new community and gain individual happiness. In the process, though one may move away from a conflict-ridden family and move up in social class, the basic hierarchical order (father as supreme followed by mother, male children, and female children) of the patriarchical family is not altered but rather reaffirmed. The "dream" of the lower-class character or oppressed person is fulfilled not through the creation of a new social order and family relations but through living up to the expectations of defined roles and gaining recognition both inside and outside the original family.

To marry and become queen and king of a realm has many sociopsychological implications that would take too long to explore at this point. However, one thing is certain: the family is constituted through marriage by a strong male head, the decision maker, whose absolute power and wisdom provide the framework within which one behaves and relates in the family and community. The male as savior is dominant and protects the virtues of the humble if not humiliated female ("King Thrushbeard"), and together they bring about the restoration of traditional family patterns, emotional bonding and interaction, in keeping with social values and patterns of identification that can be associated with those of the rising bourgeoisie. Though it is clear that the classical fairy tale is stamped by feudalism, the narrative perspective of the Grimms' "magic" fairy tales fuses a peasant worldview with the democratic-humanitarianism of the rising bourgeoisie. Thus, the treatment of family members is often differentiated by class, money, and power, but the overriding emotional pattern that emerges from the various depictions of family interaction centers on principles of moral restriction, sexual repression, and abstention set by male figures, who reward the accumulation of the proper bourgeois values with a good solid marriage or place in a secure social order. The bourgeois values are often mixed with the aristocratic ideology of might makes right, but, for the most part, justice is based on the judicious use of power by paternal leaders who know what is best for the wives and children. In some tales, especially those concerned with royalty, the notion of the family implies a kingdom as institution. Here the family takes second place to the realm, which designates what is to be valued and to assume priority in the civilizing process. It is important to have a strong leader of the realm who sets a model for the rest of society. The image of the family is closely related to the social order, as reflected in the behavior of the king and queen. Here we see again a blend of feudal absolutism and bourgeois qualities that were accepted and cultivated by the Grimms in their reworking of the folktale into the classical fairy tale. There is a pervasive sense of enlightened aristocracy in most fairy tales forging familial roles and patterns of behavior among the peasantry, bourgeoisie, and nobility that reveal that the magic and enchantment of the tales have a limited utopian function: they transform the situation of the protagonists into an improved situation so they can become parents and masters of institutions that are essentially not of their own making. The emotional patterns, roles, relations, attitudes, and goals of the exemplary family in the magic fairy tale of the Grimms resembled those that actually came to be upheld by the dominant bourgeois family type in the Weimar Republic and Third Reich. Thus, the grounds for the reception of the classical fairy tales for children were favorable in both epochs, even though different aspects and ideological components may have been stressed.

In dealing with the reception of the tales in these two epochs, there is a danger in assuming that they were always used in an ideological manner to persuade children to conform to the dominant standards in the particular socialization process or that they had (or can have) a definite sociopsychological effect on children. There is no doubt that they were and still are highly instrumental in the socialization process in Germany. Yet the fact is that it is virtually impossible to determine the specific individual meaning a fairy tale may have for a child and extremely difficult to gauge the overall meaning in a given epoch. Only by studying the general discourse on fairy tales, the fairy-tale discourse, and the mode by which fairy tales were put to use by adults can we draw some valid conclusions about their possible effect on manners, taste, and social views. In the case of the Weimar Republic we know that there were various types of families (peasant, proletarian, petit bourgeois, bourgeois, and aristocratic) and that the reception varied from class to class. Generally speaking, the actual use through picture books, radios, schools, advertisements, coupon stamps in cereal boxes and cigarette packages, plays, films, and instruction in schools stressed *Kindertümlichkeit* (childishness), the moral illusion of a *heile Welt* (harmonious world), nationalism, and such values as diligence, industry, obedience, thrift, and purity. Since the tendency had become greater in the dominant bourgeois practice of child rearing to give more care to the child and to stress orderliness and propriety, it was felt that the tales provided normative patterns for a healthy maturation of the mind and imagination and that they reinforced belief in solid *Germanic* qualities. Certainly, the roles of the female and male patterns of interaction in the tales that allowed for authoritarianism corresponded to forms of behavior that children were expected to accept in the family and society. That is, the paradigmatic structure of familial relations in the classical fairy tales did not contradict the standard bourgeois family model or policies of upbringing that were current in the Weimar Republic.

In the Nazi epoch these fairy tales assumed an even greater importance, especially those of the Grimms, which were included as part of the Nordic cultural heritage. Depending on the element to be stressed, the feudal world picture could be and was used to substantiate Nazi ideology. In regard to the family, the elements of fertility, the assertive courageous prince, the virtuous self-sacrificing mother, and industrious children could be viewed as the qualities that went into the making of an ideal Germanic family. Actually, if we look closely at the Nazi interpretations and use, we can see that they fit a policy that actually undermined solidarity within the family. As Ingeborg Weber-Kellermann pointed out,[23] the family was not to play a major role in the socialization process but considered primarily functional for production and reproduction in an economic–biological sense. Although the emotional patterns of interaction in the tales were accepted, the Nazi interpretations stressed elements that suited their policies; that is, community and race over family, the king and realm over all. All heroic qualities and actions were associated with the necessity to purify the world and establish a new Reich, whereby leadership and authority were associated with the *Führer*. The submissive role of the woman, who must sacrifice herself for the good of the king or kingdom, coincided with the shifting Nazi policy that encouraged women to remain at home, raise large families, and create a household that functioned harmoniously for the good of the Reich. When women were obliged to work in factories, plants, and offices later in the 1930s, the element of sacrifice in the fairy tale was appropriately slanted to rationalize new policies.[24]

One feature of the classical fairy tale that appealed to children and adults in Weimar and Nazi Germany was the restoration of fixed roles in a stable family blessed with good fortune. Despite the major differences in the ideology of these two periods, Weimar and Nazi leaders favored monogamy, large families, paternal domination, deference to authority figures, and family adherence to state policies. The classical fairy tale creates the illusion in its configuration that, despite conflicts among family members, the traditional family and its emotional patterns (the mildew) can be restored. The tale appears to move forward while clinging desperately to the past. That is, the traditional social order and family are viewed as goals once the friction has been resolved. The appeal and use of the fairy tale in both the Weimar and the Nazi epochs had a great deal to do with Ernst Bloch's notion of *Ungleichzeitigkeit* (nonsynchronism) and *Heimat* (home).[25] In both historical periods the classical fairy tale kept alive those unfulfilled wishes and needs of the lower strata of society and offered compensation to all classes of people who felt bypassed by swift technological progress and socioeconomic changes that uprooted them psychologically so that they were actually unable to move with the times. Moreover, they could not articulate their dissatisfaction and maladjustment concretely. They were swept off their feet, and they looked around with anxiety for footing. Thus, there was a longing for the good old times, for the stability and order of what was projected to be a more idyllic period. To this extent, the classical fairy tale with its traditional image of the family and marriage and its promise of *Heimat* was used as a stabilizing factor in the socialization process of both the Weimar and the Nazi periods in Germany.

This general tendency is also the reason why the literary fairy-tale experiments for children and adults must be taken into consideration and compared with the classical fairy tale and its use in these periods. They represent symbolic attempts to intervene in the civilizing process perceived to be destructive, to reflect artistically about competition and domination in the family and society, and to project possible alternatives to the existing state of affairs. Let us look at some of the remarkable literary fairy tales first for children, then for adults, in both the Weimar and the Nazi periods. The fact that they are barely known today is all the more reason why we should try to reconstruct their discourse.

III

In the Weimar period, the works of Bruno Schönlank, Hermynia Zur Mühlen, and Lisa Tetzner are significant.[26] Though there were differences among them, they all shared a common starting point: they wanted to depict actual social conditions as experienced by a working-class child largely in urban environments under the influence of modern technology, and they indicated that the poor conditions within the family could not be transformed unless major social changes were made. The narrative point of view is that of the oppressed. The magic and fairy-tale motifs are employed to expose (not disguise) the source of domination and real social contradictions.

Bruno Schönlank's fairy tales in *Grossstadt-Märchen* (*Big City Fairy Tales*, 1923) tend at times to be sentimental and idealistic. Nevertheless, he does manage to probe the underlying reasons for tension and friction in the family and society. In "Die geflickte Hose" ("The Patched Pants") an old widow does housework for rich people and can barely feed and clothe four sons. The youngest son Franz wears only hand-me-downs from his older brothers. Since his clothes are always patched, the other children make fun of him. One day Franz and his brothers meet an old junk dealer with two parrots. They are invited into his store where all the used garments, articles, and junk tell the boys stories about their previous owners and how hard life is. The junk dealer reveals that he was once rich and had refused to help a poor man when he wanted to sell an old picture. Because the rich man called the picture junk, the poor man sentenced him to learn the real meaning of junk. This was how the rich man became transformed into the junk dealer and his two spoiled daughters turned into parrots. In the years that followed the junk dealer tells how he discovered that sorrow, love, and joy went into the making of junk and how he came to regard used items as more valuable than jewels. After hearing this story, Franz learns to value his patched pants as the product of love, and, when he is asked to give them up to the parrots, he hesitates but then does this out of sympathy for them. This act of consideration leads to their retransformation into two beautiful girls, and the father becomes strong once again. They all head for Franz's home, where the junk dealer tells the mother that they want to live with her and make each other's burden lighter. In "Das Märchen vom Lokomotivenpfiff" ("The Fairy Tale about the Whistle of the Locomotive") the same motif of solidarity is introduced by an organ grinder man who brings the people together and gives them the feeling that they can transform themselves and the city when they are united and work and play together. This is also true of "Die bunte Stadt" ("The Colorful City"), in which an entire city is pictured as gray and the people are gloomy, with the exception of a cheerful young man apprenticed to a painter. One day, after he helps a poor old woman, he is given a magic pot containing a female painter who enables him to paint anything and everything with a wide variety of colors. So he paints the city in a colorful way, and the people begin to change their demeanor. The young man marries the female painter, and the city continues to benefit from their work. In all of Schönlank's tales the inter-action of family members among the poor is changed from domination to cooperation. Poverty and oppression are overcome only through collective action or by using one's talents and imagination for the benefit of the commu-nity. The roles of men and women are not set according to traditional patterns. The emphasis in all relations is placed on change and the possibility to effect emotional patterns so that they convey a sense of justice. The typical conserv-ative happy ending gives way to an optimistic belief in the necessity and goodness of social change.

The theme of social transformation is also stressed in most of Hermynia Zur Mühlen's innovative tales, which incidentally were translated into English as *Fairy Tales for Workers' Children* and published by the Daily Worker Publishing

Company in 1925. In "Der Spatz" ("The Sparrow") a young sparrow leaves his petit bourgeois home because he finds it too pretentious and stifling. His parents want him to admire the richer more noble birds and become like them. However—and here Zur Mühlen writes against Andersen and his "Ugly Duckling"—the young sparrow wants to show his parents and other sparrows that even the smallest birds can fly to other countries like the larger birds do and live and work under more favorable conditions. He leaves home, and through his courage, determination, and intelligence, he manages to travel thousands of miles to the south. Along the way he learns how the world is divided into the poor and the rich, oppressed and oppressors, and he wants to return and impart his knowledge to his brothers and sisters so they can free themselves from their narrow confines. However, the sparrow dies under way, and his message must be carried by a young boy, who will apparently continue his struggle.

The death of an animal who dedicates his life to the emancipation of oppressed people is also central to "Der graue Hund" ("The Gray Dog"), in which a dog dies to save the life of a young black slave in America who escapes to the North. Zur Mühlen places the motif of sacrifice in a different context from the classical fairy tale, where wives and children are generally portrayed as self-sacrificial so they can win the love of a male. Here the sacrifice is for a group of dominated people who want to do away with exploitation. Implicit is a change of traditional family relations of domination. Hence, the sparrow leaves the petit bourgeois home, and the slave and dog run away from the feudalistic plantation.

In other tales, such as "Die Brillen" ("The Glasses"), "Die Rote Fahne" ("The Red Flag"), and "Wie Said der Träumer zu Said dem Verräter wurde" ("How Said the Dreamer Became Said the Traitor"), Zur Mühlen was concerned with demonstrating how exploitation, domination, and injustice arise from the accumulation of property and wealth and how social conditions can be altered. Unlike the classical fairy tales, her tales do not portray marriage and the reestablishment of royal realms at the end. Rather she stressed permanent struggle and change. Illusions were avoided in her fairy tales to illuminate the hope for a better world. The virtues (often the same stressed by the bourgeoisie) were shaped to endorse qualitatively different emotional patterns and nonalienating social relations. Consequently, the function of the family underwent a change. Young people were depicted in her tales as moving out beyond the narrow confines of the enclosed private family and considering all people as members of one large family where collective support and struggle against oppression are regarded as the means to bring about more humane and satisfying living conditions.

The movement toward uniting in one family with all races and creatures of the world is depicted in the extraordinary fairy-tale novel *Hans Urian: The Story* of a Trip around the World (1931) by Lisa Tetzner. Similar to the structure of Brecht's play Man Is Man, in which Galy Gay goes out to buy some fish at a market and winds up learning how men are made into monsters, this fairy tale shows how Hans, a poor nine-year-old, goes out to earn bread for his starving family and then is compelled to take a trip around the world to learn under what oppressive conditions people must work to obtain bread. Once he learns from the baker that he cannot have bread without money, no matter how hungry his family is, he meets the rabbit Trillewipp, who is also looking for food to nourish his mother and family. They join forces, and, because they learn that there is money and bread to be had in America, they decide to fly there. (Trillewipp's long ears are like propellers, and he has the magic power of flying.) On the way they befriend the Eskimo Kagsgsuk, and in the States they meet Bill, whose rich father produces cannons for war efforts. Everywhere they go in the States, the children learn that people want to take advantage of them and the rabbit and exploit them without giving them money for their labor. In Africa and later in China, the children and Trillewipp are captured and treated like slaves. Finally, to save themselves, the children form a circus troupe, place Trillewipp in a cage, and pretend to be cruel to him like other human beings would be. After wandering through China and Mongolia, they make their way to Russia, where, for the first time, they are treated humanely and placed in an orphanage with other children while Trillewipp is set free. The children learn to work with other young people and determine their needs and wants. After some time, Hans and Trillewipp fly home, and Trillewipp suggests that Hans become a rabbit and live with his family because rabbits treat each other in a more humane way than humans treat each other. However, Hans refuses, arguing that he wants to improve conditions at home and help make humans more humane. Yet he encounters difficulties when he arrives. The police and his teacher want to exclude him from the community and school, whereas his mother and children from the neighborhood welcome him. After hearing his story, the children unite and insist that the school take him back because he had not broken any laws: he merely went on a long errand to bring some bread to his mother.

Written in 1928–29 and published in 1931, Tetzner's book has a curious history. It was banned by the Nazis in 1933, and, when republished in West Germany after World War II, it was banned again in 1948 by the American occupation forces because it defamed the United States. Viewed historically, it is clear that Tetzner used the Soviet Union as a model society in which children are respected, protected, and encouraged to work together so they can design their own destinies. At the time she wrote her fairy tale, such a model corresponded more to reality than it does today, though America has certainly not lost its symbolic value as a capitalist jungle. In general her symbolic act was geared to transforming Russia into a utopian construct for German children, and the configurations of the tale map out a strategy for the conception of utopia: the solidarity and trust developed between Hans the German, Kagsgsuk the Eskimo, Bill the American, and Trillewipp the rabbit, from different classes and races, represent emotional bonds of normative interaction on which future familial and social relations could be based. Again, as in the tales of Schönlank and Zur Mühlen, the family is poor and suffers because social relations are based on money, power, and exploitation. The lower-class family, as it is, must be changed and can be changed only if external social conditions are improved. The notion of family as the nucleus of society is extended in the narrative discourse along class lines of solidarity to include all oppressed people. Consequently, the value of an individual is based not on exchange value, dependent on the material wealth and power of the family, but on the use of talents to bring about equality and cooperation. The family remains to be defined; that is, redefined. The ending is open. One does not live happily ever after. The ending means struggle and insight into possible new relations.

The few examples we have of new literary fairy tales in Nazi Germany point in another direction. For instance, the volume *Geschichten aus der Murkelei* (*Stories from Murkelei*, 1937) by Hans Fallada contains tales that stress themes that recall the cruel German classic *Struwwelpeter*. Almost all the stories deal with children who are naughty or veer from the moral and ethical standards of the times. They are either punished brutally or tormented until they learn how to conform. In the very first tale, "Geschichte von der kleinen Geschichte" ("Story about the Little Story"), a child who does not want to eat his meal is sent to bed and forbidden to listen to stories by his mother. Even worse is the story of "Nuschelpeter" ("Mumbling Peter"), in which a boy is beaten up by a school comrade so that he learns to pronounce words correctly. Almost all the stories are intended to awake fear in children who might be different, pursue their own interests, or experiment with new forms of relations. In some tales like "Geschichte von Brüderchen" ("Story about the Little Brother") and "Geschichte von Murkelei" ("Story about Murkelei"), emphasis is placed on the biological function of the family as reproduction center and as place where children are socialized to respect laws out of fear. The emotional patterns elaborated in the plots center on fertility and obedience and are based on the domination of male authoritarian figures who exert their power through corporal punishment or withdrawal of love.

Whereas Fallada's tales were not explicit ideological stories and were more in keeping with the traditional bourgeois literature of *Kindertümlichkeit*, Hilde Stansch's *Das Kind im Berge* (*The Child in the Mountain*, 1944) fulfilled all the proper notions of an ideal fascist fairy tale for children. The setting is the idyllic countryside. Unna and her husband, Helge, have been married for some years and have always yearned for children, but their wishes have not been heard. Unna goes to the wise relative Erda, who reveals to her a way to have children. This involves searching for the holy mountain, and, after many adventures, she finds the holy child in the cradle. When she returns to her husband, she gives birth to twelve children in the coming years. The secret of fertility is passed on to her when Erda dies, and from Unna to her oldest daughter upon her death. The wisdom and secret remain in their blood. All the elements for a perfect Aryan fairy tale are here: the woman is mother earth, fertile, humble, wise; the man is strong and productive, portrayed in the fields. The chosen race endures and will endure unto eternity.

Not all the literary tales produced during the Nazi period were as conservative and regressive as those written by Fallada and Stansch. For instance, Paul Alverdes's *Das Männlein Mittentzwei* (*The Mannikin Mittentzwei*, 1937) has certain elements that constitute a critique of the negligent way children treat toys, objects, and other creatures. However, neither Alverdes's tale nor other fairy tales produced explicitly for children such as those by Blunck, Matthiessen, and the writers for *Auerbachs Kinderkalender* during the Nazi epoch introduced new notions of familial interaction or social behavior that suggested a break with racist prejudice, domination, authoritarianism, and false illusions about the hard realities of the Third Reich. If there were innovative experiments in the field of children's literature, then they tended to reinforce the dominant fascist ideology and emotional patterns of authoritarianism. This can be seen clearly in the primers, almanacs, and general fiction produced at that time. The literary fairy tale for children was deemed less suitable for such purposes. Besides, as we know, the classical fairy tale in its traditional format could be used to illustrate correct living in the family and community in accordance with Nazi ideology.

IV

If we now turn to the literary fairy tales produced for adults during the Weimar and Nazi periods, the picture of the family in regard to ideological roles, emotional patterns, and domination is slightly different. In the Weimar period, there was much more variety and open criticism of traditional familial conditions. In the Nazi epoch, literary fairy tales were virtually abolished, and, aside from the publication of works from the eighteenth, nineteenth, and early twentieth centuries, there was relatively little continuity of the work that had blossomed in the 1920s. A brief look at fairy-tale discourse of the 1920s and the familial interactional patterns incorporated in the tales will indicate why.

Hermann Hesse more or less set the tone for the Weimar period when he published his collection of *Märchen* (*Fairy Tales*) in 1919. Not only did they reflect his pacifistic concerns about the war but they were also influenced by his marital problems and ambivalent desire to break away from traditional bourgeois family life. In this regard Hesse harked back to the early romantics, and his work is indicative of how other German writers in the early twentieth century regarded themselves as working within the deep-rooted *Kunstmärchen* tradition. Thus, it would be misleading to argue that his tales initiated an avantgarde experiment with fairy tales in the Weimar Republic or that other German writers were breaking with conventional fairy-tale discourse. If anything, they were expanding and subverting the discourse: Hesse's fairy tales and all the rest produced in the Weimar period are significant because they use the fairytale discourse in a variety of startling imaginative ways to comment on social problems that were affecting the course of the civilizing process.

Hesse published seven fairy tales in 1919: "Augustus," "The Poet," "Strange News from Another Planet," "The Difficult Path," "A Dream Sequence," "Faldrun," and "Iris," and just as his novels all tend to repeat the same message and pattern, so too do these tales. A gifted young man senses that he has a poetic mission and feels confined by his parents or family. He breaks away from home, generally goes through two phases of sensuality and asceticism before he comes into his own; that is, before he reaches peace with himself and is satisfied with his personal development. Significantly, with few exceptions, the hero of Hesse's fairy tales does not remain within his old family or community or build a new society. He remains somewhat of an outsider, though there may be some reconciliation with the family he has spurned.

In "Augustus" the young man who never appreciated the sacrifices his mother made for him returns home after leading a decadent life for many years. There he repents and is mystically reunited with his dead mother through the intercession of his strange but saintly godfather. Still, he is nothing more than a repentant wanderer at the end. In "The Poet," Han Fook abandons his fiancée and family to lead the life of a poet. He returns home only to find everyone dead, and yet he has supposedly realized something more vital by forsaking the traditional way of family life. In "Strange News from Another Planet," Hesse has a young boy learn about the meaning of chaos and killing so that he can become dedicated to harmony and help his neighbors restore their community after an earthquake. This is Hesse's only fairy tale in which there is some sense about the necessity of social cooperation for reconstruction. Generally speaking, Hesse's tales are antisocial and especially antifamily in their description of a pattern of rebellion and self-transcendence. The family is depicted as static, the bastion of conservatism. This is not always done in a negative sense, but family forms are revealed to be outmoded, and if a young man wants to develop, he must leave this confining environment. Though Hesse may have thought of this option as liberating, there is a strong element of self-deception in his tales, for his heroes *escape* into an inner world that owes its validity only to the repressive tolerance of a society that prefers nonintrusive individuals to rebels who will not abide by its conventions in any way and who defy society through social action. Whereas Hesse's heroes reveal a pattern of behavior and action critical of authoritarian behavior and arbitrary male domination, they also make a compromise or peace with the existing state of affairs. The rejection of the traditional patriarchal family is not absolute, and only in the happy soul of the chosen hero is there a suggestion of a real alternative: the male role of guru embodies new mystical and pacifistic norms that might have an exemplary value in contrast to the Western civilizing process.

The importance of Hesse's tales in 1919 is that they signaled the twofold way that other writers would reflect on the family in the 1920s and 1930s: either there was a complete rejection of the commonplace mildew of philistinism and the traditional male authoritarian family that were mocked, parodied, or seriously criticized or there was an attempt to portray how the family could be restored with normative patterns designating strong medieval bonds with Teutonic overtones and true Christian love. Both extremes of the fairy-tale discourse must be viewed in light of the powerful and disparate tendencies among German youth since the beginning of the twentieth century. The *Wandervogel Movement*, an important youth organization, became splintered after World War I so that there were numerous youth groups mobilized *against* the older generation. Nature, purity, and independence became slogans of bourgeois youth groups, while other organizations sought party allegiances with the communists, socialists, or national socialists to articulate their protest. This was the background of the fairy-tale discourse about civilization at that time, and the various voices often spoke about patricide and protest.

For instance, in Geerken's anthology of expressionist fairy tales *Die Goldene Bombe*, the general tendency is to belittle the dominant bourgeois family and its corresponding role patterns. Most of the tales expose either explicitly or implicitly the hypocrisy of "home sweet home." The relations between human beings are portrayed as shallow and objectified because people base their behavior on competition, money, and power. The illusion of a possible restoration of the family and society is smashed in such tales as Hans von Flesch-Brunningen's "Der Metaphysische Kanarienvogel" ("The Metaphysical Canary," 1917) and Salomo Friedländer's "Die Vegetabilische Vaterschaft" ("The Vegatibilian Paternity," 1919). The classical fairy-tale happy ending with a new realm was inverted, for the expressionist writers viewed the family as an institution that cannot function to protect children or provide them with the fortitude and skills to realize their needs and dreams. In the fairy tales of other writers during the Weimar period, such as Ödön von Horváth and Oskar Maria Graf, the picture is just as bleak.

Horváth wrote a series of fairy tales titled *Sportmärchen, Fräulein Pollinger und andere Märchen* (*Sport Fairy Tales, Miss Pollinger, and Other Fairy Tales*) and *Zwei Märchen*

(*Two Fairy Tales*) during the 1920s, and they were closely related to his folk dramas that satirized the banality and lack of communication among lower-class people. In "Das Märchen in unserer Zeit" ("The Fairy Tale in Our Time") a young girl leaves her family to look for the fairy tale. No one can help her until she comes to an old horse who is about to be slaughtered because he is old and no longer useful. The horse remarks that the young girl herself is a fairy tale and that she should tell him a story. After a moment's hesitation she does. Then the horse is carted away. When the young girl returns home and refuses to eat the horse meat that is set on the table, her mother and the rest of the family call her a spoiled princess. She goes without eating and thinks about the horse and is no longer hungry. The lack of understanding that this young girl encounters is heightened in "Das Märchen vom Fräulein Pollinger." Here Horváth tells the story about an average woman with an average figure and an average face who works in the bookkeeping department of an auto-mobile repair shop. To be accepted by the men in the shop and to ride on their motor bikes, she sleeps with them every now and then. After going with one man named Fritz for a year, she becomes pregnant and is abandoned by him to shift for herself. No prince. No marriage. No family. Horváth explodes notions of the idyllic happy family life. Instead the crude and exploitative relations that depend on the commodity value of a person transforms all people into expendable merchandise.

It is the brutal aspect of life and family relations that is also stressed in Graf's collection of fairy tales titled *Licht und Schatten* (*Light and Shadow,* 1927). Like many socialist writers of this period, Graf was interested not in portraying the imminent victory of the communist movement but in showing the extent to which human beings had been made into animals and deprived of a social consciousness. All his tales—and they were directed at young people—depict how barren, savage, and destitute family and social life have become. Even the fatherland must experience this. In a bitter, ironic narrative, "Was das Vaterland einmal erlebte" ("What the Fatherland Experienced One Time"), Graf has the fatherland transform himself into a human being to see who loved him the most. To his chagrin—he visits all social types and classes—he is constantly maltreated, ignored, beaten, and driven to beg. The only person who treats him kindly and with sympathy is a beggar, who tells the fatherland his life history and how he had been accepted in society as long as he could produce and give something. But once he had become old and sick, no one cared about him. Both cry softly before they fall asleep holding hands like brothers. The notion that Germany was one big happy family is totally undermined in this tale and even more so in "Das Märchen vom König" ("Fairy Tale about the King"), in which we have a terrifying picture of a patriarch. Here the king of the realm delights in starting wars and driving people to murder. He becomes so unruly that no one wants to act as his minister and carry out his orders. All the people flee him, and only a cripple is left in the kingdom, and he turns out to be the embodiment of all the fear, need, and injustice that the king had caused. The cripple succeeds miraculously in punishing the tyrant, and peace reigns again in the devastated country.

The dissatisfaction with the brutal and exploitative way in which people appeared to treat each other inside and outside the family during the Weimar period was expressed somewhat differently by more conservative writers of fairy tales such as Hermann Stehr and Hans Friedrich Blunck, two of the more popular authors of this epoch. In 1929 three tales by Stehr were published under the title *Das Märchen vom deutschen Herzen* (*The Fairy Tale about the German Heart*), which posed an alternative to the more critical and sardonic fairy tales of radical and progressive writers. For instance, in his title story about the *German* heart, Stehr tells how God first distinguished human beings from animals by giving them the power of reason. However, this made them rich, content, and competitive. Millions of human beings die through avarice and war so that the human species is threatened with extinction. God becomes worried and decides to provide a balance for the human beings left on earth; namely, to give them more heart. He is particularly drawn to one creature with ash-blond hair. " 'You lovely German man,' he spoke into the blue eyes filled with expectation, 'I shall give you the double flame of heart so that you can serve everyone in the name of heaven and thereby in overcoming yourself you will overcome everyone.' " [27] God, who is continually referred to as the immortal housefather, watches his favorite, the blond German man, carry out his will. The racist implications of this Christian message are also imparted in the fairy tale "Wendelin Heinelt," in which the Aryan family Heinelt is set up as an exemplary unit of blessed people united in the manner by which they help poorer people. According to Stehr's fairy tales, which reek of piety, the earth lacks Christian charity, and certain groups of people are chosen to recover the path to God. Though Stehr speaks out against exploitation and maltreatment of human beings, there are obvious ideological references in the pronouncements he makes about Western civilization, especially in the tale about the German heart. The male role of patriarch parallels that of God, and it is only in following the dictates of both that one will find the divine life. The pattern of hierarchical relations in the traditional family is not altered but restored and reinforced against the decadent forces of modernism.

The restoration of familial relations and fixed roles that corresponded more to an agrarian feudal world than the German urban settings of the 1920s was one of the major themes in the fairy tales written by Hans Friedrich Blunck between 1923 and 1931. [28] Almost all his tales, directed at both adults and children, deal with the positive side of marriage and fertility and hark back with sentimental nostalgia to the folk tradition. The central characters are kings, queens, peasants, merchants, townspeople, dwarfs, nymphs, nixies, or creatures of the woods. The major magical character is Mother Holle, who often assumes the role of enchantress of love.

Typical of Blunck's pervasive ideological attitude toward the family, socialization, and domination (even if it is somewhat extreme) is the tale "Frau Holle and the Schifferfrau" ("Mother Holle and the Seaman's Wife"), which begins as follows: "There was one time that our dear God and Mother Holle came to earth again. The beautiful woman wanted to show how successful she had been in making our country into a garden. And the Lord asked how human beings were getting along with one another and whether His commands had been fulfilled. In particular, He wanted to know whether women were staying at home and whether men were moving about in life, struggling and working for their families."[29] God and Mother Holle encounter the wife of a seaman who is dissatisfied because her husband is always away from home. God transforms husband and wife into a rose garden so that they can enjoy each other under idyllic circumstances. However, when He visits her again, she is not satisfied because her children do not have the opportunity to see much of the world and achieve great things. So God again transforms the woman and her husband so that they can sail about the seas. After some years pass, God comes for a third time, and the woman complains that her children have left her and that the life they lead is too rough. Now God, as well as Mother Holle, is convinced that it would be best for all if He returned things to the way they were at the beginning. "Since then this has been the way with all good people. The women wait at home with their daughters when the men take to the wild sea."[30]

In another tale, "Frau Holle und die Liebenden" ("Mother Holle and the Lovers"), a young poet searches for Mother Holle because all the people on earth have lost their sense of love, and evil times have descended on the world. His fiancée waits patiently for him, and their own pious love and self-sacrifice bring Mother Holle back to earth, where she restores harmony to all God's creatures. In "Feinsmütterchen" ("Fein's Little Mother"), Mother Holle helps a rich councillor's wife become fertile. The woman, however, is ungrateful and disobeys Mother Holle's orders. So the good Mother Holle must punish her until the woman repents. Her reward is her transformation into a flower dedicated to her sons.

Most of Blunck's tales continually stress outworn features of the folktales: the woman is self-sacrificial; the man is courageous and hardworking. If one steers a straight and virtuous path, there is no need to fear the wrath of God or Mother Holle. This is exemplified in "Die Bräutigamseiche" ("The Oak of the Bridegroom"), where magical forces reward a woman's diligence and patience with marriage. Blunck's tales are by no means preachy or overly didactic. However, the light, witty, stale, and nostalgic atmosphere of a pastoral idyll convey a false picture of the changing family relations and socialization in the 1920s in both the agrarian and the urban areas of Germany. Indeed, it was exactly this false image of family life and the projection of fixed hierarchical roles for men and women that the Nazis exploited to undermine the real needs of the masses that might make them more secure and fulfilled. Sweet harmony, prescribed roles, and the divine sanction of supernatural forces that determine the fate of virtuous, hardworking men and women are images created by Blunck in his fairy tales that came out of his own desire in the 1920s to overcome the reified social relations and chaos that threatened to lead Germany to the brink of ruin. Yet like many other writers who sought to recall the solid German folk tradition to point to a solution of social conflict in the 1920s, he helped spread mildew that became more and more poisonous in the hands of the Nazis.

V

It is not by chance that the fairy-tale discourses of Stehr, Blunck, Matthiessen, and other writers with similar viewpoints were published during the Nazi period or is it a coincidence that Blunck became a high Nazi official of culture. In fact, even the tales of Hesse were printed, though they were not particularly promoted by the fascists. What is significant to note is that, in contrast, the lively experimentation with the literary fairy tale that raised critical questions about social problems and stimulated thinking about outmoded roles and norms of the socialization process was forced into exile or banned. It was there that Thomas Theodor Heine, former editor of *Simplicissimus*, published his sardonic collection of tales entitled *Die Märchen* (*The Fairy Tales*) in 1935. The philosopher Max Horkheimer included a couple of fairy tales in his important work *Die Dämmerung* (*Twilight*, 1935) for political purposes. Both Alfred Döblin and Joseph Roth experimented with the genre in the 1930s, while Brecht and Horváth included fairy-tale motifs in their dramas. However, nothing of major significance in the fairy-tale genre was produced in exile nor was there anything of value produced within the fascist fatherland, although there are two symbolic endeavors by Gerhart Hauptmann and Ernst Wiechert worth mentioning.

In 1941 Hauptmann wrote and published "Das Märchen" ("The Fairy Tale") in *Die Neue Rundschau*. As a conscious attempt to vary Goethe's *Das Märchen* for the purpose of commenting on fascism, his tale remains too obtuse to be considered effective. Theophrast, an old wandering pilgrim, crosses a river with two will-o'-the-wisps and arrives in a country where the old continues to live in new forms. He thinks of a lion, and suddenly it is there. He cannot wish it away, and it seems to him that the lion was always with him as part of an awesome love (*Angstliebe*). He also encounters a snake from the Garden of Eden. The pilgrim has no set goal and continues to wander with the beasts until he meets a barefoot man named Johann Operin with whom he has various esoteric, cryptic discussions and strange adventures. The will-o'-the-wisps want to lead the pilgrim to a crematorium where stupidity is burned, but Theophrast refuses because he knows that stupidity has no corpse. It has an immortal life. Thereupon, Theophrast leaves this country marked by its crematorium as a high temple, and he returns safely to his original habitat.

It is almost impossible to analyze this tale because the aesthetic structure is uniquely coded to correspond to Hauptmann's life and times. Although he had welcomed the rise of National Socialism in the early 1930s, Hauptmann had become disenchanted with the Third Reich, and he tended to become morbid in his old age. As a dramatist who had continually used fairy-tale motifs in his early works of the twentieth century to comment on social and political conditions, it is obvious that this was his intent in "Das Märchen," and that fear prevented him from enunciating his critique in easily comprehensible symbols. Yet one aspect is clear in the movement of the pilgrim who rejects a world that obviously reflects some of the more brutal aspects of Nazism. In other words, an initiation into the secrets of Nazism is refused, and the hero remains an outsider questioning a world that depends on a logic of irrationalism to rationalize its destructive tendencies.

Wiechert is much more direct in stating why he wrote his fairy tales, especially because they were published after the demise of the Third Reich: "This book was begun in the last winter of the war as hate and fire burned the earth and hearts. It was written for all the poor children of poor people and for my own heart so that I would not lose my belief in truth and justice, for the world, as it is constructed in the fairy tale, is not the world of miracles and magicians but rather one of great and lasting justice about which children and people of every epoch have dreamed."[31] Actually, Wiechert's fairy tales were written not specifically for children but more for adults, when one considers the complexity in statement and structure. Six of them, what he called his "Contemporary Fairy Tales" ("Zeitmärchen"), "Die Königsmühle" ("The King's Mill"), "Der Vogel 'Niemalsmehr'" ("The Bird 'Nevermore'"), "Die Wölfe" ("The Wolves"), "Sieben Söhne" ("Seven Sons"), "Die Liebste auf der Welt" ("The Dearest in the World"), are of particular interest because they deal with the war, exploitation, violence, and tyranny on a symbolical level. Since the settings of the tales are generally in the distant medieval past, the parallels to fascism can be drawn only if one knows the background of Wiechert's writing. He was not a socialist or radical who sought to portray the possibility of new social relations in the family. His position was that of a Christian moralist, who opposed the crimes of the Nazi period. Thus, his fairy tales carry certain contradictions with them: although they speak out for justice, they also lay the groundwork for further exploitation.

For instance, in "Die Wölfe," a brother and sister demonstrate through their courage that justice can be attained by opposing the tyranny of a king. The sister sacrifices herself to a wolf to save her people from destruction, and the wolf turns out to be an enchanted king, who is freed through her actions. He then leads an army against the tyrant and becomes the rightful ruler of the kingdom. The girl becomes his adopted daughter and will take his place once he dies. The people are to serve and honor her. Harmony and justice are restored in this medieval society, but the hierarchical pattern and social relations are not really altered, so there is an illusion of justice based simply on the moral quality of a single individual.

In "Sieben Söhne," a widow tries to protect her seven sons from being exploited by the king in a senseless war. After six of the sons die, she goes to the king to try to keep the youngest at home. In a direct critique of Nazi policy,[32] she attacks the king for not honoring motherhood. Her bravery, however, does not help save the youngest son. He, too, staunchly goes to his death, and the mother must learn to bear the burden. Implicit throughout the story is a notion of a higher judge, namely, God, who stands above all and who will make all the final decisions. When one's time is up, one must face fate as bravely as one can. Again, though the mother is presented in a dignified way, Wiechert does not suggest that basic role patterns and family socialization be altered. Though his fairy-tale protagonists act from ethical principles and pursue humane goals of mercy and justice, it is actually conceivable that even these tales might have been accepted and published during the Nazi period because there is no transformation of the patterns of domination. Power is to be used more discriminatingly and in the name of the people, and, as we know, Hitler thought of himself as a wise king who wanted to wield power for his people and to prevent sinister forces from invading the fatherland.

Hitler as fairy-tale king. Germany as glorious realm. The aesthetics of politics in the service of mystification. This fascist perversion of the bourgeois public sphere and its dire consequences for the German people conditioned the literary fairy-tale discourse during the 1930s and 1940s. As a whole, the genre was restricted and became antithetical to experimentation. The mildew of classical fairy tales that had been challenged in the 1920s was revived as a staple to legitimize racism, sexism, and authoritarianism clothed in the form of the Teutonic heritage. The atavistic designs of German fascism, however, could not conceal and repress the signs and demands for democracy that had already become so urgent in the 1920s. The Third Reich was doomed to failure from the beginning, and so too were its many cultural institutions that appear gruesomely absurd to us today. Once World War II came to a close, the debate over civilization within the literary fairy-tale discourse began to surface again. Writers recommended experimentation, and they gradually endeavored to show that the classical fairy tale for children had outlived its social purpose. They sought to liberate the form for progressive purposes, and the expansion and subversion of the fairy-tale discourse became increasingly noticeable not only in Germany but throughout the Western world during the 1960s. It is to this development of the literary genre cultivated for children that we shall now turn.

8

THE LIBERATING POTENTIAL OF THE FANTASTIC IN CONTEMPORARY FAIRY TALES FOR CHILDREN

The point is that we have not formed that ancient world—it has formed us. We ingested it as children whole, had its values and consciousness imprinted on our minds as cultural absolutes long before we were in fact men and women. We have taken the fairy tales of childhood with us into maturity, chewed but still lying in the stomach, as real identity. Between Snow-White and her heroic prince, our two great fictions, we never did have much of a chance. At some point, the Great Divide took place: they (the boys) dreamed of mounting the Greta Steed and buying Snow-White from the dwarfs; we (the girls) aspired to become that object of every necrophiliac's lust—the innocent, victimized Sleeping Beauty, beauteous lump of ultimate, sleeping good. Despite ourselves, sometimes knowing, unwilling, unable to do otherwise, we act out the roles we were taught.

—Andrea Dworkin, *Woman Hating* (1974)

Our views of child rearing, socialization, technology, and politics have changed to such a great extent since World War II that the classical folktales and fairy tales appear too backward looking to many progressive-minded critics and creative writers. Not only are the tales considered to be too sexist, racist, and authoritarian but the general contents are said to reflect the concerns of semifeudal, patriarchal societies.[1] What may have engendered hope for better living conditions centuries ago has become more inhibiting for today's children in the Western world. The discourse of classical fairy tales, its end effect, cannot be considered enlightening and emancipatory in face of possible nuclear warfare, ecological destruction, growing governmental and industrial regimentation, and intense economic crises.

Of course, there are numerous classical folktales and fairy tales that still speak to the needs of children and illuminate possibilities for attaining personal autonomy and social freedom, and it would be foolish to reject the entire classical canon as socially useless or aesthetically outmoded. Moreover, as we know, the classical fairy tale as genre has not been static. Such nineteenth-century writers as Charles Dickens, George MacDonald, John Ruskin, George Sand, Oscar Wilde, Andrew Lang, Edith Nesbit, L. Frank Baum, and others, designated now as "classical," opposed the authoritarian tendencies of the civilization process and expanded the horizons of the fairy-tale discourse for children. They prepared the way for utopian and subversive experiments that altered the fairy-tale discourse at the beginning of the twentieth century. Hope for liberating changes in social relations and political structures was conveyed through symbolic acts of writers who criticized abusive treatment of children and the repressive methods of sexual pedagogy.

Still, the innovative tales for children produced during the first three decades of the twentieth century did not successfully reutilize fantastic projections and configurations of the classical fairy tales to gain wide acceptance among children and adults. If anything, the fantastic was used to compensate for the growing rationalization of culture, work, and family life in Western society, to defend the imagination of children. The fantastic was really on the defensive while appearing to be offensive. Something else was on the march in the name of progress and civilization. The Taylorization of factory and office life; the panoptic organization of schools, hospitals, and prisons; the technical synchronization of art to create formations such as chorus lines and choreography resembling conveyer belts; the celebration of uniform military power in parade and warfare; the use of technology to promote consumerism; and the formation of a celebrity culture were the real sociopolitical tendencies against which the progressive and experimental fairy tales for children reacted at the beginning of the twentieth century. These were the forces that confined and subdued the protest elements in the fairy-tale discourse during the 1930s, 1940s, and 1950s.

Since then, the fantastic in fairy tales for children has been forced to take the offensive, and this situation has arisen not because the fantastic is assuming a more liberating role but because it is in the throes of a last-ditch battle against what many writers have described as technologically instrumental and manipulative forces that operate largely for commercial interests and cast a "totalitarian" loom over society by making people feel helpless and ineffectual in their attempts to reform and determine their own lives. "1984," "brave new world," and "one-dimensional society" have become key words in critiques of social development in both the West and the East. In commenting on the fairy tale in the postwar world, Marion Lochhead asserted that the near victory of fascism was of utmost concern to such writers as C.S. Lewis and J.R.R. Tolkien. "Myth-making continues. The renaissance of wonder has reached maturity. And we need it. The conflict between good and evil—absolute evil—in which the child heroes of fantasy are caught up and taxed to the limit of their endurance has become a common theme."[2] Yet it is not merely the survival of good that is reflected in contemporary fairy tales but the fantastic projection of possibilities for nonalienating living conditions. Hope for such a future followed the struggles of the 1960s, which were marked by civil rights movements, antiwar protests, the rise of feminism, and demands for autonomy by minority groups and small deprived nations throughout the world. Though this hope has been diminished somewhat at the beginning of the twenty-first century, and the utopian tendency has turned dystopian, many writers still envision the fairy tale as a means to critique the barbarian turns of the civilizing process—and they do this with the belief that social change is still possible.

Since it is too difficult to cover the entire development of the literary fairy tale for children in response to these struggles since 1945 and to demonstrate how and why fairy-tale writers have sought to use fantastic projections in a liberating manner, I want to limit myself to a small number of representative writers in the United Kingdom, the United States, Italy, Germany, and France who have expressly tried to make their tales more emancipatory and critical in light of restriction in advanced industrial countries. My concern is twofold: I want to depict the motifs, ideas, styles, and methods used by these writers to make the fantastic projections within the fairy tales more liberating, and I want to question if the intentions of a liberating fairy tale can actually have the effect desired by the writer in societies where socialization is concerned most with control, discipline, and rationalization.

But before I address these two points, I must discuss the "power" of the literary fairy tales in general, the classical and the innovative, to clarify the meanings of such terms as *progressive* and *regressive*, *liberating* and *inhibiting*. In other words, the classical fairy tales have not retained their appeal among children and adults simply because they comply with the norms of the civilizing process. They have an extraordinary power, and Georges Jean locates this power on the conscious level in the way all good fairy tales aesthetically structure and use fantastic and miraculous elements to prepare us for our everyday life.[3] Magic is used paradoxically not to deceive us but to enlighten us. On an unconscious level, Jean believes that the best fairy tales bring together subjective and assimilatory impulses with objective intimations of a social setting that intrigue readers and allow for different interpretations according to one's ideology and belief.[4] Ultimately, Jean argues that the fantastic power of fairy tales consists of the uncanny way they provide a conduit into social reality. Yet given the proscription of fairy-tale discourse within a historically prescribed civilizing process, a more careful distinction must be made between regressive and progressive aspects of the power of fairy tales in general to understand the liberating potential of contemporary tales for children. Here I want to discuss Sigmund Freud's concept of the "uncanny" and Ernst Bloch's concept of "home" as constitutive elements of the liberating impulse behind the fantastic projections in fairy tales, whether they be classical or experimental. I will relate their ideas to Jean Piaget's notions of how children view and adapt to the world so that we can grasp the regressive and progressive features of contemporary fairy tales as politically symbolic acts seeking to make their mark on history.

I

In his essay on the uncanny, Freud remarks that the word *heimlich* means that which is familiar and comforting *and* also that which is concealed and kept out of sight, and he concludes that *heimlich* is a word the meaning of which develops in the direction of ambivalence, until it finally coincides with its opposite, *unheimlich* or uncanny.[5] Through a close study of E.T.A. Hoffmann's fairy tale *The Sandman*, Freud argues that the uncanny or unfamiliar (*unheimlich*) brings us in closer touch with the familiar (*heimlich*) because it touches on emotional disturbances and returns us to repressed phases in our evolution:

> If psychoanalytic theory is correct in maintaining that every effect belonging to an emotional impulse, whatever its kind, is transformed, if it is repressed, into anxiety, then among instances of frightening things there must be one class in which the frightening element can be shown to be something repressed which *recurs*. This class of frightening things would then constitute the uncanny; and it must be a matter of indifference whether what is uncanny was itself originally frightening or whether it carried some *other* affect. In the second place, if this is indeed the secret nature of the uncanny, we can understand why linguistic usage has extended das *Heimliche* ("homely") into its opposite, das *Unheimliche*; for this uncanny is in reality nothing new or alien but something which is familiar and old-established in the mind and which has become alienated from it only through the process of repression. This reference to the factor of repression enables us, furthermore, to understand Schelling's definition of the uncanny as something which ought to have remained hidden but has come to light.[6]

Freud insists that one must be extremely careful in using the category of the uncanny because not everything that recalls repressed desires and surmounted modes of thinking belongs to the prehistory of the individual and the human species and can be considered uncanny. In particular, Freud mentions fairy tales as excluding the uncanny.

In fairy tales, for instance, the world of reality is left behind from the very start, and the animistic system of beliefs is frankly adopted. Wish fulfillments, secret powers, omnipotence of thoughts, and animation of inanimate objects—all the elements so common in fairy stories—can exert no uncanny influence here; for, as we have learned, that feeling cannot arise unless there is a conflict of judgment as to whether things that have been "surmounted" and are regarded as incredible may not, after all, be possible, and this problem is eliminated from the outset by the postulates of the world of fairy tales.[7]

Although it is true that the uncanny becomes the familiar and the norm in the fairy tale because the narrative perspective accepts it so totally, there is still room for *another kind of uncanny experience* within the postulates and constructs of the fairy tale. That is, Freud's argument must be qualified regarding the machinations of the fairy tale. However, I do not want to concern myself with this point at the moment. Rather, I simply want to suggest that the uncanny plays a significant role in the act of reading or listening to a fairy tale. Using and modifying Freud's category of the uncanny, I want to argue that *the very act of reading a fairy tale is an uncanny experience in that it separates the reader from the restrictions of reality from the onset and makes the repressed unfamiliar familiar once again.* Bruno Bettelheim mentioned that the fairy tale estranges the child from the real world and allows him or her to deal with deep-rooted psychological problems and anxiety-provoking incidents to achieve autonomy.[8] Whether this is true, that is, whether a fairy tale can actually provide the means for coping with ego disturbance, as Bettelheim argues,[9] remains to be seen. It is true, however, that once we begin listening to or reading a fairy tale, we experience estrangement or separation from a familiar world, inducing an uncanny feeling that can be both *frightening and comforting.*

Actually the complete reversal of the real world has already taken place before we begin reading a fairy tale on the part of the writer, and the writer invites the reader to repeat this uncanny experience. The process of reading involves dislocating the reader from his or her familiar setting and then identifying with the dislocated protagonist so that a quest for the *Heimische* or real home can begin. The fairy tale ignites a double quest for home. One occurs in the reader's mind and is psychological and difficult to interpret, because the reception of an individual tale varies according to the background and experience of the reader. The second occurs within the tale and indicates a socialization process and acquisition of values for participation in a society where the protagonist has more power of determination. This second quest for home can be *regressive* or *progressive* depending on the narrator's stance vis-à-vis society. In both quests the notion of home or *Heimat*, which is closely related etymologically to *heimlich* and *unheimlich*, retains a powerful progressive attraction for readers of fairy tales. Although the uncanny setting and motifs of the fairy tale already open us up to the recurrence of primal experiences, we can move forward at the same time because it opens us up to what Freud calls "unfulfilled but possible futures to which we still like to cling in fantasy, all the strivings of the ego which adverse external circumstances have crushed, and all our suppressed acts of volition which nourish in us the illusion of Free Will."[10]

Obviously, Freud would not condone clinging to our fantasies in reality. Yet Ernst Bloch would argue that some are important to cultivate and defend because they represent our radical or revolutionary urge to restructure society so that we can finally achieve home. Dreaming that stands still bodes no good.

> But if it becomes a dreaming ahead, then its cause appears quite differently and excitingly alive. The dim and weakening features, which may be characteristic of mere yearning, disappear; and then yearning can show what it really is able to accomplish. It is the way of the world to counsel men to adjust to the world's pressures, and they have learned this lesson; only their wishes and dreams will not hearken to it. In this respect virtually all human beings are futuristic; they transcend their past life, and to the degree that they are satisfied, they think they deserve a better life (even though this may be pictured in a banal and egotistic way), and regard the inadequacy of their lot as a barrier, and not just as the way of the world.
>
> To this extent, the most private and ignorant wishful thinking is to be preferred to any mindless goose-stepping; for wishful thinking is capable of revolutionary awareness, and can enter the chariot of history without necessarily abandoning in the process the good content of dreams.[11]

What Bloch means by the good content of dreams is often the projected fantasy and action of fairy tales with a forward and liberating look: human beings in an upright posture who strive for an autonomous existence and nonalienating setting that allows for democratic cooperation and humane consideration. Real history that involves independent human self-determination cannot begin as long as there is exploitation and enslavement of humans by other humans. The active struggle against unjust and barbaric conditions in the world leads to home, or utopia, a place nobody has known but that represents humankind coming into its own:

> *The true genesis is not at the beginning*, but at the end, and it starts to begin only when society and existence become radical: that is, comprehend their

own roots. But the root of history is the working, creating man, who rebuilds and transforms the given circumstances of the world. Once man has comprehended himself and has established his own domain in real democracy, without depersonalization and alienation, something arises in the world which all men have glimpsed in childhood: a place and a state in which no one has yet been. And the name of this something is home or homeland.[12]

Philosophically speaking, then, *the real return home or recurrence of the uncanny is a move forward to what has been repressed and never fulfilled.* The pattern in most fairy tales involves the reconstitution of home on a new plane, and this accounts for the power of its appeal to both children and adults.

In Bloch's two major essays on fairy tales, "Das Märchen geht selber in Zeit" ("The Fairy Tale Moves on Its Own in Time") and "Bessere Luftschlösser in Jahrmarkt und Zirkus, in Märchen und Kolportage" ("Better Castles in the Air in Fair and Circus, in the Fairy Tale and Popular Books"),[13] he is concerned with the manner in which the hero and the aesthetic constructs of the tale illuminate the way to overcome oppression. He focuses on the way the underdog, the small person, uses his or her wits not only to survive but also to live a better life. Bloch insists that there is good reason for the timelessness of traditional fairy tales: "Not only does the fairy tale remain as fresh as longing and love, but the demonically evil, which is abundant in the fairy tale, is still seen at work here in the present, and the happiness of 'once upon a time,' which is even more abundant, still affects our visions of the future."[14]

It is not only the timeless aspect of traditional fairy tales but also the way they are modernized and appeal to all classes and age groups in society that interests Bloch. Instead of demeaning popular culture and common appeal, Bloch endeavors to explore the adventure novels, modern romances, comics, circuses, country fairs, and the like. He refuses to make simplistic qualitative judgments of high and low art forms; rather he seeks to grasp the driving utopian impulse in the production and reception of artworks for mass audiences. Time and again he focuses on fairy tales as indications of paths to be taken in reality.

What is significant about such kinds of "modern fairy tales" is that it is reason itself which leads to the wish projections of the old fairy tale and serves them. Again what proves itself is a harmony with courage and cunning, as that earliest kind of enlightenment which already characterizes "Hansel and Gretel": consider yourself as born free and entitled to be totally happy, dare to make use of your power of reasoning, look upon the outcome of things as friendly. These are the genuine maxims of fairy tales, and fortunately for us they not only appear in the past but in the now.[15]

If Bloch and Freud set the general boundaries for helping us understand how our longing for home, which is discomforting and comforting, draws us to folktales and fairy tales, we must now become more specific and focus on the interest of children in fairy tales. In fact, we already know from sociological and psychological studies that originated after World War I that children between the ages of five and ten years are the first prime audience of fairy tales of all kinds.[16] Given this common knowledge and research, which have been variously interpreted, we must ask whether the interest of children in fairy tales can be related to their desire for an ideal home; that is, a world or state in which they come into their own.

In *Child and Tale:The Origins of Interest*, André Favat explores the usefulness of Jean Piaget's theories to explain why children are drawn to fairy tales.[17] By concentrating on the age group of children between six and eight years old, Favat demonstrates that the content and form of the "classical" fairy tales (Perrault, the Grimms, and Andersen) correspond to the way a child of this age conceives the world according to Piaget. During this particular phase of development, children believe in the magical relationship between thought and things, regard inanimate objects as animate, respect authority in the form of retributive justice and expiatory punishment, see causality as paratactic, do not distinguish the self from the external world, and believe that objects can be moved in continual response to their desires. Favat maintains that such a child's conception of the world is generally affirmed by the fairy tale, even though the tale may not have been created precisely to meet the needs of children.

Between the ages of six and eight years the child perceives his or her world tested more and more by outside forces, and it is for this reason that Favat makes careful differentiations when he talks about the response of children and their need for stability. Following Piaget, Favat also stresses that the relative development of children and their conception of the world have to be qualified by specific cultural socialization undergone by the children. Thus as the animism and egocentrism of children give way to socialization and greater conscious interaction in society, there is a general rejection of the fairy tale by age ten. About this time children have become more acclimated to the real world and view the fairy tale as an impediment to further adjustment. Only later, after adolescence is completed, do young people and adults return to fairy tales and fantasy literature, quite often to recapture the children in themselves.

To recapture the child is not a frivolous project but a serious undertaking for self-gratification and self-realization. Such earnestness can be seen in the initial attraction of children to fairy tales. As Favat maintains,

> Children's turning to the tale is no casual recreation or pleasant diversion; instead, it is an insistent search for an ordered world more satisfying than

the real one, a sober striving to deal with the crisis of experience they are undergoing. In such a view, it is even possible, regardless of one's attitude toward bibliotherapy, to see the child's turning to the tale as a salutary utilization of an implicit device of the culture. It would appear, moreover, that after reading a fairy tale, the reader invests the real world with the constructs of the tale.[18]

If we synthesize Freud's, Bloch's, and Favat's notions of Piaget in regard to home as liberation, we can now grasp the liberating potential of the fantastic in fairy tales. On a psychological level, through the use of unfamiliar (*unheimlich*) symbols, the fairy tale liberates readers of different age groups to return to repressed ego disturbances; that is, to return to familiar (*heimlich*) primal moments in their lives, but the fairy tale cannot be liberating ultimately unless it projects on a conscious, literary, and philosophical level the objectification of home as real democracy under nonalienating conditions. This means not that the liberating fairy tale must have a moral, doctrinaire resolution but that to be liberating it must reflect *a process of struggle* against all types of suppression and authoritarianism and posit various possibilities for the concrete realization of utopia. Otherwise, the words *liberating* and *emancipatory* have no aesthetical categorical substance.

Piaget notes that, from age six to age twelve, children's sense of morality and justice changes from a belief in retributive justice through expiatory punishment to distributive justice with equality. Corresponding to the early phase of development, the traditional folktales and classical fairy tales tend to reinforce a regressive notion of home by centering on arbitrary authority (generally in the form of monarchs or monarchs in the making) as the last instance of justice. Raw power is used to right wrongs or uphold a mixture of feudal and bourgeois patriarchal norms constituting a "happy end," which is not to be confused with utopia. It is exactly this configuration in the classical tales—and there are many exceptions[19]—that caused numerous authors in the course of the past two centuries to experiment with the fairy-tale discourse. And, as our own conception of what constitutes the substance of liberation in Western culture has changed, the revised literary fairy tales for children have steadily evinced a more radical and sophisticated tendency. The question we must now ask is how some contemporary writers, whom I shall designate as "countercultural," endeavor to make their tales more liberating and conducive to the progressive pursuit of home in contrast to the regressive pursuits in the tales of yesteryear.

II

In examining the unique narrative modes developed by countercultural fairy-tale writers, we will see that their experiments are connected to their endeavors to transform the civilizing process. They interject themselves into the fairy-tale discourse on civilization first by distancing themselves from conventional regressive forms of writing, thinking, and illustrating: the familiar is made unfamiliar only to regain a sense of what authenticity might be on a psycho- and sociogenetic level. Or, to put it another way, by seeking what "unadulterated" home might mean under nonalienating conditions, the fairy-tale writers transfigure classical narratives and distinguish their final constellations of home by provoking the reader to reflect critically on the conditions and limits of socialization. The countercultural intention is made manifest through alienating techniques that no longer rely on seductive, charming illusions of a happy end as legitimation of the present civilizing process but make use of jarring symbols that demand an end to superimposed illusions. The aim is to make readers perceive the actual limits and possibilities of their deep personal wishes in a social context.

The narrative voice probes and tries to uncover the disturbing repressed sociopsychological conflicts so that the young reader might imagine more clearly what forces operate in reality to curtail freedom of action. Uncomfortable questions about arbitrary authoritarianism, sexual domination, and social oppression are raised to show situations that call for change and can be changed. In contrast to the classical fairy tales of the civilizing process, the fantastic projections of the liberating tales are used not for rationalistic purposes to instrumentalize the imagination of readers but rather to subvert the controls of rationalization so that readers can reflect more freely on ego disturbances and perhaps draw parallels to the social situation of others that will enable them to conceive of work and play in a collective sense.

Needless to say, there is a multitude of ways one can write a liberating tale. Here I want to concentrate on just two major types of experimentation that have direct bearing on cultural patterns in the West. One type can be called the transfiguration of the classical fairy tale. Generally the author assumes that the young reader is already familiar with the classical tale and depicts the familiar in an estranging fashion. Consequently, the reader is compelled to consider the negative aspects of anachronistic forms and perhaps transcend them. The tendency is to break, shift, debunk, or rearrange the traditional motifs to liberate the reader from the contrived and programmed mode of literary reception. Transfiguration does not obliterate the recognizable features or values of the classical fairy tale but cancels their negativity by showing how a different aesthetic and social setting relativizes all values. To this extent the act of creative transfiguration by the author and the final artistic product as transfiguration are geared to make readers aware that civilization and life are processes that can be shaped to fulfill basic needs of the readers. Though the liberating and classical fairy tales may contain some of the same features and values, the emphasis placed on transfiguration as process, both as narrative form and as substance, makes for a qualitative difference.

The second type of experimentation, similar to transfiguration, can be called the fusion of traditional configurations with contemporary references within settings and plotlines unfamiliar to readers yet designed to arouse their curiosity and interest. Fantastic projections are used here to demonstrate the changeability of contemporary social relations, and the fusion brings together all possible means for illuminating a concrete utopia. In effect, the narrative techniques of fusion and transfiguration are aimed at disturbing and jarring readers so that they lose their complacent attitude toward the status quo of society and envision ways to realize their individuality within collective and democratic contexts. However, what distinguishes the contemporary writers of liberating tales is their strident antisexist and antiauthoritarian perspective.

For instance, Harriet Herman's *The Forest Princess* (1975) varies the traditional "Rapunzel" fairy tale to question male domination and sexual stereotypes. Her story concerns "a princess who lived alone in a tall tower deep in the woods. An invisible spirit had brought her there when she was just a little girl. The spirit watched over her bringing her food and clothing and giving her special gifts on her birthday."[20] One day after a storm she saves a prince who had been shipwrecked. At first she thinks that she too is a prince because she looks very much like him and does not know that there are differences in sex. They begin living together and teaching each other their respective skills. But the prince misses his home, and the princess agrees to go to the golden castle if he will teach her the secrets of that place. However, the princess is compelled to change at the golden castle—to wear fancy clothes and makeup and to restrict her activities to the company of other girls. Against the orders of the king she teaches them how to read, and because the prince does not want to go riding with her, she practices riding by herself. On the prince's fourteenth birthday she exhibits her astonishing riding skills to the entire court. The king decides to reward her with one wish, and she replies, "Your majesty, what I have done today could have been done by any of the boys and girls in your land. As my reward I would like the boys and girls to ride horses together, to read books together and to play together."[21] But the king refuses to grant this wish, saying that the boys and girls are happy the way they are—despite their protests. The princess realizes that she must leave the golden castle, and nobody knows where she is today. However, the narrator tells us that after her departure her wish came to be fulfilled because fairy tales must end happily.

The irony of the ending suggests a contrast: though fairy tales must end happily, life does not have to, and thus the reader is compelled to consider the reasons for a lack of happiness or home in reality.[22] Moreover, the possibility for a comparison with the traditional "Rapunzel" is given so that the author-itarian quality of the older tale becomes visible.

Similar to Herman, four women of the Merseyside Women's Liberation Movement in Liverpool, England, began publishing fairy tales to counter the values that had been carried by the traditional fairy tales: acquisitive aggres-sion in men and dutiful nurturing of this aggression by women. They argued, "Fairy tales are political. They help to form children's values and teach them to accept our society and their roles in it. Central to this society is the assump-tion that domination and submission are the natural basis of all our relation-ships."[23] In response they rewrote such well-known classics as "The Prince and the Swineherd," "Rapunzel," "Little Red Riding Hood," and "Snow White," all published in 1972. In "The Prince and the Swineherd" Samia the swineherd makes a gluttonous prince into the laughing stock of the people. In "Little Red Riding Hood" the setting is a timbermill town in the North, and the shy little girl Nadia learns to overcome her fear of the woods to save her great-grandmother from the wolf, whom she kills. His fur is used as the lining for Red Riding Hood's cloak, and the great-grandmother tells her, "This cloak now has special powers. Whenever you meet another child who is shy and timid, lend that child the cloak to wear as you play together in the forest, and then, like you, they will grow brave."[24] From then on Red Riding Hood explores and goes deeper and deeper into the forest.

In both these tales the small, oppressed protagonists learn to use their powers to free themselves from parasitical creatures. Life is depicted as an ongoing struggle and process so that the happy end is not an illusion; that is, depicted not as an end in itself but as the actual beginning of a development. The emancipatory element comes about when the fantasy (imagination) of the protagonists is projected within the tale as a means by which they can come into their own and help others in similar situations.

Like the Merseyside group, Tomi Ungerer has been drawn to rewriting "Little Red Riding Hood" (1974), which he titled "a reruminated tale."[25] Though his perspective is emancipatory, it is much different from that of the Merseyside group. In his revision of Andersen's "The Little Match Girl," which he titled "Alumette," he is irreverent, sly, and anarchistic. His wolf, dressed like a classy baron, is much different from the devious wolf of the traditional tale, and his Red Riding Hood is "the real no-nonsense one," which means that she is not gullible or afraid to voice her opinion. We learn that her grand-mother is mean and cranky and even beats her sometimes. So she stops to pick berries to delay her visit. When the wolf appears, he states candidly, "I know of your grandmother and all I can say is that her reputation is worse than mine."[26] He offers to take her to his castle and treat her like a princess in a fairy tale. Red Riding Hood is suspicious. She begins to ask questions about the wolf's jowls and tongue, and he insists that she stop asking foolish questions. He overcomes her objections and tells her that her parents and grandmother will be able to care for themselves. So the wolf and Red Riding Hood marry, have children, and live happily, and the nasty grandmother shrinks in size and remains as mean as ever.

Ungerer's tale uses irony and clever reversals to break the sexual taboos of the traditional tale. The "uncanny" wolf becomes identified with familiar sexual longings of childhood pleasure instincts, and the transformations in the tale are calculated liberating effects, measured against the superego function of the parents and grandmother. The wolf allows Red Riding Hood to grow and enter into a mature sexual relationship. What becomes home in this fairy tale is less social in implications than it is in other liberating tales, but it does make a claim for the autonomy of the young girl and wolf, who demonstrate that reputations spread through rumors of old tales no longer hold true and should not be taken at surface value today.

For the most part, the post-1945 tales of "Little Red Riding Hood" transfigure and criticize the traditional transgression perpetuated against the girl as a helpless, naive, and sweet thing and against the wolf as evil predator and troublesome male rapist. In "Little Polly Riding Hood" (1967),[27] Catherine Storr depicted a clever and independent girl, whom a bumbling wolf would like to eat. Time and again she outwits the comical wolf, who uses the old "Red Riding Hood" tale as a manual on how one should behave. Naturally his announced expectations are never fulfilled. In a more serious vein, Max von der Grün rewrote the tale to comment on prejudice and conformity.[28] His Red Riding Hood is ostracized by the community because of her red cap, which is strongly suggestive of the anti-Semitic and anti-Communist feelings that existed in Germany at one time. There also have been tales written in defense of the wolf, such as Iring Fetscher's "Little Redhead and the Wolf" (1974) and Philippe Dumas and Boris Moissard's "Little Acqua Riding Hood" (1977).[29] Fetscher gives a wry, mock-psychological interpretation that depicts the father killing the wolf because the beast had befriended Red Riding Hood's brother, whom the neurotic father disliked. In the story by Dumas and Moissard there is another ironic portrayal; this time it is Red Riding Hood's granddaughter who frees the grandnephew of the wolf from the zoo in the Jardin des Plantes because she wants to relive the classical story and become a star in Parisian society. However, the wolf is wise, for he has learned a lesson from the tragedies that have occurred in his family. He flees to Siberia and warns young wolves about the dangers of "civilization" in France.

The reversal of the classical fairy tales is at the center of the other stories in Dumas and Moissard's book *Conte à l'envers*, and it is the basis of such other collections as Jay Williams's *The Practical Princess and Other Liberating Tales* (1979),[30] Jane Yolen's *Dream Weaver* (1979),[31] and Hans-Joachim Gelberg's *Neues vom*

Rumpelstilzchen (1976).[32] The traditional stories are transfigured so that their repressive substance is subverted. The reversal of form, characters, and motifs is intended to expand the possibilities to question the fairy-tale discourse within the civilizing process.

Aside from the transfiguration of fairy tales, the second most common manner in which writers of fairy tales have endeavored to suggest options to dominant cultural patterns is through the fusion of actual references to disturbing social occurrences in contemporary society. Here I want to focus on four remarkable fairy-tale experiments in Italy, Germany, France, and England. The international quest for liberation and a new sense of home manifested in different fairy tales is clearly a reaction against international trends of domination, standardization, and exploitation.

In Italy there is a consistent protest for freedom in the creative work of Adela Turin, Francesca Cantarellis, Nella Bosnia, Margherita Soccaro, and Sylvie Selig. Seven of their books have been translated and distributed by the Writers and Readers Publishing Cooperative in London.[33] Significant here is the tale titled *Of Cannons and Caterpillars* (1975). The very first paragraph sets the dramatic predicament of modern society:

> No one in the palace of King Valour any longer remembered the first war. Not the ministers or the privy councillors, or the secretaries, observers, or the directors, or the reporters, the strategists or the diplomats; not even the generals, the colonels, the sergeants, the majors or the lieutenants. Not even Terence Wild, the very oldest soldier alive, stitched and restitched, with one glass eye, one wooden leg, and a hook in place of a hand. Because after the first war, there had been a second war, then a third, a fourth, a fifth, and then a twentieth and a twenty-first too, which was still going on. And no one in the palace of King Valour could remember anything about peaches or sparrows, or tortoise-shell cats, or bilberry marmalade, or radishes, or bed-sheets spread out to dry on green meadows. Besides, King Valour had become enthusiastic about his plans for a twenty-second war: "Not a single tree will be left standing, not a blade of grass will survive; no, not one solitary shamrock or grasshopper," so he predicted, "because we have the ultimate weapon, diabolical defoliants, death-rays, paralysing gas and cannons of perfect accuracy."[34]

Grotesque and comically exaggerated as King Valour may seem, his manner of thinking is not unlike that of some of our contemporary statesmen. His menace and madness are sadly recognized by his own wife Queen Delphina, who is sentenced to live in the modern skyscraper castle behind bulletproof windows with her daughter Princess Philippina and 174 widows and war orphans, both boys and girls. Confronted with a synthetic, suffocating technological life,

Delphina endeavors to teach her daughter about nature, including caterpillars, flowers, animals, vegetables, and so forth by writing illustrated stories for her. As her storybook expands, Philippina and all the widows and orphans of the skyscraper become less sad. Then one "evening King Valour returned in excellent humour: a new war had just been declared, and it promised to be the longest most homicidal ever. . . . So he decided that the Queen, the Princess, widows, and orphans were to leave on a Saturday morning for the Castle of King Copious, which stood further away from the battlefields."[35]

This decision turns out to be fortunate for the queen and her entourage. Along the way they stop at an abandoned castle ruined by wars, and because it is so beautifully situated in the country, they decide to renovate the buildings and cultivate the land. So they unpack the big book, and all the dreams that had been pictured in the book they now endeavor to realize in their surroundings. Many years pass, and we learn that King Valour and his wars are all but forgotten. However, the transformed castle flourishes in the middle of a busy, densely populated village, and everyone knows the name of Delphina, the legendary writer of the beautifully illustrated book.

This extraordinary antiwar fairy tale is uniquely illustrated with pictures that project a critique of authoritarianism and the possibility for collective democratic life: the entire concept of the fairy tale encourages the creative realization of peaceful coexistence. Moreover, it is a fairy tale in praise of the utopian power of fairy tales. Delphina manages to retain the principle of hope and humanism in the prison-castle of her husband by writing the illustrated book for her compatriots. Given the opportunity to escape a sick situation, they become joyful and creative. Their sterile existence is exchanged for a life without fear and oppression. Thus finally they can come into touch with their own skills and harness technology to serve their collective needs in peace.

The dangerous potential of technology and bureaucracy to create means for enslaving humankind is portrayed with even greater insight and originality in Michael Ende's 270-page fairy-tale novel Momo (1973).[36] This work won the German Youth Book Prize and has been translated into seventeen different languages and made into a film. It recalls the struggles of a little Italian orphan, a wiry, ingenuous girl named Momo, somewhere between the ages of eight and twelve years, who makes her home in the ruins of an ancient Roman amphitheater. Since she has the amazing gift of listening to people's problems in such a way that they are provided with the power to come to their own solutions, she is regarded as somewhat saintlike and is protected by everyone in the neighborhood. Surrounded by all sorts of children who play in the amphitheater and her two special friends Beppo the street cleaner and Gigi the young con artist, she lacks nothing and prospers through her wit and creativity. In general all the people in the district are poor, but they try to share and enjoy what they have with one another and struggle to improve the quality of their lives at their own pace and time. Unknown to them, however, their manner of living and playing is being threatened by the timesavers, men dressed in gray whose ash-colored faces match their suits. They wear stiff round hats, smoke gray cigars, and carry blue-gray briefcases. Nobody knows who these men are, and everyone forgets them once they enter and influence their lives to conduct themselves according to such principles as "time is money," "time is costly," or "saved time is double time." So great is their clandestine impact that the city gradually begins to transform itself into a smooth-functioning machine. Buildings and streets are torn down to make way for modern technology and automatization. Everyone rushes around seeking ways to save time and make more money. The total architecture of the city informs the psyche of people's minds that are now geared to work for work's sake. The gray men gain control over everyone and succeed in isolating Momo. Only after she finds her way to the "nowhere house" of Master Secundius Minitus Hora is she safe from the threat of the gray men, for it is Master Hora, a wizened and humane guardian of time, who can explain the essence of time to Momo—that it resides in the heart of each individual and can become as beautiful as the individual decides. Given this realization, Momo seeks to struggle against the gray men, and with the help of Master Hora and a magic turtle, she eventually undermines the nefarious plans of the gray men: time is liberated so that human beings can determine their destiny.

Ende's colorful fairy-tale novel is told in such a fashion that the events could seemingly take place in the past, present, or future. In unusual symbolical form he incorporates a critique of instrumental rationalization so that it becomes comprehensible for readers between the ages of eight and fifteen years. As is the case in most contemporary fairy tales with liberating potential, Ende has a female protagonist bring about or point a way to change. While Momo comes into her own as an individual, social relations appear to be reconstituted in a manner that will allow time to blossom for everyone. Nevertheless, there are problems with the ending of *Momo*, which is deceptively emancipatory. That is, Ende employs the fantastic to celebrate individualistic action or the privatization of the imagination. Such individualism is supposed to be the answer to the growing rationalization of everyday life, and it is celebrated in Ende's second best-seller, *Die unendliche Geschichte* (*The Neverending Story*, 1979),[37] in which a fat, fearful boy named Bastian discovers that he can use his imagination to invent a never-ending story, which helps him adjust to reality. Ende has Bastian steal a book, and, as the boy reads it in a secluded place, he feels summoned by the troubled realm of Phantásien, where he has numerous adventures. Aided by his devoted friend Atréju and magical animals, he prevents Phantásien from being destroyed. Upon returning to reality, he becomes reconciled with his father and feels strong and courageous enough to take on the world. In contrast to *Momo*, *The Neverending Story* depicts a pursuit of home as a form of regression and compromise. Moreover, there are too many traditional clichés and stereotypes in Ende's endeavor to endorse the student revolt slogan "all power to the imagination," so that, in the final analysis, his story actually deludes readers and prevents them from seeing their potential and problems against the background of social forces manipulating and exploiting both consciousness and imagination.

Such delusion is not the case in Jean-Pierre Andrevon's remarkable fairy-tale novel *La Fée et le Géometre* (*The Fairy and the Land Surveyor*, 1981).[38] Andrevon describes an idyllic verdant country filled with fairies, dwarfs, gnomes, witches, magicians, elves, dragons, and sylphs, who live in harmony with one another without rules, money, or rationalized relations of production. Nature is not threatened with gross exploitation. All creatures benefit from their interchange and exchange with one another, and sexual discrimination does not exist. Each individual works and plays according to his or her own need, that is, until Arthur Livingschwartz, an explorer, who works for an international conglomerate, discovers this paradise. From this point on, Andrevon portrays the gradual colonization of the verdant country. Technicians, scientists, soldiers, architects, and businessmen arrive and transform the small virgin land into a tourist resort with a tiny industrial capacity. Roads, towns, and factories are built. Nature is devastated and polluted. The gnomes, dwarfs, fairies, and elves are compelled to work for money and to regulate their time and lives according to the demands of outsiders, who now control the production of the country. There are intermarriages between humans and the fairy creatures, and some, like the fairy Sibialle and the land surveyor Loïc, try to oppose the onslaught of colonization and industrialization. However, it is not until their daughter and other children from mixed marriages grow up and experience human exploitation and ecological destruction in the name of progress that a strong organized protest movement develops. There are struggles over the construction of nuclear reactors, the encroachment of nature by industry and highways—all without violence. These struggles commence as Andrevon concludes his narration:

> The country of the fairies will never be as it was before. The country of the fairies will not regress. To live does not mean to move backward but to move forward. It means to be like the shark and to advance unceasingly. And the shark is not a malicious creature. He must live like all of us. That's all.
>
> The best thing that can happen to the country of the fairies is not a return to the past, nor should it seek to model itself after the human world. It can become *different*, mixing the qualities of fairies and humans alike.[39]

Whether this can happen, whether the struggle of the people in the verdant country to change their lives can succeed, remains an open question at the end of this fairy tale. Yet Andrevon manages to raise most of the significant social and political questions for today's youth in a discourse that provides an inkling of home. He does not paint rosy illusions by offering an individualistic solution to the instrumentalization of magic, fantasy, and natural needs the way Ende does in The Neverending Story. In fact, he sees the collective opposition to possible ecological and social destruction arising out of the contradictions created by capitalist colonization. In this sense he views modern technology and industrialization as revolutionary, as transformative forces that can be beneficial to living creatures and nature, only if they are not employed for profit and exploitation. Unlike some romantic anticapitalist writers of fairy tales like J.R.R. Tolkien and C.S. Lewis, who look back conservatively to the past for salvation, Andrevon knows that technology and industry are not evil per se. He assumes the viewpoint of the socialist ecologist and points with optimism toward the struggle for a qualitatively new type of "homeland."

Not all progressive fairy-tale writers are as optimistic as Andrevon is. For instance, Michael de Larrabeiti writes from the perspective of the urban lower class, and he draws different conclusions than did Andrevon in his endeavor to subvert and satirize Tolkien's Lord of the Rings and Richard Adams's Watership Down. In his first fairy-tale novel The Borribles (1978)[40] he created fictional characters from his own childhood in Battersea, who are notable for their social defiance. Borribles are outcasts or runaways who value their independence more than anything else because they take a deep delight in being what they are. They avoid adults and especially policemen, who represent arbitrary authority. Their ears grow long and pointed, a sign of their nonconformism, and if they are caught by the law, their ears are clipped and their will is broken. Borribles exist everywhere in the world, but de Larrabeiti writes mainly about the Borribles who inhabit London.

In his first novel he wrote about the Borribles' great struggle with the high and mighty Rumbles, representative of middle-class snobs, and the loss of a vast treasure in the River Wendle. In the sequel, The Borribles Go for Broke (1981),[41] he depicted the further adventures of a small group of Borribles, who are manipulated by Spiff, the irascible Horrible chief, to search for the lost treasure in the underground territory of the treacherous Wendles. Actually, the group of Borribles (consisting of the two tough girls Chalotte and Sidney, a Bangladeshi named Twilight, Stonks from Peckham, and Vulge from Stepney) primarily wants to rescue the horse Sam, who had been of immense service to them on their Great Rumble Hunt. The police, however, have created a Special Borrible Group (SBG) under the command of the fanatic inspector Sussworth, and the Borribles are pursued with vengeance. In fact, at one point they are even captured by the SBG but then are rescued by an extraordinary tramp named Ben, who is a grown-up Borrible in his own way. Though the Borribles and Ben have no difficulty in making fools of the police, it is a different story with the Wendles in the sewers of London. Spiff has instigated everything so that the Borribles must help him search for the lost treasure and eliminate the tyrannical chieftain Flinthead, who turns out to be Spiff's brother. Ultimately, Spiff and Flinthead are both killed, the Borribles escape, and Sam is rescued. However, the Borribles are not happy in the end unless they can continue bickering and arguing among themselves about their next step in opposition to the normal routine of an oppressive society.

It is difficult to do justice to the style and manner in which de Larrabeiti makes the unbelievable believable. His starting point is obviously the young *lumpenproletariat*, the down and out of the London lower classes. In this novel he begins by focusing on the interaction between Chalotte as a hard-nosed courageous girl and Twilight as a sensitive and sensible Bangladeshi. His immediate concern is to establish the integrity and skills of these two characters, generally representative of females and minority groups. Thereafter, he expands the scope of his attention by depicting the relations between Ben as an adult dropout and the Borribles as defiant young outsiders. At first the Borribles distrust Ben, but they learn quickly that his principles are similar to theirs: he lives from day to day contented with the waste and abundance of a wasteful society, abhors the deadliness of routine, shuns profit making, and minds his own business. All this is proclaimed in his special song:

Let the world roll round an' round
Wiv its hard-worked folk in fetters:
All'oo think themselves yer betters,
Money-mad and dooty bound.

Make yer choice, there ain't so many,
No ambition's worth a fart;
Freedom is a work of art—
Take yer stand with uncle Benny![42]

Together Ben and the Borribles reveal how creative and adroit one must be to gain and protect one's independence. Not only are they surrounded by powerful social forces that demand law and order just for the sake of law and order but they must contend with each other's disrespectful and suspicious natures. De Larrabeiti's fantasy projection shows lower-class life more like it is than do many so-called realistic novels for young readers. He does not mince his words or pull punches. His character portrayals and command of colloquial speech, especially cockney, are remarkable. At times his plotlines are too contrived, and he lets his imagination carry him away. (Yes, even in fantasy literature this is possible.) Still he manages to employ the fairy-tale discourse to deal with themes pertaining to racial, sexual, and political struggles of the present in such a way that young readers can comprehend the importance and urgency of protest by outsiders. There is no such thing as "home" in this fairy-tale novel. It is the refusal of the Borribles to go home, to make a regular home, that demonstrates the false promises of the classical fairy tales that celebrate regressive notions of home in their so-called happy endings.

III

Most of the tales discussed up to this point—and there are many more one could discuss[43]—provide a social and political basis for the fantastic projection so that it is instilled with a liberating potential. The configurations of the experimental fairy-tale discourse shift the perspective and meaning of socialization through reading. The active, aggressive behavior of male types in the classical fairy tales gives way to a combined activism on the part of both males and females who uncover those wishes, dreams, and needs that have been denied by social structures and institutions. The fantastic projections carried by the plots, characters, and motifs of the tales reflect the possibility for a transformation of constraining social conditions through major changes in social relations. The fairy-tale discourse in general is confronted with a demand to transform itself and become more emancipatory and innovative. The question, however, remains as to whether the experimental tales are truly liberating and can achieve their object. That is, can they have the desired effect on young readers?

Several critics have pointed to the difficulties in predicting the effect that emancipatory literature can have on children.[44] For the most part, particularly in regard to the classical fairy tales, children resist change. If they have been reared with the old tales, they do not want them altered. If their social expectations have been determined by a conservative socialization process, they find changes in fairy tales comical but often unjust and disturbing, even though the tales purport to be in their interests and seek their emancipation.

Yet it is exactly this *disturbance* that the liberating fairy tales seek on both a conscious and an unconscious level. They interfere with the civilizing process in hope of creating change and a new awareness of social conditions. This provocation is why it is more important for critics to recognize the upsetting effect of emancipatory tales and to study their uncanny insinuations for old and young readers. The quality of emancipatory fairy tales should be judged not by the manner in which they are accepted by readers but by the unique ways they bring undesirable social relations into question and force readers to question themselves. In this regard the liberating potential of the fantastic in experimental fairy tales will always be discomforting, even when concrete utopias are illuminated through the narrative perspective.

With some exceptions, the emancipatory tales are skillfully written and employ humor and artwork in original, stimulating ways to accomplish their paradoxical kind of discomforting comfort. The major difficulty facing the emancipatory fairy tales, it seems to me, lies in the system of distribution and circulation and the use of the tales, and all this is dependent on the educational views of teachers, librarians, parents, and those adults who work with children in community centers. The more regressive tales of Perrault, the Brothers Grimm, Andersen, and other conservative writers are used in schools, libraries, and homes without a blink of the eye, but the unusual, forward-looking, fantastic projections of the liberating fairy tales have not found general approval among the publishers and adults who circulate the tales. Many religious groups seek to ban fairy tales of all kinds from schools because of their putative pagan and blasphemous contents.

This is not to say that there has been no headway made by the experimental fairy tales and by adults who experiment with fairy tales. Throughout the Western world storytellers, writers, publishers, and educators have developed new methods and techniques to question and expand the classical fairy-tale discourse. In Italy, Gianni Rodari,[45] a well-known writer for children, created a series of games intended to deconstruct classical fairy tales in the hope of stimulating children to create their own modern versions. By introducing unusual elements into the fairy tale, for instance, by making Cinderella disobedient and rebellious or having Snow White meet giants instead of dwarfs and organizing a band of robbers, the child is compelled to shatter a certain uniform reception of fairy tales, to reexamine the elements of the classical tales, and to reconsider their function and meaning and whether it might not be better to alter them. Rodari published numerous innovative books such as *Venti Storie più una* (*Twenty Stories Plus One*, 1969) and *Tante Storie per giocare* (*Many Stories to Play With*, 1971), in which he either revised fairy tales in contemporary settings or proposed different plots and endings to traditional tales. As Maria Luisa Salvadori has demonstrated,[46] his influence on present-day writers of fairy tales in Italy, such as Bianca Pitzorno, Roberto Piumini, and Marcello Argilli, is immense.

In France, Georges Jean[47] has described various pedagogical means that he has used in schools to enable children to become more creative in their use of fairy tales. He describes certain card games in which children are called on to change characters or situations of the classical fairy tales so that they relate more directly to their own lives. Jean considers the reinvention of fairy tales as a means for children to become aware of traditional discourse and the necessity to modernize it. Perhaps the best example of such reinvention is the production of unusual tales by Pierre Gripari, who published three important books, *Contes de la rue Broca* (*Stories from Broca Street*, 1967), *Contes de la rue Folie-Méricourt* (*Tales from Méricourt Street*, 1983), and *Patrouille du conte* (*Fairy Tale Patrol*, 1983), which clearly comment on the norms and standards of the French civilizing process. In particular, *Patrouille du conte* is a provocative account of how eight children endeavor to humanize the world only to bring about more barbarianism with their politically correct agenda.

It is indeed the tendency toward political correctness that has engendered change, but not in a doctrinaire or destructive manner as Gripari projected in his fairy-tale novel. In the United States, for instance, writers and illustrators of fairy tales for young readers, such as Jane Yolen, William Steig, Maurice Sendak, Donna Jo Napoli, Francesca Lia Block, Gregory Maguire, and many others, have explored problems concerned with child abuse, drugs, sexism, violence, and bigotry through their transformation of the traditional fairy-tale motifs and plots. This is also true in the United Kingdom, where writers such as Philip Pullman, Anne Fine, Michael Rosen, Adèle Geras, Emma Donoghue, Michael Foreman, Diana Wynne Jones, Berlie Doherty, and others have produced tales that reflect on social conditions in humorous and yet serious ways.

One of the more exceptional picture books published in the twenty-first century, a liberating fairy tale, which owes its political and artistic profundity to the progressive experiments by writers and illustrators of the post-1945 epoch, is *Brundibar* (2003) written by Tony Kushner and illustrated by Maurice Sendak. Based on a short opera composed by Hans Krása with a libretto by Adolf Hoffmeister in 1938, the story has an important history connected to the Holocaust. It concerns a brother and sister named Pepicek and Aninku, respectively, who are sent to a nearby village by a doctor to fetch milk for their sick mother, otherwise she will die. The children have no father. Moreover, they have no money. So, when they arrive in the village, the milkman refuses to give them milk. The only way to earn money is through singing, but Brundibar, the organ-grinder man, drowns out their singing and collects all the money. Fortunately, a sparrow, a cat, and a dog come to their aid, and Pepicek and Aninku recruit the children of the village to sing with them and vanquish Brundibar. Then they take the money they received from the onlookers, buy milk, and save their mother.

In their collaborative work, Kushner and Sendak altered the story somewhat to draw parallels with the Nazi period and contemporary America. Originally Hoffmeister and Krása sought to address conditions under the Nazi occupation of Czechoslovakia, and after the opera was secretly performed in an orphanage in Prague in 1941, it was performed fifty-five times by prisoners of the concentration camp Theresienstadt without the Nazis realizing that the organ-grinder Brundibar was a symbolical representation of Hitler. There is, however, no doubt who Brundibar is in the Kushner and Sendak picturebook. Sprouting a scraggy moustache, Brundibar recalls the posturing of Hitler as a bully, and Kushner and Sendak make a major change at the end of their tale. After the children sing, "The wicked never win! We have our victory yet! Tyrants come along, but you just wait and see! They topple one-two-three! And thus we end our song. Our friends make us strong!" they add a sobering coda written by Brundibar: "They believe they've won the fight, they believe I'm gone—not quite! Nothing ever works out neatly—Bullies don't give up completely. One departs, the next appears, and we shall meet again my dears! Though I go, I won't go far. . . . I'll be back."

The clear reference is to other bullies and tyrants in the world, including the president of the United States. It is not necessary for Kushner and Sendak to name names and be overly didactic because the fairy tale, although optimistic, seeks to show how the barbarianism of the civilized world did not end with the destruction of the concentration camps and the death of Hitler. In this regard, their story is a remarkable political history lesson that offers children hope while at the same time opening their eyes to present dangers of tyranny. What is interesting are the colorful manner, the free verse, and the startling naive images in which Kushner and Sendak narrate how two children take destiny in their own hands and save their home. They return to their mother with great courage, confidence, and consciousness. Liberated from the oppressor Brundibar, they set readers free to think how they might use their creative talents and imagination to liberate themselves.

The work of Kushner and Sendak, and others before them, make it quite clear, however, that until progressive social ideas are set into practice among adults, the liberating fairy tales will remain restricted in their use and effect among children. In other words, until there is a more progressive shift within the civilizing process, the liberating potential of these tales will be confined to those social groups seeking that end. One thing, however, is certain: the writers and illustrators have experienced some sense of liberation in projecting their fantasies through the magic of the fairy tales. Home for them is achieved through the creative production of these subversive tales, which allow them to regain a sense of their familiar longings through the uncanny. It is this sensory experience that they want to share with us symbolically, for their sense of liberation can be confirmed only when others, especially children, read and benefit from the subversive power of their art.

9

WALT DISNEY'S CIVILIZING MISSION: FROM REVOLUTION TO RESTORATION

No artist and writer in the twentieth century managed to have such a profound influence on civilizing children and adults as Walt Disney. Once he discovered his utopian vision and mission and learned to organize other artists to do his bidding, he was relentless in his pursuit of the perfect clean and orderly world that was mirrored in all the fairy-tale films and books he created while he was alive and envisioned in his theme parks. His utopian vision and spirit were so powerful that, even after his death, the Disney Corporation continued to operate as though he were alive and as though it still had to shape the fairy tale to fulfill his wishes, realize his dreams, and spread his ideology. Whether the people who worked for him and the millions who watched and continue to watch Disney fairy-tale films truly shared and share his utopian vision of the good life and wholesome entertainment, he made his presence felt: it is impossible not to give him credit for revolutionizing the fairy tale through the technology of the cinema and book publishing industry. But in reality, his revolution was a major regression and caused many of the liberating aspects of the fairy tale to be tamed and to turn in against themselves. The Disney civilizing process leads to the degeneration of utopia.

But before I explain how Disney managed to domesticate the fairy tale and restore its conservative features so that it lost its rebellious and progressive features, I must summarize the status of the genre at the end of the nineteenth century, bearing in mind that it had become socially institutionalized in most

Western countries that there were distinct differences in the production and reception of the tales in these countries and that there was a marked tendency to infantilize and sanitize the genre so that children would not somehow be harmed by some of the more nefarious fairy tales that might be allegedly too violent or indecent for them. Thus the genre never lost its suspicious and pagan aura for the church and conventional educators and parents and was always censored and controlled as it became a major staple of children's culture. Some of the more ostensible functions and tendencies of the genre as social institution at the beginning of the twentieth century can be summarized as follows.

1. As the fairy tale was cultivated as a genre and social institution for children in Great Britain and America during the nineteenth century, notions of elitism and Christian meritocracy were introduced into the stories, and a select canon of tales was established for the socialization of the young, geared to children who knew how to read. These notions are easily recognizable in most of the classical tales, especially those written by Hans Christian Andersen, who had become one of the most popular writers in Europe and America during the nineteenth and early twentieth centuries. The emphasis was on extraordinarily gifted individuals who owed their rise in fortunes to God's benevolence or miracles of destiny represented metaphorically through the intervention of a fairy or powerful magical people and objects. Another aspect that appealed to children and adults was the Horatio Alger attitude that encouraged taking advantage of opportunities and pulling oneself up by one's bootstraps.

2. Though it was also told, the printed fairy tale with pictures gained more legitimacy and enduring value than the oral tale, which disappeared soon after it was told, unless it was recorded or written down. The preservation of the oral tales and the revisions made to suit a Christian and middle-class ideology were completed by the beginning of the twentieth century in Great Britain and the United States.

3. The fairy tale was often read by a parent in a nursery, library, school, or bedroom to entertain and to soothe a child's anxieties because the fairy tales for children were optimistic and had plots with closure, that is, with a happy end. By the end of the nineteenth century, fairy tales were among the first stories to be performed by adults and children and staged in the United States and Great Britain. In addition, they were read to children by librarians and teachers, and they made their way into school primers.

4. Although the plots varied and the themes and characters were altered, the classical fairy tale for children and adults reinforced the patriarchal symbolical order based on rigid notions of sexuality and gender. The stereotypes, not archetypes, depicted in printed and staged versions of fairy tales tended to follow schematic notions of how young men and

women should behave. Though it is somewhat of a simplification to say, most of the heroes are cunning, fortunate, adventurous, handsome, and daring; the heroines are beautiful, passive, obedient, industrious, and self-sacrificial. Though some are from the lower classes and though the theme of "rags to riches" plays an important role, the peasants and lower-class figures learn a certain *Habitus*, what Pierre Bourdieu describes as a set of manners, customs, normative behavior, and thinking that enables them to fulfill a social role, to rise in social status, and to distinguish themselves according to conventional social class and gender expectations.

5. In printed form the fairy tale became property (unlike the oral folktale). It was sold and marketed, and property rights were granted authors, collectors, and publishers. When bought, it could be taken by its "new" owner and read by its owner at his or her leisure for escape, consolation, or inspiration. An oral tale that once belonged to a community was gradually lifted from its context and deprived of its original social meaning and relevance.

6. There was always tension between the literary and oral traditions. The oral tales continued and continue to threaten the more conventional and classical tales because they can question, dislodge, and deconstruct the written tales. Moreover, within the literary tradition there were numerous writers in the late nineteenth century such as Charles Dickens, George MacDonald, Lewis Carroll, Oscar Wilde, Edith Nesbit, and even L. Frank Baum who questioned the standardized model of what a fairy tale should be.

7. It was through script by the end of the nineteenth century that there was a full-scale debate about what oral folktales and literary fairy tales were and what their respective functions should be. By this time the fairy tale had expanded as a high art form (opera, ballet, drama) and low art form (folk play, vaudeville, and parody) and a form developed classically and experimentally for children and adults. The oral tales continued to be disseminated through communal gatherings of different kinds, but they were also broadcast by radio and gathered in books by folklorists. Most important in the late nineteenth century was the rise of folklore, along with anthropology, as an organized field of study and inquiry. It became a social institution, and various schools of folklore began to flourish. There was hardly any literary criticism that dealt with fairy tales and folktales at this time.

8. Though many fairy-tale books and collections were illustrated, and some lavishly illustrated in the nineteenth century, the images were very much in conformity with the text. The illustrators, mainly male, were frequently anonymous and did not seem to count. Though the illustrations often enriched and deepened a tale, they were more subservient to the text and rarely presented alternative ways to read or look at a text.

However, the domination of the printed word in the development of the fairy tale as a genre was about to change. The next great revolution in the institutionalization of the genre was brought about by the technological development of the film, for the images now imposed themselves on the text and formed their own text in violation of print but also with the help of the print culture. And here is where Walt Disney and other animators enter the scene.

DISNEY'S MAGICAL RISE

By the end of the nineteenth century and the beginning of the twentieth century, there had already been a number of talented illustrators such as Gustav Doré, George Cruikshank, Ludwig Richter, Walter Crane, Charles Robinson, Alice Woodward, Charles Folkard, Arthur Rackham, Margaret Tarrant, Francis Donkin Bedford, Maxfield Parrish, Howard Pyle, W.W. Denslow, and others who had demonstrated great ingenuity in their interpretations of fairy tales through their images. In addition, the broadside, broadsheet, or image d'Epinal had spread in Europe and America during the latter part of the nineteenth century as a forerunner of the comic book, and these sheets with printed images and texts anticipated the first animated cartoons that were first produced at the beginning of the twentieth century. Actually, the French filmmaker Georges Méliès began experimenting as early as 1896 with types of fantasy and fairy-tale motifs in his féeries or trick films.[1] He produced versions of Cinderella, Bluebeard, and Red Riding Hood among others and became known for his ironic approach to the classical tradition and for his creation of extraordinary illusions that emanated from common everyday situations. In France, Méliès was not the only filmmaker with a deep interest in the fairy tale. Ferdinand Zecca, Albert Capellani, Lucien Nonguet, and Étienne Arnaud also produced unusual films based on Perrault's "Bluebeard," "Sleeping Beauty," "Puss in Boots," and "Cinderella."[2] However, because the cinema industry was still in its early phase of development, it was difficult for Méliès and these other French filmmakers to bring about a major change in the technological and cinematic institutionalization of the genre. As Lewis Jacobs remarked, Méliès's works "illustrated rather than re-created the fairy tale. Yet, primitive though it was, the order of the scenes did form a coherent, logical, and progressive continuity. A new way of making moving pictures had been invented. Scenes could now be staged and selected specially for the camera, and the movie maker could control both the material and its arrangement."[3]

During the early part of the twentieth century, Winsor McCay, John Bray, Earl Hurd, Max and Dave Fleischer, Paul Terry, Walter Booth, Anson Dyer, Lotte Reiniger, Walter Lantz, and others used fairy-tale motifs and plots in different ways in trick films and cartoons, but none of the early animators ever matched the intensity with which Disney occupied himself with the fairy tale. In fact, it is noteworthy that Disney's very first endeavors in animation (not considering the advertising commercials he made) were the fairy-tale adaptations that he produced with Ub Iwerks in Kansas City between 1922–23: *The Four Musicians of Bremen, Little Red Riding Hood, Puss in Boots, Jack and the Beanstalk, Goldie Locks and the Three Bears,* and *Cinderella,* which he called *Laugh-O-gram Films.*[4] All of these short films were highly experimental, were generally open-ended and inventive, and expressed surprising vigor and original use of animation art and technique. Moreover, they all took place in twentieth-century America, tended to be partial to the underdogs in the stories, and had heroes who often resembled Disney or Disney's aspirations. In *Little Red Riding Hood* the girl brings donuts to her grandmother and is almost raped by a "wolfish" dapper gentleman. However, an airplane pilot rescues her and disposes of the wolf by dropping him into a lake. In *Cinderella* the prince who weds the exploited hardworking ash girl bears a great resemblance to a noble Walt Disney. To a certain degree, Disney identified so closely with the fairy tales he appropriated that it is no wonder his name became virtually synonymous with the genre of the fairy tale.

In the case of the fairy-tale film at the beginning of the twentieth century, there are "revolutionary" aspects that we can note, and they prepared the way for progressive innovation that expanded the horizons of viewers and led to greater understanding of social conditions and culture. But there were also regressive uses of mechanical reproduction that brought about the cult of the personality and commoditization of film narratives. For instance, the voice in fairy-tale films is at first effaced so that the image totally dominates the screen, and the words or narrative voice can speak only through the designs of the animator, who, in the case of Walt Disney, signed his name prominently on the screen. In fact, for a long time, Disney did not give credit to the artists and technicians who worked on his films. These images were intended both to smash the aura of heritage and to celebrate the ingenuity, inventiveness, and genius of the animator. In most of the early animated films, there were few original plots, and the story lines did not count. Most important were the gags, or the technical inventions of the animators, ranging from introducing live actors to interact with cartoon characters, improving the movement of the characters so that they did not shimmer, devising ludicrous and preposterous scenes for the sake of spectacle, and so on. It did not matter what story was projected just as long as the images astounded the audience, captured its imagination for a short period of time, and left the people laughing or staring in wonderment. The purpose of the early animated films was to make audiences awestruck and to celebrate the magical talents of the animator as demigod. As a result, the fairy tale as story was a vehicle for animators to express their artistic talents, to make fun of traditional stories, and to develop the technology. The animators sought to impress audiences with their abilities to use pictures in such a way that they would forget the earlier fairy tales and remember the images that they, the new artists, were creating for them. Through these moving pictures, the animators appropriated literary and oral fairy tales to subsume the word, to have the final word, often through image and book, for Disney began publishing books during the 1930s to complement his films.

Of all the early animators, Disney was the one who truly revolutionalized the fairy tale as institution through the cinema. One could almost say that he was obsessed by the fairy-tale genre or, put another way, that Disney felt drawn to fairy tales because they reflected his own struggles in life. After all, Disney came from a relatively poor family, suffered from the exploitative and stern treatment of an unaffectionate father, was spurned by his early sweetheart, and became a success because of his tenacity, cunning, and courage and his ability to gather around him talented artists like his friend Ub Iwerks and managers like his brother Roy.

Puss in Boots, one of his early films, is crucial for grasping his approach to the literary fairy tale and for understanding how he used it to promote a notion of entrepreneurism that would mark the genre for years to come. Disney did not especially care whether one knew the original Perrault text of *Puss in Boots* or some other popular version. It is also unclear which text he actually knew. However, what is clear is that Disney sought to replace all versions with his animated version and that his cartoon is strikingly autobiographical. At the same time, it demonstrated how he began challenging the status quo of the civilizing process in general.

If we recall, Perrault wrote his tale in 1697 to reflect on a cunning cat whose life is threatened and who manages to survive by using his brains to trick a king and an ogre. On a symbolical level, the cat represented Perrault's conception of male members of the haute bourgeoisie (his own class), who composed the administrative class of Louis XIV's court and who were often the mediators between the peasantry and aristocracy. Of course, there are numerous ways to read Perrault's tale, but whatever approach one chooses, it is apparent that the major protagonist is the cat.

This is not the case in Disney's film. The hero is a young man, a commoner, who is in love with the king's daughter, and she fondly returns his affection. At the same time, the hero's black cat, a female, is having a romance with the royal white dog, the king's chauffeur. When the gigantic king discovers that the young man is wooing his daughter, he kicks him out of the palace, followed by Puss. At first, the hero does not want Puss's help nor will he buy her the boots that she sees in a shop window. Then they go to the movies together and see a film with Rudolph Vaselino, a reference to the famous Rudolph Valentino, as a bullfighter who spurs the imagination of Puss.

Consequently, she tells the hero that she now has an idea that will help him win the king's daughter, providing that he will buy her the boots. Of course, the hero will do anything to obtain the king's daughter, and he must disguise himself as a masked bullfighter. In the meantime Puss explains to him that she will use a hypnotic machine behind the scenes so he can defeat the bull and win the approval of the king. When the day of the bullfight arrives, the masked hero struggles but eventually manages to defeat the bull. The king is so overwhelmed by his performance that he offers his daughter's hand in marriage, but first he wants to know who the masked champion is. When the hero reveals himself, the king is enraged, but the hero grabs the princess and leads her to the king's chauffeur, the white dog, who jumps in front with Puss, and they speed off, with the king chasing in vain after them.

Although Puss as a cunning cat is crucial in this film, Disney focuses most of his attention on the young man who wants to succeed at all costs. In contrast to the traditional fairy tale, the hero is not a peasant or dumb. Read as a parable of Disney's life at that moment, the hero can be seen as young Disney wanting to break into the industry of animated films (the king) with the help of Ub Iwerks (Puss) or his brother Roy. The hero upsets the king and runs off with his prize possession, the virginal princess. Thus, the king is dispossessed, and the young man outraces him with the help of his friends.

But Disney's film is also an attack on the literary tradition of the fairy tale. He robs the literary tale of its voice and changes its form and meaning. Since the cinematic medium is a popular form of expression and is accessible to the public at large, Disney actually returns the fairy tale to the majority of people. The images (scenes, frames, characters, gestures, jokes) are readily comprehensible for the young and old from different social classes. In fact the fairy tale is practically infantilized, just as the jokes are infantile. The plot records the deepest oedipal desire of every young boy: the son humiliates and undermines the father and runs off with his most valued object of love, the daughter or wife. By simplifying this complex plot semiotically in black-and-white drawings and by making fun of it so that it had a common appeal, Disney also touched on other themes such as democracy, technology, and modernity. But at this point in his life, he did not realize the potential of the cinema to develop his civilizing mission. As a young man, he was very influenced by populism and he celebrated individualism. He was mainly concerned with focusing on underdogs; in particular, the small people, often anthropomorphized animals, who are oppressed, reveal great courage, and manage to pull themselves up by their bootstraps.

Disney's hero is the enterprising young man, the entrepreneur, who uses technology to his advantage. He does nothing to help the people or the community. In fact, he deceives the masses and the king by creating the illusion that he is stronger than the bull. He has learned, with the help of Puss, that one can achieve glory through deception. It is through the artful use of images that one can sway audiences and gain their favor. Animation is trickery—trick films—for still images are made to seem as if they move through automatization. As long as one controls the images (and machines) one can reign supreme, just as the hero is safe as long as he is disguised. The pictures conceal the controls and machinery. They deprive the audience of viewing the production and manipulation, and in the end audiences can no longer envision a fairy tale for themselves, as they can when they read it. The pictures deprive the audience now of visualizing their own characters, roles, and desires. At the same time, Disney offsets the deprivation with the pleasure of scopophilia and inundates the viewer with delightful images, humorous figures, and erotic signs. In general the animator, Disney, projects the enjoyable fairy tale of his life through his own images, and he realizes through animated stills his basic oedipal dream that he was to play out time and again in most of his fairy-tale films. It is the repetition of Disney's infantile anal quest to cleanse the world—the core of American mythology—that enabled him to strike a chord with American viewers from the 1920s to the present. However, instead of celebrating infantile curiosity, the child in us, Disney began insisting on taming if not instrumentalizing the imagination to serve the forces of law and order.

WHO'S AFRAID OF THE BIG BAD WOLF?

After Disney left Kansas City in 1924 and went to Hollywood, he abandoned the fairy tale as source material for his films but not for long. By 1928, when he began producing the famous Silly Symphony cartoons, he returned to the fairy-tale realm and continued to create innovative and revolutionary cartoons such as The Merry Dwarfs (1928), The Ugly Duckling (1931), Babes in the Woods (1932), Three Little Pigs (1933), The Big Bad Wolf (1934), The Flying Mouse (1934), The Golden Touch (1935), Three Little Wolves (1936), and The Brave Little Tailor (1938). Robert Sklar remarked, "The early Mickey Mouse and Silly Symphony cartoons are magical. Freed from the burdens of time and responsibility, events are open-ended, reversible, episodic, without obvious point. Outlandish events occur without fear of consequence. There is no fixed order of things: the world is plastic to imagination and will."[5] But Sklar went on to note a significant transformation in Disney's work during the 1930s that totally altered the ideology of his fairy-tale films and led to his vision of an ideal society that was eventually realized in his theme parks and EPCOT (Experimental Prototype Community of Tomorrow) Center, a model city.

Around 1932 the Disney cartoons began to change; by 1933 a whole new world view had emerged. The later cartoons are tales, many of them moral tales.

They rejoin the straight and narrow path of time. They have beginnings and endings, and everything that happens in between has consequences. The world has rules, and you'd better learn them or watch out. Don't be too imaginative, don't be too inquisitive, don't be too willful, or you'll get into trouble—though there's always time to learn your lesson and come out all right. This idea was a year or two ahead of feature films—perhaps because the features took longer to plan, produce, and market—in expressing the spirit of social purpose, the reinforcing of old values, in the culture of the later 1930s.[6]

We must remember, of course, that Disney did not direct these cartoons, but he was involved in the conception of most of the story lines and always played a major role in determining what was being produced in his studio. Therefore, he left his mark on all these cartoons that bear a similarity to the early films of the 1920s, except now he used technicolor and sound to enhance them and improved the fluidity and movement of the characters through the use of the latest technological advances in cinema. Richer in color and character, the primitive, vibrant, and raw quality of the fairy-tale films from the *Laugh-O-gram* period is still evident in a film like *Babes in the Woods*, directed by Burt Gillett. Based on an American folk song and the Grimms' "Hansel and Gretel," this short cartoon is an unusual interpretation of the traditional tale. It begins with the depiction of a sculptured Witch Rock in a forest and recounts how the wicked witch had been defeated and become petrified. Immediately after the first scene, we see two children in wooden shoes, apparently Dutch or German, wandering in a forest. They are lost and frightened, and it is not clear why they are in this predicament, because they have not been abandoned by their parents, as in "Hansel and Gretel." Fortunately, they discover a community of merry elves, who invite them to join in their festivities and to dance. However, a raggedy witch flying above them ruins the party. The elves are frightened away, but the brother and sister are intrigued by her offer to let them fly on her broom to her candy cottage. When they land, the children immediately begin to eat the house. Then the witch lures them inside, where they find all types of weird little animals in cages. All at once the witch takes a magic potion and changes the little boy into a spider and puts him into a cage. Just as she is about to grab hold of the girl, the elves appear. Before she engages them in an aerial battle, she stuffs the girl down into the cellar. While the elves fly about on white ducks and shoot arrows at the witch on her broom, the boy as spider manages to open the trap door to the cellar. The little girl escapes and changes her brother back into a human with a special potion that the two of them use in turn to transform all the pitiful caged animals into boys and girls. Finally, they carry the witch's boiling brew outside, and she falls from her broom into a potion that causes her to become petrified into a rock.

It is not clear what has happened or will happen to the two babes while the children dance around the rock, but we know that they are free to continue their journey. The exuberant colors in each frame and lively movement of the children who never become despondent reflect the optimism of the film: the children are active agents who take the initiative and thrive in the forest despite the danger of the witch. There is no suggestion that they are irresponsible or should not be curious. They are not punished for a mistake. There is no suggestion that they should tidy their act or tidy anything. They must simply learn how to survive in a world filled with danger and excitement.

However, the message in all the Disney films was about to change about the time this film was made in 1932. Indicative of the shift is Disney's greatest and most popular cartoon of this period, *Three Little Pigs*, produced in 1933 and followed by two sequels, *The Big Bad Wolf* (1934) and *Three Little Wolves* (1936), all of which convey the same moral and celebrate the popular tune of "Who's Afraid of the Big Bad Wolf?" written by Frank Churchill. Numerous critics at that time and later have commented that this particular cartoon caught the imagination of the American people because the wolf symbolized the Great Depression and the pigs were the little people who stood up to the wolf and emerged victorious. However, no matter how valid this interpretation may be for the times, it is flawed because the triumph over the wolf is not a victory of the common people over the wolf, who incidentally was first associated with a Jewish peddler (capitalism) in *Three Little Pigs* and later with Hitler (fascism) in *Three Little Wolves*. Rather, it is the triumph of the master builder, the oldest pig, who puts everyone and everything in its right place. The image of the hardworking, clean-living pig is contrasted with his dancing brothers, who are constantly afraid of being swallowed by the greedy and voracious wolf. Even when they sing the ditty "Who's Afraid of the Big Bad Wolf?" they never develop the confidence to deal with this terrifying but laughable creature. Only their brother can cope with him, not unlike Disney, who oversaw the workers in his studio and set an example as a workaholic. The one serious stalwart pig, the entrepreneur, who knows how to safeguard his interests, is the only one who can survive in a dog-eat-dog, or wolf-eat-pig, world. In *The Big Bad Wolf* the bricklaying pig even saves Little Red Riding Hood and her grandmother; he already has aspects of the dependable charming prince and is related to the cat and young hero in Disney's earlier film *Puss in Boots*. The messages that Disney now began to communicate in his fairy-tale films are as follows: don't take your risks, don't be curious, know your place in the order of things, and don't wander far from home. For instance, in *The Flying Mouse* (1934) a young mouse who desperately wants to fly like a bird is granted his wish when he rescues a butterfly from a spider. The butterfly turns into a fairy princess who grants him the power to fly. However, instead of being admired by his friends and family, he is shunned by them because he resembles a bat or vampire with his wings. In addition, the nasty bats in a cave taunt him by calling him "nothing but a nothing." The princess had told him that a mouse was never meant to fly, and he learns his lesson and pleads with the fairy to restore him to his proper station in life. In fact, he becomes a somebody, but that somebody is a tamed mouse who runs into his house to the apron strings of his mother. The film is a warning to a young child who wants to sprout wings, to be independent, or to do something extraordinary.

But this conservative Disney ideology that was developing has more to do with just conformity and conventionality in these fairy-tale films. There is a strong dose of a cleanliness fetish connected to Disney's desire to make the world more pristine and safe. The prescriptions for proper civilized behavior were becoming clearer in his mind, and the short cartoons of Silly Symphonies were only the testing ground for his monumental fairy-tale film SnowWhite and the Seven Dwarfs (1937), with which he was engaged throughout the early 1930s.

CASTING THE COMMODITY SPELL WITH SNOW WHITE

From 1933 to 1937 Disney worked closely with all the animators and technicians assigned to the production of SnowWhite. By now, Disney had divided his studio into numerous departments such as animation, layout, sound, music, storytelling, and so forth, and there were even subdivisions so that certain animators were placed in charge of developing the characters of Snow White, the prince, the dwarfs, and the queen/crone. Disney spent thousands of dollars on a multiplane camera to capture the live action depictions that he desired, the depth of the scenes, and close-ups. In addition he had his researchers experiment with using colored gels, blurring focus, and filming through frosted glass, and he employed the latest inventions in sound and music to improve the synchronization with the characters on the screen. Throughout the entire production of this film, Disney had to be consulted, and his approval had to be granted for each stage of development. After all, Snow White was his story that he had taken from the Brothers Grimm and changed completely to suit his tastes and beliefs.[7] He cast a spell over this German tale and transformed it into something peculiarly American.

Just what were the changes he induced?

1. Snow White is an orphan. Neither her father nor her mother is alive, and she is at first depicted as a kind of Cinderella, cleaning the castle as a maid in a patched dress. In the Grimms' version there is the sentimental death of her mother. Her father remains alive, and she was never forced to do the work of commoners such as wash the steps of the castle.

2. The prince appears at the very beginning of the film on a white horse and sings a song of love and devotion to Snow White. He plays a negligible role in the Grimms' version and appears only at the end of the tale.

3. Not only is the queen jealous that Snow White is more beautiful than she is but she also sees the prince singing to Snow White and is envious because her stepdaughter has such a handsome suitor.

4. Though the forest and the animals do not speak, they are anthropomorphized. In particular the animals befriend Snow White and become her protectors. They assist her in cleaning the house, and they are all degendered and made as soft as stuffed animals.

5. The dwarfs are hardworking and rich miners. They all have names—Doc, Sleepy, Bashful, Happy, Sneezy, Grumpy, and Dopey—representative of certain human characteristics, and they are fleshed out so that they become the star attractions of the film. Their actions are what count in defeating evil. They also provide comic relief. In the Grimms' tale, the dwarfs are anonymous and play a humble role.

6. The queen comes only one time instead of three as in the Grimms' version, and she is killed almost accidentally while trying to destroy the dwarfs by rolling a huge stone down a mountain to crush them. The punishment in the Grimms' tale is more horrifying because she must dance in red-hot iron shoes at Snow White's wedding.

7. Snow White does not return to life when a dwarf stumbles while carrying the glass coffin as in the Grimms' tale. She returns to life when the prince, who has searched far and wide for her, arrives and bestows a kiss on her lips. His kiss of love is the only antidote to the queen's poison.

At first glance, it seems that the changes that Disney made were not momentous. If we recall Sandra Gilbert and Susan Gubar's penetrating analysis in their book *The Madwoman in the Attic*,[8] the film follows the classic sexist narrative about the framing of women's lives through a male discourse. Such male framing drives women to frustration and some women to the point of madness. It also pits women against women in competition for male approval (the mirror) of their beauty, which is short-lived. No matter what they do, women cannot chart their own lives without male manipulation and intervention, and in the Disney film the prince plays even more of a framing role because he is introduced at the beginning while Snow White is singing "I'm Wishing for the One I Love to Find Me Today." He also appears at the end of the film as the fulfillment of her dreams.

There is no doubt that Disney retained key ideological features of the Grimms' fairy tale that reinforce nineteenth-century patriarchal notions, which Disney shared with the Grimms. In some way, he can even be considered their perfect "disciple," for he preserves and carries on many of their benevolent stereotypical attitudes toward women. For instance, in the Grimms' tale, when Snow White arrives at the cabin, she pleads with the dwarfs to allow her to remain and promises that she will wash the dishes, mend their clothes, and clean the house. In Disney's film, she arrives and notices that the house is dirty. So, she persuades the animals to help her make the cottage tidy so that the dwarfs will perhaps let her stay there. Of course, the house for the Grimms and Disney was the place where good girls remained, and one aspect of the fairy tale and the film is about the domestication of women.

However, Disney went much further than the Grimms to make his film more memorable than the tale, for he does not celebrate the domestication of women so much as the triumph of the banished and the underdogs. That is, he celebrates his destiny, and insofar as he had shared marginal status with many Americans, he also celebrated an American myth of Horatio Alger: it is a male myth about perseverance, hard work, dedication, loyalty, and justice— key features of the Protestant Ethic, which forms the basis of the so-called American civilizing process.

It may seem strange to argue that Disney perpetuated a male myth through his fairy-tale films when, with the exception of *Pinocchio* (1940), they all featured young women as heroines, as in *Cinderella* (1950) and *Sleeping Beauty* (1959). However, despite their beauty and charm, these figures are pale and pathetic compared with the more active and demonic characters in the film. The witches not only are agents of evil but also represent erotic and subversive forces that are more appealing both for the artists who drew them and for the audiences.[9] The young women are like helpless ornaments in need of protection, and when it comes to the action of the film, they are omitted. In *Snow White and the Seven Dwarfs*, the film does not really become lively until the dwarfs enter the scene. They are the mysterious characters who inhabit a cottage, and it is through their hard work and solidarity that they are able to maintain a world of justice and restore harmony to the world. The dwarfs can be interpreted as the humble American workers, who pull together during a depression. They keep their spirits up by singing "Hi Ho, it's home from work we go" or "Hi Ho, it's off to work we go," and their determination is the determination of every worker, who will succeed just as long as he does his share while women stay at home and keep the house clean. Of course, it is also possible to see the workers as Disney's own employees, on whom he depended for the glorious outcome of his films. In this regard, the prince can be interpreted as Disney, who directed the love story from the beginning. If we recall, it is the prince who frames the narrative. He announces his great love at the beginning of the film, and Snow White cannot be fulfilled until he arrives to kiss her. During the major action of the film, he, like Disney, is lurking in the background and waiting for the proper time to make himself known. When he does arrive, he takes all the credit as champion of the disenfranchised, and he takes Snow White to his castle while the dwarfs are left as keepers of the forest.

But what has the prince actually done to deserve all the credit? What did Disney actually do to imprint his name as a brand, signifying the appropriation of the fairy tale in his name? As producer of the fairy-tale films and major owner of the Disney Studio, he wanted to figure in the film, and he accomplished this by stamping his signature as owner on the frame with the title of the film and then by having himself embodied in the figure of the prince. It is Prince Disney, or master builder, who made inanimate figures come to life through his animated films, and it is the prince who is glorified in *Snow White and the Seven Dwarfs* when he resuscitates Snow White with a magic kiss. Afterward he holds Snow White in his arms, and in the final frame he leads her off on a white horse to his golden castle on a hill. His golden castle—every woman's dream—transcends the dark, sinister castle of the queen. The prince becomes her reward, and his power and wealth are glorified in the end.

There are obviously mixed messages or multiple messages in *Snow White and the Seven Dwarfs*, but the overriding sign, in my estimation, is the signature of Disney's self-glorification as organizer, sanitizer, and entrepreneur. Disney wants the world *cleaned up*, and the pastel colors with their sharply drawn ink lines create images of cleanliness, just as each sequence reflects a clearly conceived and preordained destiny for all the characters in the film. Peter Brunette talks about the anal-obsessive features of the film. For instance, "the continual emphasis on washing and cleaning and turning the dwarfs' cottage into a nice little middle-class suburban habitation clearly leads in this direction,"[10] that is, in the direction of the anal stage of development, something that Brunette likens to the tenacity of the Puritan mind-set in American culture. Unlike his earlier more experimental fairy-tale shorts, Disney brings absolute closure to the tale—purifying the forest for innocent love and stamping the story with a patriarchal imprint. For Disney, the Grimms' tale is not a vehicle to explore the deeper implications of the narrative and its history or to question its classical status[11] but a vehicle to spread his message about proper sex roles, behavior, manners, and customs. If there is a major change in the plot, it centers on the power of the prince, the only one who can save Snow White, and he becomes the focal point by the end of the story.

In Disney's early work with fairy tales in Kansas City, he had a wry and irreverent attitude toward the classical narratives, and there was a strong suggestion in the manner in which he and Iwerks rewrote and filmed the tales that they were revolutionaries, the new boys on the block, who were about to introduce innovative methods of animation into the film industry and speak for the outcasts. However, by 1934 Disney is already one of the kingpins of animation, and he uses all that he had learned to reinforce his power and command of fairy-tale animation. The manner in which he copied the musical plays and films of his time and his close adaptation of fairy tales with patriarchal codes indicate that all the technical experiments would be used not to foster social change in America but to keep power in the hands of individuals like himself, who felt empowered to design and create new worlds. As Richard Schickel perceptively remarked, Disney "could make something his own, all right, but that process nearly always robbed the work at hand of its uniqueness, of its soul, if you will. In its place he put jokes and songs and fright effects, but he always seemed to diminish what he touched. He came always as a conqueror, never as a servant. It is a trait, as many have observed, that many Americans share when they venture into foreign lands hoping to do good but equipped only with knowhow instead of sympathy and respect for alien traditions."[12] [13]

Disney always wanted to do something new and unique just as long as he had absolute control. He also knew that novelty would depend on the collective skills of his employees, whom he had to keep happy or indebted to him in some way. Therefore, from 1934 onward, about the time that he conceived his first feature-length fairy-tale film, Disney became the master builder and orchestrator of a corporate network that changed the function of the fairy-tale genre in America. The power of Disney's fairy-tale films resides not in the uniqueness or novelty of the productions but in Disney's great talent for holding still many antiquated views of the civilizing process through animation and his use to his advantage of the latest technological developments in cinema. His adaptation of the literary fairy tale for the screen led to the following changes in the institution of the genre:

1. Technique takes precedence over the story, and the story is used to celebrate the technician as master builder and his means of operating. In this case, though many hands contributed to a Disney fairy-tale film, it was Disney who designated how technique and technology were to be used.
2. The carefully arranged images narrate through seduction and imposition by the animator's hand and the camera. Viewers are not to think for themselves. They are to be carried away by the spectacle controlled by the master builder.
3. The images and sequences engender a sense of wholeness, seamless totality, and harmony that is orchestrated by a savior/technician on and off the screen.
4. Though the characters are fleshed out to become more realistic, they are also one-dimensional and are to serve functions in the film. There is no character development because the characters are stereotypes, arranged according to a credo of domestication of the imagination.

5. The domestication is related to colonization insofar as the ideas and types are portrayed as models of behavior to be emulated. Exported through the screen as models, the so-called American fairy tale colonizes other national audiences. What is good for Disney is good for the world, and what is good in a Disney fairy tale is good in the rest of the world. This generalization may seem simplistic, but it refers to a practice that is continually exercised by major corporations throughout the world, whether they are American, European, or global.

6. The thematic emphasis on cleanliness, control, and organized industry reinforces the technics of the film: the clean frames with attention paid to every detail, the precise drawing and manipulation of the characters as real people, and the careful plotting of the events that focus on salvation through the male hero.

7. Private reading pleasure is replaced by pleasurable viewing in an impersonal cinema. Here one is brought together with other viewers not to develop the community but to be diverted in the French sense of *divertissement* and the American sense of diversion.

8. The diversion of the Disney fairy tale is geared toward nonreflective viewing. Everything is on the surface, one-dimensional, and we are to delight in one-dimensional portrayal and thinking, for it is adorable, easy, and comforting in its simplicity.

Once Disney realized how successful he was with his formula for feature-length fairy tales, he never abandoned it, and in fact it appears as if the motif and motive of tidying the fairy tale and tidying the world run throughout all the cinematic adaptations during his lifetime and beyond. His mission to restore a conservative ideology through plots that exemplified a traditional civilizing process and to conventionalize the fairy tale through the repetition of diverting spectacles was firmly set by 1940 with the production of *Pinocchio*. Here it is a gawky wooden boy who must prove that he is obedient, responsible, docile, and sweet if he is to be accepted into a so-called civilized society that resembles more a Bavarian dollhouse than the rough villages and cities of nineteenth-century Italy. Pinocchio must clean up his act to be granted clemency from the Blue Fairy. The gentle cuteness of Jiminy Cricket, who is actually killed in Carlo Collodi's original fairy-tale novel, is the voice of reason that establishes the ethical and moral principles of behavior that are once again set according to a code of the Protestant Ethic and principles of a patriarchal tradition.

This is also true in *Mary Poppins* (1964), in which a magical governess answers a newspaper ad to save the Banks family from chaos; she does not serve the imagination or cultivate the talents of the children. On the contrary, though she is a fairy figure, she acts as the stereotypical nanny or cleaning woman to clean up a messy upper-class family. Though the musical is charming, the charm conceals how Disney restores the conservative tendencies of the classical fairy tale. Mary Poppins uses her magic and imagination to tame the children, enable Mr. Banks to procure a better position at the bank, and minimize Mrs. Banks's involvement in the suffragette movement. What passes for a happy end can be compared to a dampening of curiosity and diversity, even though the film was regarded as an uplifting sensation. As Steven Watts notes,

> The portrait of *Mary Poppins* as a virtuous moral exercise gained added luster from the publicity accorded to its two biggest stars. Both Julie Andrews, portrayed as a devoted mother who demurely confessed that "I suspect my best talent is being a housewife," and Dick Van Dyke, pictured as an ardent churchgoer and family man, were presented in national publications as paragons of wholesome values. . . . The favorable moral critique of *Mary Poppins*, however, triggered a skirmish in a larger cultural war. On one side stood ordinary Americans, who generally adored the innocent fun, fantasy, moral uplift, and sentimental emotion of Disney's productions. On the other stood many critics, who increasingly loathed his work as morally naïve, socially conservative, and artistically appalling.[14]

What makes the artistry appalling, no matter how delightful some of the characters and scenes are, is the repetition of a pattern typical of Hollywood and Broadway musicals that repeat the same romantic happy endings. From *Snow White and the Seven Dwarfs* up through *Beauty and the Beast*, the writers and directors in Disney's studio have operated with a formula: there is an opening song that announces the yearning of a heroine; the young woman, always virginal and sweet, is victimized and is captured or imprisoned by evil forces; at the same time comical animals or animated objects, as in the case of *Beauty and the Beast*, provide comic relief and try to assist the persecuted heroine; at one point a male hero is introduced along with a romantic song or two; and because the girl cannot save herself, the hero is called on to overcome sinister forces represented by a witch, scheming minister, or dumb brute. Of course, there are variations to the pattern, but they are minor. The message in these "black-and-white" films is simplistic: evil is represented by the dark forces of discord, impropriety, and overreaching. There is no complexity in a Disney fairy-tale film, no exploration of character or the causes that create obstacles for the protagonists in the narratives. The emphasis is on purification, preparing oneself to become chosen, a member of the elite, and this American cleansing process based on meritocracy replaces the old schemata of the European fairy tale while at the same time it restores notions of hierarchy and elitism, reinforces a kind of redundant behavior controlled by a master builder such as Disney, and leads to a static dystopian vision of the world, that is, a degeneration of utopia.

There is a strong connection between the type of behavior and thinking fostered by the Disney fairy-tale films and the Disney theme parks, EPCOT Center, and the town of Celebration, constructed by the Disney Corporation. If we focus on the implicit ideological assumptions in Disney's appropriation of the fairy tale and how he desexualized and ordered the world through images and music that suggest wholeness, innocence, alacrity, cleanliness, and obedience, we can see how he tried to implant the same ideas of the perfect happy world in his theme parks and even managed to animate people in his corporation to carry them forward after his death in 1966. For example, after his initial creation of the California Disneyland in 1955, he began working on plans for EPCOT, which he described as "a planned, controlled community, a showcase for American industry and research, schools, cultural and educational communities."[15] The emphasis, as in all of Disney's operations and films, was on control, and when EPCOT came into being after Disney's death, it was apparent that freedom of the imagination and movement was to be limited. As Alexander Wilson commented, "The organizing principle of the EPCOT landscape is control. Direction is given to the gaze of the spectator; visual perspectives, aural terrains, the kinds of movement permitted—all reinforce and reinterpret the various themes of the Center. . . . EPCOT is a seamless environment; there is never a moment of space that is not visually, aurally, and olfactorily programmed by the Disney resort managers."[16] Eventually, the experiment of EPCOT led to the creation of a real town called Celebration that has manifested the same homogenized and static features of EPCOT and the theme parks and loss of control by the inhabitants.[17]

Despite the deprivation of civil rights, the continual instrumentalization of the imagination, and the increased security measures to contain the violence of American life, the appeal of Disney's vision of how the world should be ordered symmetrically and controlled has not abated.[18] Louis Marin, the great French philosopher, long ago put his finger on why Disney's utopian verve is still popular, highly significant, and alarming not only in the United States but throughout the world:

> Disneyland is the representation realized in a geographical space of the imaginary relationship that the dominant groups of American society maintain with their real conditions of existence, with the *real* history of the United States, and with the space outside of its borders. Disneyland is a fantasmatic projection of the history of the American nation, of the way in which this history was conceived with regard to other peoples and to the natural world. Disneyland is an immense and displaced metaphor of the system of representation and values unique to American society. This function has an obvious ideological function. It alienates the visitor by a distorted and fantasmatic representation of daily life, by a fascinating image of the past and

future, of what is estranged and what is familiar: comfort, welfare, consumption, scientific and technological progress, superpower, and morality. These are values obtained by violence and exploitation; here they are projected under the auspices of law and order.[19]

Marin was concerned with the degeneration of utopia and how it was turned into the form of a myth. In the case of Disney, the degeneration of utopia in his fairy-tale films began during the 1930s when he became more conscious of the civilizing influence of his works and how he actually captured and portrayed American values in his films. To what extent Disney influenced people, young and old, through his myriad and diverse films is a matter of debate, but the development of his civilizing mission and his use of the fairy tale as a means to convey this mission cannot be debated. Disney came to represent the essence of American ideology—its populism, Puritanism, elitism, and consumerism—and he felt that these values should be spread throughout the world by all his products. His feature fairy-tale films, those he produced and those produced by his corporation after his death, were never propagandistic films, but they did change the civilizing function of the fairy tale and they did reflect Disney's personal ideology.

Fortunately, Disney's use of fairy tales in the cinema has not been uncontested, but like the Brothers Grimm in the nineteenth century, he set a worldwide standard in the twentieth century against which all fairy-tale films, whether animated or live action, were measured. It is to his credit that he developed innovative and experimental modes of animation to restore the fairy tale as a staple of family entertainment, but his ideological premises have long since outlived their validity and justification. The recent fairy-tale films *Shrek* (2001) and *Shrek 2* (2003) produced by the American film company Dreamworks and *Spirited Away* (2001) and *Howl's Moving Castle* (2004) created by the Japanese filmmaker Hayao Miyazaki suggest that the fairy-tale film is now being used to question the degeneration of utopia. In particular, the two Shrek films make obvious reference to the Disney Corporation and ideological world to critique and question it. In the first film all the fairy-tale characters from the Grimms' tales up through the Disney films are banished to Shrek's swamp, where they are happy and find refuge from the brutal puritanical force of Lord Farquaad—who resembles Michael Eisner, former head of the Disney Corporation—who hates fantasy and strange characters that look like mutants. What is neat, clean, and beautiful at his court, which resembles the antiseptic Disneyland, masks the violence and ugliness of the Farquaad's empire. Eventually, the lord is exposed as a petty tyrant and made into a laughing stock while the ugly Shrek and ugly Fiona can retire to the messy swamp—but not to live happily ever after, for there is a sequel. In the second Shrek film, notions of beauty, consumerism, and celebrity are undercut by the behavior of Shrek, the princess Fiona, and a cunning Puss in Boots. In this hilarious film, the parents of Fiona live in a kingdom that resembles Hollywood, and Prince Charming is the son of a witch, who creates an artificial world that she controls until Shrek and his friends reveal her methods of blackmail and pretension. Once again, at the end, Fiona chooses to remain with Shrek and live in a swamp with marginalized creatures.

In the Shrek fairy-tale films, handsome princes do not save helpless virgins, and the unusual qualities of intrepid young women are fully represented in Miyazaki's Spirited Away and Howl's Moving Castle. In the first film, the young Chihiro enters a haunted town and proves herself to be dauntless as she rescues her parents who have been turned into pigs by a greedy witch. In the second, based on a fantasy novel by Diana Wynne Jones, Sophie, a young hatmaker, joins with the wizard Howl to defeat the Witch of the Waste. Throughout all Miyazaki's films one senses a liberation of the imagination that counters social reality and the manner in which fairy-tale films for children have traditionally been produced. In a 2001 interview with Tom Mes, he stated,

> I believe that fantasy in the meaning of imagination is very important. We shouldn't stick too close to everyday reality but give room to the reality of the heart, of the mind and of the imagination. Those things can help us in life. But we have to be cautious in using this word fantasy. In Japan, the word fantasy these days is applied to everything from TV shows to video games, like virtual reality. But virtual reality is a denial of reality. We need to be open to the powers of the imagination, which brings something useful to reality. Virtual reality can imprison people. It's a dilemma I struggle with in my work, that balance between imaginary worlds and virtual worlds.[20]

Clearly such unusually imaginative and subversive fairy-tale films of the twenty-first century, such as the works by Miyazaki and Dreamworks, must contend with the hundreds of conventional fairy-tale films in which the imagination is instrumentalized so they can continue to formulate and disseminate the Disney American ideology, whether the film is made by the Disney Corporation or a clone company. However, it is significant that Disney's civilizing mission has been shown to be flawed and has led to a degeneration of utopia. Whether the exposure will lead to a different, more open-ended type of utopian fairy-tale film in America will depend not so much on changes in the culture industry but more on real social changes in the civilizing process and on the ideological bent of the American people and how they try to impose their values of democracy on other countries in the world.

NOTES

INTRODUCTION TO THE ROUTLEDGE CLASSICS EDITION

1   E. Taylor, *Grimms' Goblins. Grimms' Household Stories, Translated from the Kinder und Haus Marchen*, illustr. George Cruikshank (London: R. Meek & Co., 1876).
2   George Lakoff and Mark Johnson, *Metaphors We Live By*, 2nd ed. (Chicago: University of Chicago Press, 2003), 247.

1 FAIRY-TALE DISCOURSE: TOWARD A SOCIAL HISTORY OF THE GENRE

1   Fredric Jameson, *The Political Unconscious: Narrative as a Socially Symbolic Act* (Ithaca: Cornell University Press, 1981), 35.
2   Ibid., 40.
3   Ibid., 77.
4   Ibid., 79.
5   Cf. Marc Soriano, "From Tales of Warning to Formulettes: The Oral Tradition in French Children's Literature," *Yale French Studies* 43 (1969): 24–43, and *Guide de littérature pour la jeunesse* (Paris: Flammarion, 1975); Isabelle Jan, *Essai sur la littérature enfantine* (Paris: Éditions Ouvrières, 1969); Dieter Richter and Johannes Merkel, *Märchen, Phantasie und soziales Lernen* (Berlin: Basis, 1974); and F.J. Darton, *Children's Books in England*, 2nd ed. (Cambridge: Cambridge University Press, 1960). There are numerous other studies that touch on this point.
6   See Robert Mandrou, *De la culture populaire aux XVIIe et XVIIIe siècles* (Paris: Stock, 1964).
7   See Teresa DiScanno, *Les Contes de Fées à l'époque classique (1680–1715)* (Naples: Liguori, 1975), 20–30.
8   Cf. Claudia Schmölders, ed., *Die Kunst des Gesprächs* (Munich: Deutscher Taschenbuch Verlag, 1979), 9–67.
9   *The Political Unconscious*, 106–107.
10 Vladimir Propp, *Morphology of the Folktale*, ed. Louis Wagner and Alan Dundes (Austin: University of Texas Press, 1968).

11   Algirdas-Julien Greimas, *Sémantique structurale* (Paris: Larousse, 1964).
12   Marie-Louise Tenèze, ed., "Du Conte merveilleux comme genre," in *Approches de nos traditions orales* (Paris: G.-P. Maisonneueve et Larse, 1970), 11–65.
13   Ibid., 23–24.
14   Claude Lévi-Strauss, *Tristes Tropiques* (Paris: Plon, 1955), 29–30.
15   "Du Conte merveilleux comme genre," 28–29.
16   Ibid., 65.
17   August Nitschke, *Soziale Ordnungen im Spiegel der Märchen*, 2 vols. (Stuttgart: Frommann-Holzborg, 1977).
18   Heide Göttner-Abendroth, *Die Göttin und ihr Heros* (Munich: Frauenoffensive, 1980).
19   Cf. the chapter "Might Makes Right—The Politics of Folk and Fairy Tales" in the revised and expanded edition of my book *Breaking the Magic Spell: Radical Theories of Folk and Fairy Tales* (Lexington: University Press of Kentucky, 2002), 23–46.
20   Cf. Eugen Weber, "Fairies and Hard Facts: The Reality of Folktales," *Journal of the History of Ideas* XLII (1981): 93–113.
21   See Max Lüthi, *Das europäische Volksmärchen*, 2nd rev. ed. (Bern: Francke, 1960) and *Die Gabe im Märchen* (Bern: Francke, 1943).
22   Denise Escarpit, *La Littérature d'enfance et de jeunesse en Europe* (Paris: Presses Universitaires de France, 1981), 39–40.

2 THE ORIGINS OF THE FAIRY TALE IN ITALY: STRAPAROLA AND BASILE

1   For an excellent study of the influence of Straparola and Basile on the French fairy-tale writers, see Charlotte Trinquet, "La Petite Histoire des Contes de Fées Littéraires en France (1690–1705)" (diss., University of North Carolina, Chapel Hill, 2001).
2   Giambattista Basile, *The Pentamerone of Giambattista Basile*, trans. N.M. Penzer, Vol. 1 (London: Bodley Head, 1932), 5. This edition has a superb introduction by Benedetto Croce about the life and works of Basile.
3   See Nancy Canepa, "Basile e il Carnavalesco," in *Giovan Battista Basile e l'invenzione della fiaba*, ed. Michelangelo Picone and Alfred Messerli (Ravenna: Longo Editore, 2004), 41–60.
4   For a full discussion of the influence, see Trinquet, "La Petite Histoire des Contes de Fées Littéraires (1690–1705)."
5   In recent years, more attention has been paid to Mme d'Aulnoy, and she has gained more recognition as the driving force behind the fairy-tale vogue of the 1690s. See Jean Mainil, *Madame d'Aulnoy et Le Rire des Fées: Essai sur la Subversion féerique et le Merveilleux Comique sous l'Ancien Régime* (Paris: Kimé, 2001); Anne Duggan, *Salonnières, Furies, and Fairies: The Politics of Gender and Cultural Change in Absolutist France* (Newark: University of Delaware Press, 2005); and Allison Stedman, "D'Aulnoy's *Histoire d'Hypolite, comte de Duglas* (1690): A Fairy-Tale Manifesto," *Marvels & Tales* 19, no. 1 (2005): 32–53. See also the excellent bibliography in the special issue of *Marvels & Tales*, "Reframing the Early French Fairy Tale," 19, no. 1 (2005), edited by Holly Tucker.
6   See Joan DeJean, *Tender Geographies: The Politics of Female Authorship under the Late Ancien Régime* (New York: Columbia University Press, 1991).
7   See Patricia Hannon, *Fabulous Identities: Women's Fairy Tales in Seventeenth-Century France* (Atlanta: Rodopi, 1998).

8 See Norbert Elias, "The Retreat of Sociologists into the Present," *Theory, Culture & Society* 4 (1987): 223–47.

9 Ibid., 243.

10 Pierre Bourdieu, *Masculine Domination*, trans. Richard Nice (Stanford, CA: Stanford University Press, 2001), 11.

11 Michele Rak, "Il Sisemta dei racconti nel *Cunto de li cunti* di Basile," in *Giovan Battista Basile e l'innvenzione della fiaba*, ed. Michelangelo Picone and Alfred Messerli (Ravenna: Longo Editore, 2004), 13. "L'opera è stata allestita prevendeno le sue modalità d'uso nell'ottica del passatempo (*intrattenimento*) e delle pratiche della *conversazione* di corte con i suoi generi registri teatrali, comici, devianti, neil limiti di una situazione sociale prevista nel catalogo del costume corrente e delle sue maniere. L'opera è uno degli anelli barccchi della tradizione del raconto di gruppo europeo che va dalle veglie medievali intorno al fuoco al racconto di fate dei salotti francesi del Settecento."

12 Jack Zipes, ed., *The Great Fairy Tale Tradition: From Straparola and Basile to the Brothers Grimm* (New York: Norton, 2001), 106.

13 Ibid., 132.

14 Ibid., 205.

3 SETTING STANDARDS FOR CIVILIZATION THROUGH FAIRY TALES: CHARLES PERRAULT AND THE SUBVERSIVE ROLE OF WOMEN WRITERS

1 Philippe Ariès, *Centuries of Childhood: A Social History of Family Life* (New York: Knopf, 1962), 43.

2 Among the more important works, in chronological order, dealing with this vogue are Mary Elizabeth Storer, *La Mode des contes des fées (1685–1700)* (Paris: Champion, 1928); Jacques Barchilon, *Le Conte merveilleux français de 1690 à 1790* (Paris: Champion, 1975); Raymonde Robert, *Le conte de fées littéraire en France de la fin du XVIIe à la fin du XVIIIe siècle* (Nancy: Presses Universitaires de Nancy, 1982); Lewis Seifert, *Fairy Tales, Sexuality and Gender in France, 1690–1715: Nostalgic Utopias* (Cambridge: Cambridge University Press, 1996); Patricia Hannon, *Fabulous Identities: Women's Fairy Tales in Seventeenth-Century France* (Amsterdam: Rodopi, 1998); and Charlotte Trinquet, "La Petite Histoire des Contes de Fées Littéraires en France (1690–1705)" (diss., University of North Carolina, Chapel Hill, 2001).

3 See Allison Stedman, "D'Aulnoy's *Histoire d'Hypolite, comte de Duglas* (1690): A Fairy-Tale Manifesto," *Marvels & Tales* 19, no. 1 (2005): 32–53.

4 For an excellent anthology that covers not only this period but also the entire literary tradition in France, see Francis Lacassin, *Si les fées m'étaient contées . . . 140 contes de fées de Charles Perrault à Jean Cocteau* (Paris: Omnibus, 2003).

5 Gilbert Rouger, ed., *Contes de Perrault* (Paris: Garnier, 1967), 3. All translations in this chapter are my own unless otherwise indicated.

6 Ibid., 5–6.

7 Ibid., 89.

8 Robert Samber, *The Authentic Mother Goose Fairy Tales and Nursery Rhymes*, ed. Jacques Barchilon and Henry Petit (Denver: Swallow, 1960), iv–v.

9 Edmund Jephcott, trans., *The History of Manners*, 2 vols. (New York: Urizen, 1978). This fascinating study was first published as *Über den Prozess der Zivilisation* (Basel: Haus zum Falken, 1939) and received scant attention because of World War II and the author's difficulties during emigration. It was rediscovered and reissued in 1969 by

Francke Verlag in Bern. Since then it has had a profound influence on major European sociologists and historians. See the essays by Wolf Lepenies, "Norbert Elias: An Outsider of Unprejudiced Insight," 57–64, and Andreas Wehowsky, "Making Ourselves More Flexible Than We Are—Reflections on Norbert Elias," 65–82, and the review by George Mosse, 178–83, all in *New German Critique* 15 (Fall 1978).

10 Christian Zimmer, *Cinéma et politique* (Paris: Seghers, 1974), 138.

11 Norbert Elias, *The Civilizing Process* (New York: Urizen, 1978), xiii.

12 The most thorough and stimulating account of Perrault's life and works is Marc Soriano's *Les Contes de Perrault, Culture savante et traditions populaires* (Paris: Gallimard, 1968). See also his other book *Le Dossier Perrault* (Paris: Hachette, 1972).

13 *The Civilizing Process*, 36. See also Donata Elschenbroich, *Kinder werden nicht geboren* (Bensheim: päd. extra, 1980).

14 Ibid., 59–143.

15 Pierre Bourdieu, *La Distinction* (Paris: Minuit, 1979). There are very important connections between the works of Elias and Bourdieu that explain how literature actually incorporates and fleshes out social attitudes and behaviors.

16 *The Civilizing Process*, 108.

17 Cf. Andrea Dworkin, *Woman Hating* (New York: Dutton, 1974); Claudia Honnegger, *Die Hexen der Neuzeit. Studien zur Sozialgeschichte eines kulturellen Deutungsmusters* (Frankfurt am Main: Suhrkamp, 1978); Sylvia Bovenschen, "The Contemporary Witch, the Historical Witch, and the Witch Myth," *New German Critique* 15 (Fall 1978): 83–120; and Hans Peter Duerr, *Traumzeit. Über die Grenze Zwischen Wildnis und Zivilisation* (Frankfurt am Main: Syndikat, 1978), 13–90.

18 H.R. Trevor-Roper, "The European Witch-Craze of the Sixteenth and Seventeenth Centuries," in *Religion, the Reformation and Social Change* (London: Macmillan, 1967), 90–192.

19 Cf. Michel Foucault, *Discipline and Punish* (New York: Pantheon, 1979).

20 Cf. Rudolf Zur Lippe, *Naturbeherrschung am Menschen*, 2 vols. (Frankfurt am Main: Suhrkamp, 1974).

21 *The Civilizing Process*, 143.

22 Lilyane Mourey, *Introduction aux contes de Grimm et de Perrault* (Paris: Minard, 1978), 40.

23 *Contes de Perrault*, 102.

24 See Philip Lewis's excellent study, *Seeing through the Mother Goose Tales: Visual Turns in the Writings of Charles Perrault* (Stanford, CA: Stanford University Press, 1996). He demonstrates how Perrault's thinking and style owe a great deal to Cartesian philosophy.

25 I have endeavored to develop this concept more thoroughly in my book *Breaking the Magic Spell: Radical Theories of Folk and Fairy Tales*, 2nd rev. ed. (Lexington: University Press of Kentucky, 2000).

26 Cf. Paul Delarue, "Le Petit Chaperon Rouge," in *Le Conte Populaire Français*, vol. I (Paris: Editions Erasme, 1957), 337–38; Marianne Rumpf, "Rotkäppchen. Eine vergleichende Märchenuntersuchung" (diss., Universität Göttingen, 1951), and "Ursprung und Entstehung von Warn- und Schreckmärchen," *FF Communications* 160 (1955): 3–16; Marc Soriano, "From Tales of Warning to Formulettes: The Oral Tradition in French Children's Literature," *Yale French Studies* 43 (1969): 24–43; and Jack Zipes, *The Trials and Tribulations of Little Red Riding Hood*, 2nd ed. (New York: Routledge, 1993).

27 See Elliott O'Donell, *Werewolves* (London: Methuen, 1912); Konrad Müller, *Die Werwolfsage* (Karlsruhe: Macklotsche, 1937); and Montague Summers, *The Werewolf* (Hyde Park: University Books, 1966).

28 Ibid.

29 Paul Delarue, *The Borzoi Book of French Folk Tales* (New York: Knopf, 1956), 383.

30 Yvonne Verdier, "Grands-mères, sie vous saviez: le Petit Chaperon Rouge dans la tradition orale," *Cahiers de Littérature Orale* 4 (1978): 17–55.

31 *Traumzeit*, 82 (cited in *The Civilizing Process*; see note 16).

32 For an exhaustive study of the countless Cinderella versions, see Marian Roalfe Cox, *Cinderella: Three Hundred and Forty-Five Variants* (London: Publications of the Folklore Society, 1892). There are also important essays in Alan Dundes, ed., *Cinderella: A Folklore Casebook* (New York: Garland, 1982). Jane Yolen's article "America's Cinderella," *Children's Literature in Education* 8 (1977): 21–29, demonstrates that the positive depiction of Cinderella as an active heroine in the folk tradition becomes warped by Perrault's time. The matriarchal basis of the tale is confirmed in August Nitschke's *Soziale Ordnungen im Spiegel der Märchen*, 2 vols. (Stuttgart: Frommann-Holzborg, 1977) and in Heide Göttner-Abendroth's *Die Göttin und ihr Heros* (Munich: Frauenoffensive, 1980).

33 *Introduction aux contes de Grimm et de Perrault*, 36.

34 Bruno Bettelheim, *The Uses of Enchantment* (New York: Knopf, 1976), 307–308.

35 *Le Conte merveilleux français de 1690 à 1790*, 10.

36 Cf. Foucault's *The History of Sexuality* (New York: Pantheon, 1979); Elias's *The Civilizing Process*; and van Ussel's *Sexualunterdruckung: Geschichte der Sexualfeindschaft* (Giessen: Focus, 1977).

37 Heide Göttner-Abendroth, "Matriarchale Mythologie," in *Weiblich-Männlich*, ed. Brigitte Wartmann (Berlin: Ästhetik & Kommunikation, 1980), 224. See also her book *Die Göttin und ihr Heros*, 134–71.

38 Cf. Detlev Fehling, *Amor und Psyche: Die Schöpfung des Apuleius und ihre Einwirkung auf das Märchen* (Wiesbaden: Steiner, 1977).

39 *Contes de Perrault*, 180.

40 See Claudia Honegger, *Die Hexen der Neuzeit*, and Sylvia Bovenschen, "The Contemporary Witch, the Historical Witch, and the Witch Myth" (cited in *La Distinction*; see note 15).

41 See Jeanne Roche-Mazon, *Autor des contes de fées* (Paris: Didier, 1968), 61–91.

42 "Riquet à la houppe," in *Contes de fées du grand siècle*, ed. Mary Elizabeth Storer (New York: Publications of the Institute of French Studies, Columbia University, 1934), 78.

43 Jack Zipes, ed. and trans., "The Ram," in *Beauties, Beasts and Enchantment: Classic French Fairy Tales* (New York: New American Library, 1989), 399.

44 Madame d'Aulnoy had great difficulties with her own husband, whom she found extremely disagreeable. She accused him of a crime and brought him to trial. The case turned against her, however, and she was banished from Paris. Two of her accomplices in the conspiracy against her husband were beheaded. Another one of her friends, Madame Ticquet, was executed for killing her own husband. Somehow Mme d'Aulnoy was involved in this murder and barely escaped with her life. See Storer, *La Mode des contes de fées*, 18–41; Jeanne Roche-Mazon, *En marge de "l'Oiseau bleu"* (Paris: L'Artisan du Livre, 1930); and the chapter "Le voyage d'Espagne de Madame d'Aulnoy," in *Autor des contes de fées*, 7–20.

45 For instance, when the merchant and his family move to the country, the narrator in Mme Leprince de Beaumont's tale remarks,

   At first she [Beauty] had a great deal of difficulty because she was not accustomed to working like a servant. But after two months she became stronger, and the hard work improved her health. After finishing her chores, she generally read, played the harpsichord, or sung while spinning. On the other hand, her two sisters were bored to death. They rose at ten, took walks the entire day, and entertained themselves by bemoaning the loss of their beautiful clothes and the fine company they used to have.

"Look at our little sister," they would say to each other. "She's so thick and stupid that she's quite content in this miserable situation."

The good merchant did not agree with them. He knew that Beauty was more suited to stand out in company than they were. He admired the virtues of this young girl—especially her patience, for her sisters were not content merely to let her do all the work in the house, but also insulted her every chance they had.

46 See *Beauty, Beasts and Enchantment: Classic French Fairy Tales*, 234.

47 *Le Conte merveilleux français de 1690 à 1790*, 92.

4 WHO'S AFRAID OF THE BROTHERS GRIMM? SOCIALIZATION AND POLITICIZATION THROUGH FAIRY TALES

1 It has always been fashionable to try to rewrite folktales and the classical ones by the Grimms. However, the recent trend is more international in scope, not just centered in Germany, and more political in intent. For some examples see Jay Williams, *The Practical Princess and Other Liberating Fairy Tales* (London: Chatto & Windus, 1979); Astrid Lindgren, *Märchen* (Hamburg: Oetingen, 1978), which first appeared in Swedish; *The Prince and the Swineherd, Red Riding Hood,* and *Snow White* by the Fairy Story Collective (Liverpool, 1976), three different publications by four women from the Merseyside Women's Liberation Movement. I discuss this international trend in my chapter 8, "The Liberating Potential of the Fantastic in Contemporary Fairy Tales for Children."

2 My focus is on the development in West Germany only. The official attitude toward fairy tales in East Germany has gone through different phases since 1949. At first they were rejected, but there was a more favorable policy during the 1980s, so long as the tales did not question the existing state of affairs. Thus, the older fairy tales by the Grimms were accorded due recognition whereas reutilization of the tales in a manifest political manner critical of the state and socialization was not condoned. See Sabine Brandt, "Rotkäppchen und der Klassenkampf," *Der Monat* 12 (1960): 64–74. I have also written more extensively about the development in East and West Germany in "The Struggle for the Grimms' Throne: The Legacy of the Grimms' Tales in the FRG and GDR since 1945," in *The Reception of Grimms Fairy Tales: Responses, Reactions, Revisions*, ed. Donald Haase (Detroit: Wayne State University Press, 1993), 167–206.

3 See Dieter Richter and Jochen Vogt, eds., *Die heimlichen Erzieher, Kinderbücher und politisches Lernen* (Reinbek bei Hamburg: Rowohlt, 1974), and Linda Dégh, "Grimms' Household Tales and Its Place in the Household: The Social Relevance of a Controversial Classic," *Western Folklore* 38 (April 1979): 83–103.

4 See Erich Kaiser, " 'Ent-Grimm-te' Märchen," *Westermanns Pädagogische Beiträge* 8 (1975): 448–59, and Hildegard Pischke, "Das veränderte Märchen," *Literatur für Kinder*, ed. Maria Lypp (Göttingen: Vandenhoeck & Ruprecht, 1977), 94–113.

5 See Heinz Rölleke's introduction and commentaries to the 1810 manuscript written by the Grimms in *Die älteste Märchensammlung der Brüder Grimm* (Cologny-Geneva: Fondation Martin Bodmer, 1975); Werner Psaar and Manfred Klein, *Wer hat Angst vor*

der bösen Geiss? (Braunschweig: Westermann, 1976), 9–30; and Ingeborg Weber-Kellermann's introduction to *Kinder- und Hausmärchen gesammelt durch die Brüder Grimm*, vol. I (Frankfurt am Main: Insel, 1976), 9–18.

6 Weber-Kellermann, *Kinder- und Hausmärchen gesammelt durch die Brüder Grimm*, vol. I, 14.

7 Ibid., 23–24. This is taken from the 1819 preface by the Brothers Grimm.

8 Ibid., 24.

9 Rölleke, ed., *Die älteste Marchensammlung der Brüder Grimm*, 144. Unless otherwise indicated, all the translations in this chapter are my own. In most instances I have endeavored to be as literal as possible to document the historical nature of the text.

10 Ibid., 145.

11 *Kinder- und Hausmärchen gesammelt durch die Brüder Grimm*, 35–36.

12 Gilbert Rouger, ed., *Contes de Perrault* (Paris: Garnier, 1967), 113.

13 Brüder Grimm, *Kinder- und Hausmärchen. In der ersten Gestalt* (Frankfurt am Main, 1962), 78.

14 Carole Hanks and D.T. Hanks Jr., "Perrault's 'Little Red Riding Hood': Victim of Revision," *Children's Literature* 7 (1978): 68.

15 For the best analysis of Perrault and his times, see Marc Soriano, *Les Contes de Perrault* (Paris: Gallimard, 1968).

16 The word *sittsam* is used in the 1857 edition and carries with it a sense of chastity, virtuousness, and good behavior.

17 *Die älteste Märchensammlung der Brüder Grimm*, 246, 248 (see note 5).

18 Ibid., 249, 251.

19 Ibid., 250.

20 Psaar and Klein, *Wer hat Angst vor der bösen Geiss?* 112–36.

21 See *The Uses of Enchantment: The Meaning and Importance of Fairy Tales* (New York: Knopf, 1976). For a critique of Bettelheim's position, see James W. Heisig, "Bruno Bettelheim and the Fairy Tales," *Children's Literature* 6 (1977): 93–114, and my own criticism in the chapter "On the Use and Abuse of Folk and Fairy Tales: Bruno Bettelheim's Moralistic Magic Wand," in *Breaking the Magic Spell: Radical Theories of Folk and Fairy Tales* (London: Heinemann, 1979), 160–82.

22 Helmut Fend, *Sozialisation durch Literatur* (Weinheim: Beltz, 1979), 30, remarks,

Socialization proves itself to be a process of resubjectification of cultural objectifications. In highly complex cultures and societies this involves the learning of complex sign systems and higher forms of knowledge as well as the general comprehension of the world for dealing with natural problems and the general self-comprehension of human beings. Through the process of resubjectification of cultural objectifications, structures of consciousness, that is, subjective worlds of meaning, are constructed. Psychology views this formally as abstraction from particular contents and speaks about the construction of cognitions, about the construction of a "cognitive map," or a process of internalization. In a depiction of how cultural patterns are assumed in a substantive way, the matter concerns what conceptions about one's own person, which skills and patterns or interpretations, which norms and values someone takes and accepts in a certain culture relative to a sub-sphere of a society. Generally speaking, what happens in the socialization process is what hermeneutical research defines as "understanding." Understanding is developed and regarded here as an interpretative appropriation of linguistically transmitted meanings which represent socio-historical forms of life. To be sure, this understanding has a differentiated level of development which is frequently bound by social class.

23 See Richard Hoggart, *The Uses of Literacy* (London: Chatto & Windus, 1957); R.A Houston, *Literacy in Early Modern Europe: Culture and Education 1500–1800*, 2nd ed. (London: Longman, 2002).

24 Rudolf Schenda, *Volk ohne Buch* (Frankfurt am Main: Klostermann, 1970).

25 Emanuel K. Schwartz, "A Psychoanalytical Study of the Fairy Tale," *American Journal of Psychotherapy* 10 (1956): 755. See also Julius E. Heuscher, *A Psychiatric Study of Fairy Tales* (Springfield, IL: Thomas, 1963).

26 The terms are from Victor Laruccia's excellent study, "Little Red Riding Hood's Metacommentary: Paradoxical Injunction, Semiotics and Behavior," *Modern Language Notes* 90 (1975): 517–34. Laruccia notes (p. 520), "All messages have two aspects, a command and a report, the first being a message about the nature of the relationship between sender and receiver, the second the message of the content. The crucial consideration is how these two messages relate to each other. This relationship is central to all goal-directed activity in any community since all human goals necessarily involve a relation with others." Laruccia's essay includes a discussion of the way male domination and master–slave relationships function in the Grimms' tales.

27 See Dieter Richter, ed., *Das politische Kinderbuch* (Darmstadt: Luchterhand, 1973). Various writers such as Kurd Lasswitz began creating political fairy tales at the end of the nineteenth century. One of the first collections of political fairy tales published during the Weimar period is Ernst Friedrich, ed., *Proletarischer Kindergarten* (Berlin: Buchverlag der Arbeiter-Kunst-Ausstellung, 1921), which contains stories and poems as well.

28 All these writers either wrote political fairy tales or wrote about them during the 1920s and early part of the 1930s. One could add many other names to this list, such as Ernst Bloch, Bruno Schönlank, Berta Lask, Oskar Maria Graf, Kurt Held, Robert Grötzsch, and even Bertolt Brecht. The most important fact to bear in mind, aside from the unwritten history of this development, is that German writers of the 1970s began to hark back to this era.

29 See my article "Down with Heidi, Down with Struwwelpeter, Three Cheers for the Revolution: Towards a New Children's Literature in West Germany," *Children's Literature* 5 (1976): 162–79.

30 Friedrich Karl Waechter was one of the most gifted writers and illustrators for children in Germany during the latter part of the twentieth century. He died in 2005. He is particularly known for the following books: *Der Anti-Struwwelpeter* (1973), *Wir können noch viel zusammenmachen* (1973), *Die Kronenklauer* (1975), and *Die Bauern im Brunnen* (1978).

31 The publisher of *Der Feuerdrache Minimax* is Rowohlt in Reinbek bei Hamburg. Angela Hopf has written several interesting books related to political fairy tales: *Fabeljan* (1968), *Die grosse Elefanten-Olympiade* (1972), *Die Minimax-Comix* (1974), and *Der Regentropfen Pling Plang Pling* (1981).

32 For a thorough and most perceptive analysis of this book, see Hermann Hinkel and Hans Kammler, "Der Feuerdrache Minimax—ein Märchen?—ein Bilderbuch," *Die Grundschule* 3 (1975): 151–60.

33 Among the more interesting studies related to the fairy tale are Dieter Richter and Johannes Merkel, *Märchen, Phantasie und soziales Lernen* (Berlin: Basis, 1974); Andrea Kuhn, *Tugend und Arbeit. Zur Sozialisation durch Kinder- und Jugendliteratur im 18. Jahrhundert* (Berlin: Basis, 1975); and Andrea Kuhn and Johannes Merkel, *Sentimentalität und Geschäft. Zur Sozialisation durch Kinder- und Jugendliteratur im 19. Jahrhundert* (Berlin: Basis, 1977).

34 The publisher of *Janosch erzählt Grimms Märchen* is Beltz and Gelberg in Weinheim. Janosch, whose real name is Horst Eckert, is considered one of the most inventive and

provocative illustrators and writers for young people in Germany. Among his many titles, the most important are *Das Auto heisst Ferdinand* (1964), *Wir haben einen Hund zu Haus* (1968), *Flieg Vogel flieg* (1971), *Mein Vater ist König* (1974), *Das grosse Janosch-Buch* (1976), *Ich sag, du bist ein Bär* (1977), *Oh, wie schön ist Panama* (1978), and *Die Maus hat rote Strümpfe an* (1978). Many of his books have been filmed and translated into English.

35 A good example is *Erstes Jahrbuch der Kinderliteratur. "Geh und spiel mit dem Riesen,"* ed. Hans-Joachim Gelberg (Weinheim: Beltz, 1971), which won the German Youth Book Prize of 1972.

36 Many of the tales were printed in other books edited by Gelberg, or they appeared elsewhere, indicative of the great trend to reutilize fairy tales.

37 Translations of the tales by Brender and Künzler have been published in my book *Breaking the Magic Spell*, 180–82.

38 Gmelin, in particular, has been active in scrutinizing the value of fairy tales and has changed his position in the course of the past eight years. See Otto Gmelin, "Böses kommt aus Märchen," *Die Grundschule* 3 (1975): 125–32.

39 Lerche and Gmelin, *Märchen für tapfere Mädchen* (Giessen: Schlot, 1978), 16.

5 HANS CHRISTIAN ANDERSEN AND THE DISCOURSE OF THE DOMINATED

1 "Er kam mir vor, wie ein Schneider; er sieht auch wirklich ganz so aus. Er ist ein hagerer Mann mit einem hohlen, eingefallenen Gesichte und verrät in seinem äußeren Anstande ein ängstliches, devotes Benehmen, so wie die Fürsten es gern lieben. Daher hat Andersen auch bei allen Fürsten eine so glänzende Aufnahme gefunden. Er repräsentiert vollkommen die Dichter wie die Fürsten sie gern haben wollen." Heinrich Teschner, "Hans Christian Andersen und Heinrich Heine: Ihre literarischen und persönlichen Beziehungen" (diss., Münster: Westfällische Vereinesdruckerei, 1914), 177–78.

2 Niels Kofoed, "Hans Christian Andersen and the European Literary Tradition," in *Hans Christian Andersen: Danish Writer and Citizen of the World* (Amsterdam: Rodopi, 1996), 216–17.

3 Elias Bredsdorff, *Hans Christian Andersen: The Story of His Life and Work* (London: Phaidon, 1975), 152.

4 Ibid., 179. Many more statements like this can be found in Andersen's letters and diaries. See *Hans Christian Andersen's Correspondence with the Late Grand-duke of Saxe-Weimar, Charles Dickens, Etc.*, ed. Frederick Crawford (London: Dean, 1891); *The Diaries of Hans Christian Andersen*, ed. Patricia Conroy and Sven Rossel (Seattle: University of Washington Press, 1990); *Das Märchen meines Lebens. Briefe. Tagebücher*, ed. Erling Nielsen (Munich: Winkler, 1961); and *Aus Andersens Tagebüchern*, ed. Heinz Barüske, 2 vols. (Frankfurt am Main: Fischer, 1980).

5 Ibid., 132–33.

6 Noëlle Bisseret, *Education, Class Language and Ideology* (London: Routledge Kegan Paul, 1979), 1–2.

7 See Jeffrey M. Blum, *Pseudoscience and Mental Ability* (New York: Monthly Review Press, 1978), and Stephan L. Chorover, *From Genesis to Genocide: The Meaning of Human Nature and the Power of Behavior Control* (Cambridge: MIT Press, 1979).

8 For the general development in Europe, see Jürgen Habermas, *Strukturwandel der Öffentlichkeit. Untersuchungen zu einer Kategorie der bürgerlichen Gesellschaft* (Neuwied: Luchterhand, 1962), and Charles Morazé, *The Triumph of the Middle Classes: A Political*

and *Social History of Europe in the Nineteenth Century* (London: Weidenfeld and Nicolson, 1966). For Denmark, see W. Glyn Jones, *Denmark* (New York: Praeger, 1968).

9 Michel Foucault, *Discipline and Punish* (New York: Pantheon, 1968).

10 *Education, Class Language and Ideology*, 26.

11 *Hans Christian Andersen*, 54.

12 Ibid., 69.

13 Cf. *The Fairy Tale of My Life*, trans. W. Glyn Jones (New York: British Book Centre, 1955). Andersen wrote three autobiographies during his life, and each one is filled with distortions and embellishments of his life.

14 *Denmark*, 66–67.

15 Cf. Paul V. Rubow, "Idea and Form in Hans Christian Andersen's Fairy Tales," in *A Book on the Danish Writer Hans Christian Andersen*, ed. Sven Dahl and H.G. Topsøe-Jensen (Copenhagen: Det Berlingske Bogtrykkeri, 1995), 97–136.

16 *Education, Class Language and Ideology*, 63–64.

17 Ibid., 65.

18 Bengt Holbek, "Hans Christian Andersen's Use of Folktales," in *A Companion to the Fairy Tale*, ed. Hilda Ellis Davidson and Anna Chaudri (Cambridge: D.S. Brewer, 2003), 153.

19 Finn Hauberg Mortensen, *A Tale of Tales: Hans Christian Andersen and Children's Literature*, parts III and IV (Minneapolis: Center for Nordic Studies, University of Minnesota, 1989), 16–17.

20 See Lutz Röhrich, "Dankbarer Toter (AaTh-508)," in *Enzyklopädie des Märchens*, ed. Kurt Ranke, vol. 3 (Berlin: De Gruyter, 1999), 306–22.

21 Antti Aarne and Stith Thompson, *The Types of the Folktale*, 2nd rev. ed. (Helsinki: Suomalainen Tiedeaktatemia, 1991), 171–75.

22 "Hans Christian Andersen's Use of Folktales," 155.

6 INVERTING AND SUBVERTING THE WORLD WITH HOPE: THE FAIRY TALES OF GEORGE MACDONALD, OSCAR WILDE, AND L. FRANK BAUM

1 Cf. Jürgen Habermas, *Strukturwandel der Öffentlichkeit* (Berlin: Luchterhand, 1962). English translation: *The Structural Transformation of the Public Sphere*, trans. Thomas Burger (Cambridge, MA: MIT Press, 1989).

2 Brian Alderson, "Tracts, Rewards and Fairies," in *Essays in the History of Publishing*, ed. Asa Briggs (London: Longman, 1977), 248–82. See also Roger Lancelyn Green, *Tellers of Tales* (London: Ward, 1965), 23–73.

3 Jonathan Cott, *Beyond the Looking Glass: Extraordinary Works of Fairy Tale and Fantasy* (New York: Stonehill, 1973). See also Jack Zipes, ed., *Victorian Fairy Tales* (New York: Methuen, 1987); Michael Patrick Hearn, ed., *The Victorian Fairy Book* (New York: Pantheon, 1988); and Nina Auerbach and Ulrich Knoepfelmacher, eds., *Forbidden Journeys: Fairy Tales and Fantasies by Victorian Women Writers* (Chicago: University of Chicago, 1993).

4 *Beyond the Looking Glass*, xlvi.

5 Michel Butor, "On Fairy Tales," in *European Literary Theory and Practice*, ed. Vernon W. Gras (New York: Delta, 1973), 352.

6 Rosemary Jackson, *Fantasy: The Literature of Subversion* (London: Methuen, 1981), 91.

7 Ibid., 33.

8   Ibid., 35.
9   Ibid.
10 For an extensive discussion of MacDonald's life, see Greville MacDonald, *George MacDonald and His Wife* (New York: Dial, 1924); and Richard H. Reis, *George MacDonald* (New York: Twayne, 1972).
11 *George MacDonald*, 45.
12 *Unspoken Sermons*, Second Series (London: Longmans, Green, 1885), 49.
13 Quoted in Reis, *George MacDonald*, 43.
14 *The Complete Fairy Tales of George MacDonald*, intr. Roger Lancelyn Green (New York: Schocken, 1977), 17.
15 Ibid., 35.
16 For a thorough and stimulating psychoanalytic examination of the sexual implications in MacDonald's works, see Robert Lee Wolff, *The Golden Key: A Study of the Fiction of George MacDonald* (New Haven, CT: Yale University Press, 1961).
17 *The Complete Fairy Tales of George MacDonald*, 267.
18 Ibid., 271.
19 See E.H. Mikhail, *Oscar Wilde: An Annotated Bibliography of Criticism* (Totowa, NJ: Rowman & Littlefield, 1978), and also the useful bibliography in H. Montgomery Hyde, *Oscar Wilde* (London: Methuen, 1977), 520–31.
20 Philippe Jullian, *Oscar Wilde* (London: Paladin, 1971), 62.
21 George Woodcock, *The Paradox of Oscar Wilde* (London: T.V. Boardman, 1949), 139.
22 Cf. Jullian, *Oscar Wilde*, 283–97, and Hyde, *Oscar Wilde*, 376–410.
23 Isobel Murray, *Introduction to Oscar Wilde, Complete Shorter Fiction* (Oxford: Oxford University Press, 1979), 10–11.
24 Oscar Wilde, *The Soul of Man under Socialism*, ed. Robert Ross (London: Humphreys, 1912), 18.
25 Ibid., 32.
26 Ibid., 43.
27 Ibid., 45.
28 Ibid., 92.
29 Ibid., 97.
30 See Volker Klotz's excellent short essay on the major ideological differences between Andersen and Wilde, "Wie Wilde seine Märchen über Andersen hinwegerzählt," in *Der zerstückte Traum: Für Erich Arendt zum 75. Geburtstag*, ed. Gregor Laschen and Manfred Schlosser (Berlin: Agora, 1978), 219–28.
31 *Complete Shorter Fiction*, 182.
32 See "Wie Wilde seine Märchen über Andersen hinwegerzählt," 225–28.
33 *Complete Shorter Fiction*, 252.
34 See Frank Joslyn Baum and Russel P. MacFall, *To Please a Child: A Biography of L. Frank Baum* (Chicago: Reilly & Lee, 1961), which contains important biographical and historical material.
35 See Aljean Harmetz, *The Making of the Wizard of Oz* (New York: Knopf, 1978).
36 In addition to the biography by Frank Joslyn Baum and Russel P. MacFall, see Raylyn Moore's *The Wonderful Wizard, Marvelous Land* (Bowling Green, OH: Bowling Green University Press, 1974), for valuable insights for the study of Baum's life.
37 Henry M. Littlefield, "The Wizard of Oz: Parable on Populism," in *American Culture*, ed. Hennig Cohen (New York: Houghton Mifflin, 1968), 370–81. See also Fred Erisman, "L. Frank Baum and the Progressive Dilemma," *American Quarterly* 20 (Fall 1968): 616–23.
38 Ibid., 373, 380.

39 Numerous critics have discussed the censorship exercised by American librarians against Baum. In particular, see Martin Gardner and Russel B. Nye, *The Wizard of Oz and Who He Was* (East Lansing: Michigan State University Press, 1957). This study was one of the first to reestablish Baum's significance for American culture.

40 L. Frank Baum, *The Emerald City* (New York: Ballantine, 1979), 22. Reprint of the original 1910 edition.

41 See Gore Vidal's two-part essay "The Wizard of the 'Wizard,' " *New York Review of Books*, September 29, 1977, 10–15, and "On Rereading the Oz Books," *New York Review of Books*, October 13, 1977, 38–42.

42 See Marius Bewley, "The Land of Oz: America's Great Good Place," in *Masks and Mirrors* (New York: Atheneum, 1970), 255–67.

43 "On Rereading the Oz Books," 42.

7 THE BATTLE OVER FAIRY-TALE DISCOURSE: FAMILY, FRICTION, AND SOCIALIZATION IN THE WEIMAR REPUBLIC AND NAZI GERMANY

1 Within the past thirty-five years there has been a veritable deluge of studies on Weimar and Nazi literature and culture, but none has investigated the significance of the fairy tale. Among the best works for reference and background material are George Mosse, *Nazi Culture: Intellectual and Social Life in the Third Reich* (London: W.H. Allen, 1966); Peter Gay, *Weimar Culture: The Outsider as Insider* (London: Secker & Warburg, 1969); Wolfgang Rothe, ed., *Die deutsche Literatur in der Weimarer Republik* (Stuttgart: Reclam, 1974); Horst Denkler and Karl Prümm, *Die deutsche Literatur im Dritten Reich* (Stuttgart: Reclam, 1976); Jost Hermand and Frank Trommler, *Die Kultur der Weimarer Republik* (Munich: Nymphenburg, 1978); John Willett, *The New Sobriety, 1917–1933: Art and Politics in the Weimar Period* (London: Thames and Hudson, 1978); and Ernst Alker, *Profile und Gestalten der deutschen Literatur nach 1914*, ed. Eugen Thurnher (Stuttgart: Kröner, 1979).

2 The most exhaustive treatment of the debates is to be found in Ulrike Bastian, *Die Kinderund Hausmärchen der Brüder Grimm in der literaturpädagogischen Diskussion des 19. und 20. Jahrhunderts* (Giessen: Haag & Herchen, 1981). See also Bernd Dolle, "Märchen und Erziehung. Versuch einer historischen Skizze zur didaktischen Verwendung Grimmscher Märchen," in *Und wenn sie nicht gestorben sind ... Perspektiven auf das Märchen*, ed. Helmut Brackert (Frankfurt am Main: Suhrkamp, 1980), 165–92.

3 For other significant studies, see Ernst Linde, *Die Bildungsaufgabe der deutschen Dichtung* (Leipzig: Brandstetter, 1927); Alois Jalkotzy, *Märchen und Gegenwart* (Vienna: Jungbrunnen, 1930); Alois Kunzfeld, *Vom Märchenerzähler und Märchenillustrieren* (Vienna: Deutscher Verlag für Jugend und Volk, 1926); Max Troll, *Der Marchenunterricht* (Langensalza: Beyer, 1928); and Walter Wenk, *Das Volksmärchen als Bildungsgut* (Langensalza: Beyer, 1929).

4 See Ernst Bloch, "Das Märchen geht selber in der Zeit" (1930) in *Die Kunst, Schiller zu sprechen und andere literarische Aufsätze* (Frankfurt am Main: Suhrkamp, 1969), 10–14. For a translation and discussion of this essay, see Jack Zipes, "The Utopian Function of Fairy Tales and Fantasy: Ernst Bloch the Marxist and J.R.R. Tolkien the Catholic," in *Breaking the Magic Spell: Radical Theories of Folk and Fairy Tales* (London: Heinemann, 1979). All Bloch's essays on fairy tales can be found in Ernst Bloch, *The Utopian Function of Art and Literature*, trans. Jack Zipes and Frank Mecklenburg (Cambridge, MA: MIT Press, 1988).

5 See Walter Benjamin, "Der Erzähler," in *Gesammelte Schriften*, vol. 2, ed. Rolf Tiedemann and Hermann Schweppenhäuser (Frankfurt am Main: Suhrkamp, 1977), 438–65. For a translation, see Walter Benjamin, "The Storyteller," in *Illuminations*, trans. Harry Zohn (New York: Harcourt Brace, 1968).

6 See Helmut Mörchen, "Notizen zu Wolgast," in *Literatur für Kinder*, ed. Maria Lypp (Göttingen: Vandenhoeck & Ruprecht, 1977), 13–20.

7 Edwin Hoernle, "Die Arbeit in den kommunistischen Kindergruppen" (1923), in *Das politische Kinderbuch*, ed. Dieter Richter (Darmstadt: Luchterhand, 1973), 220–21.

8 Christa Kamenetsky, "Folktale and Ideology in the Third Reich," *Journal of American Folklore* 90 (1977): 169. See also Christa Kamenetsky, "Folklore as a Political Tool in Nazi Germany," *Journal of American Folklore* 85 (1972): 221–35.

9 For more information about the trends at this time, see Peter Aley, *Jugendliteratur im Dritten Reich* (Gütersloh: Bertelsmann, 1967), and Wolfgang Emmerich, *Germanistische Volkstumsideologie, Genese und Kritik der Volksforschung im Dritten Reich* (Reutlingen: Tübingen Vereinigung für Volkskunde, 1968). For two of the many publications on the fairy tale and film, see Adolf Reichwein, "Märchen und Film," *Film und Bild* 2 (April 10, 1926): 114–18, and Max Meurer, "Das Märchen in Bild und Film, von der Schule aus gesehen," *Film und Bild* 5 (May 15, 1939): 121–24.

10 Josef Prestel, *Märchen als Lebensdichtung* (Munich: Hueber, 1938), 86.

11 Cited in *Jugendliteratur im Dritten Reich*, 102.

12 See Irene Dyhrenfurth, *Geschichte des deutschen Jugendbuches* (Zurich: Atlantis, 1967), 262.

13 Hartmut Geerken, *Die goldene Bombe* (Darmstadt: Agora, 1970). Reprinted as *Fischer-Taschenbuch* (Frankfurt am Main: Fischer, 1979).

14 Christoph Eykmann, "Das Märchen im Expressionismus," in *Denk- und Stilformen des Expressionismus* (Munich: Fink, 1974), 126.

15 "Folktale and Ideology in the Third Reich," 177 (see note 8).

16 Max Lüthi, "Familie und Natur im Märchen," in *Volksliteratur und Hochliteratur* (Bern: Francke, 1970), 63–78.

17 Ibid., 77.

18 Eleasar Meletinsky, "Die Ehe im Zaubermärchen," *Acta Ethnographica Academiae Scientarum Hungaricae* 19 (1970): 288.

19 Mark Poster, *Critical Theory of the Family* (London: Pluto, 1978).

20 Ibid., 155.

21 Ibid.

22 Charlotte Bühler, *Das Märchen und die Phantasie des Kindes* (Berlin: Springer, 1977), 27–29. Reprint of the 1919 edition with an essay by Josephine Belz.

23 Ingeborg Weber-Kellermann, *Die deutsche Familie* (Frankfurt am Main: Suhrkamp, 1974), 176–92.

24 See Renate Bridenthal, "Something Old, Something New: Women in Nazi Germany" and Claudia Koonz, "Mothers in the Fatherland: Women in Nazi Germany," in *Becoming Visible: Women in European History*, ed. Renate Bridenthal and Claudia Koonz (Boston: Houghton Mifflin, 1977), 422–44, 445–71, and Jill McIntyre Stephenson, *Women in Nazi Society* (New York: Barnes and Noble, 1976).

25 See Ernst Bloch, "Non-Synchronism and the Obligation to Its Dialectics," *New German Critique* 11 (Spring 1977): 22–38. Also important is Anson Rabinbach's analysis of nonsynchronism in the same issue of *New German Critique*, "Ernst Bloch's Heritage of Our Times and the Theory of Fascism," 5–21.

26 There were numerous attempts to radicalize fairy tales and to make them more socially relevant for children. The works of Zur Mühlen, Schönlank, and Tetzner are among the

best examples of this movement. For other significant writers and their tales, see the stories by Berta Lask, Karl Ewald, and Robert Grötzsch, *Proletarischer Kindergarten, Ein Märchen- und Lesebuch für Gross und Klein*, ed. Ernst Friedrich (Berlin: Buchverlag der Arbeiter-Kunst-Austellung, 1921); Bela Balázs, *Das richtige Himmelblau* (Munich: Drei-Masken Verlag, 1925) and *Sieben Märchen* (Vienna: Rikola, 1921); Robert Grotzsch, *Der Zauberer Burufu* (Berlin: Dietz, 1922); Bela Illes, *Rote Märchen* (Leipzig: Freidenker-Verlag, 1925); Kurd Lasswitz, *Traumkristalle* (Berlin: Emil Felber, 1928); József Lengyel, *Sternekund und Reinekind* (Dresden: Verlags-Anstalt proletarischer Freidenker Deutschlands, 1923); Eugen Lewin-Dorsch, *Die Dollarmännchen* (Berlin: Malik, 1923); Irene Rona, *Was Paulchen werden will* (Berlin: Vereinigung Internationaler Verlagsanstalten, 1926); Maria Szucisich, *Die Träume des Zauberbuches* (Dresden: Verlags-Anstalt proletarischer Freidenker Deutschlands, 1923), and *Silavus* (Berlin: Malik, 1924); and Julius Zerfass, *Die Reise mit dem Lumpensack* (Berlin: Dietz, 1925).

27 Hermann Stehr, *Das Märchen vom deutschen Herzen* (Berlin: Horen, 1929), 13.
28 See Hans Friedrich Blunck, *Gesammelte Werke*, 10 vols. (Hamburg: Hanseatische Verlagsanstalt, 1937).
29 Ibid., vol. 8, 32.
30 Ibid., vol. 8, 34.
31 Ernst Wiechert, *Sämtliche Werke*, vol. 8 (Vienna: Desch, 1957), 9.
32 Ibid., 212–13.

8 THE LIBERATING POTENTIAL OF THE FANTASTIC IN CONTEMPORARY FAIRY TALES FOR CHILDREN

1 See Claire R. Farrer, ed., *Women and Folklore* (Austin: University of Texas Press, 1975); Madonna Kolbenschlag, *Kiss Sleeping Beauty Good-bye: Breaking the Spell of Feminine Myths and Models* (New York: Doubleday, 1979); Marcia Lieberman, " 'Some Day My Prince Will Come': Female Acculturation through the Fairy Tale," *College English* 34 (1972): 383–95; Allison Lurie, "Fairy Tale Liberation," *New York Review of Books*, December 17, 1970, 42; Heather Lyons, "Some Second Thoughts on Sexism in Fairy Tales," in *Literature and Learning*, ed. Elizabeth Grugeon and Peter Walden (London: Ward Lock Educational, 1978), 42–58; Robert Moore, "From Rags to Witches: Stereotypes, Distortions and Anti-Humanism in Fairy Tales," *Interracial Books for Children* 6 (1975): 1–3; Jane Yolen, "America's Cinderella," *Children's Literature in Education* 8 (1977): 21–29; and Heide Göttner-Abendroth, *Die Göttin und ihr Heros* (Munich: Frauenoffensive, 1981).
2 Marion Lochhead, *The Renaissance of Wonder in Children's Literature* (Edinburgh: Canongate, 1977), 154.
3 Georges Jean, *Le Pouvoir des Contes* (Paris: Casterman, 1981), 153–54.
4 Ibid., 206–209.
5 Reprinted in Sigmund Freud, "The Uncanny," *New Literary History* 7 (Spring 1976): 619–45. See also Helene Cixous, "Fiction and Its Phantoms: A Reading of Freud's *Das Unheimliche*," in this same issue, pp. 525–48.
6 Ibid., 634.
7 Ibid., 640.
8 See Bruno Bettelheim, *The Uses of Enchantment: The Meaning and Importance of Fairy Tales* (New York: Knopf, 1976).
9 See my critique of Bettelheim's book, "On the Use and Abuse of Folk and Fairy Tales with Children: Bruno Bettelheim's Moralistic Magic Wand," in *Breaking the Magic Spell: Radical Theories of Folk and Fairy Tales* (London: Heinemann, 1979), 160–82.

10 Freud, "The Uncanny," *New Literary History*, 630.

11 Ernst Bloch, "Karl Marx and Humanity: The Material of Hope," in *On Karl Marx* (New York: Seabury, 1971), 30–31.

12 Ibid., 44–45.

13 For a detailed discussion of Bloch's essays, see my "Introduction: Toward a Realization of Anticipatory Illumination," in Ernst Bloch, *The Utopian Function of Art and Literature*, trans. Jack Zipes and Frank Mecklenburg (Cambridge, MA: MIT Press, 1988), xi–xliii, and my chapter "The Utopian Function of Fairy Tales and Fantasy: Ernst Bloch the Marxist and J.R.R. Tolkien the Catholic," in *Breaking the Magic Spell*, 129–59.

14 Ibid., 133.

15 Ibid., 135.

16 See Charlotte Bühler, *Das Märchen und die Phantasie des Kindes* (Berlin: Springer, 1977), based on the original 1918 edition; Alois Jalkotzy, *Märchen und Gegenwart* (Vienna: Jungbrunnen und Verlagsbuchhandlung, 1930); Alois Kunzfeld, *Vom Märchenerzähler und Marchenillustrieren* (Vienna: Deutscher Verlag für Jugend und Volk, 1926); Wilhelm Ledermann, *Das Märchen in Schule und Haus* (Langensalza: Schulbuchhandlung von F.G.L. Gressler, 1921); Erwin Müller, *Psychologie des deutschen Volksmärchens* (Munich: Kösel and Pustet, 1928); and Reinhard Nolte, *Analyse der freien Märchenproduktion* (Langensalza: Beyer, 1931).

17 André Favat, *Child and Tale: The Origins of Interest* (Urbana, IL: National Council of Teachers of English, 1977).

18 Ibid., 54.

19 There is a tendency to think that the patterns of folktales and classical fairy tales do not vary much. However, this widespread belief, based on Vladimir Propp's *Morphology of the Folk Tale*, 2nd rev. ed. (Austin: University of Texas Press, 1968), fails to consider the effects of cultural differences on the contents and configurations of the tales. For a more differentiated viewpoint, see August Nitzschke, *Soziale Ordnungen im Spiegel der Märchen*, 2 vols. (Stuttgart: Frommann-Holzborg, 1976–77).

20 Harriet Herman, *The Forest Princess* (Berkeley: Rainbow Press, 1975), 1–2.

21 Ibid., 38.

22 Herman wrote a sequel to this story, *Return of the Forest Princess* (Berkeley: Rainbow Press, 1975), which is, however, not as stimulating and open-ended as her first tale.

23 Merseyside Women's Liberation Movement, *Red Riding Hood* (Liverpool: Fairy Story Collective, 1972), 6.

24 Ibid., 5.

25 For the manifold ways that "Little Red Riding Hood" has been revised in the course of history, see my book *The Trials and Tribulations of Little Red Riding Hood: Versions of the Tale in Sociocultural Context*, rev. ed. (New York: Routledge, 1993). For the most recent commentary, see Sandra Beckett, *Recycling Red Riding Hood* (New York: Routledge, 2002), and Catherine Orenstein, *Little Red Riding Hood Uncloaked: Sex, Morality, and the Evolution of a Fairy Tale* (New York: Basic Books, 2002).

26 Tomi Ungerer, *A Storybook* (New York: Watts, 1974), 88.

27 Catherine Storr, *Clever Polly and the Stupid Wolf* (Harmondsworth: Puffin Books, 1967), 17–23.

28 Max von der Grün, "Rotkäppchen," in *Bilderbogengeschichten. Märchen, Sagen, Abenteuer*, ed. Jochen Jung (Munich: dtv, 1976), 95–100.

29 See Iring Fetscher, *Wer hat Dornröschen wachgeküßt?* (Frankfurt am Main: Fischer, 1974), 28–32, and Philippe Dumas and Boris Moissard, *Contes à l'envers* (Paris: L'École des Loisirs, 1977), 15–26.

30 Jay Williams, *The Practical Princess and Other Liberating Tales* (London: Chatto & Windus, 1979).

31 Jane Yolen, *Dream Weaver* (Cleveland: Collins, 1979).

32 Hans-Joachim Gelberg, *Neues vom Rumpelstilzchen* (Weinheim: Beltz & Gelberg, 1976).

33 See Adela Turin and Margherita Saccaro, *The Breadtime Story;* Adela Turin, Francesca Cantarelli, and Nella Bosnia, *The Five Wives of Silverbeard;* Adela Turin and Sylvie Selig, *Of Cannons and Caterpillars;* Adela Turin and Nella Bosnia, *Arthur and Clementine, A Fortunate Catastrophe, The Real Story of the Bonobos Who Wore Spectacles,* and *Sugarpink Rose.* All were published by the Writers and Readers Publishing Cooperative between 1975 and 1977. There also have been translations in German and French.

34 *Of Cannons and Caterpillars,* 1.

35 Ibid., 17.

36 Michael Ende, *Momo* (Stuttgart: Thienemann, 1973).

37 Michael Ende, *The Neverending Story* (Stuttgart: Thienemann, 1979).

38 Jean-Pierre Andrevon, *The Fairy and the Land Surveyor* (Paris: Casterman, 1981).

39 Ibid., 264.

40 Michael de Larrabeiti, *The Borribles* (London: Bodley Head, 1978).

41 Michael de Larrabeiti, *The Borribles Go for Broke* (London: Bodley Head, 1981).

42 Ibid., 80.

43 For example, see Christine Nöstlinger, *Wir pfeifen auf den Gurkenkönig* [We Don't Give a Hoot for the Pickle King] (Weinheim: Beltz & Gelberg, 1972); Ursula LeGuin, *The Wizard of Earthsea* (1968) and *Orsinian Tales* (1976); John Gardner, *Dragon, Dragon and Other Tales* (1975), *Gudgekin the Thistle Girl and Other Tales* (1976), and *The King of the Hummingbirds and Other Tales* (1977); and Robin McKinley, *Beauty* (1980).

44 Cf. Nicholas Tucker, "How Children Respond to Fiction," in *Writers, Critics, and Children* (New York: Agathon, 1976), 177–78, and Maximilian Nutz, "Die Macht des Faktischen und die Utopie. Zur Rezeption emanzipatorischen Märchen," *Diskussion Deutsch* 48 (1979): 397–410.

45 See Gianni Rodari, *The Grammar of Fantasy,* ed. and trans. Jack Zipes (New York: Teachers and Writers Collaborative, 1996).

46 Maria Luisa Salvadori, "Apologizing to the Ancient Fable: Gianni Rodari and His Influence on Italian Children's Literature," *The Lion and the Unicorn* 26, no. 2 (2002): 169–202.

47 *Le Pouvoir des Contes,* 203–32.

9 WALT DISNEY'S CIVILIZING MISSION: FROM REVOLUTION TO RESTORATION

1 See Lewis Jacobs, "Georges Méliès: Artificially Arranged Scenes," in *The Emergence of Film Art: The Evolution and Development of the Motion Picture as an Art, from 1900 to the Present,* ed. Lewis Jacobs, 2nd ed. (New York: Norton, 1979), 10–19, and François de la Bretèque, "Les contes de Georges Méliès," in *Contes et légendes à l'écran* (Condé-sur-Noireau, France: Corlet Éditions Diffusion, 2005), 62–71.

2 Bernard Bastide, "Présence de Perrault dans le cinéma français des premiers temps (1897–1912)," in *Contes et légendes à l'écran,* 24–33.

3 Jacobs, "Georges Méliès: Artificially Arranged Scenes," 13.

4 See Russell Merritt and J.B. Kaufman, *Walt in Wonderland: The Silent Films of Walt Disney* (Baltimore: Johns Hopkins University Press, 1993), 39–52.

5   Robert Sklar, "The Making of Cultural Myths—Walt Disney," in *The American Animated Cartoon: A Critical Anthology,* ed. Danny Peary and Gerald Peary (New York: Dutton, 1980), 61.

6   Ibid.

7   For a careful examination of the differences between the Grimms' tale and Disney's film, see Peter Brunette's essay, "Snow White and the Seven Dwarfs," in *The American Animated Cartoon: A Critical Anthology,* 66–73.

8   See Sandra Gilbert and Susan Gubar, *The Madwoman in the Attic: The Woman Writer and the Nineteenth-Century Literary Imagination* (New Haven, CT: Yale University Press, 1979).

9   Cf. Charles Solomon, "Bad Girls Finish First in Memory of Disney Fans," *Milwaukee Journal,* TV Section, August 17, 1980, 28. This article cites the famous quote by Woody Allen in *Annie Hall:* "You know, even as a kid I always went for the wrong women. When my mother took me to see 'Snow White,' everyone fell in love with Snow White; I immediately fell for the Wicked Queen."

10 Peter Brunette, "Snow White and the Seven Dwarfs," 72.

11 See Karen Merritt, "The Little Girl/Little Mother Transformation: The American Evolution of 'Snow White and the Seven Dwarfs,'" in *Storytelling in Animation: The Art of the Animated Image,* ed. John Canemaker (Los Angeles: American Film Institute, 1988), 105–21. Merritt makes the interesting point that

> Disney's *Snow White* is an adaptation of a 1912 children's play (Disney saw it as a silent movie during his adolescence) still much performed today, written by a male Broadway producer under a female pseudonym; this play was an adaptation of a play for immigrant children from the tenements of lower East Side New York; and that play, in turn, was a translation and adaptation of a German play for children by a prolific writer of children's comedies and fairy tale drama. Behind these plays was the popularity of nineteenth and early twentieth century fairy tale pantomimes at Christmas in England and fairy tale plays in Germany and America. The imposition of childish behavior on the dwarves, Snow White's resulting mothering, the age ambiguities in both Snow White and the dwarves, the "Cinderella" elements, and the suppression of any form of sexuality were transmitted by that theatrical tradition, which embodied a thoroughly developed philosophy of moral education in representations for children. . . . By reading Disney's *Snow White* by the light of overt didacticism of his sources, he no longer appears the moral reactionary disdained by contemporary critics. Rather, he is the entertainer who elevates the subtext of play found in his sources and dares once again to frighten children. (p. 106)

12 Though it may be true that Disney was more influenced by an American theatrical and film tradition, the source of all these productions, one acknowledged by Disney, was the Grimms' tale. And, as I have argued, Disney was not particularly interested in experimenting with the narrative to shock children or provide a new perspective on the traditional story. For all intents and purposes his film reinforces the didactic messages of the Grimms' tale, and it is only in the technical innovations and designs that he did something startlingly new. The object of critique is not to "disdain" or "condemn" Disney for reappropriating the Grimms' tradition to glorify the great designer but to understand those cultural and psychological forces that led him to map out his narrative strategies in fairy-tale animation.

13 Richard Schickel, *The Disney Version* (New York: Simon and Schuster, 1968), 227.

14 ibid., 213.

15 Steven Watts, *The Magic Kingdom: Walt Disney and the American Way of Life* (Boston: Houghton Mifflin, 1997), 408.

16 Quoted in Alexander Wilson, "The Betrayal of the Future: Walt Disney's EPCOT Center," in *Disney Discourse: Producing the Magic Kingdom*, ed. Eric Smoodin (New York: Routledge, 1994), 118.

17 Ibid., 121–22.

18 See Henry Giroux, *The Mouse That Roared: Disney and the End of Innocence* (New York: Rowman & Littlefield, 1999), 63–81.

19 Louis Marin, *Utopics: Spatial Play*, trans. Robert Vollrath (Highland, NJ: Humanities Press, 1984), 240.

20 Tom Mes, "Interview with Hayao Miyazaki," *Midnight Eye*, January 7, 2002, 4. Also published on the Internet: http://midnighteye.com/interviews/hayao_miyazaki.shtml.

BIBLIOGRAPHY

PRIMARY WORKS

Andersen, Hans Christian. *The Complete Fairy Tales and Stories*. Trans. by Erik Christian Haugaard. New York: Doubleday, 1974.

Auerbach, Nina, and Ulrich Knoepflmacher, eds. *Forbidden Journeys: Fairy Tales and Fantasies by Victorian Women Writers*. Chicago: University of Chicago Press, 1993.

Aulnoy, Marie-Catherine Le Jumel de Barneville, Baronne de. *Les Contes de fées*. 4 vols. 1st ed. Paris: Claude Barbin, 1697.

——. *Contes Nouveaux ou les Fées à la mode*. 2 vols. Paris: Veuve de Théodore Girard, 1698.

——. *Suite des Contes Nouveaux ou des Fées à la mode*. 2 vols. Paris: Veuve de Théodore Girard, 1698.

——. *The Fairy Tales of Madame d'Aulnoy*. Trans. Annie Macdonell. Intro. Anne Thackeray Ritchie. London: Lawrence & Bullen, 1895.

——. *Contes*. Ed. Philippe Houcade. Intr. Jacques Barchilon. 2 vols. Paris: Société des Textes Français Modernes, 1997–98.

Barchilon, Jacques, ed. *Nouveau Cabinet des fées*. 18 vols. Geneva: Slatkine Reprints, 1978. Partial reprint of *Le Cabinet des fées*, ed. Charles-Joseph Mayer.

Basile, Giambattista. *Lo cunto de li cunti overo Lo trattenemiento de peccerille. De Gian Alessio Abbattutis*. 5 vols. Naples: Ottavio Beltrano, 1634–36.

——. *The Pentamerone of Giambattista Basile*. Trans. N.M. Penzer. 2 vols. London: Bodley Head, 1932.

——. *Lo cunto de li cunti*. Ed. Michele Rak. Milan: Garazanti, 1986.

——. *Il racconto dei racconti*. Ed. Alessandra Burani and Ruggero Guarini. Trans. Ruggero Guarini. Milan: Adelphi Edizioni, 1994.

——. *The Pentamerone*. Trans. Richard Burton. London: Spring, n.d.

Baum, L. Frank. *The Emerald City*. New York: Ballantine, 1979. Reprint of the original 1910 edition.

Bernard, Catherine. *Inès de Cardoue, nouvelle espagnole*. Paris: Jouvenol, 1696; Geneva: Slatkine Reprints, 1979.

Galland, Antoine. *Les Milles et une nuit*. 12 vols. Vols. 1–4. Paris: Florentin Delaulne, 1704; vols. 5–7, ibid., 1706; vol. 8, ibid., 1709; vols. 9–10, Florentin Delaulne, 1712; vols. 11–12, Lyon: Briasson, 1717.

Grimm, Jacob, and Wilhelm Grimm. *Kinder- und Hausmärchen. Gesammelt durch die Brüder Grimm*. Berlin: Realschulbuchhandlung, 1812.

——. *Kinder- und Hausmärchen. Gesammelt durch die Brüder Grimm*. Vol. 2. Berlin: Realschulbuchhandlung, 1815.

——. *Kinder- und Hausmärchen. Gesammelt durch die Brüder Grimm*. 2 vols. 7th rev. and exp. edition. Göttingen: Dieterich, 1857.

——. *The Complete Fairy Tales of the Brothers Grimm*. Ed. and trans. Jack Zipes. New York: Bantam, 1987.

Hearn, Michael Patrick, ed. *The Victorian Fairy Tale Book*. New York: Pantheon, 1988.

La Force, Charlotte-Rose Caumont de. *Les Contes des contes par Mlle de ****. Paris: S. Bernard, 1698.

——. *Les Jeux d'esprit ou la promenade de la Princesse de Conti à Eu par Mademoiselle de La Force*. Ed. M. le Marquis de la Grange. Paris: Auguste Aubry, 1862.

Le Noble, Eustache. *Le Gage touché, histoires galantes*. Amsterdam: Jaques Desbordes, 1700.

Le Prince de Beaumont, Marie. *Magasin des enfans, ou Dialogue d'une sage gouvernante avec ses élèves de la première distinction*. Lyon: Reguilliat, 1756.

Lhéritier de Villandon, Marie-Jeanne. *Oeuvres meslées, contenant l'Innocente tromperie, l'Avare puni, les Enchantements de l'éloquence, les Aventures de Finette, nouvelles, et autres ouvrages, en vers et en prose, de Mlle de L'H***—avec le Triomphe de Mme Des-Houlières tel qu'il a été composé par Mlle****. Paris: J. Guignard, 1696.

——. *La Tour ténébreuse et les jours lumineux, contes anglois, accompagnés d'historiettes et tirés d'une ancienne chronique composée par Richard, surnommé Coeur de Lion, roi d'Angleterre, avec le récit des diverse aventures de ce roi*. Paris: Veuve de Claude Barbin, 1705.

MacDonald, George. *The Complete Fairy Tales of George MacDonald*. Ed. Roger Lancelyn Green. New York: Schocken, 1977.

Mailly, Jean de. *Les Illustres fées, contes galans. Dédié aux dames*. Paris: M.-M. Brunet, 1698.

Mayer, Charles-Joseph, ed. *Le cabinet des fées; ou Collection choisie des contes des fées, et autres contes merveilleux*. 41 vols. Amsterdam: s.n., 1785.

Murat, Henriette Julie de Castelnau, Comtesse de. *Contes de fées dédiez à S. A. S. Madame la princesse douairière de Conty, par Mad, la comtesse de M****. Paris: Claude Barbin, 1698.

——. *Les Nouveaux Contes de fées par Mme de M****. Paris: Claude Barbin, 1698.

——. *Histoires Sublimes et Allégoriques*. Paris: Floentin Delaulne, 1699.

Perrault, Charles. *Histoires ou contes du temps passé*. Paris: Claude Barbin, 1697.

——. *Contes de Perrault*. Ed. Gilbert Rouger. Paris: Garnier, 1967.

——. *Contes*. Ed. Jean Pierre Collinet. Folio, 1281. Paris: Gallimard, 1981.

——. *Contes*. Ed. Marc Soriano. Paris: Flammarion, 1989.

——. *Contes*. Ed. Catherine Magnien. Paris: Le Livre de Poche, 1990.

Rölleke, Heinz, ed. *Die älteste Märchensammlung der Brüder Grimm*. Cologny-Geneva: Fondation Martin Bodmer, 1975.

Straparola, Giovan Francesco. *Le Piacevoli Notti*. 2 vols. Venice: Comin da Trino, 1550/1553.

——. *The Facetious Nights of Straparola*. Trans. William G. Waters. Illus. Jules Garnier and E.R. Hughes. 4 vols. London: Lawrence and Bullen, 1894.

——. *Le Piacevoli Notti*. Ed. Giovanni Macchia. Milan: Bompiani, 1943.

——. *Le Piacevoli Notti*. Ed. Bartolomeo Rossetti. Rome: Avanzini e Torraca, 1966.

——. *Le Piacevoli Notti*. Ed. Pastore Stocchi. Rome-Bari: Laterza, 1979.

Warner, Marina, ed. *Wonder Tales: Six Stories of Enchantment*. London: Chatto & Windus, 1994.

Wilde, Oscar. *Complete Shorter Fiction*. Ed. Isobel Murray. Oxford: Oxford University Press, 1979.

Zipes, Jack, ed. *Victorian Fairy Tales*. New York: Methuen, 1987.

——. ed. *Beauties, Beasts, and Enchantment: French Classical Fairy Tales*. New York: New American Library, 1989.

——. ed. *Fairy Tales and Fables from Weimar Days*. Hanover, NH: University Press of New England, 1989.

——. ed. *Spells of Enchantment: The Wondrous Fairy Tales of Western Culture*. New York: Viking, 1991.

——. ed. *The Outspoken Princess and the Gentle Knight: A Treasury of Modern Fairy Tales*. New York: Bantam, 1994.

——. ed. *The Great Fairy Tale Tradition: From Straparola and Basile to the Brothers Grimm*. New York: Norton, 2001.

SECONDARY WORKS

Aarne, Antti, and Stith Thompson. *The Types of the Folktale*. 2nd rev. ed. Helsinki: Suomalainen Tiedeaktatemia, 1991.

Alderson, Brian. "Tracts, Rewards and Fairies: The Victorian Contribution to Children's Literature." In *Essays in the History of Publishing*, ed. Asa Briggs, 248–82. London: Longman, 1977.

Aley, Peter. *Jugendliteratur im Dritten Reich*. Gütersloh: Bertelsmann, 1967.

Alker, Ernst. *Profile und Gestalten der deutschen Literatur nach 1914*. Ed. Eugen Thurnher. Stuttgart: Kröner, 1979.

Andersen, Hans Christian. *The Fairy Tale of My Life*. Trans. W. Glyn Jones. New York: British Book Centre, 1955.

——. *Das Märchen meines Lebens. Briefe. Tagebücher*. Ed. Erling Nielsen. Munich: Winkler, 1961.

——. *Aus Andersens Tagebüchern*. Ed. Heinz Barüske. 2 vols. Frankfurt am Main: Fischer, 1980.

Apel, Friedmar. *Die Zaubergärten der Phantasie. Zur Theorie und Geschichte des Kunstmärchens*. Heidelberg: Winter, 1978.

Ariès, Philippe. *Centuries of Childhood: A Social History of Family Life*. New York: Knopf, 1962.

——. "At the Point of Origin." *Yale French Studies* 43 (1969): 15–23.

Armstrong, Nancy, and Leonard Tennenhouse, eds. *The Violence of Representation: Literature and the History of Violence*. New York: Routledge, 1989.

Aurouet, Carole, ed. *Contes et legends à l'écran*. Condé-sur-Noireau, France: Corlet Éditions Diffusion, 2005.

Avery, Gillian. *Childhood's Pattern: A Study of Heroes and Heroines of Children's Fiction 1770–1950*. London: Hodder and Stoughton, 1975.

Azzara, Claudio. *Le civiltà del Medievo*. Bologna: Mulino, 2004.

Barchilon, Jacques. *Le Conte merveilleux français de 1690 à 1790*. Paris: Champion, 1975.

Barchilon, Jacques, and Peter Flinders. *Charles Perrault*. Boston: Twayne, 1981.

Barchilon, Jacques, and Henry Petit. *The Authentic Mother Goose Fairy Tales and Nursery Rhymes*. Denver: Swallow, 1960.

Barthes, Roland. *Elements of Semiology*. Trans. Annette Lavers and Colin Smith. New York: Hill and Wang, 1968.

——. *Writing Degree Zero*. Trans. Annette Lavers and Colin Smith. New York: Hill and Wang, 1968.

Bastian, Ulrike. *Die Kinder und Hausmärchen der Brüder Grimm in der literaturpädagogischen Diskussion des 19. und 20. Jahrhunderts*. Giessen: Haag & Herchen, 1981.

Bastide, Bernard. "Présence de Perrault dans le cinéma français des premiers temps (1897–1912)." In *Contes et legends à l'écran*, ed. Carole Aurouet, 24–33. Condé-sur-Noireau, France: Corlet Éditions Diffusion, 2005.

Baum, Frank Joslyn, and Russel P. MacFall. *To Please a Child: A Biography of L. Frank Baum.* Chicago: Reilly & Lee, 1961.

Beckett, Sandra. *Recycling Red Riding Hood.* New York: Routledge, 2002.

Beckwith, Osmond. "The Oddness of Oz." *Children's Literature* 5 (1976): 74–91.

Belmont, Nicole. *Mythes et croyances dans l'ancienne France.* Paris: Flammarion, 1973.

Benjamin, Walter. *Illuminations.* Trans. Harry Zohn. New York: Harcourt, Brace & World, 1968.

——. *Gesammelte Schriften.* Ed. Rolf Tiedemann and Hermann Schweppenhäuser. 6 vols. Frankfurt am Main: Suhrkamp, 1977.

Berendsohn, Walter A. *Grundformen volkstümlicher Erzählkunst in den Kinder- und Hausmärchen der Brüder Grimm.* 2nd rev. ed. Wiesbaden: Sändig, 1968.

——. *Phantasie und Wirklichkeit in den Märchen und Geschichten Hans Christian Andersen.* Wiesbaden: Sändig, 1973.

Bettelheim, Bruno. *The Uses of Enchantment: The Meaning and Importance of Fairy Tales.* New York: Knopf, 1976.

Bewley, Marius. "The Land of Oz: America's Great Good Place." In *Masks and Mirrors,* 255–67. New York: Atheneum, 1970.

Bibliothèque Nationale. *Au temps des Précieuses. Les salons littéraires au XVIIe siècle.* Paris: Bibliothèque Nationale, 1968.

Bisseret, Noëlle. *Education, Class Language and Ideology.* London: Routledge Kegan Paul, 1979.

Bloch, Ernst. *Das Prinzip Hoffnung.* 3 vols. Frankfurt am Main: Suhrkamp, 1959.

——. "Das Märchen geht selber in der Zeit." In *Die Kunst, Schiller zu sprechen und andere literarische Aufsätze,* 10–14. Frankfurt am Main: Suhrkamp, 1969.

——. *Erbschaft dieser Zeit.* Frankfurt am Main: Suhrkamp, 1973.

——. *Ästhetik des Vor-Scheins.* Ed. Gert Ueding. 2 vols. Frankfurt am Main: Suhrkamp, 1974.

——. *The Utopian Function of Art and Literature.* Trans. Jack Zipes and Frank Mecklenburg. Cambridge, MA: MIT Press, 1988.

Blount, Margaret. *Animal Land: The Creatures of Children's Fiction.* New York: Avon, 1974.

Blum, Jeffrey M. *Pseudoscience and Mental Ability.* New York: Monthly Review Press, 1978.

Bollème, Geneviève, ed. *La Bibliothèque Bleue.* Paris: Julliad, 1971.

Book, Fredrik. *Hans Christian Andersen: A Biography.* Trans. George C. Schoolfield. Norman: University of Oklahoma Press, 1962.

Bourdieu, Pierre. *La Distinction: Critique Sociale du jugement.* Paris: Minuit, 1979.

——. *Distinction: A Social Critique of the Judgment of Taste.* Trans. Richard Nice. Cambridge, MA: Harvard University Press, 1984.

——. *Masculine Domination.* Trans. Richard Nice. Stanford, CA: Stanford University Press, 2001.

Brackert, Helmut, ed. *Und wenn sie nicht gestorben sind . . . Perspektiven auf das Märchen.* Frankfurt am Main: Suhrkamp, 1980.

Bredsdorff, Elias. *Hans Christian Andersen.* London: Phaidon, 1975.

Brémond, Claude. "Les bons récompensés et les méchants punis. Morphologie du conte merveilleux français." In *Sémiotique narrative et textuelle,* ed. Claude Chabrol, 96–121. Paris: Larousse, 1973.

——. "Le méccano du conte." *Magazine littéraire* 150 (July–August 1979): 13–15.

Bretèque, François de la. "Les contes de Georges Méliès." In *Contes et legends à l'écran,* ed. Carole Aurouet, 62–71. Condé-sur-Noireau, France: Corlet Éditions Diffusion, 2005.

Bridenthal, Renate, and Claudia Koonz, eds. *Becoming Visible: Women in European History.* Boston: Houghton Mifflin, 1977.

Briggs, K.M. *The Fairies in Tradition and Literature.* London: Routledge Kegan Paul, 1967.

Bühler, Charlotte, and Josefine Belz. *Das Märchen und die Phantasie des Kindes.* Berlin: Springer, 1977.

Bülow, Werner von. *Märchendeutungen durch Runen. Die Geheimsprache der deutschen Märchen.* Hellerau bei Dresden: Hakenkreuz–Verlag, 1925.

Bürger, Christa. "Die soziale Funktion volkstümlicher Erzählformen—Sage und Märchen." In *Projekt Deutschunterricht I,* ed. Heinz Ide, 26–56. Stuttgart: Metzler, 1971.

Butor, Michel. "On Fairy Tales." In *European Literary Theory and Practice,* ed. Vernon W. Gras, 351–56. New York: Delta, 1973.

Canepa, Nancy. "Basile e il Carnavalesco." In *Giovan Battista Basile e l'invenzione della fiaba,* ed. Michaelangelo Piccone and Alfred Messerli, 41–60. Ravenna: Longo Editore, 2004.

Chorover, Stephan. *From Genesis to Genocide: The Meaning of Human Nature and the Power of Behavior Control.* Cambridge, MA: MIT Press, 1979.

Coffin, Tristram Potter. *The Female Hero in Folklore and Legend.* New York: Seabury, 1975.

Conroy, Patricia, and Sven Rossel, eds. *The Diaries of Hans Christian Andersen.* Seattle: University of Washington Press, 1990.

Cook, Elizabeth. *The Ordinary and the Fabulous.* Cambridge: Cambridge University Press, 1969.

Corten, Irina H. "Evgenii Shvarts as an Adapter of Hans Christian Andersen and Charles Perrault." *Russian Review* 37 (1978): 51–67.

Cott, Jonathan, ed. *Beyond the Looking Glass: Extraordinary Works of Fairy Tale and Fantasy.* New York: Stonehill, 1973.

Coveney, Peter. *The Image of Childhood.* London: Penguin, 1967.

Cox, Marian Roalfe. *Cinderella: Three Hundred and Forty-five Variants.* London: Publications of the Folklore Society, 1892.

Crafton, Donald. *Before Mickey: The Animated Film 1898–1928.* Cambridge, MA: MIT Press, 1982.

Craveri, Benedetta. *La civiltà della conversazione.* Milan: Adelphi, 2001.

———. *The Age of Conversation.* Trans. Teresa Waugh. New York: New York Review of Books, 2005.

Crawford, Frederick, ed. *Hans Christian Andersen's Correspondence with the Late Grand-duke of Saxe-Weimar, Charles Dickens, Etc.* London: Dean, 1891.

Dahl, Svend, and H.G. Topsøe-Jensen, eds. *A Book on the Danish Writer Hans Christian Andersen: His Life and Work.* Copenhagen: Det Berlingske Bogtrykkeri, 1955.

Dal, Erik. "Hans Christian Andersen's Tales and America." *Scandinavian Studies* 40 (1968): 1–25.

Darton, F.J. *Children's Books in England.* Cambridge: Cambridge University Press, 1960.

Defrance, Anne. *Les contes de fées et les nouvelles de Madame d'Aulnoy (1690–98).* Geneva: Droz, 1998.

Dégh, Linda. *Folktales and Society.* Bloomington: Indiana University Press, 1969.

———, ed. *Folklore Today.* Bloomington: Indiana University Research Center for Language and Semiotic Studies, 1976.

———. "Grimm's Household Tales and Its Place in the Household: The Social Relevance of a Controversial Classic." *Western Folklore* 38 (1979): 83–103.

Dejean, Joan. *Tender Geographies: Women and the Origins of the Novel in France.* New York: Columbia University Press, 1991.

Denkler, Horst, and Karl Prümm, eds. *Die deutsche Literatur im Dritten Reich.* Stuttgart: Reclam, 1976.

Dewald, Jonathan. *The European Nobility 1400–1800*. Cambridge: Cambridge University Press, 1996.

Di Scanno, Teresa. *Les Contes de fées à l'époque classique (1680–1715)*. Naples: Liguori, 1975.

Dixon, Bob. *Catching Them Young: Vol. 1, Sex, Race and Class in Children's Fiction; Vol. 2, Political Ideas in Children's Fiction*. London: Pluto, 1977.

Doderer, Klaus, ed. *Klassische Kinder und Jugendbücher*. Weinheim: Beltz, 1969.

Dolle, Bernd. "Märchen und Erziehung. Versuch einer historischen Skizze zur didaktischen Verwendung Grimmscher Märchen." In *Und wenn sie nicht gestorben sind . . . Perspektiven auf das Märchen*, ed. Helmut Brackert, 165–92. Frankfurt am Main: Suhrkamp, 1980.

Dorson, Richard M. *Folklore and Fakelore*. Cambridge, MA: Harvard University Press, 1976.

Drews, Jörg, ed. *Zum Kinderbuch*. Frankfurt am Main: Insel, 1975.

Duerr, Hans Peter. *Traumzeit. Über die Grenze zwischen Wildnis und Zivilisation*. Frankfurt am Main: Syndikat, 1978.

Duffy, Maureen. *The Erotic World of Faery*. London: Hodder and Stoughton, 1972.

Duggan, Anne. *Salonnières, Furies, and Fairies: The Politics of Gender and Cultural Change in Absolutist France*. Newark: University of Delaware Press, 2005.

Duindam, Jeroen. *Myths of Power: Nobert Elias and Early-Modern European Court*. Amsterdam: Amsterdam University Press, 1994.

Dulong, Claude. *La vie quotidienne des femmes au grand siècle*. Paris: Hachette, 1984.

Dundes, Alan, ed. *The Study of Folklore*. Englewood Cliffs, NJ: Prentice Hall, 1965.

——, ed. *Cinderella: A Folklore Casebook*. New York: Garland, 1982.

Durand, Gilbert. *Les Structures anthropologiques de l'Imaginaire*. Paris: Bordas, 1969.

Dworkin, Andrea. *Woman Hating*. New York: Dutton, 1974.

Elias, Norbert. *Über den Prozess der Zivilisation*. 2 vols. Frankfurt am Main: Suhrkamp, 1977.

——. *The Civilizing Process*. Trans. Edmund Jephcott. Vol. 1. New York: Urizen, 1978.

——. *The Court Society*. New York: Pantheon, 1983.

——. "The Retreat of Sociologists into the Present." *Theory, Culture & Society* 4 (1987): 223–47.

——. *The Civilizing Process: Sociogenetic and Psychogenetic Investigations*. Eds. Eric Dunning, Johann Godsblom, and Stephen Mennell. Trans. Edmund Jephcott. Rev. ed. Oxford: Blackwell, 2000.

Eliot, Marc. *Walt Disney: Hollywood's Dark Prince*. New York: Birch Lane, 1993.

Elschenbroich, Donata. *Kinder werden nicht geboren*. Bensheim: päd. extra, 1980.

Emmerich, Wolfgang. *Germanistische Volkstumsideologie. Genese und Kritik der Volksforschung im Dritten Reich*. Reutlingen: Tübingen Vereinigung für Volkskunde, 1968.

Erisman, Fred. "L. Frank Baum and the Progressive Dilemma." *American Quarterly* 20 (1968): 616–23.

Escarpit, Denise. *La littérature d'enfance et de jeunesse en Europe*. Paris: Presses Universitaires de France, 1981.

Eschbach, Walter. *Märchen der Wirklichkeit*. Leipzig: Oldenburg, 1924.

Eykmann, Christoph. "Das Märchen im Expressionismus." In *Denk- und Stilformen des Expressionismus*, 125–43. Munich: Fink, 1974.

Farrer, Claire R., ed. *Women and Folklore*. Austin: University of Texas Press, 1975.

Favat, André F. *Child and Tale: The Origins of Interest*. Urbana, IL: National Council of Teachers of English, 1977.

Fehling, Detler. *Armor und Psyche: Die Schöpfung des Apuleius und ihre Einwirkung auf das Märchen*. Wiesbaden: Steiner, 1977.

Fend, Helmut. *Sozialisation durch Literatur*. Weinheim: Beltz, 1979.

Filstrup, Jane Merrill. "Thirst for Enchanted Views in Ruskin's *The King of the Golden River*." *Children's Literature* 8 (1979): 68–79.

Fink, Gonthier-Louis. *Naissance et apogée du conte merveilleux en Allemagne 1740–1800*. Paris: Les Belles Lettres, 1966.

Fischer, Maria. *Es war einmal—es ist noch. Das deutsche Märchen in seinen charakterlichen und sittlichen Werten*. Stuttgart: Union Deutsche Verlagsgesellschaft, 1944.

Foucault, Michel. *Discipline and Punish: The Birth of the Prison*. Trans. Alan Sheridan. New York: Pantheon, 1978.

———. *The History of Sexuality*. New York: Pantheon, 1978.

Fox, Geoff, et al., eds. *Writers, Critics, and Children*. New York: Agathon, 1976.

France, Peter. "The Pleasure of Their Company." *New York Review of Books*, June 23, 2005, 16–18.

Fraser, James H. *Society and Children's Literature*. Boston: David Godine, 1978.

Gardner, Martin, and Russel B. Nye. *The Wizard of Oz and Who He Was*. East Lansing: Michigan State University Press, 1957.

Gay, Peter. *Weimar Culture: The Outsider as Insider*. London: Secker and Warburg, 1969.

Gerstner, Hermann. *Brüder Grimm in Selbstzeugnissen und Bilddokumenten*. Hamburg: Rowohlt, 1973.

Gilbert, Sandra, and Susan Gubar. *The Woman Writer and the Nineteenth-Century Literary Imagination*. New Haven, CT: Yale University Press, 1979.

Giroux, Henry A. *The Mouse That Roared: Disney and the End of Innocence*. New York: Rowman & Littlefield, 1999.

Göttner-Abendroth, Heide. *Die Göttin und ihr Heros*. Munich: Frauenoffensive, 1980.

———. "Matriarchale Mythologie." In *Weiblich-Männlich*, ed. Brigitte Wartmann, 202–40. Berlin: Ästhetik & Kommunikation, 1980.

Graff, Harvey. *The Legacies of Literacy: Continuities and Contradictions in Western Culture and Society*. Bloomington: University of Indiana Press, 1987.

Green, Roger Lancelyn. *Tellers of Tales*. New York: Watts, 1965.

Greene, David L. "The Concept of Oz." *Children's Literature* 3 (1974): 173–76.

Greene, David L., and Dick Martin. *The Oz Scrapbook*. New York: Random House, 1977.

Greimas, A.J. *Sémantique structurale*. Paris: Larousse, 1964.

Grenz, G. "Vom Märchenerzählen." *Die Neue Gemeinschaft* (December 1943): 123–26.

Griswold, Jerome J. "Sacrifice and Mercy in Wilde's 'The Happy Prince,' " *Children's Literature* 3 (1974): 103–106.

Grønbech, Bo. *Hans Christian Andersen*. Boston: Twayne, 1980.

Grugeon, Elizabeth, and Peter Walden, eds. *Literature and Learning*. London: Open University Press, 1978.

Haase Dubosc, Danielle, and Eliane Viennot, eds. *Femmes et pouvoirs sous l'Ancien Régime*. Paris: Rivages/Histoire, 1991.

Habermas, Jürgen. *Strukturwandel der bürgerlichen Öffentlichkeit*. Neuwied: Luchterhand, 1962.

———. *Legitimation Crisis*. Trans. Thomas McCarthy. Boston: Beacon, 1975.

———. *The Structural Transformation of the Public Sphere*. Trans. Thomas Burger. Cambridge, MA: MIT Press, 1989.

Hannon, Patricia Ann. *Fabulous Identities: Women's Fairy Tales in Seventeenth-Century France*. Amsterdam: Rodopi, 1998.

Harmetz, Haljean. *The Making of the Wizard of Oz*. New York: Knopf, 1978.

Harth, Erica. *Ideology and Culture in Seventeenth-Century France*. Ithaca, NY: Cornell University Press, 1983.

———. "The Salon Woman Goes Public. Or Does She?" In *Going Public: Women and Publishing in Early Modern France*, ed. Elisabeth C. Goldsmith and Dena Goodman, 179–93. Ithaca, NY: Cornell University Press, 1995.

Hearn, Michael Patrick, ed. *The Annotated Wizard of Oz.* New York: Potter, 1973.

Held, Jacqueline. *L'imaginaire au pouvoir.* Paris: Les Éditions Ouvrières, 1975.

Hermand, Jost, and Frank Trommler. *Die Kultur der Weimarer Republik.* Munich: Nymphenburg, 1978.

Herrmann, Ulrich. "Literatursoziologie und Lesergeschichte als Bildungsforschung. Historische Sozialisationsforschung im Medium der Kinder- und Jugendliteratur." *Internationales Archiv für Sozialgeschichte der deutschen Literatur* 2 (1977): 187–98.

Heuscher, Julius E. *A Psychiatric Study of Fairy Tales.* Springfield, IL: Thomas, 1963.

Heyden, Franz. *Volksmärchen und Volksmärchenerzähler.* Hamburg: Hanseatische Verlagsanstalt, 1922.

Hoernle, Edwin. *Grundfragen proletarischer Erziehung.* Ed. Lutz von Werder and Reinhart Wolff. Darmstadt: März, 1969.

Hoggart, Richard. *The Uses of Literacy.* London: Chatto & Windus, 1957.

Holbek, Bengt. "Hans Christian Andersen's Use of Folktales." In *A Companion to the Fairy Tale,* ed. Hilda Ellis Davidson and Anna Chaudri, 149–58. Cambridge: D.S. Brewer, 2003.

Honegger, Claudia. *Die Hexen der Neuzeit. Studien zur Sozialgeschichte eines kulturellen Deutungsmusters.* Frankfurt am Main: Suhrkamp, 1978.

Houston, R.A. *Literacy in Early Modern Europe: Culture and Education 1500–1800.* 2nd ed. London: Longman, 2002.

Hurrelmann, Bettina, ed. *Kinderliteratur und Rezeption.* Baltmannsweiler: Burgbücherei Schneider, 1980.

Hyde, H. Montgomery. *Oscar Wilde.* London: Methuen, 1976.

Jackson, Rosemary. *Fantasy: The Literature of Subversion.* London: Methuen, 1981.

Jacobs, Lewis. "Georges Méliès: Artificially Arranged Scenes." In *The Emergence of Film Art: The Evolution and Development of the Motion Picture as an Art from 1900 to the Present,* ed. Lewis Jacobs, 10–19. 2nd ed. New York: Norton, 1979.

Jalkotzy, Alois. *Märchen und Gegenwart.* Vienna: Jungbrunnen, 1930.

Jameson, Fredric. *The Political Unconscious: Narrative as a Socially Symbolic Act.* Ithaca, NY: Cornell University Press, 1981.

Jan, Isabelle. *On Children's Literature.* New York: Schocken, 1974.

——. *Andersen et ses contes.* Paris: Aubier, 1977.

Jean, Georges. *Le Pouvoir des Contes.* Paris: Casterman, 1981.

Jolles, André. *Einfache Formen.* Tübingen: Niemeyer, 1958.

Jones, W. Glyn. *Denmark.* New York: Praeger, 1970.

Jullian, Philippe. *Oscar Wilde.* London: Constable, 1969.

Kaiser, Erich. " 'Ent-Grimm-te' Märchen." *Westermanns Pädagogische Beiträge* 8 (1975): 448–59.

Kamenetsky, Christa. "Folklore as a Political Tool in Nazi Germany." *Journal of American Folklore* 85 (1972): 221–35.

——. "Folktale and Ideology in the Third Reich." *Journal of American Folklore* 90 (1977): 168–78.

Karlinger, Felix, ed. *Wege der Märchenforschung.* Darmstadt: Wissenschaftliche Buchgesellschaft, 1973.

Klotz, Volker. "Wie Wilde seine Märchen über Andersen hinwegerzählt." In *Der zerstückte Traum: Für Erich Arendt zum 75. Geburtstag,* ed. Gregor Laschen and Manfred Schlösser, 219–28. Berlin: Agora, 1978.

Kofed, Niels. "Hans Christian Andersen and the European Literary Tradition." In *Hans Christian Andersen: Danish Writer and Citizen of the World,* ed. Sven Rossel, 209–56. Amsterdam: Rodopi, 1996.

Kolbenschlag, Madonna. *Kiss Sleeping Beauty Good-bye: Breaking the Spell of Feminine Myths and Models.* New York: Doubleday, 1979.

Kuhn, Andrea. *Tugend und Arbeit. Zur Sozialisation durch Kinder- und Jugendliteratur im 18. Jahrhundert.* Berlin: Basis, 1975.

Kuhn, Andrea, and Johannes Merkel. *Sentimentalität und Geschäft.* Zur Sozialisation durch *Kinderund Jugendliteratur im 19. Jahrhundert.* Berlin: Basis, 1977.

Kunzfeld, Alois. *Vom Märchenerzahlen und Märchenillustrieren.* Vienna: Deutscher Verlag für Jugend und Volk, 1926.

Labatut, Jean-Pierre. *Les noblesses européennes de la fin du XVe à la fin de XVIIIe siècle.* Paris: Presses Universitaires de France, 1978.

Laiblin, Wilhelm, ed. *Märchenforschung und Tiefenpsychologie.* Darmstadt: Wissenschaftliche Buchgesellschaft, 1969.

Lanes, Selma G. *Down the Rabbit Hole.* New York: Atheneum, 1971.

Laruccia, Victor. "Little Red Riding Hood's Metacommentary: Paradoxical Injunction, Semiotics and Behavior." *Modern Language Notes* 90 (1975): 517–34.

Ledermann, Wilhelm. *Das Märchen in Schule und Haus.* Langensalza: Schulbuchhandlung, 1921.

Lewis, Philip. *Seeing through the Mother Goose Tales: Visual Turns in the Writings of Charles Perrault.* Stanford: Stanford University Press, 1996.

Leyen, Friedrich von der. *Das Märchen.* Leipzig: Quelle & Meyer, 1917.

Lieberman, Marcia. " 'Some Day My Prince Will Come': Female Acculturation Through the Fairy Tale." *College English* 34 (1972): 383–95.

——. "The Feminist in Fairy Tales—Two Books from the Jung Institute, Zurich." *Children's Literature* 2 (1973): 217–18.

Linde, Ernst. *Die Bildungsaufgabe der deutschen Dichtung.* Leipzig: Brandstetter, 1927.

Littlefield, Henry M. "The Wizard of Oz: Parable on Populism." In *American Culture,* ed. Hennig Cohen, 370–81. New York: Houghton Mifflin, 1968.

Lochhead, Marion. *The Renaissance of Wonder in Children's Literature.* Edinburgh: Canongate, 1977.

Lurie, Alison. "Fairy Tale liberation." *New York Review of Books,* December 17, 1970, 42.

——. "Witches and Fairies: Fitzgerald to Updike." *New York Review of Books,* December 2, 1971, 6.

——. "Ford Madox Ford's Fairy Tales." *Children's Literature* 8 (1979): 7–21.

Lüthi, Max. *Die Gabe im Märchen und in der Sage.* Bern: Francke, 1943.

——. *Das europäische Volksmärchen.* 2nd rev. ed. Bern: Francke, 1960.

——. *Volksmärchen und Volkssage.* 2nd rev. ed. Bern: Francke, 1966.

——. *Märchen.* 3rd rev. ed. Stuttgart: Metzler, 1968.

——. "Familie und Natur im Märchen." In *Volksliteratur und Hochliteratur,* 63–78. Bern: Francke, 1970.

——. *Once upon a Time: On the Nature of Fairy Tales.* New York: Ungar, 1970.

——. *Das Volksmärchen als Dichtung.* Cologne: Diederichs, 1975.

Lyons, Heather. "Some Second Thoughts on Sexism in Fairy Tales." In *Literature and Learning,* ed. Elizabeth Grugeon and Peter Walden, 42–58. London: Open University Press, 1978.

Lypp, Maria, ed. *Literatur für Kinder.* Göttingen: Vandenhoeck & Ruprecht, 1977.

Lystad, Mary. *From Dr Mather to Dr Seuss: 200 Years of American Books for Children.* Boston: G.K. Hall, 1980.

MacDonald, Greville. *George MacDonald and His Wife.* London: Allen & Unwin, 1924.

——. *Reminiscences of a Specialist.* London: Allen & Unwin, 1932.

Mainil, Jean. *Madame d'Aulnoy et le Rire des Fées: Essai sur la Subversion Féerique et le Merveilleux Comique sous L'Ancien Régime.* Paris: Klimé, 2001.

Mandrou, Robert. *De la culture populaire aux XVIIe et XVIIIe siècles.* Paris: Stock, 1964.

Manlove, C.N. *Modern Fantasy*. London: Cambridge University Press, 1975.

Marin, Louis. "Puss-in-Boots: Power of Signs—Signs of Power." *Diacritics* (Summer 1977): 54–63.

——. *Utopics: Spatial Play*. Trans. Robert Vollrath. Atlantic Highlands, NJ: Humanities Press, 1984.

Martin, Robert K. "Oscar Wilde and the Fairy Tale: 'The Happy Prince' as Self-Dramatization." *Studies in Short Fiction* 16 (1979): 74–77.

Mayer, Hans. "Vergebliche Renaissance: Das 'Märchen' bei Goethe und Gerhart Hauptmann." In *Von Lessing bis Thomas Mann*, 357–82. Pfullingen: Neske, 1959.

——. *Aussenseiter*. Frankfurt am Main: Suhrkamp, 1975.

Meletinsky, Eleasar. "Die Ehe im Zaubermärchen." *Acta Ethnographica Academiae Scientiarum Hungaricae* 19 (1970): 281–92.

Merritt, Karen. "The Little Girl/Little Mother Transformation: The American Evolution of 'Snow White and the Seven Dwarfs.' " In *Storytelling in Animation: The Art of the Animated Image*, ed. John Canemaker, 105–21. Los Angeles: American Film Institute, 1988.

Merritt, Russell, and J.B. Kaufman. *Walt in Wonderland: The Silent Films of Walt Disney*. Baltimore: Johns Hopkins University Press, 1993.

Mes, Tom. "Interview with Hayao Miyazaki." *Midnight Eye*, January 7, 2002, 1–4. See also http://www.midnighteye.com/interviews/hayao_miyazaki.shtml.

Meyer, Rudolf. *Die Weisheit der deutschen Märchen*. Stuttgart: Verlag der Christengemeinschaft, 1935.

Michaelis-Jena, Ruth. *The Brothers Grimm*. London: Routledge Kegan Paul, 1970.

Mieder, Wolfgang, ed. *Grimms Märchen—modern*. Stuttgart: Reclam, 1979.

Mikhail, E.H. *Oscar Wilde: An Annotated Bibliography of Criticism*. Totowa, NJ: Rowman & Littlefield, 1978.

Moore, Raylyn. *Wonderful Wizard, Marvelous Land*. Bowling Green, OH: Bowling Green University Popular Press, 1974.

Moore, Robert. "From Rags to Witches: Stereotypes, Distortions and Anti-humanism in Fairy Tales." *Interracial Books for Children* 6 (1975): 1–3.

Morazé, Charles. *The Triumph of the Middle Classes: A Political and Social History of Europe in the Nineteenth Century*. London: Weidenfeld and Nicolson, 1966.

Mörchen, Helmut. "Notizen zu Wolgast." In *Literatur für Kinder*, ed. Maria Lypp, 13–20. Göttingen: Vandenhoeck & Ruprecht, 1977.

Mortensen, Finn Hauberg. *A Tale of Tales: Hans Christian Andersen and Children's Literature*. Part III and IV. Minneapolis: Center for Nordic Studies, University of Minnesota, 1989.

Mosely, Leonard. *Disney's World*. New York: Stein and Day, 1985.

Mosse, George. *Nazi Culture: Intellectual and Social Life in the Third Reich*. London: W.H. Allen, 1966.

Mourey, Lilyane. *Introduction aux contes de Grimm et de Perrault*. Paris: Minard, 1978.

Moynihan, Ruth B. "Ideologies in Children's Literature." *Children's Literature* 2 (1973): 166–72.

Muir, Pery. *English Children's Books 1600–1900*. New York: Praeger, 1954.

Müller, Erwin. *Psychologie des deutschen Volksmärchens*. Munich: Kösel & Pustet, 1928.

Müller, Konrad. *Die Werwolfsage*. Karlsruhe: Macklotsche, 1937.

Niedlich, Kurd. *Das Mythenbuch*. Leipzig: Dürr'sche Buchhandlung, 1927.

Nielsen, Erling. *Hans Christian Andersen in Selbstzeugnissen and Bilddokumenten*. Hamburg: Rowohlt, 1958.

Nisard, Charles. *Histoires des Livres Populaires ou de la Littérature du Colportage*. Paris: Maisonneuve & Larose, 1968.

Nitschke, August. *Soziale Ordnungen im Spiegel der Märchen*. 2 vols. Stuttgart: Frommann-Holzborg, 1976–77.

Nolte, Reinhard. *Analyse der freien Märchenproduktion.* Langensalza: Beyer, 1931.

Nye, Russel B. "The Wizardress of Oz—And Who She Is." *Children's Literature* 2 (1973): 119–22.

O'Dell, Felicity Ann. *Socialisation through Children's Literature.* Cambridge: Cambridge University Press, 1978.

O'Donnell, Elliott. *Werwolves.* London: Methuen, 1912.

Opie, Iona, and Peter Opie. *The Classic Fairy Tales.* New York: Oxford University Press, 1974.

Orenstein, Catherine. *Little Red Riding Hood Uncloaked: Sex, Morality, and the Evolution of a Fairy Tale.* New York: Basic Books, 2002.

Peary, Gerald, and Danny Peary, eds. *The American Animated Cartoon: A Critical Anthology.* New York: E.P. Dutton, 1980.

Peppard, Murray B. *Paths through the Forest: A Biography of the Brothers Grimm.* New York: Holt, Rinehart and Winston, 1971.

Piaget, Jean. *The Language and Thought of the Child.* Cleveland, OH: World Publishing, 1955.

———. *The Child's Conception of the World.* Totowa, NJ: Littlefield, Adams, 1967.

Piccone, Michelangelo, and Alfred Messerli, eds. *Giovan Battista Basile e l'Invenzione della Fiaba.* Ravenna: A Longo, 2004.

Pinchbeck, Ivy, and Margaret Hewitt. *Children in English Society.* 2 vols. London: Routledge Kegan Paul, 1969.

Poster, Mark. *Critical Theory of the Family.* London: Pluto, 1977.

Prestel, Josef. *Handbuch zur Jugendliteratur.* Freiburg i. Brsg.: Herder, 1933.

———. *Märchen als Lebensdichtung. Das Werk der Brüder Grimm.* Munich: Hueber, 1938.

Propp, Vladimir. "Les transformations des contes fantastiques." In *Théorie de la littérature,* ed. Tzvetan Todorov, 234–62. Paris: Seuil, 1965.

———. *Morphology of the Folktale.* Ed. Louis Wagner and Alan Dundes. 2nd rev. ed. Austin: University of Texas Press, 1968.

Psaar, Werner, and Manfred Klein. *Wer hat Angst vor der bösen Geiss? Zur Märchendidaktik und Märchenrezeption.* Braunschweig: Westermann, 1976.

Quintus, J.A. "The Moral Prerogative in Oscar Wilde: A Look at the Tales." *Virginia Quarterly Review* 53 (1977): 708–17.

Rak, Michele. "Il Sistema dei racconti nel Cunto de li cunti di Basile." In *Giovan Baattista Basile e l'Invenzione della Fiaba,* ed. Michelangelo Piccone and Alfred Messerli, 13–40. Ravenna: Longo Editore, 2004.

Reis, Richard H. *George MacDonald.* New York: Twayne, 1972.

Richardson, Selma K., ed. *Research about Nineteenth-Century Children and Books.* Champaign: University of Illinois Graduate School of Library Science, 1980.

Richter, Dieter. "Kinderbuch und politische Erziehung. Zum Verständnis der neuen linken Kinderliteratur." *Ästhetik und Kommunikation* 4 (1971): 5–12; 5/6 (1972): 23–32.

———, ed. *Das politische Kinderbuch.* Darmstadt: Luchterhand, 1973.

———. "Schöne Kindheit." *päd. extra* 1 (1979): 20–23.

Richter, Dieter, and Johannes Merkel. *Märchen, Phantasie und soziales Lernen.* Berlin: Basis, 1974.

Richter, Dieter, and Jochen Vogt, eds. *Die heimlichen Erzieher. Kinderbücher und politisches Lernen.* Reinbek: Rowohlt, 1974.

Robert, Marthe. *Sur le papier.* Paris: Grasset, 1967.

Robert, Raymonde. *Le conte de fées en France de la fin du XVIIe à la fin du XIIIe siècle.* Nancy: Presses Universitaires de Nancy, 1982.

Roche-Mazon, Jeanne. *Autour des Contes des Fées.* Paris: Didier, 1968.

Rodari, Gianni. *Grammatica della fantasia.* Turin: Einaudi, 1973.

———. *The Grammar of Fantasy: An Introduction to the Art of Inventing Stories.* Ed. and trans. Jack Zipes. New York: Teachers & Writers Collaborative, 1996.

Röhrich, Lutz. "Zwölfmal Rotkäppchen." In *Gebärden—Metapher—Parodie*, 130–52. Dusseldorf: Schwann, 1967.

——. *Märchen und Wirklichkeit*. Wiesbaden: Steiner, 1974.

——. "Dankbarer Toter (AaTh–508)." In *Enzyklopädie des Märchens*, ed. Kurt Ranke, 306–22. Vol. 3. Berlin: De Gruyter, 1999.

Rölleke, Heinz, ed. *Die älteste Märchensammlung der Brüder Grimm*. Cologny-Geneva: Fondation Martin Bodmer, 1975.

Rothe, Wolfgang, ed. *Die deutsche Literatur in der Weimarer Republik*. Stuttgart: Reclam, 1974.

Rubow, Paul V. "Idea and Form in Hans Christian Andersen's Fairy Tales." In *A Book on the Danish Writer Hans Christian Andersen*, ed. Sven Dahl and H.G. Topsøe-Jensen, 97–135. Copenhagen: Det Berlingske Bogtrykkeri, 1995.

Rüttgers, Severin. *Die Dichtung in der Volksschule*. Leipzig: R. Voigtländers Verlag, 1914.

——. *Erweckung des Volkes durch seine Dichtung*. Leipzig: Verlag der Dürr'schen Buchhandlung, 1933.

Saintyves, P. *Les Contes de Perrault et les récits parallèles*. Paris: Nourry, 1923.

Sale, Roger. *Fairy Tales and After: From Snow White to E.B. White*. Cambridge, MA: Harvard University Press, 1978.

Salvadori, Maria Luisa. "Apologizing to the Ancient Fable: Gianni Rodari and His Influence on Italian Children's Literature." *The Lion and the Unicorn* 26 (April 2002): 169–202.

Schenda, Rudolf. *Volk ohne Buch*. Frankfurt am Main: Klostermann, 1970.

——. *Die Lesestoffe der Kleinen Leute*. Munich: Beck, 1976.

Scherf, Walter. "Family Conflicts and Emancipation in Fairy Tales." *Children's Literature* 3 (1974): 77–93.

Schickel, Richard. *The Disney Version*. New York: Simon and Schuster, 1968.

Schmidt, Kurt. *Das Märchen*. Berlin: Matthiessen, 1940.

Schmitz, Victor August. *H.C. Andersens Märchendichtung*. Greifswald: L. Bamberg, 1925.

Schmölders, Claudia, ed. *Die Kunst des Gesprächs*. Munich: Deutscher Taschenbuch Verlag, 1979.

Schoof, Wilhelm. *Zur Entstehungsgeschichte der Grimmschen Märchen*. Hamburg: Hauswedell, 1959.

Schott, Georg. *Weissagung und Erfüllung im Deutschen Volksmärchen*. Munich: Wiechmann, 1925.

——. *Das Volksbuch vom Hitler*. Munich: Eher, 1933.

Schwartz, Emanuel K. "A Psychoanalytic Study of the Fairy Tale." *American Journal of Psychotherapy* 10 (1956): 740–62.

Smoodin, Eric. *Animating Culture: Hollywood Cartoons from the Sound Era*. New Brunswick, NJ: Rutgers University Press, 1993.

——, ed. *Disney Discourse: Producing the Magic Kingdom*. New York: Routledge, 1994.

Solomon, Charles. "Bad Girls Finish First in Memory of Disney Fans." *Milwaukee Journal*, TV Section, August 17, 1980, 28.

Soriano, Marc. "Le petit chaperon rouge." *Nouvelle Revue Française* 16 (1968): 429–43.

——. *Les Contes de Perrault. Culture savante et traditions populaires*. Paris: Gallimard, 1968.

——. "From Tales of Warning to Formulettes: The Oral Tradition in French Children's Literature." *Yale French Studies* 43 (1969): 24–43.

——. *Le Dossier Charles Perrault*. Paris: Hachette, 1972.

——. *Guide de littérature pour la jeunesse*. Paris: Flammarion, 1975.

Spiess, Karl von. *Das deutsche Volksmärchen*. Leipzig: Teubner, 1917.

——. "Was ist ein Volksmärchen?" *Jugendschriftenwarte* 7 (1938): 143–50.

Spiess, Karl von, and Edmund Mudrak. *Deutsche Märchen—Deutsche Welt.* 2nd ed. Berlin: Stubenrauch, 1939.

Spink, Reginald. *Hans Christian Andersen and His World.* London: Thames & Hudson, 1972.

Stedman, Allison. "D'Aulnoy's *Histoire d'Hypolite, comte de Duglas* (1690): A Fairy-Tale Manifesto." *Marvels & Tales* 19, no. 1 (2005): 32–53.

Steinlein, Rüdiger. *Die domestizierte Phantasie: Studien zur Kinderliteratur, Kinderlektüre und Literaturpädagogik des 18. und frühen 19. Jahrhunderts.* Heidelberg: Carl Winter, 1987.

Stephenson, Jill McIntyre. *Women in Nazi Society.* New York: Barnes and Noble, 1976.

Stirling, Monica. *The Wild Swan: The Life and Times of Hans Christian Andersen.* London: Collins, 1965.

Stone, Kay. "Things Walt Disney Never Told Us." In *Women and Folklore,* ed. Claire R. Farrer, 42–50. Austin: University of Texas Press, 1975.

Storer, Mary Elizabeth. *La Mode des contes de fées.* Paris: Champion, 1928.

———. *Contes de Fées du Grand Siècle.* New York: Publications of the Institute of French Studies, Columbia University, 1934.

Summers, Montague. *The Werewolf.* Hyde Park: University Books, 1966.

Tenèze, Marie-Louise, ed. *Approches de nos traditions orales.* Paris: Maisonneuve et Larose, 1970.

Teschner, Heinrich. *Hans Christian Andersen und Heinrich Heine: Ihre literarischen und persönlichen Beziehungen.* Münster: Westfällische Vereinsdruckerei, 1914.

Thomas, Bob. *Disney's Art of Animation: From Mickey Mouse to Beauty and the Beast.* New York: Hyperion, 1991.

Thompson, Stith. *The Folktale.* New York: Holt, Rinehart and Winston, 1946.

Tilley, Arthur. *The Decline of the Age of Louis XIV.* Cambridge: Cambridge University Press, 1929.

Tismar, Jens. *Kunstmärchen.* Stuttgart: Metzler, 1977.

———. *Das deutsche Kunstmärchen des zwanzigsten Jahrhunderts.* Stuttgart: Metzler, 1981.

Traxler, Hans. *Die Wahrheit über Hänsel und Gretel.* Frankfurt am Main: Zweitausendeins, 1978.

Trevor-Roper, H.R. *Religion, the Reformation and Social Change.* London: Macmillan, 1967.

Trigon, Jean de. *Histoire de la littérature enfantine.* Paris: Hachette. 1950.

Trinquet, Charlotte. "La Petite Histoire des Contes de Fées Littéraires en France (1690–1705)." Diss., University of North Carolina, Chapel Hill, 2001.

Troll, Max. *Der Märchenunterricht.* 2nd ed. Langensalza: Beyer, 1928.

Tucker, Holly, ed. "Reframing the Early French Fairy Tale." Special issue, *Marvels & Tales* 19, no. 1 (2005).

Ussel, Jos van. *Sexualunterdrückung. Geschichte der Sexualfeindschaft.* Giessen: Focus, 1977.

Velten, Harry. "The Influence of Charles Perrault's *Contes de ma Mère L'Oie* on German Folklore." *Germanic Review* 5 (1930): 14–18.

Verdier, Yvonne. "Grands-mères, sie vous saviez: le Petit Chaperon Rouge dans la tradition orale." *Cahiers de Littérature Orale* 4 (1978): 17–55.

Vidal, Gore. "The Wizard of the 'Wizard.'" *New York Review of Books,* September 29, 1977, 10–15.

———. "On Rereading the Oz Books." *New York Review of Books,* October 13, 1977, 38–42.

Viergutz, Rudolf F. *Von der Weisheit unserer Märchen.* Berlin: Widukind-Verlag, 1942.

Watts, Steven. *The Magic Kingdom: Walt Disney and the American Way of Life.* New York: Houghton Mifflin, 1997.

Weber, Eugen. "Fairies and Hard Facts: The Reality of Folktales." *Journal of the History of Ideas* XLII (1981): 93–113.

Weber-Kellermann, Ingeborg. *Die deutsche Familie.* Frankfurt am Main: Suhrkamp, 1974.

——. *Die Kindheit*. Frankfurt am Main: Insel, 1979.

Wenk, Walter. *Das Volksmärchen als Bildungsgut*. Langensalza: Beyer, 1929.

Wilde, Oscar. *The Soul of Man under Socialism*. Ed. Robert Ross. London: Humphreys, 1912.

Wisser, Wilhelm. *Das Märchen im Volksmund*. Hamburg: Im Quick-born Verlag, 1927.

Woeller, Waltraut. "Der soziale Gehalt und die soziale Funktion der deutschen Volksmärchen." Habilitations-Schrift der Humboldt-Universität zu Berlin, 1955.

Wolff, Robert Lee. *The Golden Key: A Study of the Major Fiction of George MacDonald*. New Haven, CT: Yale University Press, 1961.

Wolgast, Heinrich. *Das Elend unserer Jugendliteratur*. 7th ed. Worms: Wunderlich, 1950.

Wollenweber, Bernd. "Märchen und Sprichwort." In *Projektunterricht 6*, ed. Heinz Ide, 12–92. Stuttgart: Metzler, 1974.

Woodcock, George. *The Paradox of Oscar Wilde*. London: Boardman, 1950.

Yearsley, Macleod. *The Folklore of Fairy-tale*. London: Watts, 1924.

Yolen, Jane. "America's Cinderella." *Children's Literature in Education* 8 (1977): 21–29.

Ziegler, Matthes. *Die Frau im Märchen*. Leipzig: Koehler & Amelang, 1937.

Zimmer, Christian. *Cinéma et politique*. Paris: Seghers, 1974.

Zipes, Jack. "Down with Heidi, Down with Struwwelpeter, Three Cheers for the Revolution: Towards a New Socialist Children's Literature in West Germany." *Children's Literature* 5 (1976): 162–79.

——. *Breaking the Magic Spell: Radical Theories of Folk and Fairy Tales*. London: Heinemann, 1979. 2nd rev. ed. Lexington: University Press of Kentucky, 2002.

——. *The Trials and Tribulations of Little Red Riding Hood: Versions of the Tale in Socio-Cultural Context*. London: Heinemann, 1982.

——. *The Brothers Grimm: From Enchanted Forests to the Modern World*. New York: Routledge, 1988. 2nd rev. ed. New York: Palgrave, 2002.

——. "The Rise of the French Fairy Tale and the Decline of France." In *Beauties, Beasts and Enchantment: Classic French Fairy Tales*, trans. Jack Zipes, 1–15. New York: New American Library, 1989.

——. "The Struggle for the Grimms' Throne: The Legacy of the Grimms' Tales in the FRG and GDR since 1945." In *The Reception of Grimms Fairy Tales: Responses, Reactions, Revisions*, ed. Donald Haase, 167–206. Detroit: Wayne State University Press, 1993.

——. *Happily Ever After: Fairy Tales, Children, and the Culture Industry*. New York: Routledge, 1997.

——. *When Dreams Came True: Classical Fairy Tales and Their Tradition*. New York: Routledge, 1999.

Zur Lippe, Rudolf. *Naturbeherrschung am Menschen*. 2 vols. Frankfurt am Main: Suhrkamp, 1974.

INDEX

Please note that page numbers relating to Notes will have the letter 'n' following the page number

CPSIA information can be obtained at www.ICGtesting.com
Printed in the USA
LVOW11s1742240316

480603LV00007B/675/P

MAY 0 1 2016